Routledge Revivals

On Constructive Interpretation of Predictive Mathematics

First published in 1990, this book consists of a detailed exposition of results of the theory of "interpretation" developed by G. Kreisel — the relative impenetrability of which gives the elucidation contained here great value for anyone seeking to understand his work. It contains more complex versions of the information obtained by Kreisel for number theory and clustering around the no-counter-example interpretation, for number-theorectic forumulae provide in ramified analysis. It also proves the omega-consistency of ramified analysis. The author also presents proofs of Schütte's cut-elimination theorems which are based on his consistency proofs and essentially contain them — these went further than any published work up to that point, helping to squeeze the maximum amount of information from these proofs.

T0398050

On Constructive Interpretation of Predictive Mathematics

Charles Parsons

ROUTLEDGE REVIVALS

Routledge
Taylor & Francis Group

First published in 1990
by Garland

This edition first published in 2017 by Routledge
2 Park Square, Milton Park, Abingdon, Oxon, OX14 4RN
and by Routledge
711 Third Avenue, New York, NY 10017

Routledge is an imprint of the Taylor & Francis Group, an informa business

© 1990 Charles Parsons

The right of Charles Parsons to be identified as the author of this work has been asserted by them in accordance with sections 77 and 78 of the Copyright, Designs and Patents Act 1988.
All rights reserved. No part of this book may be reprinted or reproduced or utilised in any form or by any electronic, mechanical, or other means, now known or hereafter invented, including photocopying and recording, or in any information storage or retrieval system, without permission in writing from the publishers.

Publisher's Note
The publisher has gone to great lengths to ensure the quality of this reprint but points out that some imperfections in the original copies may be apparent.

Disclaimer
The publisher has made every effort to trace copyright holders and welcomes correspondence from those they have been unable to contact.

A Library of Congress record exists under LC control number: 8949571

ISBN 13: 978-1-138-22652-4 (hbk)
ISBN 13: 978-1-315-39706-1 (ebk)
ISBN 13: 978-1-138-22667-8 (pbk)

On Constructive Interpretation of Predicative Mathematics

Charles Parsons

Garland Publishing
New York & London
1990

Copyright © 1990 by
Charles Parsons
All Rights Reserved

Library of Congress Cataloging-in-Publication Data

Parsons, Charles, 1933–
On constructive interpretation of predicative mathematics / Charles Parsons.
p. cm. — (Harvard dissertations in philosophy)
Thesis (Ph.D.)—Harvard University, 1961.
Includes bibliographical references.
ISBN 0-8240-5091-6
1. Proof theory. 2. Number theory. 3. Mathematics—Philosophy. I. Title. II. Series.
QA9.54.P37 1990
512'.72'01—dc20 89-49571

All volumes printed on acid-free, 250-year-life paper
Manufactured in the United States of America

Design by Julie Threlkeld

PREFACE, 1989

This dissertation arose from my efforts to understand the proof theory of the Hilbert school, as it had been presented programmatically by Hilbert in the 1920's and systematically in the classic Grundlagen der Mathematik of Hilbert and Bernays.[1] At the time I began my work, the actual research done in this program was little known in the English-speaking world, although Georg Kreisel was beginning to change that state of affairs. In the 1950's Kreisel and Kurt Schütte were the only logicians who pursued this program very actively. Kreisel had given Hilbert's program a new twist, by showing how the consistency proofs that Hilbert had sought to construct could be used to give a finitary or constructive meaning to provable formulae in formalized systems of arithmetic and, eventually, analysis. Since other readers had found Kreisel's papers difficult, a systematic exposition of Kreisel's theory of "interpretation" seemed a worthwhile task. This is the overall framework of the dissertation, which is explained in the Introduction.

A word should be added about the connection between Kreisel's idea of turning Hilbert's program into a theory of interpretation of classical theories and the problem, much discussed both before and after this work, of how to rescue Hilbert's program from the limitations imposed by Gödel's incompleteness theorems. Hilbert aspired to prove the consistency of classical arithmetic and analysis by what he called the "finitary method." There have been some disputes about just what that method permitted, but there is little

---

[1] For items such as this one listed in the Bibliography of the dissertation, I refer the reader there for bibliographical information. (But see now Hilbert-Bernays 1968/70.) Works referred to by author and date are described in the list of references for this Preface.

doubt that any proof conforming to this method can be translated into a proof in some part of classical first-order arithmetic (called below Z). Gödel's second incompleteness theorem implies that a proof of the consistency of Z cannot be formalized in Z, and thus it seems evident that it cannot be finitary by Hilbert's standard.

Already in the 1930's it was proposed to replace Hilbert's standard by a weaker standard, that of constructivity. It is still philosophically useful to prove the consistency of a classical theory by constructive means, but this can in many cases already be done more simply than by the kind of proof-theoretic analysis developed by Hilbert and his co-workers. For example, in the case of Z that end is accomplished by Gödel's translation of Z into the same theory with intuitionistic logic, what is now called Heyting's arithmetic (see Gödel 1933). In Kreisel's early work, more important than the specific concept of interpretation was probably his emphasis on the ability of the Hilbert type of proof theory to give additional information in the form of more explicit, computational cashing in of existence statements. A simple example is statements of the form $\forall x \exists y A(x, y)$, where A is, say, a primitive recursive predicate of natural numbers. If such a statement is true, there is a general recursive function that gives for each x the least y such that A(x, y) ($\mu y A(x, y)$). But as an algorithm, this description of the function tells us only to keep trying values of y until one turns up such that A(x, y) is true. If $\forall x \exists y A(x, y)$ has been proved in Z, the consistency proof gives a more informative algorithm, described in terms of ordinal recursion.[2] This kind of

---

[2] Ordinal recursion is rather poorly and unperspicuously described in the dissertation. The idea of ordinal recursion in the present setting is that for each x, the problem of determining $\mu y A(x, y)$ is reduced to that of determining $\mu y A(z, y)$ for values of z preceding y in a given primitive recursive well-ordering of the natural numbers. But see below.

result was made possible by sharper demands on the methods of proof theory than simply that they be constructive; although the formalisms in which consistency and other results might be proved would unavoidably extend Hilbert's finitism, they would share with it its explicit character, in that existence of an object satisfying some condition could only be stated by actually giving a term designating such an object, whose meaning carries with it a method of computation. (For recent surveys of what has been accomplished in this program, see Sieg 1984 and Feferman 1988.)

Apart from exposition, the significance of what was accomplished in the dissertation is narrower and more technical. In chapter VI, §3, a proof of the ω-consistency of ramified analysis is given (published in Parsons 1962). It contains a proof of the ω-consistency of Z by Schütte's method of cut-elimination in proofs in which induction has been replaced by the effective ω-rule.[3]

In chapters IV and V of the dissertation, I undertook to obtain by Schütte's methods the results that Kreisel had obtained for arithmetic using the consistency proof of Ackermann [2].[4] Schütte's methods had the advantage of extending to ramified analysis.[5] I gave a very explicit treatment of

---

[3] In note 3, p. 255, it is stated that the latter proof uses transfinite induction up to ε_1, the second ε-number, and that this ordinal is not the best possible. But in fact it is; Kreisel's claim in [5] to have proved the ω-consistency of Z by transfinite induction up to $\varepsilon_0{}^2$ is false. See Kreisel 1964 and, for a more detailed and refined treatment, Goldfarb 1974.

[4] This proof is presented in Hilbert-Bernays 1968/70, vol. II, pp. 535-555. However, this presentation does not include the calculation of ordinal bounds, which could be used for an alternative proof of (1) of the theorem below.

[5] Only finite levels of the ramified hierarchy are treated in the dissertation, though in [4], published when my work was far advanced, Schütte had extended his analysis to transfinite levels.

The effective ω-rule, the central element in Schütte's methods, is treated thoroughly in Sundholm 1983, from a more modern point of view than that of the dissertation.

Schütte's consistency proof, so that in particular it could be seen how one defines by ordinal recursion the function which, given a proof in elementary number theory of a variable-free formula, reduces it to a purely computational proof, . The main accomplishment of this explicit treatment (theorems 13 (p. 126) and 17 (p. 210)) was to show how the length of the ordinal recursion needed to define this function depended basically on the complexity in terms of quantifiers of induction formulae, number of quantifiers corresponding to ordinal exponentiation, and in the case of ramified analysis, increase of a level in the hierarchy corresponding to going from an ordinal α to the αth ε-number. Theorems of a similar kind were proved in the reverse direction. Kreisel had proved that functions recursive on ordinals $< \varepsilon_0$ are povably recursive in Z, and it was clear that it would follow from Schütte's derivations of transfinite induction in ramified analysis that functions ordinal recursive on ordinals less than the first critical ε-number κ_0 are provably recursive in ramified analysis with finite levels. Theorems 15 and 19 of the dissertation refine these results to show how the complexity of induction required depends on the ordinal of the recursion.

In the number theoretic case, in neither direction did the dissertation give the best possible result. Only after returning to the subject several years later did I prove the following theorem. To fix ideas, let R be a standard primitive recursive well-ordering of the natural numbers of type $\geq \varepsilon_0$ (such as that of Schütte [4], §11, or Schütte 1977, §14[6]). We will say that a function φ is definable by simple (nested) ordinal recursion of type α if it is definable by simple (nested) recursion on the ordering $\{x\colon\ xR\alpha\}$ in the sense of Tait 1961, p.

---

[6] The method of chapter V, §3 is adequate to define such a well-ordering but less elegant and powerful than those of Schütte.

236. (It is assumed that α is represented in a canonical way by a numerical term.)

<u>Theorem</u> (Parsons 1966a). Let $\beta_0(\alpha) = \alpha$, $\beta_{n+1}(\alpha) = \beta \exp \beta_n(\alpha)$. Let Z_n be Z with the induction axiom restricted to formulae with $\leq$ n nested quantifiers.[7]

(1) If $\forall x_1 \ldots x_m \exists y A(x_1 \ldots x_m, y)$ is provable in Z_n for $n \neq 0$, then an $\alpha < \omega_n(\omega)$ can be found so that the function φ giving $\mu y A(x_1 \ldots x_m, y)$ for each $x_1 \ldots x_m$ is definable by simple (not nested) ordinal recursion on α. (If $n = 0$, primitive recursion; it follows that φ is also primitive recursive if $n = 1$.)

(2) If φ is a function of m arguments definable by simple ordinal recursion on some $\alpha < \omega_n(\omega)$ for $n \neq 0$, then φ is provably recursive in Z_n; that is there is a formula $A(x_1 \ldots x_m, y)$ which represents φ such that for A the recursion equations for φ are provable in Z_n.

The proof of (1) can be extracted from the proof of theorem 13 below. The infinite proof resulting from a proof in Z_n has binding degree[8] $\leq$ n and order $\alpha < \omega^2$ (pp. 140-141). Note that in the cut-elimination procedure for proofs using Schütte's rule of infinite induction, the step that reduces by the binding degree by 1 increases the order from, say, β to $2^{\beta \cdot k}$ for some number k (lemma 13.4). It then follows that elimination of all cuts increases the order

---

[7] We may, as in the work of Parsons 1970 and 1972, assume that primitive symbols and recursion equations are given for all Kalmár elementary functions. Then what is here called Z_n is what is there called IA_n. By Theorem 1 of Parsons 1972, however, we may disregard bounded quantifiers.

The statement of Parsons 1966a refers only to the rule of induction, and the analysis of the dissertation is carried out for the rule as well. It applies to the axiom with minor modifications, or (1) can be extended to the axiom by the observation (Parsons 1972, p. 474) that Z_n for $n \neq 0$ is a conservative extension for Π_{n+1} sentences of the corresponding system with the rule.

(1) for the rule of induction is also proved (independently) in Mints 1971.

[8] That is, maximum number of nested quantifiers in cuts.

from γ to some number $< 2_n(\gamma \cdot q)$ (for some q) $< 2_n(\omega^2)$. Since $2^{\omega^2} = \omega^\omega$, if $n \neq 0$ this bound is $\omega_n(\omega)$.[9]

To prove (2), suppose that φ is definable by simple ordinal recursions on an ordinal $\beta < \omega_n(\omega)$ for $n \neq 0$, say $n = p + 1$. Then $\beta < \omega_p(\omega^\alpha)$ for some α, $0 < \alpha < \omega$. If $p = 0$, φ is primitive recursive, and it is straightforward to show that φ is provably recursive in Z_1. If $p \neq 0$, observe that by Tait 1961, theorem 5, φ is definable by nested ordinal recursion on some $\gamma < \omega_p(\omega)$. Such functions can be straightforwardly seen to be provably recursive by means of transfinite inductions on γ applied to Π_2 formulae. Standard derivations of transfinite induction in formal number theory (such as those in the proof of theorem 14) show that these inductions are provable in Z_{p+1}, i. e. Z_n. It follows that φ is provably recursive in Z_n.

Although chapters IV and V of the dissertation were not in a satisfactory state, they led me into a systematic proof-theoretic study of subsystems of first-order arithmetic defined by restrictions on the occurrence of quantifiers in the rule or axiom of induction or in other possible axiom schemata. The main results of this work are in Parsons 1966a, 1970, and 1972; see also Parsons 1966, 1971, and 1973. Toward the end of the 1970's, after I had left the subject, similar questions began to be investigated by model-theoretic methods, beginning with Paris and Kirby 1978 and Paris 1981. Those of my own results that do not involve transfinite induction or recursion are proved in an elegant and uniform way in Sieg 1985. The line of research initiated by Paris and others has been considerably elaborated, with the result that questions about elementary fragments of arithmetic have turned out to be

---

[9] One also has to observe that the ordinal recursion involved is simple and not nested.

connected with problems in computational complexity theory.

REFERENCES

Gödel, Kurt, 1933. Zur intuitionistischen Arithmetik und Zahlentheorie. Ergebnisse eines mathematischen Kolloquiums 4 (1933), 34-38. Reprinted with English translation and introductory note by A. S. Troelstra in Gödel 1986.

Gödel, Kurt, 1986. Collected Works, Volume I: publications 1929-36. Edited by Solomon Feferman, John W. Dawson, Jr., Stephen C. Kleene, Gregory H. Moore, Robert M. Solovay, and Jean van Heijenoort. New York: Oxford University Press.

Feferman, Solomon, 1988. Hilbert's program relativized: proof-theoretical and foundational reductions. The Journal of Symbolic Logic 53, 364-384.

Goldfarb, Warren D., 1974. Ordinal bounds for k-consistency. The Journal of Symbolic Logic 39, 693-699.

Hilbert, David, and Paul Bernays, 1968/70. Grundlagen der Mathematik. Second edition. Berlin, Heidelberg, New York: Springer-Verlag.

Kreisel, G., 1964. Review of Parsons 1962. Zentralblatt für Mathematik und ihre Grenzgebiete 106, 238.

Mints, G. E., 1971. Exact estimates of the provability of transfinite induction in the initial segments of arithmetic. Journal of Soviet Mathematics 1 (1973), 85-91. Russian original in Zapiski Nauchnykh Seminarov Leningradskogo Otdeleniya Matematicheskogo Instituta im. V. A. Steklova Akademii Nauk SSSR 20 (1971), 134-144.[10]

Paris, J. B., and L. A. S. Kirby, 1978. Σ_n-Collection schemas in arithmetic. In Angus Macintyre, Leszek Pacholski, and J. B. Paris (eds.), Logic Colloquium '77, pp. 199-209. Amsterdam: North-Holland.

Paris, J. B., 1981. Some conservation results for fragments of arithmetic. In Chantal Berline, Kenneth McAloon, and Jean-Pierre Ressayre (eds.),

Model Theory and Arithmetic, pp. 251-262. Lecture Notes in Mathematics, 890. Berlin, Heidelberg, New York: Springer-Verlag.

Parsons, Charles, 1962. The ω-consistency of ramified analysis. Archiv für mathematische Logik und Grundlagenforschung 6, 30-34.

---------------, 1966. Reduction of inductions to quantifier-free induction (abstract). Notices of the American Mathematical Society 13, 740.

---------------, 1966a. Ordinal recursion in partial systems of number theory (abstract). Notices of the American Mathematical Society 13, 857-858.

---------------, 1970. On a number-theoretic choice schema and its relation to induction. In John Myhill, Akiko Kino, and Richard E. Vesley (eds.), Intuitionism and Proof Theory, pp. 459-473. Amsterdam: North-Holland.

---------------, 1971. On a number-theoretic choice schema II (abstract). The Journal of Symbolic Logic 36, 587.

---------------, 1972. On n-quantifier induction. The Journal of Symbolic Logic 37, 466-482.

---------------, 1973. Transfinite induction in subsystems of number theory (abstract). The Journal of Symbolic Logic 38, 544-545.

Sieg, Wilfried, 1984. Foundations of analysis and proof theory. Synthese 60, 159-200.

Sieg, Wilfried, 1985. Fragments of arithmetic. Annals of Pure and Applied Logic 28, 33-71.

Sundholm, Göran, 1983. Proof Theory: A Survey of the ω-Rule. D. Phil. Thesis, Oxford.

Tait, W. W., 1961. Nested recursion. Mathematische Annalen 143, 236-250.

---

[10] The reference [6] (to me) in the translation is mixed up, probably by the translator; it should be to Parsons 1966a. In the previous translation in the same journal, also of a paper by Mints, there is a similar mixup; the reference [6] (on p. 84) should be to Parsons 1966.

TABLE OF CONTENTS

Preface

Chapter I. INTRODUCTION 1

1. Statement of the Problem 1

2. Systems considered 10

3. Metamathematical Methods of Proof 22

Chapter II. OVER-SIMPLE INTERPRETATIONS 26

1. Trivial Interpretation 26

2. Failure of Interpretation by Recursive Satisfaction 27

3. Dependence on the Proof of the Verifiable Formula corresponding to a Theorem 31

Chapter III. HERBRAND INTERPRETATION 40

1. The Concept of Herbrand Interpretation 40

2. Herbrand Interpretation of Elementary Number Theory without Induction 43

3. Properties of the Interpretation 51

4. Impossibility of an Herbrand Interpretation of Number Theory with Induction 57

Chapter IV. THE NO-COUNTER-EXAMPLE INTERPRETATION OF NUMBER THEORY 76

1. Non-constructive considerations 76

2. No-counter-example Interpretation of Number Theory without Induction 80

3. No-counter-example Interpretation, 1*-consistency, and External Consistency 94

4. Ordinal Recursive Functionals. 1*-consistency of Number Theory with Induction 118

5. Representation of Ordinal Recursive Functionals in Elementary Numbér Theory 162

Chapter V. RAMIFIED ANALYSIS 187

1. Description of Systems 187

2. Ramified Analysis without Induction 190

3. Recursive Well-orderings and Ordinal Recursive Functionals 198

4. Ramified Analysis with Induction 209

5. Representation of Ordinal Recursive Functionals in Ramified Analysis 230

Chapter VI. Ω-CONSISTENCY

1. Critique of the Concept of ω-consistency 243

2. Ω-consistency, External Consistency, and 1*-consistency 246

3. Ω-consistency of Ramified Analysis 252

Appendix I. Arithmetization of Schütte's Cut-elimination theorems 260

Appendix II. Ordinal Functions 317

Bibliography 334

Index of Definitions 340

PREFACE

The great bulk of this dissertation consists of detailed exposition of results of the theory of "interpretation," developed by G. Kreisel. Enough readers have found Kreisel's own papers impenetrable for there to be some excuse for this presentation. We hope, moreover, that the results have more unity than they could possibly have in research papers.

We also give proofs (of theorems 13 and 17) which are based on Schütte's consistency proofs and which essentially contain them. Since Schütte's own exposition is quite lucid, the purpose of this is quite different, namely to squeeze the maximum amount of information from them. Our proofs go farther in this respect than any published work.

We offer as new results our obtaining, in chapter V, more complex versions of the information obtained by Kreisel for number theory and clustering around the no-counter-example interpretation, for number-theoretic formulae proved in ramified analysis. We also prove the ω-consistency of ramified analysis (theorem 22).

I wish to thank Profs. G. Kreisel, W. V. Quine, J. R. Shoenfield, and Hao Wang for their assistance or advice at various points, and expecially Prof. Burton

Dreben for his frequent consultation, encouragement, and helpful criticism.

In addition, I wish to thank the Department of Philosophy for financial assistance in the years 1956-58, and the Society of Fellows for its support since then.

C. D. P.

April 3, 1961

CHAPTER I

INTRODUCTION

1. Statement of the Problem

Our purpose is to find constructive interpretations for parts of classical mathematics.

It is impossible to be completely precise about the concepts of constructive statement and constructive proof. But we generally say that a proof is constructive if whenever the existence of some mathematical object is asserted, the proof enables us to find out just what this object is. We can say we know what an object is if we have an expression for it which is especially standard, informative, or explicit. For example, if in a proof in number theory a statement of the form $(Ex)A(x)$ is asserted, where x ranges over natural numbers, we should expect to find a numeral denoting an x such that $A(x)$ holds. If $(E\alpha)A(\alpha)$ is asserted, where α ranges over number-theoretic functions, the most informative expression would be one which enabled us to compute all the values of α, or which at least gave the rule by which the values are determined.

We could say that we had given a constructive interpretation of a theorem of classical mathematics if we found a constructive proof of a statement which was sufficiently close in meaning to the original theorem to serve as its "constructive content." For example, if the theorem was $(Ex)A(x)$, we should be making an advance if we were to produce a proof of $A(0^{(n)})$ for some n, where $0^{(n)}$ is the numeral denoting n . If the theorem is $(x)(Ey)A(x, y)$, we might seek a computable term $t(a)$ and a proof of $(x)A[x, t(x)]$, for then for any n we should be able to compute an m such that $A(0^{(n)}, 0^{(m)})$ is true, and we should have a proof of $A(0^{(n)}, 0^{(m)})$.

In a moment we shall discuss the question what is the criterion of sufficient closeness in meaning. First we must point out that we could avoid the possibility of making proofs which were not constructive by so limiting our language that we could not make a statement without at the same time giving, for objects which are asserted to exist, expressions which have the requisite degree of explicitness. This means first of all avoiding the existential quantifier: instead of saying "there is an x such that $A(x)$" we should say $A(0^{(n)})$ for some n . However, the case of $(x)(Ey)A(x, y)$ shows that we cannot expect every existential quantifier to be cashed in by a constant; if we did then in the reduced language we should be unable to make any but the most trivial generalizations. The next best thing is to admit computable terms involving variables. Then we should be assured that if constants are substituted for the variables, then we shall always be able to find constants which are values of the terms.

There are also reasons to limit the use of universal quantification in the constructive language. A second, philosophically more fundamental meaning of constructivity is that the proof should never use any hypothesis which refers to a completed infinite totality, or whose verification would require an infinity of information. But by this criterion, the interpretation of statements of the form

$$(x)A(x) \supset B$$

is problematic.[1]

Universal quantifiers which do not lie within other logical connectives do not present the same difficulty, and their meaning can be expressed by free variables with the generality interpretation. For a formula with free variables and no quantifiers can, if any variable-free formula can be decided with finitely much information, be decided in each particular case. If we can show how to verify it in each case, we shall call the formula <u>verifiable</u>.

It follows that the problem of constructive interpretation is closely related to that of finding satisfactions for formulae with quantifiers. <u>A satisfaction</u> of a prenex formula is an assignment of a function to each existential quantifier which gives the value of the existentially quantified variable in terms of the values of preceding universally quantified variables; i. e. given a formula

---

[1]Brouwer's solution was to interpret the antecedent as stating the existence of a hypothetical <u>construction</u> which would prove $(x)A(x)$. It is then, however, no longer obvious that the laws of classical logic are valid, and in fact Brouwer showed that on this interpretation they are not.

$$(x)(Ey)(z)A(x, y, z) \tag{1}$$

we have a satisfaction of the formula if we have a function f of one variable such that

$$A[a, f(a), b] \tag{2}$$

is true for all a, b in the range of the variables.

If A is a formula of our constructive language, and f is computable, then (2) is the sort of formula which might be taken to embody the constructive content of (1).

If (1) is a formula of elementary number theory and f is a recursive function, we shall say we have a <u>recursive satisfaction</u> of (1). In our subsequent work we shall obtain recursive satisfactions of all formulae of elementary number theory which we consider whose general form leads us to expect, from a non-constructive point of view, that they will possess recursive satisfactions.

We know that if the formula of elementary number theory

$$(x)(Ey)B(x, y), \tag{3}$$

where $B(x, y)$ expresses a recursive predicate, is true, then it is recursively satisfied by the function

$$\lambda x\ \mu y B(x, y).$$

We cannot regard such a term as this as sufficient for a satisfaction which is to serve as a constructive interpretation, for our knowledge that it <u>is</u> computable is dependent on a proof of (3) which may be non-constructive. It follows that any computable terms admitted for the purpose of interpreting must be shown to be computable by methods which are already seen to be constructive.

We have implicitly supposed that an interpretation involves associating with a classical proof of a theorem A a constructive statement which is to be the interpretation of A . This corresponding statement A' is itself to be constructively proved.

Since our objective is to find general methods of interpretation for theorems proved by certain types of methods, and since we do not wish to assume the soundness or even the intelligibility of classical methods and theorems, we shall represent the fragments of classical mathematics with which we deal as formal systems. Then our informal talk of "formulae" will hereafter, when it is a question of classical mathematics, refer to some formal system $\mathfrak{F}$.

Now we intend for the statements A' to be expressible by the reduced means, without quantifiers, which we described roughly above and will describe more precisely in section 2. These statements will be thus expressed by formulae without quantifiers which we take to have an immediate intuitive meaning. We do not formalize the constructive methods of proof, but since we obtain A' by syntactical transformations from A (that is, we obtain a formula expressing the (constructive, unproblematic) statement A' by transformation of (in fact the proof of) a formula expressing the (non-constructive, problematic) theorem A), we wish A' to be expressed by a formula. Therefore we shall hereafter use the letters to refer to formulae, but we must understand that we interpret from a formal system in which formulae are provable, unprovable, refutable, etc., into a formalized language (with limited means of expression) in which formulae are true, false, verifiable, etc.[2]

Thus the first condition for an interpretation of a system $\mathcal{F}$ is

(a') From any proof of a formula A in the system $\mathcal{F}$ we obtain a quantifier-free formula A' which is verifiable.

We might ask whether A' can be associated directly with A instead of with a proof of A . Our examples cast doubt on this: if from a proof of, say (1), we can find a recursive satisfaction, we might well expect that different proofs will yield different satisfactions. We shall show (theorem 3) that there is in fact a difficulty in principle, and that in any useful interpretation, the formula A' will depend essentially on the proof.

It is clear that (a') is a minimal condition and that others will have to be added. One might be a condition which will insure consistency and that A' is not a com-

---

[2]This terminology, if I have understood it correctly, is Burton Dreben's.

pletely arbitrary verifiable formula. In order to formulate such a condition, we modify (a') to

(a) For any formula A of $\mathfrak{F}$ and any n we can effectively obtain a quantifier-free formula A_n. From a proof of A we can find an m such that A_m is verifiable.

Then we add

(b) From a proof of - A (the negation of A) in $\mathfrak{F}$, we can find for each n a substitution-case of A_n which is false.

Then if A and - A were both provable, the formula A_m obtained from the proof of A would be verifiable, and yet have a false substitution-case, which is impossible. Therefore if we can satisfy (a) and (b), we shall have shown the consistency of $\mathfrak{F}$.

<u>Definition 1</u>. If (a) and (b) are satisfied, then we say we have a <u>finitary interpretation</u> of $\mathfrak{F}$.[3] Of course the methods of our metamathematical investigation will be constructive (see below, section 3); it follows that the proof of (a) will in fact give us a constructive

---

[3]Kreisel in [2] discusses a general concept in which the A_n are formulae in a second formal system F and "verifiable" is replaced by "true". This concept has a certain architectonic value (see [5]), but it does not have enough structure for a general theory to be built around it, and outside the finitary case there seems to be no utility in using the sequence A_n instead of a single formula. [The numerals in brackets of course refer to the bibliography at the end of this dissertation.]

proof of A_m.

The quest for finitary interpretations of classical formal systems is a generalization of, and historically an outgrowth of, Hilbert's program of proving by "finitary methods" the consistency of formal systems of classical mathematics. For an interpretation establishes the consistency of the system (so that if Gödel's second undecidability theorem applies to a system $\mathfrak{F}$, the proof of the existence of an interpretation of $\mathfrak{F}$ is not formalizable in $\mathfrak{F}$), and we shall see that the methods used to prove consistency by extensions of Hilbert's methods not only yield the most interesting interpretations but are the basic tools we have for obtaining them.

There is a closer relation between our program and Hilbert's philosophy of mathematics. Hilbert suggested looking at non-constructive existence proofs and axioms on the analogy of the introduction of ideal elements in affine and projective geometry. A consistency proof supports this picture in thefollowing way: Suppose that $\mathfrak{F}$ has a class of formulae all of which express finitary decidable statements, and such that every true one is provable. Then if the system is consistent, no false formula of the class is provable; moreover any formula obtained by replacing terms in one of the class by free variables is verifiable. Thus from the consistency proof we obtain a constructive proof of any generalization of a formula of the class which was provable in the system.[4] Then the non-constructive proof could be viewed as, according to one's point of view, a detour or a short-cut, a detour in that it goes through "ideal points" and a short cut in terms of length an d complexity.

This picture incidentally suggests a further condition which can be imposed on an interpretation, namely that if (as is true of elementary number theory) the formulae of $\mathfrak{F}$ are obtained by adding certain further devices (e. g. quantifiers) to formulae in our constructive language, then the interpretation assigns to any quantifier-free formula A of $\mathfrak{F}$ itself for each n . This condition will be clearer in the light of section 2.

Definition 2. We shall say that an interpretation is strong if it satisfies

(c) If B is deduced from A in $\mathfrak{F}$, and with A, B are associated the sequences A_n , B_n under (a), then for any n we can find an m such that if A_n is verifiable, so is B_m .

---

[4]Hilbert himself apparently thought of the matter more narrowly, for in [1] (p. 281 of the abridged reprint in [2]) he says that all but the variable-free numerical formulae are ideal elements. The sense in which the consistency proof eliminates ideal elements must be that it effectively obtains from the formal proof of a numerical formula a numerical computation. The free variables of a formula of recursive number theory have "in themselves" no meaning; they are schematic letters.

If $\mathfrak{F}$ satisfies (c), then if we add to $\mathfrak{F}$ as an axiom a formula A for which some A_n is verifiable, the same assignment of quantifier-free formulae will be an interpretation of the extension.

2. Systems considered

In this section we describe precisely both the vocabulary of the quantifier-free formulae A_n and the classical systems which we seek to interpret.

The systems $\mathfrak{F}$ which we interpret will be extensions of a "finitary core" of decidable numerical formulae which they have in common with the constructive vocabulary. We shall seek interpretations by which any formula of this core is mapped onto itself.

Definition 3. By a numerical scheme we mean an effective specification of a constant 0 , a function symbol S a predicate symbol = , other constants, predicates and function symbols, but no other primitive symbols, such that

I. Term and formula are defined as follows:

A. 0 and any other constant is a term.

B. If α is a function symbol with n argument places, and $t_1 \ldots t_n$ are terms, then so is $\alpha(t_1 \ldots t_n)$. In particular, if t is a term, so is St .

C. If P is an n-place predicate symbol, and $t_1 \ldots t_n$ are terms, then $P(t_1 \ldots t_n)$ is a formula. In particular, if s and t are terms, then s = t is a formula.

II. With each constant there is associated a natural number; with each n-argument function symbol is associated an n-place recursive function; with each n-place predicate symbol is associated a recursive class of n-tuples, such that

A. 0 is assigned 0 .

B. S is assigned the successor function

C. = is assigned $\hat{x}\hat{y}(x = y)$.

III. To each term is assigned a <u>value</u>, inductively as follows:

A. A constant is assigned the number under II.

B. If $t_1 \ldots t_n$ have values $v_1 \ldots v_n$ respectively, and α is assigned the function $\bar{\alpha}$ under II, then $\alpha(t_1 \ldots t_n)$ has the value $\bar{\alpha}(v_1 \ldots v_n)$. In particular, if t has the value v , then St has the value v + 1 .

IV. To each formula is assigned a <u>truth-value</u>: If P is assigned the class p under II, and $t_1 \ldots t_n$ have the values $v_1 \ldots v_n$ respectively, then $P(t_1 \ldots t_n)$ has the value True if $v_1 \ldots v_n \varepsilon p$, otherwise False .[5] In particular, if s and t have the values v and w , then s = t has the value True if v = w , otherwise

[5]Note that we use simply the sequence as a notation for ordered n-tuples. v, w is a sample notation for an ordered pair.

False

The set of true formulae of a numerical scheme is recursive if the functions and classes of the above-described evaluation procedure are recursively enumerable in the following sense: We have two recursive functions f and g, each of two variables, such that

(a) If $\bar{\alpha}$, with k_n arguments, is the function assigned to the n th function symbol, then for each y

$$f(n, y) = \bar{\alpha}[(y)_0 \dots (y)_{k_n - 1}].^6$$

(b) If p is the class (of j_n-tuples) assigned to the n th predicate symbol, then for each y

$$g(n, y) = 0 \text{ if } (y)_0 \dots (y)_{j_n - 1} \in p ;$$
$$g(n, y) = 1 \text{ if } (y)_0 \dots (y)_{j_n - 1} \notin p .$$

In point of fact, every specification of a class of recursive functions and relations which is satisfactory from our methodological point of view will have these properties. See section 3.

Definition 5. By a numerical system N we mean a system formalized in the classical propositional calculus whose non-logical axioms are exactly the true formulae of some numerical scheme and the negations of the false formulae.

---

[6] $(y)_i$ is the exponent of the i th prime p_i ($p_0 = 2$) in the prime decomposition of y. See Kleene, Introduction to Metamathematics ([3], but hereafter referred to as IM in order to avoid repeated mention of the author), p. 230, where p_i and $(y)_i$ are both seen to be primitive recursive (as functions of i and y, i, respectively).

We suppose that (a) and (b) above are satisfied. Since it follows that the set of axioms of N is recursive, whether a formula is provable can simply be decided by the usual truth-tables. Therefore we speak of truth rather than of provability, particularly since the assignment of truth-values is simply an extension by adding the truth-tables of the valuation of the original numerical scheme.

If N is a numerical system, we can consider extensions of the notation of N by adding free number variables.

Definition 6. A formula of the extension is verifiable if every formula A* obtained by substituting numerals for the free variables of A is true.

We shall also use extensions which add free function variables. To extend the notion of valuation, and of verifiability, we must consider assignments of functions to function variables.

Definition 7. A substitution for a free function variable f, with k argument places, in a formula of an extension by variables of a numerical system, is an assignment of numerical values to terms of the form

$$f(0^{(n_1)} \dots 0^{(n_k)}) \qquad (1)$$

Then given a substitution for each of the variables of a formula A (including number variables), then the procedure under III of def. 3 assigns a numerical value to each term in A, and then the procedure under IV assigns a truth-value to each prime subformula of A, for if $\alpha(t_1 \ldots t_n)$ is a term such that the values of $t_1 \ldots t_n$ are $v_1 \ldots v_n$, then if α is a function symbol of N, the value of $\alpha(t_1 \ldots t_n)$ is givon by IIIB; if α is a function variable f, then the value of α will be that of $\alpha(0^{(v_1)} \ldots 0^{(v_n)})$, which is given by the substitution. Thus at each stage in computing the value of a term we can proceed. Thus we can make

Definition 8. A formula of an extension of N by number and function variables is verifiable if it is true for every substitution for its number and function variables.

To determine the truth-value of a formula for given substitutions for its variables, we need only a finite number of values of terms (1) for each function variable. Therefore it could be that the value of every other such term under the substitution is 0. It follows that whatever the class of functions from which those giving the values of the terms (1) are chosen, a formula will be verifiable if it is true for all substitutions where the terms are 0 for all but a finite number of arguments. I. e. if a formula is verifiable for all functions 0 except for finitely many arguments, it is verifiable for all functions.

Such functions can be represented by numbers in a very simple way.

Definition 9. $\nu_2(a, b) = 2^a(2b + 1) - 1$

$\nu_2^1(a) = (a + 1)_0$ $\qquad \nu_2^2(a) = (a + 1)/(a + 1)_0$

where a/b is the quotient function (the $[a/b]$ of IM, p. 223). ν_2 is a one-to-one mapping of ordered pairs of natural numbers onto the natural numbers, $\nu_2^1(a)$ is the first element of the pair number a ; $\nu_2^2(a)$ is the second element.

Definition 10. For any $n \geq 2$,

$\nu_{n+1}(a_1 \ldots a_{n+1}) = \nu_2[\nu_n(a_1 \ldots a_n), a_{n+1}]$

$\nu_{n+1}^i(a) = \nu_n^i[\nu_2^1(a)]$ if $i \leq n$; $\nu_{n+1}^{n+1}(a) = \nu_2^2(a)$.

Then ν_n is for each $n \geq 2$ a one-to-one mapping of ordered n-tuples of natural numbers onto the natural numbers, and $\nu_n^i(a)$ is the i-th element of the n-tuple number a .

Then if $\beta(a_1 \ldots a_n) = 0$ unless each $a_i \leq p$, then the function β is represented by the number $w =$ $\prod_{i \leq k} p_i \exp \beta[\nu_n^1(i) \ldots \nu_n^n(i)]$, where $k = \max_{x_i \leq p}[\nu_n(x_1 \ldots x_n)]$.

It is plain that if $x_i \leq p$, then $(w)_{\nu_n(x_1 \ldots x_n)} =$ $\beta(\nu_n^1[\nu_n(x_1 \ldots x_n)] \ldots \nu_n^n[\nu_n(x_1 \ldots x_n)]) = \beta(x_1 \ldots x_n)$. Moreover if $k < \nu_n(x_1 \ldots x_n)$, then $(w)_{\nu_n(x_1 \ldots x_n)} = 0$, and since by the definition of k , for some i, $p < x_i$, $\beta(x_1 \ldots x_n) = 0$ also.

Thus every function of n variables which is 0 except for finitely many arguments is of the form $\lambda x_1 \ldots x_n (w)_{\nu_n(x_1 \ldots x_n)}$, for some w (and is of course primitive recursive; indeed the class of all these functions is obviously primitive recursively enumerable).

The introduction of function variables also makes possible the introduction of ~~functional~~ symbols which have function variables as arguments, as well as number variables, ~~and~~ for functionals whose values are to be natural numbers. These will be introduced according to the following principle: If recursion schemata are admitted to define recursive functions of a given degree of complexity (we do not attempt here to make this expression precise; see chapter IV, section 4; also Kleene [6]), then we define a corresponding class of functionals by admitting function variables as parameters in the schemata and adding the further schema

$$H(f_1 \ldots f_p, a_1 \ldots a_q) = f_1[H_1(f_1 \ldots f_p, a_1 \ldots a_q) \ldots H_{n_1}(f_1 \ldots f_p, a_1 \ldots a_q)] , \qquad (2)$$

where n_1 is the number of arguments of f_1 .

It follows that in order to <u>compute</u> the value of a functional for given arguments, all we need is to have at certain points (when evaluating the H of (2) having already evaluated each H_i) the value of terms (1). Therefore a substitution in the sense of definition 8 is sufficient to permit this computation, and the assignment of values to the terms and of truth-values to formulae can be extended to terms and formulae containing functional symbols. The definitions of substitution and of verifiability are still adequate.

It is still true that the value of a term for a given substitution for all its variables depends on only a finite number of values of terms (1) for each function argument. For only finitely many such terms would appear in the computation of a functional if its number arguments are given as numerals,[7] and therefore if for each i a numerical value of t_i can be obtained on the basis of finitely many values of terms (1), so can a numerical value of $K(f_1 \ldots f_p, t_1 \ldots t_q)$, if K is a functional symbol of the system. It is therefore also still true that if a formula is verifiable for functions 0 except for finitely many arguments, then it is verifiable for all functions.

We might remark parenthetically that if a class of functions defined by recursion schemata is closed under explicit definition, then no new functions can be obtained by substituting functions of the class for function variables in functionals of the corresponding class. For only the schema (2) could produce a jump out of the class, and if we assume that the substitution of $\bar{f}_1 \ldots \bar{f}_p$ for $f_1 \ldots f_p$ in $H_1 \ldots H_{n_1}$ yields functions $\bar{H}_j$ of the class, ~~and~~ then (2) becomes an explicit definition

---

[7]The definition of a functional $K(f_1 \ldots f_p, a_1 \ldots a_q)$ is essentially the same as that of a function $k(a_1 \ldots a_q)$ recursive relative to $f_1 \ldots f_p$, and therefore the computation can be in Kleene's formalism of recursive functions. See below ch. IV, §5, and IM §54, also pp. 274-5, 290-5.

$$\overline{H}(a_1 \ldots a_q) = \overline{f}_1[\overline{H}_1(a_1 \ldots a_q) \ldots \overline{H}_{n_1}(a_1 \ldots a_q)].$$

(When we speak of substitution here, we speak informally of substituting the symbols in the functional expressions; in view of the computable character of the functions involved, this yields a substitution in the sense of def. 7.)

Definition 11. By a formula of recursive number theory we mean a formula of an extension of a numerical system N by free number variables only.

We note that if t is a term and A(x) a formula of recursive number theory, then the formulae $(x)[x \leq t \supset A(x)]$ and $(Ex)[x \leq t \& A(x)]$ express recursive predicates (primitive recursive in the function exp ressed by t and the predicate expressed by A(x); IM, p. 228), and the term $\mu x[x \leq t \& A(x)]$ expresses a recursive function. It follows that the addition of bounded quantification and the bounded μ-symbol to a recursive number theory is equivalent to adding additional functions and predicates, and therefore we can enlarge the notion of recursive number theory to include these devices.

The same considerations apply if t and A(x) contain function variables and functional symbols. Therefore we make the following definition:

Definition 12. A (full) finitary formula is a formula of an extension of a numerical system by function variables, functional symbols, and bounded quantification.

The most important <u>non-finitary</u> extensions of numerical systems are those which add at least the classical predicate calculus of first order with equality.

<u>Definition 13</u>. A <u>formula of elementary number theory</u> is a formula obtained from formulae of an extension of a numerical system by number and function variables (but not functionals) by the formation rules of the first-order predicate calculus.

<u>Definition 14</u>. A <u>system of elementary number theory</u> is a system whose formulae are formulae of elementary number theory, whose rules of proof are those of the classical predicate calculus with equality, and whose theorems include all the true formulae of the underlying numerical system.

<u>Definition 15</u>. A <u>system of elementary number theory without induction</u> is a system of elementary number theory whose axioms are verifiable quantifier-free formulae.[8] A <u>system of elementary number theory with induction</u> is an extension of an elementary number theory without induction by the axiom schema of ordinary induction, or by the rule of inference

$$\frac{\mathfrak{A}(0) \qquad \mathfrak{A}(a) \supset \mathfrak{A}(Sa)}{\mathfrak{A}(t)}$$

---

[8]The axiom schema $a = b \supset . \mathfrak{A}(a) \supset \mathfrak{A}(b)$ can be replaced by (verifiable) quantifier-free axioms. See Hilbert and Bernays, <u>Grundlagen der Mathematik</u> (hereafter referred to as HB), I, 373-5.

where a of course does not occur in $\mathfrak{a}(0)$

It follows that not every system of elementary number theory is either a system of elementary number theory without induction or a system of elementary number theory with induction.

We know that extensions of elementary number theory by the description operator, and therefore by the least

number operator (μ-symbol) and Hilbert's ε-symbol are inessential in the sense that if a formula not containing these symbols is provable with their use, then it is also provable without them. For the description operator this is shown in HB I, §8 (and from a different point of view in IM §74), and the μ-symbol and the ε-symbol are explicitly definable by the description operator. We can therefore count such extensions as elementary number theory, but our proofs of reduction theorems will presuppose that they have been eliminated.

We can also consider systems of elementary number theory with higher induction principles such as transfinite induction on recursive well-orderings.

We shall defer the description of systems beyond elementary number theory, and of the apparatus for their interpretation, until chapter V.

Let N_0 be the numerical scheme which consists only of 0 , S , $=$, $+$, and $\cdot$, the latter two symbols having their standard valuations. The most important system without induction is one based on this scheme, namely the system Q of Tarski, Mostowski, and Robinson, p. 51. Since this system has the property that every general recursive function is numeralwise representable in it,[9] it in effect contains

[9] In the sense of IM p. 200. If we are to avoid quantifiers in our metalanguage, we ought not to put the matter in precisely this way. The proof that every general recur-

every numerical system as a subsystem. Namely if we extend Q by adding the description operator, then for any numerical scheme N we can associate to each function ymbol a term, to each constant a numeral, to each predicate a formula, such that if the symbols of N are introduced by explicit definitions, then every true formula of N becomes provable, and the negation of each false formula becomes provable.[10]

The standard elementary number theory, e. g. the Z of HB (I, 371), or the classical system of Kleene (IM, p. 82) is in effect an extension of Q by adding an axiom or rule of induction. Although these systems are well known, we shall give their non-logical axioms here.

Q:[11] Q_1 $Sx = Sy \supset x = y$

---

sive function is numeralwise representable in Q (as given in IM 41, not in Tarski et al.) gives for every set of recursion equations a formula $A(a_1 \ldots a_n, b)$ (where n is the number of places of the principal function letter) and a method which, given any $m_1 \ldots m_n$, k and a computation from the equations of an equation $f(0^{(m_1)} \ldots 0^{(m_n)}) = 0^{(j)}$, yields a proof of $A(0^{(m_1)} \ldots 0^{(m_n)}, 0^{(k)})$ if $k = j$, and a proof of $-A(0^{(m_1)} \ldots 0^{(m_n)}, 0^{(k)})$ if $k \neq j$. It will then follow that from a computation of a truth-value for a formula of N, we obtain a proof either of the corresponding formula of Q or of its negation.

[10]The numeral for a constant is simply the assigned value. If α is a function symbol assigned the function $\bar{\alpha}$ of n variables, and $A(a_1 \ldots a_n, b)$ numeralwise represents this function in Q, then the term is $\imath x A(a_1 \ldots a_n, x)$; each predicate symbol is assigned the formula which numeralwise expresses its associated class.

[11]We deviate from Tarski et al. in using the function

$Q_2 \quad 0 \neq Sy$

$Q_3 \quad x \neq 0 \supset S[\delta(x)] = x$

$Q_4 \quad x + 0 = x$

$Q_5 \quad x + Sy = S(x + y)$

$Q_6 \quad x \cdot 0 = 0$

$Q_7 \quad x \cdot Sy = (x \cdot y) + x$

Z:[12] adds $\mathcal{A}(0)$ & $(x)[\mathcal{A}(x) \supset \mathcal{A}(Sx)]. \supset (x)\mathcal{A}(x)$.

It follows that Z also has the property of implicitly including every numerical system. This is a kind of completeness property which is of course the root of the incompleteness properties discovered by Gödel.

3. Metamathematical methods of proof

It is, as we have said, essential that the methods of our investigation should be constructive. In fact, if it were arithmetized, its vocabulary should properly be that of finitary formulae, so that the possibility of non-constructiveness does not arise in it.

We shall not actually adhere to this, but there will be two types of deviations. The first is stylistic; the second

---

symbol δ (predecessor) to replace the quantifier in Q_3, and in taking the free variable axioms instead of their universal closures.

[12]The axiom Q_3 is no longer independent and is not included in either HB I, 371 or IM p. 82. It is noteworthy that it must be assumed in the system Z_μ (HB II, 293) in order to get induction from the schema

$$\mathcal{A}(a) \supset (\mu x)\mathcal{A}(x) < Sa .$$

the second is more fundamental.

With respect to the first, consider the definition of finitary interpretation (def. 1). We have used such phrases as "we can effectively obtain" where the existence of an effective procedure is asserted without the procedure being explicitly described. We can state (a) and (b) of def. 1 more strictly thus:

A finitary interpretation of a system $\mathfrak{F}$ is a triple f, g, h, of recursive functions, f and g of two variables, h of one variable, such that

(a) If a is the number of a formula A of $\mathfrak{F}$, then $f(n, a)$ is the number of a finitary formula A_n; if b is the number of a proof of A in $\mathfrak{F}$, then $f[h(b), a]$ is the number of a verifiable formula.

(b) If b is the number of a proof of $-A$ in $\mathfrak{F}$, then $g(b, n)$ is the number of a false substitution-case of the formula A_n.

Then in our proofs, we shall describe these functions so that routine arithmetization and formalization will yield explicit expressions for them.

The second deviation is that universal quantification will be used in a more essential way in connection with such things as the rule of (effective) infinite induction: If for each n we can effectively obtain a proof of $A(0^{(n)})$ then $A(a)$ is provable. These uses of quantifiers in conditionals will be such that in the unpacking necessary to show that a particular case of a formula whose verifiability is claimed is true, the quantifications will have been proved, and therefore the innermost ones will be verifiable. Howver, in order to justify the transfinite inductions which we shall use, it is necessary to go one step further; and, the proofs of such inductions can be formalized only by bound predicate or relation variables, but with the same restriction as above, so that we need no concept of the negation of a universal quantification. (See below, theorem 18; HB II, 344-5, 363-7; Schütte [4], pp. 113-4.)

We shall conclude with a remark about what functions and functionals are admitted and what induction principles we use in our metamathematics. The functions will be a recursively enumerable subclass of the general recursive functions; in fact, we do not need to mention any functions which are not primitive recursive relative to a function which enumerates all ordinal recursive functions of finite level and order, described in chapters IV and V. In order to prove statements involving these functions, we shall need transifinite induction on certain well-orderings defined in those chapters. The considerations of the last paragraph imply that an axiomatization of our metamathematics which did not use higher-type bound variables would have to take such transfinite inductions as axioms. Conversely, with sufficiently powerful such inductions it ought to be possible to eliminate all quantifiers from the proofs of finitary formulae by our methods.

This entire description of a constructive metalanguage is of one in which we can carry out the interpretation (or other metamathematical studies concerning) of particular systems; in this language the functions f , g, h , of the sharpened def.1 are constants, not variables. We do not describe the vocabulary of a "general theory of systems". It follows that if this constructive language is to be regarded as the "real elements", then much of our text is "ideal" and schematic. But this is inescapable.

CHAPTER II

OVER-SIMPLE INTERPRETATIONS

1. Trivial Interpretation

The following theorem is formally analogous to Gödel's completeness theorem, and its triviality and unfruitfulness shows how much less structure the *general* concept of finitary interpretation has than that of model.

Theorem 1 (Kreisel [1], [2]). Let $\mathfrak{F}$ be a consistent system which has a negation and for which the predicate $Pr(a, b)$: " a is the number of a proof in $\mathfrak{F}$ of a formula with number b " is recursive. Then $\mathfrak{F}$ has an interpretation by a single free variable formula.

Proof. If a is the number of A, let $neg(a)$ be the number of $-A$. Let A_n be the formula $Pr[b, neg(0^{(a)})]$ for each n.

If A is provable, then by consistency $-A$ is unprovable, and $-Pr[b, neg(0^{(a)}]$ is verifiable.

If $-A$ is provable, then if b is the number of a proof of it, $-Pr[0^{(b)}, neg(0^{(a)})]$ is false, q. e. d.

Note that if $\mathfrak{F}$ has the deduction theorem, then this interpretation is strong (def. 2, p. 9), if $neg(a)$ is now the number of $-Cl(A)$, where $Cl(A)$ is the closure of A. If B is deducible in $\mathfrak{F}$ from A, then $Cl(A) \supset Cl(B)$ is provable; so is $-Cl(B) \supset -Cl(A)$. Let p be the number of a proof of the last formula. Then if $Pr[m, neg(b)]$ holds, so does $Pr\{k[neg(b), neg(a), m, p], neg(a)\}$, where $k(x, y, z, w)$ is the number of a proof of Y, if x is the number of X, y of Y, z of a proof of X, and w of a proof of $X \supset Y$. Therefore is $-\Pr[m, neg(0^{(a)})]$ is verifiable, so is $-\Pr[m, neg(0^{(b)})]$.

2. Failure of Interpretation by Recursive Satisfaction

We mentioned in the Introduction, §1, as one possibility for interpreting prenex formulae of a system $\mathcal{F}$ of elementary number theory, obtaining recursive satisfactions of such formulae. In this section, we show that any system in which every general recursive predicate is numeralwide expressible has a theorem which has no recursive satisfaction.

We remind the reader that a recursive satisfaction of a formula

$$(x)(Ey)(z)A(x, y, z) \qquad (1)$$

is an assignment of a recursive function $f(a)$ such that

$$A[a, f(a), b]$$

is verifiable.

Definition 16. Let $\mathfrak{A}$ be a prenex formula of elementary number theory (perhaps with free function variables). Let $x_1 \ldots x_{n_i}$ be the universally quantified variables whose quantifiers precede in the prefix the i th existential quantifier, whose variable is y_i. Then a recursive satisfaction of $\mathfrak{A}$ is an assignment to each y_i of a recursive functional whose arguments are the free variables of $\mathfrak{A}$ and $x_1 \ldots x_{n_1}$, such that the result of dropping the quantifiers and substituting the symbol for the assigned functional for y_1 is verifiable. (A functional of 0 function arguments is a function; a function of 0 number arguments is a number.)

We can think of the expectation of a recursive satisfaction for each provable formula of $\mathfrak{A}$ as a "naive reading" of these formulae, for what we do is to interpret the quantifiers in the same way as we do the informal use of quantifiers in finitary mathematics. We could justify this expectation if we could produce an interpretation of $\mathfrak{F}$ which assigned to each formula $\mathfrak{A}$ a sequence A_n such that if $\mathfrak{A}$ is a theorem, then a recursive satisfaction of $\mathfrak{A}$ can be effectively found.

Essentially the same argument as for Gödel's incompleteness theorem shows that if the system is sufficiently rich, no such interpretation can be found.

Theorem 2 (Kreisel [1], appendix I). Let $\mathfrak{F}$ be a consistent system of elementary number theory, whose class of proofs is recursive, and in which every general recursive predicate is numeralwise expressible. (IM, p. 197.) Then we can find a formula of the form (1), where $A(x, y, z)$ numeralwise expresses a recursive predicate, which is provable in $\mathfrak{F}$ but which has no general recursive satisfaction.

<u>Proof.</u>[1] Let Pr(a, b) be the "proof" predicate of the system (cf. theorem 1). Let s(x, y) be the (recursive) function whose value is the number of the formula obtained by substituting $0^{(x)}$ for every occurrence of the free variable b in the formula whose number is y . Let Ps(x, y, z) be the formula which represents in the system the predicate Pr[x, s(y, z)] . Consider the formula

$$(x)[(Ey)Ps(y, x, x) \vee -(Ey)Ps(y, x, x)] .$$

This is provable in $\mathfrak{F}$, since it is an instance of the schema $(x)[\mathfrak{A}(x) \vee -\mathfrak{A}(x)]$, provable in the pure predicate calculus. Then its prenex normal form

$$(x)(Ey)(z)[Ps(y, x, x) \vee - Ps(z, x, x)] \qquad (2)$$

is also provable in $\mathfrak{F}$. (This is not strictly prenex, but since Ps(y, x, x) expresses a recursive predicate, the quantifiers in it do not count for the purpose of interpretation.)

Consider any recursive function f and the formula

$$Ps[f(a), a, a] \vee - Ps(b, a, a) \qquad (3)$$ [2]

If the number of the formula - Ps[f(a), a, a] is p , then the number of the formula

---

[1]A stricter statement of the theorem is: For every set of recursion equations with a one-place principal functionletter f we can find a number p such that if a value can be computed from the equations for the argument p , then we can find a number q such that A[p, f(p), q] is false.

[2]By the first alternand we mean the formula of $\mathfrak{F}$ which expresses Pr[f(a), s(a, a)] .

$$- Ps[f(0^{(p)}), 0^{(p)}, 0^{(p)}] \tag{4}$$

is s(p, p) . What this formula expresses, namely

$$- Pr[f(p), s(p, p)] \tag{5}$$

must be true. For otherwise f(p) must be the number of a proof of it, for it has number s(p, p) . Then evidently both (4) and

$$Ps[f(0^{(p)}), 0^{(p)}, 0^{(p)}]$$

must be provable in $\mathfrak{F}$, which contradicts the hypothesis that $\mathfrak{F}$ is consistent. Therefore (5) holds.

Then (4) is provable. Let q be the number of a proof of it. Then since Pr[q, s(p, p)] holds, the formula (3) expresses a falsehood if $0^{(p)}$ is substituted for a and $0^{(q)}$ is substituted for b . It follows that f does not satisfy (2). Note that we suppose that f is computable at p , but not that it is computable for any other arguments.

It follows that (2) can also not have a "non-standard" recursive satisfaction in which quantifiers which might occur in the formula Ps(a, b, c) are brought into the prefix. For the function assigned to y would still yield a recursive satisfaction in the sense in which we have shown it to be impossible, for the formula (3) would be deducible from the alleged satisfying formula by restoring the existential quantifiers whose variables had been replaced by recursive terms.

The failure of this naive interpretation is an indication that there are real difficulties about giving a finitary interpretation to classical mathematics. The naive interpretation is the most plausible reading of the quantifiers in intuitionist mathematics. Brouwer showed that there are certain instances of the one-quantifier law of the excluded middle which are intuitionistically false (see [2], [4]). It is precisely this law for which the naive interpretation fails in number theory. However, because of its appeal to the concept of recursive function, to take the interpretation as <u>the</u> reading of the quantifiers from an intuitionist point of view would involve an appeal to Church's thesis, which is intuitionistically problematic. (See Heyting.) Thus we cannot say that we have shown that the formula (2) is intuitionistically <u>false</u>, and indeed we still do not know of any truth of classical elementary number theory which is intuitionistically false.[3]

3. <u>Dependence on the Proof of the Verifiable Formula Corresponding to a Theorem</u>

In this section we prove the theorem referred to on page 6, which says that interpretations by a single free

---

[3]Kleene and Nelson (IM §82) have obtained an interpretation of intuitionist elementary number theory which gives a recursive satisfaction to each prenex theorem. It follows that (2) is not provable in Kleene's intuitionist system. They also obtain what is called a recursive "realization" to theorems of any logical form. This is extended to analysis in Kleene [9].

variable formula are not adequate for our purposes. Why this is will be clear in a moment.

First we must assume that the system $\mathfrak{F}$ has a property of number-theoretic "standardness" or "soundness" which we might describe as follows: If $A(x)$ is a quantifier-free formula of elementary number theory with no free variables except x, then there is an effective method for deciding for each n whether $A(0^{(n)})$, which is now a formula of the underlying numerical scheme, is true. If $(Ex)A(x)$ is provable, then we should hope that there is an n such that $A(0^{(n)})$ is true; and if there is, then from the point of view of non-constructive recursive function theory, the least such n is given effectively. Hence we might hope to find an effective procedure whereby, given any proof of such a formula $(Ex)A(x)$, we can find an n such that $A(0^{(n)})$ is true; and then we could find a numerical computation showing $A(0^{(n)})$ to be true, from which we could find a proof of it in $\mathfrak{F}$, by the definition of elementary number theory (defs. 14, 15).

Definition 17. $\mathfrak{F}$ is 1-consistent if there is an effective method by which, given a quantifier-free formula $A(x)$ of $\mathfrak{F}$, with no other free variables, we can find an n such that $A(0^{(n)})$ is true from any proof of $(Ex)A(x)$.

If $\mathfrak{F}$ is 1-consistent, then $\mathfrak{F}$ is consistent. For if C is a numerical formula provable in $\mathfrak{F}$, then clearly

(Ex)(x = x & C) is also provable. Then by 1-consistency, we can find an n such that $0^{(n)} = 0^{(n)}$ & C is true. Therefore C is true.[4]

If $\mathfrak{F}$ is 1-consistent, then every provable formula of the form (x)(Ey)B(x, y), where B(x, y) is quantifier-free and has noother free variables, has a recursive satisfaction. For we can effectively find a proof of (Ey)B($0^{(m)}$, y) for each m, and from that by 1-consistency an n such that B($0^{(m)}$, $0^{(n)}$) is true. Then the function f(m) giving n as a function of m is such that B[m, f(m)] is verifiable.

Definition 18. $\mathfrak{F}$ is 1*-consistent if there is an effective method by which, given a quantifier-free formula A(x_1 ... x_k) with no other free variables, and a proof of (Ex_1) ... (Ex_k)A(x_1 ... x_k), we can find n_1 ... n_k such that A($0^{(n_1)}$ ... $0^{(n_k)}$).

If $\mathfrak{F}$ is 1*-consistent, then every provable formula of the form (x_1) ... (x_j)(Ey_1) ... (Ey_k)B(x_1 ... x_j, y_1 ... y_k) has a recursive satisfaction.

---

[4] We use the expression "1-consistency" because it might be taken as a specialization to one-quantifier formulae of ω-consistency. The latter property has complications which we discuss in chapter VI, §1. 1-consistency is closely related to external consistency (HB II, 282-3; see also below, ch. IV, §3, and Kreisel [3]).

The analogous property of formulae (x)A(x) follows from simple consistency. For if (x)A(x) is provable, then for every n A($0^{(n)}$) is provable, and, by consistency, it is true.

Lemma 3.1. If $\mathfrak{F}$ is 1*-consistent, and $B(a_1 \ldots a_k)$ is a verifiable quantifier-free formula of $\mathfrak{F}$, then the system $\mathfrak{F}_1$ obtained from $\mathfrak{F}$ by adding $B(a_1 \ldots a_k)$ as an axiom is 1*-consistent.

Proof. Let $A(x_1 \ldots x_m)$ be a quantifier-free formula of $\mathfrak{F}$ with no other free variables and suppose that

$$(Ex_1) \ldots (Ex_m)A(x_1 \ldots x_m)$$

is provable in $\mathfrak{F}_1$. Then by the deduction theorem

$$(x_1) \ldots (x_k)B(x_1 \ldots x_k) \supset (Ex_1) \ldots (Ex_m)A(x_1 \ldots x_m)$$

is provable in $\mathfrak{F}$, and therefore so is

$$(Ex_1) \ldots (Ex_k)(Ey_1) \ldots (Ey_m)[-B(x_1 \ldots x_k) \vee A(y_1 \ldots y_m)].$$

By the 1*-consistency of $\mathfrak{F}$, we can find $n_1 \ldots n_{k+m}$ such that

$$-B(0^{(n_1)} \ldots 0^{(n_k)}) \vee A(0^{(n_{k+1})} \ldots 0^{(n_{k+m})})$$

is true. Since $B(a_1 \ldots a_k)$ is verifiable, the first alternand is false, and therefore $A(0^{(n_{k+1})} \ldots 0^{(n_{k+m})})$ is true, q. e. d.

Lemma 3.2. For each m let ν_m, ν_m^i $(i \leq m)$, be the mappings of m-tuples of defs. 9, 10. Suppose that $\mathfrak{F}$ has symbols for these functions and that

$$\nu_m^i[\nu_m(a_1 \ldots a_m)] = a_i \qquad (1_{im})$$

is provable in $\mathfrak{F}$ for each m and each $i \leq m$. Then if $\mathfrak{F}$ is 1-consistent, then $\mathfrak{F}$ is 1*-consistent.

Proof. Suppose $(Ex_1) \ldots (Ex_m)A(x_1 \ldots x_m)$ is provable in $\mathfrak{F}$, $A(x_1 \ldots x_m)$ quantifier-free. Then by (1_{im}) for each $i \leq m$ and the axioms of equality

$$A(a_1 \ldots a_m) \supset A\{\nu_m^1[\nu_m(a_1 \ldots a_m)] \ldots \nu_m^m[\nu_m(a_1 \ldots a_m)]\}$$

is provable, whence

$$(Ex_1) \ldots (Ex_m)A(x_1 \ldots x_m) \supset (Ex)A[\nu_m^1(x) \ldots \nu_m^m(x)] ,$$

whence

$$(Ex)A[\nu_m^1(x) \ldots \nu_m^m(x)]$$

is provable.

By the 1-consistency of $\mathfrak{F}$, we can find an n such that

$$A[\nu_m^1(0^{(n)}) \ldots \nu_m^m(0^{(n)})]$$

is true. But then

$$A[0^{(\nu_m^1(n))} \ldots 0^{(\nu_m^m(n))}]$$

is also true, which is what definition 18 requires.

Theorem 3 (Kreisel [1], appendix II). Let $\mathfrak{F}$ be a 1*-consistent formal system which has quantifier-free expressions which numeralwise express certain primitive recursive predicates specified below. Then any interpretation of $\mathfrak{F}$ by a single free variable formula (i. e. in which the A_n of def. 1 is independent of n) fails to be an interpretation of an extension of $\mathfrak{F}$ by a verifiable quantifier-free formula, provided that the interpreting formulae have no free function variables.

Proof. Let $s(x, y)$ be the substitution function of $\mathfrak{F}$ (see theorem 2).

Tr(a) be the predicate " a is the number of a true

formula of the numerical system of which the instances of the formulae which the interpretation associates with those of $\mathfrak{F}$ are formulae"

$T_1(e, x, y)$, $T_2(e, x, y, z)$, $U(x)$ be as in Kleene's normal form for partial recursive functions (IM, p. 289)

Let $Ts(e, a, b, c)$ be the formula which (numeralwise) expresses $T_2[e, a, s(b, b), c]$ in $\mathfrak{F}$.

$U'(c, d)$ be the formula which expresses $U(c) = d$ in $\mathfrak{F}$.

$T_1'(e, x, y)$ be the formula which expresses $T_1(e, x, y)$ in $\mathfrak{F}$.

$T_2'(e, x, y, z)$ be the formula which expresses $T_2(e, x, y, z)$ in $\mathfrak{F}$.

We assume that these four formulae are quantifier-free.

Let e be the Gödel number of a general recursive function which is 0 if $Tr(x)$, 1 if $- Tr(x)$.

Since the interpretation effectively associates with a formula $\mathfrak{A}$ of $\mathfrak{F}$ a formula A which is finitary without function variables, we can, using an effective enumeration of the numerical instances of A, obtain from the interpretation a recursive function $f(n, a)$ such that if a is the number of $\mathfrak{A}$, then $f(n, a)$ is the number of the n th numerical instance of A. If $\mathfrak{A}$ is provable, then each of these instances is true; if $\mathfrak{A}$ is refutable, then we can find a false one.

Let p be the Gödel number of f, so that $f(n, a) = U[\mu y T_2(e, n, a, y)]$.

Consider the formula

$$(Ex)(Ey)(Ez)(Ew)[Ts(0^{(p)}, x, b, y) \& U'(y, z) \& T_1'(0^{(e)}, z, w) \& U'(w, 1)] . \quad (2)$$

Let c_0 be the Gödel number of this formula. Let c be the number of the formula

$$(Ex)(Ey)(Ez)(Ew)[Ts(0^{(p)}, x, 0^{(c_0)}, y) \& U'(y, z) \& T_1'(0^{(e)}, z, w) \& U'(w, 1)]. \quad (3)$$

Then $c = s(c_0, c_0)$.

If (3) is provable in $\mathcal{F}$, then by the 1*-consistency of $\mathcal{F}$, numbers q, r, s, t can be found such that

$$T_2(p, q, c, r) \& U(r) = s \& T_1(e, s, t) \& U(t) = 1$$

from which $-Tr(s)$ follows.

But then $s = f(q, c)$ and s is the number of a false numerical formula. This is impossible, since (3) was assumed to be provable and s is the number of (3). Therefore (3) is not provable.

This implies that the formula

$$Ts(0^{(p)}, x, 0^{(c_0)}, y) \& U'(y, z) \& T_1'(0^{(e)}, z, w) . - U'(w, 1) \quad (4)$$

with free variables x, y, z, w is verifiable. For any substitution of numerals for the free variables yields a decidable formula. But the resulting formula cannot be false, for if it were for some n, m, r, v , then

$$Ts(0^{(p)}, 0^{(n)}, 0^{(c_o)}, 0^{(m)}) \& U'(0^{(m)}; 0^{(r)}) \& T_1'(0^{(e)}, 0^{(r)}, 0^{(v)}) \& U'(0^{(v)}, 1)$$

would be provable, and (3), which we have shown to be unprovable, could be inferred by existential generalization. Therefore the substitution in (4) is true, and (4) is verifiable. Since $f(n, c)$ is defined for every n , for each n an m and an r can be found such that

$$T_2(p, n, c, m) \& U(m) = r .$$

And moreover, a v can be found such that $T_1(e, r, v)$. Since $s(c_o, c_o) = c$, the antecedent of (4) is true with $0^{(n)}$ for x , $0^{(m)}$ for y , $0^{(r)}$ for z , and $0^{(v)}$ for w . It follows by (4) that $U(v) \neq 1$, that is that $U(v) = 0$ and $Tr(r)$. Since $r = f(n, c)$, it follows that each formula associated with (3), whose number was c , is true.

But if (4) is added to $\mathcal{F}$ as an axiom, then (3) becomes refutable. But by the last paragraph, it will be impossible to find a counterinstance to the formula associated wihh it by the interpretation. Moreover, by lemma 3.1 the extension is 1*-consistent.

This completes the proof of theorem 3. A somewhat elaborated version of the same argument would show that theorem 3 holds if free function variables are allowed in A . This would turn on the fact (see page 14) that if a finitary formula has a counterinstance at all, it has one where the functions are zero except for finitely many arguments, and are therefore representable by numbers.

If we wish to avoid the situation described in theorem 3, the formula A_n which the interpretation assigns to $\mathfrak{a}$ must depend on n, and therefore the verifiable formula which the interpretation assigns to a proof of $\mathfrak{a}$ must depend on the proof of $\mathfrak{a}$ and not simply on $\mathfrak{a}$.

Finally we note that although such systems as Q and Z do not directly contain quantifier-free expressions for the primitive recursive predicates used in the proof of theorem 3, it would be very shocking if these systems became 1*-inconsistent with the addition of recursive or explicit definitions of recursive predicates, and in fact this does not happen (theorems 4 and 13 below).[5]

---

[5] I do not know whether every system which is 1*-consistant remains such with the addition of explicit or recursive definitions, the former of recursive functions and predicates. In speaking of the 1*-consistency of an extension by explicit definition, the defined symbol must be a new symbol such that the biconditional or equation of its ambiguous value and the definiens is a new axiom (as in HB I, 292), so that a formula counts as quantifier-free even if it does not remain so if defined symbols are eliminated.

CHAPTER III

HERBRAND INTERPRETATION

As we have intimated, the proofs of the consistency of formal systems obtained by the methods of the Hilbert school yielded more information than the consistency of the system, or even Hilbert's objective of eliminating non-finitary methods from the proofs of finitary statements. For example, the general consistency theorem of HB (II, 36-7) explicitly mentions what we have called 1*-consistency.

1. The concept of Herbrand interpretation

For systems without induction, i. e. those to which the general consistency theorem applies, Herbrand obtained a stronger result which immediately yields an interpretation of these systems. This interpretation is a reflection of the proof-theoretic fact, discovered by Herbrand, that in a proof in the first order predicate calculus from quantifier-free axioms, the proof can be divided into two parts, of which the first consists of quantifier-free steps and the second essentially of the attaching of quantifiers. If we regard the quantifier-free formula obtained in the first part of the proof as the formula interpreting the proved formula, then we shall (it turns out) have given an interpretation of the system in the subsystem obtained by dropping the apparatus of quantification. We can then think of quantification as an abbreviative or simplifying device, where the full statement of which the theorem is a "partial statement" is given by the quantifier-free "midformula" of the special proof.

Let $\mathcal{A}$ be any prenex formula of the first order predicate calculus, perhaps with function symbols. Let $A(x_1 \ldots x_k)$ be the scope of the innermost quantifier of $\mathcal{A}$, called the scope of $\mathcal{A}$, so that $\mathcal{A}$ is of the form $Q_1 \ldots Q_k A(x_1 \ldots x_k)$, where Q_i is either a universal or an existential quantifier of x_i. Suppose we have an alternation of substitution-cases of the scope of $\mathcal{A}$, i. e. a formula

$$A(t_{11} \ldots t_{1k}) \vee \ldots \vee A(t_{m1} \ldots t_{mk}) . \qquad (1)$$

Definition 19. (1) is called an Herbrand alternation of $\mathcal{A}$ if its free variables $c_1 \ldots c_\mu$ can be so indexed that the free variables of $\mathcal{A}$ come first and

(a) If Q_j is universal, then t_{ij} is a free variable $c_{p_{ij}}$. If Q_s is also universal, then if $c_{p_{ij}} = c_{p_{rs}}$, then $p_{ij} = p_{rs}$ and $j = s$.

(b) If Q_j is universal, and c_q occurs in t_{ik} where $k < j$, then $q < p_{ij}$.

(c) If Q_j is universal, then $p_{ij} = p_{rj}$ if and only if $t_{ih} = t_{rh}$ for each $h < i$.

It is instructive to consider what these conditions imply in the simple case of a three-quantifier formula

$$(x)(Ey)(z)A(x, y, z) \ . \qquad (2)$$

By (a), in each alternand x is replaced by a free variable which, by (c), is the same for each alternand. By (a) and (c), z is replaced by a free variable which is different for every alternand (assuming no two alternands are the same). If we index the alternands A_i so that $i < j$ if the variable replacing z in A_i precedes the variable replacing z in A_j, then by (b) the variable replacing z in the i th alternand does not occur in any previous alternand or in the term replacing y. Therefore (1) is of the form

$$A[\underline{a}, t_1(a), a_1] \vee A[\underline{a}, t_2(a, a_1), a_2] \vee \ldots \vee A[a, t_m(\underline{a}, a_1 \ldots a_{m-1}), a_m] \ .$$

If this formula is verifiable, we can interpret it in the following way: Suppose we attempt to find a recursive satisfaction of (2) by a term $t_1(a)$ and fail for certain values of a and a_1. Then t_2 gives us a new value for y such that if this fails for a_2, ... eventually we obtain a value given by t_m which succeeds for any a_m if all previous attempts have failed.

We can very easily find a verifiable alternation for the formula of theorem 2 which we showed not to have a recursive satisfaction. We choose $t_1(a)$ arbitrarily and let $t_2(a, a_1)$ be just a_1. Thenwe have (cf. p. 29)

$$Ps[\underline{t}_1(a), a, a] \vee - Ps(a_1, a, a) \vee Ps(a_1, a, a) \vee$$

$Ps(a_2, a, a)$,

which is a tautology.

Definition 20. An Herbrand interpretation of a system $\mathfrak{F}$ of elementary number theory is an interpretation in which if $\mathfrak{A}$ is a pre nex formula, then every A_n associated with it is an Herbrand alternation of $\mathfrak{A}$, so that from a proof of $\mathfrak{A}$ we can effectively find a verifiable Herbrand alternation of $\mathfrak{A}$.

Neither definition 19 nor definition 20 requires that the terms substituted in (1) be terms of $\mathfrak{F}$, although they must of course be terms of an extension of a numerical system by free (number and function) variables. Theorem 4 will give for a system without induction an interpretation in which the terms are terms of the system, but theorem 7 will show that even if arbitrary terms of recursive number theory are admitted, this interpretation does not carry over to Z .

2. Herbrand interpretation of elementary number theory without induction

Theorem 4 (Herbrand, Kreisel [1]). Let $\mathfrak{F}$ be an elementary number theory without induction. Let F be the subsystem obtained by omitting quantifiers. Then $\mathfrak{F}$ has an Herbrand interpretation such that if the formula A_n associated with $\mathfrak{A}$ is (1), then each t_{ij} is a term of F , and from a proof of $\mathfrak{A}$ we can find an A_n which is provable in F .

If $-\mathcal{A}$ is provable, then each A_n is refutable in F ; i. e. a substitution-case of its negation can be proved.

Proof. This is, in effect, an almost immediate consequence of Herbrand's theorem.

Given any formula $\mathcal{A}'$, let $\mathcal{A}$ be a prenex equivalent of $\mathcal{A}'$ under some standard (effective) procedure. Then from a proof of $\mathcal{A}'$ we can find a proof of $\mathcal{A}$. Let $B(a_1 \ldots a_p)$ be the conjunction of all the axioms, including equality axioms, used in this proof, where $a_1 \ldots a_p$ are all its free variables. Of course there are no bound variables. Then by the deduction theorem

$$(x_1) \ldots (x_p)B(x_1 \ldots x_p) \supset \mathcal{A} \quad (3)$$

is provable in the predicate calculus. Then by Herbrand's theorem[1] we can find a tautology of the form

$$B_1(s_{11} \ldots s_{1p}) \;\&\; \ldots \;\&\; B_r(s_{r1} \ldots s_{rp}) \,. \supset . \, A(t_{11} \ldots t_{1k}) \vee \ldots \vee A(t_{m1} \ldots t_{mk}) \quad (4)$$

where the consequent satisfies (a)-(c) of def. 19 and is therefore an Herbrand alternation of $\mathcal{A}$. The terms are all constructed of symbols which occurred in the proof of (3) and are therefore terms of $\mathfrak{F}$ and a fortiori of F . Since the conjuncts of the antecedent of (4) are conjunctions of substitution-cases of axioms of $\mathfrak{F}$, which are quantifier-free, it follows that (4) is provable in $\mathfrak{F}$ by

[1] That, if function symbols are present, the form of the terms t_{ij} is according to (a)-(c) is shown in HB II, 151 ff. That function symbols have recursive valuations is not assumed.

the propositional calculus and the rule of substitution for number variables, i. e. by the "elementary calculus with free variables" of HB (I, 295), i. e. in F .

The only essential step in completing the interpretation is, for (b) of def. 1, to show that from a proof of $-\mathfrak{A}$ we can find a counter-example to every Herbrand alternation. This follows from

Lemma 4.1 (Kreisel [1]). If C is an Herbrand alternation of the prenex formula $\mathfrak{A}$, then from a proof of $-\mathfrak{A}$ we can effectively obtain terms $s_{i1} \ldots s_{i\mu}$ of F (if the terms of C are of F), $i = 1 \ldots h$, such that if C_i is the result of substituting s_{ij} for c_j , $j = 1 \ldots \mu$ (these, as with (1), are to be all the free number variables of C), then

$$- C_1 \vee \ldots \vee - C_h$$

is provable in F , and for any substitution of terms representing recursive functions (e. g. 0 except for finitely many arguments; see p. 15) for the free function variables of C we can find an $i \leq h$ such that the resulting formula $C_i{*}$ is false, and if the terms are terms of F , refutable in F .

Proof. By Herbrand's theorem,, we can deduce $\mathfrak{A}$ from C in the predicate calculus of $\mathfrak{F}$, in a variant, to cover function symbols, of what Dreben calls a proof in "Herbrand normal form" (see Dreben, HB II, 152-5). Then by the deduction theorem,

$$(c_1) \ldots (c_\mu)\ C \supset \mathcal{A}$$

is provable in the predicate calculus. Using the given proof of $-\mathcal{A}$, we obtain a proof in $\mathcal{F}$ of

$$(Ec_1) \ldots (Ec_\mu) - C .$$

Then by Herbrand's theorem, we obtain from this a proof in F of a formula of the form (5).

Now for any substitution of recursive terms for the free function variables of (5), the result is an alternation which must have at least one true alternand, since every theorem of F is verifiable. If the true alternand is $-C_1{*}$, then if the terms are terms of F, $-C_1{*}$ is provable (by def. 14). This proves lemma 4.1.

Thus if $\mathcal{A}$ does not have free function variables, one can certainly find from a proof of $-\mathcal{A}$ an instance of C which is refutable in F. In the case where there are function variables, there is certainly a <u>false</u> instance for any substitution for the function variables (by the verifiability of (5)). One might regard a proof of (5) as a refutation of C in F; if one insists on a provable $-C_1{*}$, then it is necessary in this case to assume that $\mathcal{F}$ has at least one function symbol of more than one place, so that for any n we can find a term with n free variables to substitute for a free function variable.

Without doing more work, we might describe an Herbrand

interpretation of $\mathcal{F}$ as follows: Let A_1 be some arbitrary Herbrand alternation of $\mathcal{A}$. Then the sequence A_1, A_2 ... of formulae associated with an arbitrary formula $\mathcal{A}'$ is defined as follows: If n is not the number of a proof of $\mathcal{A}'$, let A_n be A_1; if n is the number of a proof of $\mathcal{A}'$, let A_n be the consequent of the conditional (4) obtained from the proof of $\mathcal{A}$ which we can effectively obtain from that of $\mathcal{A}'$ by the transformation into prenex form. Then A_n is provable in F, and since the axioms of F are verifiable, A_n is verifiable. Therefore (a) of def. 1 holds.

Since each A_n is an Herbrand alternation of $\mathcal{A}$, and $\mathcal{A}$ is equivalent to $\mathcal{A}'$, it follows from lemma 4.1 that if $-\mathcal{A}'$ is provable, then every A_n has an instance which is false and refutable in F.

If the interpretation is defined in this way, then (b) says no more than that $\mathcal{F}$ is consistent, for if $-\mathcal{A}'$ is provable, no n is the number of a proof of $\mathcal{A}'$, and therefore every A_n is A_1.

(b) will contain more of the information of lemma 4.1 (and therefore of Herbrand's theorem), but will follow in the same way, if we take for the sequence A_n an enumeration of all the Herbrand alternations of $\mathcal{A}$ made with terms of $\mathcal{F}$. This has the further advantage that the formulae are independent of any particular arithmetizations of the metamathematics of $\mathcal{F}$. We shall describe an enumeration of Herbrand alternations of $\mathcal{A}$ such that every Herbrand alternation of $\mathcal{A}$ is essentially a subalternation of one in the enumeration. Then if the A_n are this sequence, (b) will be proved in the same way, and the A_n of which the consequent of (4) is a subalternation will be truth-functionally implied by it and therefore provable in F.

Lemma 4.2 (cf. Dreben). Given any prenex formula $\mathcal{A}$, we can generate a sequence of Herbrand alternations of $\mathcal{A}$ such that if (1) is any Herbrand alternation of $\mathcal{A}$, then by renaming free variables it becomes a subalternation of some A_i.

Proof. Let $y_1 \ldots y_p$ be the existentially quantified variables of $\mathcal{A}$; let $z_1 \ldots z_q$ be the universally quantified variables of $\mathcal{A}$. Let d_j be the number of existential variables preceding z_j in the prefix of $\mathcal{A}$. Let f_j be a function symbol with d_j argument places, or a new number variable if $d_j = 0$. Let $r_1, r_2 \ldots$ be an enumeration of all terms obtained using the constants and function symbols of $\mathcal{F}$, the free (number and function) variables of $\mathcal{A}$, and the symbols f_j, so ordered that each term is preceded by all its proper parts, and if $j < j'$, then $f_j(t_1 \ldots t_{d_j})$ precedes $f_j(t_1 \ldots t_{d_{j'}})$ (where evidently $d_j \leq d_{j'}$). Let the p-tuples of these terms be so ordered that $r_{i_1} \ldots r_{i_p}$ precedes $r_{j_1} \ldots r_{j_p}$

if $\max_{k \le p} i_k < \max_{k \le p} j_k$ or $\max i_k = \max j_k$ and for some $p' < p$, $i_k = j_k$ for each $k \le p'$ while $i_{p'+1} < j_{p'+1}$. Let $A'(y_1 \ldots y_p)$ be obtained from $A(x_1 \ldots x_n)$ (the scope of $\mathcal{A}$; see p. 41) by substituting $f_j(y_1 \ldots y_{d_j})$ for z_j, $j = 1 \ldots q$. Let C^i be obtained from $A'(y_1 \ldots y_p)$ by substituting the i th p-tuple in the above ordering for $y_1 \ldots y_p$.

Let r_1', r_2' ... be an enumeration in the same order of the terms r_v of the form $f_j(t_1 \ldots t_{d_j})$, $0 \le d_j$. Let c_1, c_2 ... be a list of number variables, none of which is an f_j or is free in $\mathcal{A}$. Let A^i be the formula obtained from C^i by replacing each occurrence of a term r_m' which is not an occurrence as a proper part of another such term by the variable c_m.

Then A_n is $A^1 \vee \ldots \vee A^n$.

It is evident that A_n is of form (1). Clearly the term $f_j(t_{i1} \ldots t_{id_j})$ which replaces z_j in C^i is not a proper part of another term r_m'; therefore in A^i z_j is replaced by a free variable. Moreover different z_j must be replaced by different variables, for the terms replacing them in C^i have different outermost symbols. Hence (a) of def. 19 is satisfied.

(b) If Q_m is existential, Q_j universal, and $k < j$, let s_{im} be the term replacing x_m in C^i, t_{im} in A^i.

Then the term replacing x_j in C^1 is of the form $f_j(\ldots s_{1m} \ldots)$. In the series of r_1 , it must come after s_{1m} , and therefore after any proper part of s_{1m} . Since c_q replaces such a part, $q < p_{1j}$.

If Q_m and Q_j are both universal, then x_m and x_j are replaced in C^1 by terms $f_m(t_1 \ldots t_v)$ and $f_j(u_1 \ldots u_w)$, where $v \leq w$ and $t_\beta = u_\beta$ for $\beta \leq v$. Therefore the one replacing x_m precedes the one replacing x_j in the series of r_α , and therefore also in the series of r_α' . It follows that $q = p_{1m} < p_{1j}$.

(c) If $p_{1j} = p_{rj}$, then in C^1 and C^r , x_j must have been replaced by the same term. This is possible only if the preceding existential variables were also replaced by the same terms, which implies that the same is the case in A^1 and A^r . Since this argument works backwards, the converse also holds.

By def. 19, A_n is an Herbrand alternation of $\mathcal{A}$.

Now for every alternand of a formula of the form (1), we shall find a number i such that with a suitable renaming of all the variables of (1), it becomes A^i .

Let B_1 be obtained from (1) by replacing $c_{\beta+1}$ (where $c_1 \ldots c_\beta$ are the free variables of $\mathcal{A}$) by $f_1(t_1 \ldots t_{d_1})$ (by (b), $c_{\beta+1}$ must replace z_1), where t_s is the term replacing y_s in any alternand where $c_{\beta+1}$ replaces z_1 . B_1 is still of the form (1) and satisfies (a)-(c) of def. 19 except that z_1 is not always replaced by a variable.

Let B_{v+1} be obtained from B_v by the same process, where instead of $\beta + 1$ we have the lowest c_w not yet replaced; instead of 1 we have the j for which c_w replaces z_j.

Let B be the result of replacing all c_w, $\beta < w$, in this way. Then each alternand is clearly one of the formulae C^i defined above. If the terms $f_j(\ldots)$ not proper parts of others are replaced by variables as above, each alternand will become an A^i, but the whole will be an alphabetic variant of (1), because the effect will be simply to put back variables where they were removed.

This completes the proof of lemma 4.2, and therefore of theorem 4.

3. Properties of the interpretation

That the interpretation is strong also follows easily from Herbrand's theorem. For suppose $\mathcal{B}$ is deduced from $\mathcal{A}$ in $\mathcal{F}$, where both are prenex formulae. Then given any A_n, let $c_1 \ldots c_\mu$ be its free variables. Then by Herbrand's theorem, $\mathcal{A}$ and therefore $\mathcal{B}$ is deducible from A_n; and by the deduction theorem

$$(w_1)\ldots(w_r)(c_1)\ \ldots\ (c_\mu)[A_n \,\&\, D] \supset \mathcal{B}$$

is provable in the predicate calculus, where D is the

conjunction of the axioms used in the derivation of $\mathcal{B}$ from $\mathcal{A}$, and $w_1 \ldots w_r$ are their free variables.

Then by Herbrand's theorem we can find a tautology

A_n^1 & D^1 & ... & A_n^q & D^q . ⊃ . $B^1 \vee \ldots \vee B^r$

where A_n^1 & D^1 is a substitution-instance of A_n & D , and the consequent is an Herbrand alternation of $\mathcal{B}$. It follows that if A_n is verifiable, then each A_n^i is also verifiable, and since certainly D is, it follows that

$$B^1 \vee \ldots \vee B^r \qquad (1)$$

is a verifiable Herbrand alternation of $\mathcal{B}$. If B_n is the sequence associated with $\mathcal{B}$, then any B_n which has (1) as a subalternation (of which there is at least one by lemma 4.2) is verifiable, and in fact provable in F with A_n as a new axiom.

The case for non-prenex formulae follows from their equivalence with prenex formulae.

The fact that the interpretation is strong reflects the fact that with the addition of new verifiable axioms, theorem 4 still applies in the same way.

Analysis of the proof of Herbrand's theorem, which we shall not carry out here, would show that the functions which generate the sequence A_n and finds one provable in F if $\mathcal{A}'$ is provable in $\mathcal{F}$ are primitive recursive.[2]

---

[2]One way of obtaining the normal proof is to use a Gentzen-type logic (e. g. those of IM ch. XV or Schütte [1];

Now consider the special case of the formula

$$(z_1) \ldots (z_q)(Ey_1) \ldots (Ey_p)A(z_1 \ldots z_q, y_1 \ldots y_p) \ . \quad (2)$$

By (c) ofdef. 19, an Herbrand alternation of (2) is of the form

$$A(a_1 \ldots a_q, t_{11} \ldots t_{1p}) \vee \ldots \vee A(a_1 \ldots a_q, t_{m1} \ldots t_{mp}) \quad (3)$$

where t_{ij} contains only $a_1 \ldots a_q$ and free variables of (2).

Then (2) is satisfied by the function(al)s

$$\nu_p^j\{\mu x[x \leq \max_{i \leq m} \nu_p(t_{i1} \ldots t_{ip}) \ \& \ A(a_1 \ldots a_q, \nu_p^1(x) \ldots \nu_p^p(x))]\} \quad (4)$$

for if, in (3), each t_{ij} is replaced by its equal $\nu_p^j[\nu_p(t_{i1} \ldots t_{ip})]$, we can infer from (3)

$$(Ex)[x \leq \max_{i \leq m} \nu_p(t_{i1} \ldots t_{ip}) \ \& \ A(a_1 \ldots a_q, \nu_p^1(x) \ldots \nu_p^p(x))] \ .$$

The functionals (4) are clearly primitive recursive in the functions and predicates expressed by the symbols of $\mathcal{F}$. Thus we have

Corollary 4.1. Every theorem of $\mathcal{F}$ of the form (2), where A is quantifier-free, is satisfiable by functions primi-

---

see below, ch. IV 4). One proves first that cuts can be eliminated and then, by permutation, produces a proof in which all inferences of the propositional calculus, except certain "structural" inferences, precede all predicate inferences. Our arithmetization of Schütte's cut-elimination for the case with infinite induction, in appendix I, shows that the cut-elimination function for the present case is primitive recursive, by dropping the clauses in our definitions which concern infinite induction.

tive recursive in the functions and predicates expressed by the symbols of $\mathfrak{F}$.

If we consider that (3) is obtained effectively, then by looking at the case where (2) is closed and $q = 0$, we see that $\mathfrak{F}$ is 1*-consistent. For then each t_{ij} is a closed term, and one of the alternands of (3) must be true. Suppose it is the i th. If m_j is the numerical value of t_{ij}, then

$$A(0^{(m_1)} \ldots 0^{(m_p)})$$

is true. Since the m_j are obtained effectively, this shows that $\mathfrak{F}$ is 1*-consistent. However, we can prove more than that.

Definition 21. $\mathfrak{F}$ is uniformly 1*-consistent if for any finite set $\bar{h}$ of number and function variables, there is a recursive functional $F(\bar{h}, b)$ such that if b is the number of a proof of a formula

$$(Ey_1) \ldots (Ey_p)A(\bar{h}, y_1 \ldots y_p) \tag{5}$$

with no other free variables, then

$$A\{\bar{h}, \nu_p^1[F(\bar{h}, b)] \ldots \nu_p^p[F(\bar{h}, b)]\} \tag{6}$$

is verifiable.[3]

---

[3]In fact if this holds for $\bar{h}$ a single one-place function variable β, then it holds for any set. For let x_{11} x_{1n_1}, $\alpha_{21} \ldots \alpha_{2n_2}$, $\ldots$ $\alpha_{k1} \ldots \alpha_{kn_k}$ be an arbitrary set in which α_{ij} has $m_1 + \ldots + m_{i-1}$ arguments. Given the functional $F(\beta, b)$, we set $F_1(\bar{x}_1, \bar{\alpha}_2 \ldots \bar{\alpha}_k, b)$ (where

Then in fact, our considerations show that $\mathcal{F}$ is uniformly 1*-consistent. For we can define $F(\bar{h}, b)$ to be 0 if b is not the number of a proof of a formula of the form (5), and to be the functional which is the argument of ν_p^j in (4), if b <u>is</u> the number of a proof of (5) $(q = 0)$, where t_{ij} are obtained from an alternation (3) which is obtained from the proof number b by Herbrand's theorem. Then clearly in the latter case (6) is verifiable. Thus we have

<u>Corollary 4.2.</u> $\mathcal{F}$ is uniformly 1*-consistent.

The mentioned possible analysis of the proof of Herbrand's theorem would show that F is primitive recursive in the functions and predicates of $\mathcal{F}$, or if there are infinitely many, primitive recursive in a function which enu-

---

$\bar{\alpha}_1$ is an abbreviation for the sequence) = $F(\beta_o, b_o)$, where

$$\beta_o(x) = \nu_k\{\nu_{n_1}(x_{11} \ldots x_{1n_1}), \nu_{n_2}(\alpha_{21}[\nu^1_{m_1}\nu^1_{k-1}(x) \ldots \nu^{m_1}_{m_1}\nu^1_{k-1}(x)] \ldots \alpha_{2n_2}[\nu^1_{m_1}\nu^1_{k-1}(x) \ldots \nu^{m_1}_{m_1}\nu^1_{k-1}(x)]) \ldots \nu_{n_k}(\alpha_{k1}[\nu^1_{m_1}\nu^1_{k-1}(x) \ldots \nu^{m_1}_{m_1}\nu^1_{k-1}(x) \ldots \nu^1_{m_{k-1}}\nu^{k-1}_{k-1}(x) \ldots \nu^{m_{k-1}}_{m_{k-1}}\nu^{k-1}_{k-1}(x)])\} .$$

If b is the number of a proof of (5) ($\bar{h}$ our arbitrary set), then b_o is the number of a proof of the result of substituting

$\nu^j_{n_1}\nu^1_k[\beta(0)]$ for x_{1j}

$\nu^j_{n_2}\nu^2_k\, \beta(\nu_{k-1}[\nu_{m_1}(y_{11} \ldots y_{1m_1}), 0 \ldots 0])$ for α_{2j}

$\nu^j_{n_k}\nu^k_k\, \beta(\nu_{k-1}[\nu_{m_1}(\quad " \quad) \ldots \nu_{m_{k-1}}(y_{k-1,1} \ldots y_{k-1,n_{k-1}})])$

for α_{kj}, where the y_{rs} are argument terms, i. e. replaced at each occurrence by the arguments at that occurrence.

merates all of them. Note that F enumerates the recursive satisfactions of <u>all</u> provable formulae (5).

<u>Theorem 5</u> (Kreisel [2]). The interpretation of theorem 4 is complete in the sense that if $\mathcal{A}'$ is assigned the sequence A_n, then from any proof in F of a formula A_m we can find a proof of $\mathcal{A}'$ in $\mathcal{F}$.

<u>Proof</u>. Let $\mathcal{A}$ be the prenex equivalent of $\mathcal{A}'$. Since F is a subsystem of $\mathcal{F}$, the proof of A_m in F followed by the Herbrand normal derivation of $\mathcal{A}$ from A_m, followed by the deduction of $\mathcal{A}'$ from $\mathcal{A}$ inthe predicate calculus, is a proof of $\mathcal{A}'$ in $\mathcal{F}$.

<u>Theorem 6</u>. If $\mathcal{F}$ has an Herbrand interpretation, then $\mathcal{F}$ is a subsystem of an elementary number theory without induction.

<u>Proof</u>. We describe a system $\mathcal{F}_1$ as follows: For each prenex formula $\mathcal{A}$ of $\mathcal{F}$, consider the sequence A_n associated with it, which by def. 20 consists of Herbrand alternations of $\mathcal{A}$. Let h be the function of page 23, so that if b is the number of a proof of $\mathcal{A}$, then $A_{h(b)}$ is verifiable. For each such b, $A_{h(b)}$ is to be an axiom of $\mathcal{F}_1$. The set of such formulae is recursively enumerable, and a recursive set which defined the same system is obtainable by Craig's method.

Then by Herbrand derivation, each prenex theorem of $\mathcal{F}$ is provable in $\mathcal{F}_1$. Therefore so is every theorem.

4. Impossibility of an Herbrand interpretation of number theory with induction

Naturally our main interest in these investigations is to find finitary interpretations of systems at least as strong as the full elementary number theory Z , although it is of some value to have interpretations of systems for whose theorems we cannot always find recursive satisfactions, such as Q . Therefore it is well to ask whether the methods of this chapter might suffice to interpret Z . The answer is no. We can prove directly either that a certain theorem of Z is not a theorem of any elementary number theory without induction, or that a certain theorem of Z has no verifiable Herbrand alternation. By Herbrand's theorem, these are equivalent, and we shall therefore prove directly only the first.

Theorem 7.[4] There is a theorem of Z which is not a theorem of any elementary number theory without induction.

Proof. If A is any theorem of a system without induction, then only finitely many of the axioms are used in the proof of A . It follows that A is a consequence in the pred-

---

[4]In [2] Kreisel gives an example of a theorem of Z_μ with no verifiable Herbrand alternation. The present example, which is in effect a new proof of the result of [2], was communicated to me by Kreisel in a letter dated February 3, 1959. This contained two errors. Lemma 7.1, supplied by me, corrects the first, and lemma 7.2, supplied by Kreisel, replaces the inadequate lemma of the original letter.

icate calculus of their conjunction. Thus if A is a theorem of a system without induction, it is deducible in the predicate calculus from a single verifiable formula of recursive number theory (if A does not contain function variables, for then they can be eliminated from the proof).

The idea of the proof is to construct a formula by Gödel's method which "says" ofitself that it is not deducible in the predicate calculus from a verifiable formula of recursive number theory. However, this process has certain complications. We prove first two lemmas.

Lemma 7.1. Let A be an arbitrary formula of recursive number theory. Then we can find a number e such that A can be deduced from

$$(x)(Ey)[T_1(0^{(e)}, x, y) \ \& \ U(y) = 0] \tag{1}$$

in a system S which can be obtained from Q by the following additions:

1. For each k, S has a symbol for Kleene's predicate T_k (IM, p. 281), likewise for his function U. " S has a symbol for f " means that f also has symbols for each function which enters into its recursive definition, and that the recursion equations themselves are axioms. We may suppose a predicate to be givenas a formula f(...) = 0, so that we shall have no formal predicates except = .

We also have the axiom

$$T_k(e, a_1 \ldots a_k, y) \,\&\, T_k(e, a_1 \ldots a_k, z) \,.\supset y = z \qquad (2)$$

(By IM p. 281, this is verifiable.)

2. Let e be the Gödel number of a system of recursion equations in Kleene's formalism with n-place principal function letter g. Let $e_1 \ldots e_n$ be the Gödel numbers of systems of equations with k-place principal function letters $h_1 \ldots h_n$, so none of these systems have letters in common. Let $\alpha_{kn}(e, e_1 \ldots e_n)$ be the number of the system obtained by stringing these together and adding the explicit definition

$$f(a_1 \ldots a_k) = g[h_1(a_1 \ldots a_k) \ldots h_n(a_1 \ldots a_k)]$$

where f is new.

Let β^i_{kn} be a function such that, if y is the number of a deduction in the formalism of an evaluation of f, then $\beta^i_{kn}(y)$ is the number of a computation of h_i for the same arguments ($i = 1 \ldots n$); let $\gamma_{kn}(y)$ be the number of a computation of g for the arguments $U[\beta^1_{kn}(y)] \ldots U[\beta^n_{kn}(y)]$, i. e. the results of the computations of h. The functions α_{kn}, β^i_{kn}, and γ_{kn} are all primitive recursive.

We suppose S has symbols for these functions with the axioms

$$T_k[\alpha_{kn}(e, e_1 \ldots e_n), a_1 \ldots a_k, y] \supset$$
$$.T_k[e, a_1 \ldots a_k, \beta^1_{kn}(y)] \,\&\, \ldots \,\&\, T_k[e_k, a_1 \ldots a_k, \beta^n_{kn}(y)]$$

$\& \ T_n\{e, U[\beta^1_{kn}(y)] \ \ldots\ldots \ U[\beta^n_{kn}(y)], \gamma_{kn}(y)\} \ \&$

$$U(y) = U[\gamma_{kn}(y)] \qquad (3)$$

which are, in view of what was said above, evidently verifiable.

3. If $i \leq n$, let e_{ni} be the Gödel number of the equation $f(a_0 \ldots a_n) = a_i$. Then S has the axioms

$$T_{n+1}(0^{(e_{ni})}, a_0 \ \ldots\ldots \ a_n, y) \supset U(y) = a_i \qquad (4)$$

4. Let e^0_n be the Gödel number of the equation $f(a_0 \ldots a_n) = 0$. Then S has the axioms

$$T_{n+1}(0^{(e^0_n)}, a_0 \ \ldots\ldots \ a_n, y) \supset U(y) = 0 \qquad (5)$$

5. Let $S_1(e)$ be the function which assigns to the number of an arbitrary set of equations whose principal function letter is g and has k places, the number of this set with $f(a_1 \ \ldots\ldots \ a_k) = Sg(a_1 \ldots a_k)$ added, where f is a new letter.

Let $S^*(y)$ be a function which from an evaluation of $\{S_1(e)\}$ for arguments $a_1 \ldots a_k$ gives one of e for these arguments. Then S contains symbols for these functions and has the axioms

$$T_k[S_1(e), a_1 \ldots a_k, y] \supset . \ T_k[e, a_1 \ldots a_k, S^*(y)]$$

$$\& \ U(y) = SU[S^*(y)] \qquad (6)$$

6. Let v be the Gödel number of multiplication. Then S has the axiom

$$T_2(0^{(v)}, a, b, y) \supset : a = 0 \vee b = 0 \ . \equiv U(y) = 0 \qquad (7)$$

7. Let w be the Gödel number of the function $\overline{sg}$

$[\overline{sg}(0) = 1;\ \overline{sg}(n + 1) = 0$ (IM, p. 223)]. Then S has the axiom

$$T_1(0^{(w)}, a, y) \supset .\ a \neq 0 \equiv U(y) = 0 \qquad (8)$$

8. Let $\psi_n(e)$ be the function which if e is the Gödel number of a set of equations with n -place function letter, say g , assigns to e the number of the juxtaposition of this set with the equation

$$f(a) = g[\nu(0, a) \ldots \nu(0^{(n-1)}, a)]$$

plus equations with a new principal function letter ν for the function $\lambda xy(y)_x$. Let $\varphi_n(y)$ be the function which from an evaluation of $\{\psi_n(e)\}$ for the argument a yields an evaluation of $\{e\}$ for the arguments $(a)_0 \ldots (a)_{n-1}$. We suppose S has these functions and the axioms

$$T_1[\psi_n(e), a, y] \supset .\ T_n[e, (a)_0 \ldots (a)_{n-1}, \varphi_n(y)] \ \& \ U(y) = U[\varphi_n(y)] \qquad (9)$$

9. S contains the exponential function, the function $(a)_b$, and the axioms (for $j \leq n$)

$$(2^{a_0} \cdot \ldots \cdot {}_n{}^{a_n})_0(j) = a_j \qquad (10)$$

10. Let $\pi(e_1, e_2)$ be a function which gives a Gödel number of $(f \dot{-} g) + (g \dot{-} f)$ in terms of the Gödel numbers of f and g respectively ($a \dot{-} b = 0$ if $a \leq b$; otherwise $b + (a \dot{-} b) = a$; IM p. 223). Let $\pi_1(y)$ and $\pi_2(y)$ be functions which give, from a computation of $\{\pi(e_1, e_2)\}$ for the argument a , computations for $\{e_1\}$ and $\{e_2\}$ respectively for the same argument. We suppose

that S has symbols for these functions and the axiom

$$T_1[\pi(e_1, e_2), a, y] \supset : T_1[e_1, a, \pi_1(y)] \; \& \; T_1[e_2, a, \pi_2(y)] \; \& . U(y) = 0 \equiv U[\pi_1(y)] = U[\pi_2(y)] \quad (11)$$

Proof. By induction on the construction of A , we show the following: If the Hilbert ε-operator[5] and certain explicit definitions are added to S , then if the variables of A are among $a_0 \ldots a_n$, we can find an e such that

$$T_1[0^{(e)}, 2^{a_0} \cdot \ldots \cdot p_n^{a_n}, y] \supset . U(y) = 0 \equiv A \quad (12)$$

is provable.

I. A is a prime formula s = t . By induction on the construction of s , we first find a number d such that

$$T_{n+1}(0^{(d)}, a_0 \ldots a_n, y) \supset U(y) = s \quad (13)$$

is provable.

(a) s is 0 . Let $d = e_n^o$. Then (13) is (5).

(b) s is a_i . Let $d = e_{ni}$. Then (13) is (4)

(c) s is Sr , where we have a d' such that

---

[5]The use of the ε-symbol can be avoided if we use the assumption that every symbol of A expresses a general recursive function. Let f_i be the i th function occurring in A ; suppose it has r_i variables (i = 1 ... q). Let g be the function expressed by the e of (12). If we replace this by the Gödel number of $g + (f_1 \dot{-} f_1) + \ldots + (f_q \dot{-} f_q)$, then from (12) we can deduce $(x_1) \ldots (x_{r_i})(Ey)T_{r_i}(0^{(e_i)}, x_1 \ldots x_{r_i}, y)$, where e_i is the Gödel number of f_i . Then we can use the -operator instead of the ε-operator.

$$T_{n+1}(0^{(d')}, a_o \dots a_n, y) \supset U(y) = r \qquad (14)$$

is provable. Then $d = s_1(d')$. Then $0^{(d)} = S_1(0^{(d')})$ is provable, and by (6) we have

$$T_{n+1}(0^{(d)}, a_o \dots a_n, y) \supset . T_{n+1}[0^{(d')}, a_o \dots a_n, S^*(y)] \\ \& \; U(y) = SU[S^*(y)] \\ \supset . U(y) = s$$

by (14) with $S^*(y)$ substituted for y .[6]

(d) s is $f(t_1 \dots t_k)$, where for $i = 1 \dots k$ we have d_i such that

$$T_{n+1}(0^{(d_i)}, a_o \dots a_n, y) \supset U(y) = t_i \qquad (15)$$

If f is not a given function of Z , we add the explicit definition

$$f(b_1 \dots b_k) = U[\varepsilon z T_k(0^{(e_f)}, b_1 \dots b_k, z)] \qquad (16)$$

where e_f is the Gödel number of the function f expresses.[7]

Let $d = \alpha_{n+1,k}(e_f, d_1 \dots d_k)$. Then since

$$\alpha_{n+1,k}(0^{(e_f)}, 0^{(d_1)} \dots 0^{(d_k)}) = 0^{(d)}$$

is provable, by (3)

$$T_{n+1}(0^{(d)}, a_o \dots a_n, y) \supset . T_{n+1}[0^{(d_1)}, a_o \dots a_n, \beta^1_{n+1,k}(y)] \\ \& \dots \& \; T_{n+1}[0^{(d_k)}, a_o \dots a_n, \beta^k_{n+1,k}(y)] \;\&$$

---

[6] Following Quine ([1], p. 92), we use

$$A \supset B \\ \supset C$$

to mean: $A \supset B$ is provable; $B \supset C$ is provable; therefore so is $A \supset C$.

[7] See note 5. Note that if the procedure there outlined were followed, the η-terms introduced would all be of rank 1, Kleene's procedure for eliminating them (IM §74) will suffice.

$$T_k\{0^{(e_f)}, U[\beta^1_{n+1,k}(y)] \ldots U[\beta^k_{n+1,k}(y)], \gamma_{n+1,k}(y)\}$$
$$\& \ U(y) = U[\gamma_{n+1,k}(y)] \qquad (17)$$

By the ε-formula (HB II, 13)

$$T_k(0^{(e_f)}, b_1 \ldots b_k, z) \supset T_k[0^{(e_f)}, b_1 \ldots b_k, \varepsilon z T_k(0^{(e_f)}, b_1 \ldots b_k, z)]$$

and therefore by (2)

$$T_k(0^{(e_f)}, b_1 \ldots b_k, z) \supset z = \varepsilon z T_k(0^{(e_f)}, b_1 \ldots b_k, z)$$
$$\supset U(z) = f(b_1 \ldots b_k) \qquad (18)$$

by (16), from which follows

$$T_k(0^{(e_f)}, b_1 \ldots b_k, z) \ \& \ b_1 = t_1 \ \& \ldots \& \ b_k = t_k \,.$$
$$\supset U(z) = s \,.$$

By (15) with $U[\beta^1_{n+1,k}(y)]$ for y

$$T_{n+1}[0^{(d_1)}, a_0 \ldots a_n, \beta^1_{n+1,k}(y)] \ \& \ldots$$
$$\& \ T_{n+1}[0^{(d_k)}, a_0 \ldots a_n, \beta^k_{n+1,k}(y)]$$
$$\& \ T_k\{0^{(e_f)}, U[\beta^1_{n+1,k}(y)] \ldots U[\beta^k_{n+1,k}(y)], \gamma_{n+1,k}(y)\}.$$
$$\supset U[\gamma_{n+1,k}(y)] = s$$

Then (13) now follows by (17). [If f is a symbol of Z, we suppose (18) is an axiom of S.]

This completes the proof of (13). By (13) with $\varphi_n(y)$ for y, and by (9) and (10), we can prove

$$T_1[\psi_{n+1}(0^{(d)}), 2^{a_0} \cdot \ldots \cdot p_n{}^{a_n}, y] \supset U(y) = s \,. \qquad (19)$$

By the same argument we can find a number g such that

$$T_1[\psi_{n+1}(0^{(g)}), 2^{a_0} \cdot \ldots \cdot {}_n{}^{a_n}, z] \supset U(z) = t \qquad (20)$$

Then from (25) and (26) evidently follows

$$L19 \ \& \ L20 \,. \supset . \ U(y) = U(z) \equiv s = t \,.^8 \qquad (21)$$

Now we set $e = \pi[\psi_{n+1}(d), \psi_{n+1}(g)]$. Then evidently $0^{(e)} = \pi[\psi_{n+1}(0^{(d)}), \psi_{n+1}(0^{(g)})]$ is provable. Then by (11), with $2^{a_0} \cdot \ldots \cdot p_n^{a_n}$ for a , and (21) with $\pi_1(y)$ for y and $\pi_2(y)$ for z , we have

$$T_1(0^{(e)}, 2^{a_0} \cdot \ldots \cdot p_n^{a_n}, y) \supset .U(y) = 0 \equiv s = t ,$$

i. e. (12).

II. A is $-$ B , where we have found an e' such that

$$T_1(0^{(e')}, 2^{a_0} \cdot \ldots \cdot p_n^{a_n}, y) \supset .U(y) = 0 \equiv B \qquad (22)$$

is provable. Let e be $\alpha_{11}(w, e')$. Then

$$0^{(e)} = \alpha_{11}(0^{(w)}, 0^{(e')})$$

is evidently provable, and by (3) we have

$$\begin{aligned} &T_1(0^{(e)}, 2^{a_0} \cdot \ldots \cdot p_n^{a_n}, y) \quad . \\ &\quad \supset . T_1[0^{(e')}, 2^{a_0} \cdot \ldots \cdot p_n^{a_n}, \beta_{11}^1(y)] \qquad (23) \\ &\qquad \& \; T_1\{0^{(w)}, U[\beta_{11}^1(y)], \gamma_{11}(y)\} \;\&\; U(y) = U[\gamma_{11}(y)] \; . \end{aligned}$$

By (8)

$$T_1\{0^{(w)}, U[\beta_{11}^1(y)], \gamma_{11}(y)\} \supset . U[\beta_{11}^1(y)] \neq 0 \equiv U[\gamma_{11}(y)] = 0$$

By (23)

$$\begin{aligned} L23 \supset : &T_1[0^{(e')}, 2^{a_0} \cdot \ldots \cdot p_n^{a_n}, \beta_{11}^1(y)] \\ &\qquad \&. U[\beta_{11}^1(y)] \neq 0 \equiv U(y) = 0 \end{aligned}$$

By (22) wihh $\beta_{11}^1(y)$ for y

$$L23 \supset . U(y) = 0 \equiv - B \text{ , q. e. d.}$$

III. A is B v C , where we have e' such that (22) and e'' such that

---

[1] [8] "L19" stands for the formula on the left of the main connective in (19); the letter "R" will be used analogously. See Quine [1], p. 129.

$$T_1(0^{(e'')}, 2^{a_0} \cdot \ldots \cdot p_n{}^{a_n}, y) \supset . U(y) = 0 \equiv C . \qquad (24)$$

Let $e = \alpha_{12}(v, e', e'')$. Then since

$$0^{(e)} = \alpha_{12}(0^{(v)}, 0^{(e')}, 0^{(e'')})$$

is evidently provable, by (3) we have

$$\begin{aligned} L29 \supset . T_1[0^{(e')}, 2^{a_0} \cdot \ldots \cdot p_n{}^{a_n}, \beta^1_{12}(y)] \\ \& \; T_1[0^{(e'')}, 2^{a_0} \cdot \ldots \cdot p_n{}^{a_n}, \beta^2_{12}(y)] \qquad (25) \\ \& \; T_2\{0^{(v)}, \bar{U}[\beta^1_{12}(y)], \bar{U}[\beta^2_{12}(y)], \gamma_{12}(y)\} \; \& \; U(y) = \bar{U}[\gamma_{12}(y)] \end{aligned}$$

By (7)

$$T_2\{0^{(v)}, U[\beta^1_{12}(y)], U[\beta^2_{12}(y)], \gamma_{12}(y)\}$$
$$\supset : \bar{U}[\beta^1_{12}(y)] = 0 \vee \bar{U}[\beta^2_{12}(y)] = 0 . \equiv U[\gamma_{12}(y)] = 0 .$$

By (22) with $\beta^1_{12}(y)$ for y and $\beta^2_{12}(y)$ for y in (24),

$$R25 \supset : B \vee C . \equiv U(y) = 0 ,$$

and (12) follows by (25).

If A contains propositional connectives other than $-$ and $\vee$, then it is truth-functionally equivalent to a formula A' which does not, and clearly if e can be found such that (12) holds for A' , then the same e suffices for A . Therefore (12) holds in general.

By (12) evidently

$$L12 \; \& \; U(y) = 0 . \supset A ;$$

since y can be chosen not to be among $a_0 \ldots a_n$,

$$(Ey)[L12 \; \& \; U(y) = 0] \supset A , \text{ whence}$$
$$(x)(Ey)[T_1(0^{(e)}, x, y) \; \& \; U(y) = 0] \supset A$$

is provable in S . This completes the proof of lemma 7.1.

Lemma 7.2. Let $Pr(a, b)$ be the predicate " a is the number of a proof in S of a formula whose number is b "; let $Ps(a, b, c)$ be a formula of Z which expresses $Pr[a, s(b, c)]$, where s is the Gödel substitution function (see theorem 2). Let k be the number of some formula of Z of the form $A(b)$ with no other free variables. Then we can prove in Z

$$Ps(a, 0^{(k)}, b) \supset A(b) \tag{26}$$

Proof. We shall not give the derivation in detail. (26) says that for any a and b , $A(b)$ follows from the statement that a is the number of a proof of $A(0^{(b)})$; i. e. if $A(0^{(b)})$ is provable, then it is true. Thus the proof proceeds by formalizing a partial truth definition in Z for formulae of S .

Definition 22. The logical degree of a first order formula A is defined inductively as follows:

1. If A is prime, its degree is 0 .
2. If B has degree p , then $-B$ has degree $p + 1$.
3. If B has degree p , C has degree q , then $B \vee C$, $B \& C$, $B \supset C$, and $B \equiv C$ have degree $\max(p, q) + 1$.
4. If $B(x)$ has degree p , then $(x)B(x)$ and $(Ex)B(x)$ have degree $p + 1$.

Now suppose p is the logical degree of $A(b)$. Then if $A(0^{(n)})$ is proved in S by a proof with number m , then we can find a proof in a suitable logic in which no formula occurs which is not an alternation of formulae of degree $\leq p$. This follows by the normal form theorem of Schütte [1] if the logic is the one described there and in chapter IV, §4 below.[9]

We can give in Z a truth-definition for formulae of degree $\leq p$. For inspection of the definition of $T_n(z, x_1 \ldots x_n, y)$ shows that each predicate T_n could be defined by substituting, say $\prod_{0<i\leq n} p_i^{x_i}$ for x in a single predicate $T(z, x, y)$.[10] Likewise, the functions α_{kn}, β^1_{kn} could be defined explicitly from a small number of primitive recursive functions. Therefore we can set up S with finitely many function symbols, say $f^0_1 \ldots f^0_k$, representing primitiverecursive functions. Then if Val is the truth-value functional of appendix I (def. 26), where f_i has the right number of arguments, then

$$\mathrm{Val}(a, f^0_1 \ldots f^0_k) = 0 \tag{27}$$

---

[9] An alternative is to use a logic in which a proof of a formula $\mathfrak{a}$ consists of a quantifier-free proof of an Herbrand alternation of a prenex of $\mathfrak{a}$, an Herbrand normal derivation of the prenex, and then equivalences leading to $\mathfrak{a}$. That we can obtain such a proof follows from Herbrand's theorem. Here it is best to define the truth of $\mathfrak{a}$ in terms of the truth of the prenex of $\mathfrak{a}$ (as HB II, 333-4). (27) works for all quantifier-free formulae.

[10] IM, pp. 277-81. Change Df13 (of S_n) on p. 278 to $D(z, y)$ & $FL[(y)_{010}]$ & $(y)_{010} = (z)_{lh\, z \dot{-} 1, 10}$ & $(w)\{0 < w < lh[(y)_{01}] \supset Nu[(y)_{01w}, (x)_w]\}$, and set $T(z, x, y) \equiv . S(z, x, y)$ & $(w)[w < y \supset - S(z, x, w)]$. Then $T_n(z, x_1 \ldots x_n, y) \equiv . T[z, \prod_{0<i\leq n} p_i^{x_i}, y]$ & $lh[(y)_{01}] = n + 1$.

is a truth-predicate for prime formulae of S . Let (27) be $Tr_0(a)$. Then we can define $Tr_{p+1}(a)$ from $Tr_p(a)$ by cases according to definition 22.[11]

Now we can prove in Z , by induction on the length of the proof, that every line in the proof of $A(0^{(n)})$ is an alternation of which at least one alternand is true.[12] That is, we can prove in Z

$$Ps(a,\ 0^{(k)},\ b) \supset Tr_p[s(0^{(k)},\ b)] \ . \tag{28}$$

Finally, from the truth-definition we should be able to derive in Z

$$Tr_p[s(0^{(k)},\ b)] \equiv A(b) \ , \tag{29}$$

and then (26) follows by (28).

We shall not give the construction of the actual formalization. The fact, shown in appendix I, that the cut-elimination function for the normal form theorem is primitive recursive encourages us to believe that this proof can be given in Z . (Cf. HB II, 340-7.) The basic step is an induction on the logical degree of cut terms (as in the proof of theorem 13 below, where, however, things are more complicated because of infinite induction).

---

[11] $Tr_{p+1}(a) \equiv :.\ a = 40 \cdot 7^{(a)_3} \cdot 11^{(a)_4}\ \&.\ Tr_p[(a)_3] \vee Tr_p[(a)_4]:$ $v.\ 3 | a\ \&\ -\ Tr_p(a/3).v.\ a = 50 \cdot p_{lh(a) \dot{-} 1}^{(a)_{lh(a) \dot{-} 1}}\ \&$ $(x) Tr_p\{st[(a)_{lh(a) \dot{-} 1},\ 2 \cdot 3^x,\ p_{lh(a) \dot{-} 1}]\}.v.\ a = 100 \cdot$ etc.

[12] If we follow the method of note 9, then this applies to the proof of the prenex, and then the truth of $\mathfrak{a}$ itself follows from the definition.

For more details on the construction of a truth-definition and derivation of (29), see HB II, 328-340. See also Kreisel and Wang.

Proof of theorem 7. We construct by Gödel's method a formula of an extension of Z_μ by explicit definitions for recursive functions a formula C which "says" that it is not provable in S from any true formula of form (1).

Let r(e, a) be the primitive recursive function which gives, if a is the Gödel number of the formula A , the number of the formula

$$(x)(Ey)[T_1(0^{(e)}, x, y) \& U(y) = 0] \supset A \tag{30}$$

where T_1 and U have been added to Z_μ by explicit definitions. We also introduce the proof predicate Pr(a, b) of S and the substitution function s . Then a is the number of a formula derivable in S from a true formula of form (1) if and only if

$$(Ee)(Ez)(x)(Ey)\{T_1(e, x, y) \& U(y) = 0 \& Pr[z, r(e, a)]\} \tag{31}$$

Let p be the number of the negation of (31) with a replaced by s(b, b) . Then if t is the term $s(0^{(p)}, 0^{(p)})$, s(p, p) is the number of the formula C :

$$- (Ee)(Ez)(x)(Ey)\{T_1(e, x, y) \& U(y) = 0 \& Pr[z, r(e, t)]\} \tag{32}$$

We show first that C is provable in Z_μ . By lemma 7.2

$$\Pr[z, r(e, t)] \supset . (x)(Ey)[T_1(e, x, y) \ \&\ U(y) = 0] \supset C \quad (32)$$

(using the provable formula $t = 0^{(s(p,p))}$). By the predicate calculus this implies

$$\Pr[z, r(e, t)] \supset . LR32 \supset - \{(x)(Ey)[T_1(e, x, y) \ \& \ U(y) = 0] \ \& \ \Pr[z, \bar{r}(e, t)]\} \text{, i. e.}$$

$$\Pr[z, r(e, t)] \ \& \ LR32 . \supset - \Pr[\bar{z}, r(e, t)] \text{, i. e.}$$

$$- (\bar{x})(Ey)\{T_1(e, x, y) \ \& \ U(y) = \bar{0} \ \& \ \Pr[z, r(e, t)]\} ,$$

from which C follows.

Suppose C is provable in S from (1). Then if m is the number of the resulting proof of (30), where A is now C , we have in S

$$\Pr[0^{(m)}, r(0^{(e)}, t)]$$

which with ($\bar{1}$) implies

$$(x)(Ey)[T_1(0^{(e)}, x, y) \ \& \ U(y) = 0 \ \& \ \Pr(0^{(m)}, r(0^{(e)}, t))]$$

which implies - C by existential generaliztion. Therefore the negation of (1) is provable in S . (We may for this purpose add the functions r and s to S . However, they can be eliminated from the resulting refutation of (1).)

Suppose A_0 is a formula of recursive number theory from which C is derivable in the predicate calculus. Let e be determined by lemma 7.1 so that A_0 is derivable in S from (1). It is evident from the construction of e that if A_0 is verifiable, then (1) is true. But by the last paragraph, since C is now derivable in S from (1),

(1) is false. Therefore A_0 is not verifiable.

Given a derivation of C from A_0 in the predicate calculus, we can find a counterexample to A_0 in the following manner. By adding some more verifiable axioms to S and following the procedure of note 5, we can derive (1) from A_0 and formulae $(x)(Ey)T_{r_1}(0^{(e_f)}, x_1 \ldots x_{r_1}, y)$ for the function symbols f_1 of A_0.[13] It follows that one can derive both (1) and its negation from A_0 in the expanded S. By applying the Herbrand interpretation to the proof of their conjunction, we can find numerical terms of S for which A_0 is refutable in S and therefore numerically false. It is assumed that the functions represented by f_1 are general recursive.

Thus we have produced a formula C of an inessential extension of Z which is derivable in the extension but not provable in the predicate calculus from a verifiable formula of recursive number theory. Let C' be the formula obtained from C by eliminating defined symbols and replacing μ-terms by their representing predicates. C' is evidently provable in Z.

Suppose A' is a formula of recursive number theory from which C' follows by the predicate calculus. Then

[13] The additional axioms are axioms which allow us to construct derivations in the opposite direction from that provided by the given axioms, e. g. in addition to (11)

$T_1(e_1, a, y) \,\&\, T_1(e_2, a, z). \supset T_1[\pi(e_1, e_2), a, \pi_3(y, z)]$

with a suitable added function π_3.

C' is provable in S from a formula of the form (1) which is true if A' is verifiable. But then with the addition of the functions r and s, and definitions of the predicates and functions of C in terms of their representing formulae, C will be provable from (1). Therefore (1) cannot be true, and A' cannot be verifiable.

Thus C' is a theorem of Z which is not derivable in the predicate calculus from a verifiable formula of recursive number theory.

Since neither C nor C' contains free function variables, they are not derivable in the predicate calculus from any finitary formulae.

Corollary 7.1. Neither C nor C' has a verifiable Herbrand alternation.

We shall make one final remark. Let S be an elementary number theory without induction to which we have added the induction rule

$$\frac{\mathcal{A}(0) \qquad \mathcal{A}(a) \supset \mathcal{A}(Sa)}{\mathcal{A}(t)}$$

so restricted that the formula $\mathcal{A}(a)$ must be quantifier-free. Then S has an Herbrand interpretation. Let S' be the system obtained from S by adding as axioms all conclusions of inductions in proofs of S. The set of these formulae is clearly recursively enumerable, so that S' is a proper formal system. Moreover, the axioms of S' are verifiable. Suppose $\mathfrak{a}(t)$ is the conclusion of an induction such that there is no induction above it in the proof. Then by Herbrand's theorem, its premisses are provable by the elementary calculus with free variables from the axioms of S. Therefore $\mathfrak{a}(t)$ is provable in the system of recursive number theory which has the axioms of S, and the elementary calculus with free variables and quantifier-free induction as rules of proof. Suppose this is true of all conclusions of inductions in S such that in each branch of the proofsof their premisses, there are no more than n inductions. Let $\mathfrak{a}(t)$ now be the conclusion of an induction in the proof of whose premisses there are no more than n + 1 inductions in each branch. Then the conclusions of the next inductions upward are all provable in the recursive number theory, by the hypothesis of induction, and the derivations of the premisses of our induction can, by Herbrand's theorem, be carried out in the elementary calculus with free variables. Therefore $\mathfrak{a}(t)$ is provable in the recursive number theory.

It follows by induction on n that every axiom of S' is provable in the recursive number theory and is therefore verifiable. By theorem 4, S' has an Herbrand interpretation, and since S and S' are equivalent, so has S.

It follows that no matter what new recursive function symbols and verifiable axioms are added to Z, the formula

C' will not only not be provable without induction, but it will not be provable by quantifier-free inductions. It is essential that the formula $\mathfrak{A}(a)$ of at least one induction in the proof of C should represent a non-recursive predicate. In fact, the intuitive argument which would be formalized in a full proof of lemma 7.2 refers to an induction on the statement "the n th line of the proof has at least one true alternand". Since the predicate "true" is non-recursive if the limit on the logical degree is sufficiently large (since S contains the T-predicates, the limit is 1; IM pp. 282-3), this inference is the necessary induction on a non-recursive predicate.

CHAPTER IV

THE NO-COUNTER-EXAMPLE INTERPRETATION OF NUMBER THEORY

1. Non-constructive considerations

We have seen that the quest for an Herbrand interpretation, and indeed for any interpretation which gives a verifiable formula from which the original formula can be derived in the predicate calculus, fails for elementary number theory with induction. The more general intent of Herbrand interpretation, namely to find a finitary formula which is closely related logically to a given one, can from a non-constructive point of view be easily seen to be achievable for quite arbitrary formulae of elementary number theory.

For let $\mathfrak{a}$ be a prenex formula of the form[1]

$$(x_1)(Ey_1) \ldots (x_k)(Ey_k)A(x_1 \ldots x_k, y_1 \ldots y_k) \qquad (1)$$

($0 \leq k$; x_1 or y_k may be missing). We note that in the predicate calculus with bound function variables, (1) is equivalent to

$$(x_1)(\alpha_2) \ldots (\alpha_k)(Ey_1) \ldots (Ey_k)A[x_1, \alpha_2(y_1) \ldots \alpha_k(y_1 \ldots y_{k-1}), y_1 \ldots y_k] . \qquad (2)$$

We shall state this equivalence more precisely

Theorem 8. In the predicate calculus of first order with

---

[1] In this chapter and the next we shall work in terms of prenex formulae of this form. The reader may regard this as a paradigm for the general case, in which each quantifier would be replaced by a sequence of the same kind, or suppose that we add to the systems the functions ν_m, ν_m^1 of defs. 9 & 10, the formulae (1_{1m}) of p. 34, and regard the collapsing of adjacent quantifiers of the same kind as part of the transformation into normal form.

free function variables, (1) implies

$$(Ey_1) \ldots (Ey_k) \quad A[x_1,\ \alpha_2(y_1) \ldots \alpha_k(y_1 \ldots y_{k-1}),\ y_1 \ldots y_k] \; . \tag{3}$$

Proof. We note first that

$$(x_k)(Ey_k)A(x_1 \ldots x_k,\ y_1 \ldots y_k) \supset (Ey_k)A[x_1 \ldots x_{k-1},\ \alpha_k(y_1 \ldots y_{k-1}),\ y_1 \ldots y_k] \tag{4}$$

is valid. Therefore (1) implies

$$(x_1)(Ey_1) \ldots (x_{k-1})(Ey_{k-1})(Ey_k) \quad A[x_1 \ldots x_{k-1},\ \alpha_k(y_1 \ldots y_{k-1}),\ y_1 \ldots y_k]. \tag{5}$$

Suppose we have derived

$$1 \supset (x_1)(Ey_1) \ldots (x_i)(Ey_i)(Ey_{i+1}) \ldots (Ey_k) \tag{6}$$

$$A[x_1 \ldots x_i,\ \alpha_{i+1}(y_1 \ldots y_i) \ldots \alpha_k(y_1 \ldots y_{k-1}),\ y_1 \ldots y_k]$$

for some $i < k$. If $i = 1$, the consequent is simply (3) quantified by (x_1) , and therefore we are done. Ohher-wise we note that we have

$$(x_i)(Ey_i)(Ey_{i+1}) \ldots (Ey_k)[\text{scope of (6)}]$$

$$\supset (Ey_i) \ldots (Ey_k)A[x_1 \ldots x_{i-1},\ \alpha_i(y_1 \ldots y_{i-1}),$$

$$\alpha_{i+1}(y_1 \ldots y_i) \ldots \alpha_k(y_1 \ldots y_{k-1}),\ y_1 \ldots y_k]$$

and therefore (R6) implies itself with i replaced by $i - 1$. It follows that (1) implies this also, so that (6) holds with $i - 1$ replacing i .

It follows by induction on $k - i$ that (1) implies (3), q. e. d.

Theorem 9. In the predicate calculus with bound function variables, (2) implies (1).

Proof. We use the principle

$$(x_1) \ldots (x_n)(Ey)B(x_1 \ldots x_n, y) \supset (E\beta)(x_1) \ldots (x_n)B[x_1 \ldots x_n, \beta(x_1 \ldots x_n)]$$

from which follows for any $i = 1 \ldots k - 1$

$$(y_1) \ldots (y_i)(Ex_{i+1})(y_{i+1}) \ldots (Ex_k)(y_k)$$
$$- A[x_1, \alpha_2(y_1) \ldots \alpha_i(y_1 \ldots y_{i-1}), x_{i+1} \ldots x_k, y_1 \ldots y_k]$$
$$\supset (E\alpha_{i+1})(y_1) \ldots (y_{i+1})(Ex_{i+2})(y_{i+2}) \ldots (Ex_k)(y_k)$$
$$- A[x_1, \alpha_2(y_1) \ldots \alpha_{i+1}(y_1 \ldots y_i), x_{i+2} \ldots x_k, y_1 \ldots y_k] \quad (7)$$

$$(Ex_1)(E\alpha_2) \ldots (E\alpha_i)L7 \supset (Ex_1)(E\alpha_2) \ldots (E\alpha_i)R7$$

Then by a chain of inferences, using induction on i

$$(Ex_1)(y_1) \ldots (Ex_k)(y_k) - A(x_1 \ldots x_k, y_1 \ldots y_k)$$
$$\supset (Ex_1)(E\alpha_2) \ldots (E\alpha_k)(y_1) \ldots (y_k) \quad (8)$$
$$- A[x_1, \alpha_2(y_1) \ldots \alpha_k(y_1 \ldots y_{k-1}), y_1 \ldots y_k] .$$

That (2) implies (1) follows by contraposition and distributing the negations through the quantifiers, q. e. d.

Now the formula (3) has the property that if its universal closure (2) is true, then (3) (and in an obvious extended sense, (2)) is recursively satisfiable. (See def. 16, pp. 27-8.), for the functionals

$$F_1(x_1, \alpha_2 \ldots \alpha_k) =$$
$$\nu_k^1[\mu y A\{x_1, \alpha_2[\nu_k^1(y)] \ldots \alpha_k[\nu_k^1(y) \ldots \nu_k^{k-1}(y)], \nu_k^1(y) \ldots \nu_k^k(y)\}]$$

satisfy (3), for (3) implies

$$(Ey)A\{x_1, \alpha_2[\nu^1_k(y)] \dots \alpha_k[\nu^1_k(y) \dots \nu^{k-1}_k(y), \nu^1_k(y) \dots \nu^k_k(y)\} .$$

Moreover, these are recursive functionals.[2] It follows that if (2) is true, then substituting $F_1(x_1, \alpha_2 \dots \alpha_k)$ for y_1 in the scope of (3) yields a verifiable formula.

This argument is simply an elaborated version of the usual non-constructive proof that if $(x)(Ey)A(x, y)$ is true, then it is recursively satisfiable. It suffers from the defect mentioned on page 4, namely that only a non-constructive proof of (2) or (1) assures us that the functionals F_1 are general recursive. It does, however, show that to seek recursive satisfactions for formulae (3) is a promising line to take in seeking interpretations of number-theoretic systems.

We note that if the system $\mathfrak{F}$ which we seek to interpret is uniformly 1*-consistent, then we obtain a satisfaction of (3) from the functional F of def. 21, p. 54. For we can replace F_1 by $\nu^1_p[F(x_1, \alpha_2 \dots \alpha_k, b)]$, where b is the number of a proof of (3) in

<u>Definition 23</u>. If $\mathfrak{F}$ is a system of elementary number theory, an interpretation of $\mathfrak{F}$ which assigns to each theorem of the form (1) a verifiable formula of the form

$$A[x_1, \alpha_2(Y_1) \dots \alpha_k(Y_1 \dots Y_{k-1}), Y_1 \dots Y_k] \qquad (9)$$

where $Y_1 = Y_1(x_1, \alpha_2 \dots \alpha_k)$ is a recursive functional, is called a no-counter-example interpretation of $\mathfrak{F}$.

---

[2]This follows from the <u>uniform</u> recursiveness of $\mu yR(x, y)$ in R (cf. IM pp. 279-80).

To explain the phrase "no-counter-example", we note that the formula (8) says that if (1) is <u>false</u>, then there are $x_1, a_2 \ldots a_k$ to satisfy the negation of (1). But if (9) is verifiable, then from any such purported satisfaction we can effectively find values of $y_1 \ldots y_k$ such that it fails, namely the $Y_1(x_1, a_2 \ldots a_k)$. Thus the functionals effectively defeat any would-be counter-example to (1).

For a practical example of a no-counter-example interpretation of a single formula, the reader should turn to the discussion of ω-consistency at the beginning of chapter VI.

In view of the non-constructive considerations above, it would be very shocking if there were any impossibility in principle, analogous to that of theorem 2 or 7, of obtaining a no-counter-example of Z. By the remark on page 79, to prove (a) of the definition of interpretation it will suffice to prove the 1*-consistency of the system. After some work which we do in section 3, this will be altogether sufficient.

2. <u>No-counter-example interpretation of number theory without induction</u>

It turns out that Herbrand's theorem also supplies us with a no-counter-example interpretation.

<u>Theorem 10</u> (Kreisel [1], [3]). If $\mathfrak{F}$ is an elementary

number theory without induction, then F has a no-counter-example interpretation.

Proof. Let $\mathcal{A}'$ again be an arbitrary formula of $\mathcal{F}$, which we shall suppose to have the prenex equivalent (1).[1] Then the formula A_n associated with $\mathcal{A}'$ is the n the in the enumeration of the Herbrand alternations of (3) by lemma 4.2. It is of the form

$$A[x_1, \alpha_2(t_{11}) \ldots \alpha_k(t_{11} \ldots t_{1,k-1}), t_{11} \ldots t_{1k}] \vee \ldots$$
$$\vee\ A[x_1, \alpha_2(t_{n1}) \ldots \alpha_k(t_{n1} \ldots t_{n,k-1}), t_{n1} \ldots t_{nk}] \quad (10)$$

The free variables of t_{ij} are among the free variables of $\mathcal{A}'$ and $x_1, \alpha_2 \ldots \alpha_k$.

Given a proof of $\mathcal{A}'$, we can find a proof of (1) and, by theorem 8, of (3). Then by Herbrand's theorem we can find a proof in F of one of the alternations (10), where free function variables are added to F if it does not already have them. This proves (a) of def. 1.

If (10) is verifiable, it serves the purpose of effectively defeating any purported satisfaction of the negation of (1), for any $x_1, \alpha_2 \ldots \alpha_k$ will fail for the values of $t_{i1} \ldots t_{ik}$ for some i. More formally, the functionals

$$\nu_k^j\big[\mu y\{y \le \max_{1 \le p} \nu_p(t_{11} \ldots t_{1k}) \ \&\ A[x_1, \alpha_2(\nu_k^1(y)) \ldots$$
$$\alpha_{k-1}(\nu_k^1(y) \ldots \nu_k^{k-1}(y)), \nu_k^1(y) \ldots \nu_k^k(y)]\}\big]$$

as Y_j make (9) verifiable.

The relation between (10) and the Herbrand alternations

of (1) is as follows: If we replace α_1 by the f_1 of lemma 4.2 (which has the same number of argument places), then (10) is simply $C^1 \vee \ldots \vee C^n$.[2]

To complete the proof we must show how to find a counter-instance of an arbitrary Herbrand alternation of (3) if (1) is refutable in $\mathfrak{F}$. This is less simple than in the case of theorem 4 because we must substitute for function variables, and because no deduction of (1) from (10) is at hand. In order to obviate this difficulty, we associate with (10) a formula without function variables (except perhaps some occurring in (1)), from which (1) is deducible, and from a counter-instance of which one of (10) can be found. The idea is that a set of functions satisfying (10) is the same as a set of numbers satisfying the resulting Herbrand alternation of (1) but subject to certain equality conditions to allow for the fact that we have function variables.[3]

---

[2]This fact can be used in the proof of Herbrand's theorem. See HB II, 151 ff.

[3]Kreisel's method of resolving the difficulty is mistaken. The proof of the lemma on p. 254 of [1] or of the corresponding theorem I of [3] is incorrect, for both are based on the false assumption that the procedure for eliminating ε-terms given by Hilbert's first ε-theorem has the property that if $\varepsilon x A(x, a)$ is an ε-term, then there is a term $t(a)$ such that if s is any term and is replaced by s' under the procedure, then $\varepsilon x A(x, s)$ is replaced by $t(s')$.

If the system $\mathfrak{F}$ with which we work has sparse enough notation, then the lemma of [1] is actually false. Suppose

~ has only the predicate = and one function symbol f which represents the function

$$f(a) = a \dot{-} 1 \quad \text{if} \quad a \text{ is odd}$$
$$\quad\;\; = a + 1 \quad \text{if} \quad a \text{ is even.}$$

Let $A(a, b)$ be the formula

$$a = 0 \,\&\, b = 0 \;.\text{v}.\; a = 1 \,\&\, b = 0 \;.\text{v}.\; a \neq 0 \,\&\, a \neq 1 \,\&\, b \neq 0 \,.$$

Then $-A(a, b)$ is equivalent to

$$a = 0 \,\&\, b \neq 0 \;.\text{v}.\; a = 1 \,\&\, b \neq 0 \;.\text{v}.\; a \neq 0 \,\&\, a \neq 1 \,\&\, b = 0 \,.$$

The formula

$$A(a, a) \vee A[a, f(a)]$$

is a verifiable Herbrand alternation of $(x)(Ey)A(x, y)$. It is clearly true if $1 < a$. If $a = 0$, the first alternand is true; if $a = 1$, the second alternand is true because $f(a) = 0$. It follows from Kreisel's lemma that we can find a term $t(b)$ of which when substituted for α makes

$$A[0, \alpha(0)] \,\&\, A[1, \alpha(1)] \,\&\, A[2, \alpha(2)] \qquad (1)$$

true. The possible terms t are b, 0, St for given t, and $f(t)$ for given t.

1. If b is tried, the second conjunct becomes $A(1, 1)$, which is false.

2. If 0 is tried, the third conjunct becomes $A(2, 0)$, which is false.

3. If St is tried, then the first conjunct becomes $A(0, Su)$ for some u, which is false whatever the value of u.

4. We observe that no term $t(b)$ in which b actually occurs has the value 1 or 0 for <u>both</u> $b = 0$ and $b = 1$. This is clearly true for b itself, and if it is true of t, it is true of St and $f(t)$. [We mean that $-(t(0) = t(1) = 0 \vee t(0) = t(1) = 1)$.] The latter could have 0 for both only if t had 1 for both and vice versa.

Suppose $t(b)$ has been tried and consider $f[t(b)]$. By the above, either $ft(b)$ is identically 1, in which case it fares like 1 and is covered by case 3, or it is identically 0 and is covered by case 2, or either $t(0)$ has value $\neq 1$ or $t(1)$ has value $\neq 0$.

In the first case, $f[t(0)]$ has value $\neq 0$ and the first conjunct is false.

In the second case, $f[t(1)]$ has value $\neq 0$ and the second conjunct is false.

<u>Lemma 10.1</u>. Let C be an Herbrand alternation of (3). Then from C we can effectively find formulae of the form $K_v \supset C_v$, $v = 1 \ldots g$, where

(i) K_v is a conjunction of equations and negations of equations of terms composed of constants and function symbols of $\mathfrak{F}$, free variables of (1), and the variables $x_1, \alpha_2 \ldots \alpha_k$.

(ii) If $K_v' \supset A_v'$ is the result of replacing outermost terms r_j' (with α_j playing the role of f_j) by free variables as in lemma 4.2, then (1) is deducible from the conjunction of these formulae.

(iii) If C is provable in F, then so is $K_v' \supset A_v'$.

<u>Proof</u>.[4] By induction on n, we define a sequence $K_{vn} \supset C_{vn}$, where $v = 1 \ldots g_n$. Suppose $r_1' \ldots r_u'$ include all the terms of the form x_1 or $\alpha_j(t_1 \ldots t_{j-1})$ in C (or, for (iii), in the given proof of C). Then (i) is true of K_{vn} and moreover

(iv) C is deducible from the conjunction of $K_{vn} \supset C_{vn}$ without the use of equality axioms of the form

$$s = t \supset \alpha_j(s_1 \ldots s_{h-1}, s, s_{h+1} \ldots s_{j-1}) = \alpha_j(s_1 \ldots s_{h-1}, t, s_{h+1} \ldots s_{j-1}) \text{ . (11)}$$

Thus, for every substitution of a term t(b) of $\mathfrak{F}$ for α in (A), (A) is false, contrary to Kreisel's lemma.

[4]This argument is an adaptation of the elimination of "Formeln der ε-Gleichheit" in the proof of the first ε-theorem. Cf. HB II, 56-79.

(v) Let $P_1 \ldots P_{\mu*}$ $(\mu* < \mu^2)$ be the (unordered) pairs of terms (r_p', r_q') where the elements differ with respect to exactly one argument and have the same function variable, ordered first according to $\max(p, q)$ and then according to $\min(p, q)$. Then we can obtain from the given proof of C a proof of $K_{vn} \supset C_{vn}$ in which if an axiom (11) occurs in the proof, the pair of terms equated in the consequent has index $\leq \mu* - n$.

If $n = 0$, K_{vn} is vacuous and C_{vn} is simply C. $g_0 = 1$. Then (i) is vacuous and (iv) and (v) trivial.

Now suppose we have defined the formulae $K_{vn} \supset C_{vn}$. From each formula we shall define two formulae $K_{2v-1,n+1} \supset C_{2v-1,n+1}$ and $K_{2v,n+1} \supset C_{2v,n+1}$, so that $g_{n+1} = 2g_n$.

Let the pair $P_{\mu*-n}$ be (r_p', r_q'), where $q < p$. Let $K_{vn}* \supset C_{vn}*$ be the result of replacing r_p' by r_q' wherever it may occur in $K_{vn} \supset C_{vn}$. Suppose r_q' is $\alpha_j(\ldots s' \ldots)$ and r_p' is $\alpha_j(\ldots t' \ldots)$. Then

$K_{2v-1,n+1}$ is $s' = t' \;\&\; K_{vn}*$

$K_{2v,n+1}$ is $s' \neq t' \;\&\; K_{vn}$

$C_{2v-1,n+1}$ is $C_{vn}*$

$C_{2v,n+1}$ is C_{vn}.

(i) is obvious from the hypothesis of induction.

(iv) In view of the hypothesis of induction, it suffices to deduce $K_{vn} \supset C_{vn}$ from the conjunction

$$K_{2v-1,n+1} \supset C_{2v-1,n+1} \;.\&.\; K_{2v,n+1} \supset C_{2v,n+1} ,$$

without axioms (11). Clearly from this we have

$$s' \neq t' \supset . K_{vn} \supset C_{vn} . \tag{12}$$

From equality axioms of the form

$$s' = t' \supset . P(\ldots s' \ldots) \supset P(\ldots t' \ldots) \tag{13}$$

where $P(a_1 \ldots a_w)$ is a prime formula, we can obtain by the propositional calculus

$$s' = t' \supset : K_{vn}^* \supset C_{vn}^* . \supset . K_{vn} \supset C_{vn}$$

from which, usigg $K_{2v-1,n+1} \supset C_{2v-1,n+1}$, we obtain

$$s' = t' \supset . K_{vn} \supset C_{vn} .$$

With (12), this yields the result.

(v}) Suppose we have a proof of $K_{vn} \supset C_{vn}$ which satisfies the condition. If an axiom (11) occurs in this proof, either the pair of terms in the consequent has index $< \mu^* - n$ or s is s' and t is t' . In that case, (11) is deducible in the propositional calculus from $s' \neq t'$. Therefore by the deduction theorem, $s' \neq t' \;\& K_{vn} . \supset C_{vn}$ is provable without it; i. e. $K_{2v,n+1} \supset C_{2v,n+1}$ is provable subject to the condition for $n + 1$.

Suppose that in the given proof of $K_{vn} \supset C_{vn}$ we replace r_p' wherever it occurs by r_q' . The proof connection is preserved except for axioms (11). In view of the condition on the proof and our ordering of pairs, the terms in the consequent of any formula (11) both have indices $\leq p$. Their proper parts have indices $< p$. Hence they are unaffected unless one or both of the terms is r_p', and unless this holds the pair has index $< \mu^* - n$, so that their remaining is in accordance with the condition for $n + 1$.

If, say, the t of (11) is t', (11) becomes

$$s = t' \supset \alpha_j(\ldots s \ldots) = \alpha_j(\ldots s' \ldots) \qquad (14)$$

Using only equality axioms of the same type as (13), we can deduce

$$s' = t' \supset : s = s' \supset R14. \supset 14$$

Supposing that s is not t' (for in that case (11) could have been eliminated at the outset, for its consequent would have been an instance of $a = a$), it follows that we can deduce (14) from $s' = t'$ and the axiom

$$s = s' \supset R14$$

where the consequent terms both have indices $< p$, and therefore the pair of consequent terms has index $< u^* - n$. Thus we can deduce $K_{vn}{}^* \supset C_{vn}{}^*$ from $s' = t'$ by a proof in which thataxioms (11) satisfy the condition for $n + 1$. By the deduction, theorem, we can so deduce $K_{2v-1,n+1} \supset C_{2v-1,n+1}$.

By induction, we can obtain $K_{vn} \supset C_{vn}$ for each n and $v = 1 \ldots 2^n$, provided $n \leq \mu^*$, to satisfy (i), (iv), and (v). Let K_v be $K_{v\mu^*}$ and C_v be $C_{v\mu^*}$. If in a deduction in $\mathfrak{F}$ we replace outermost erms r_p' by free variables, the proof connection will be preserved except from axioms (11). Thus if we do this to the deduction of C from the conjunction of $K_v \supset C_v$ which we obtain from (iv) for $n = \mu^*$, the proof connection is undisturbed, and we obtain a deduction from the conjunction of the $K_v' \supset A_v'$ of an Herbrand alternation A of (1). Since we can deduce $\mathfrak{a}$ from A, it follows that (ii) holds.

(iii) By (v) for $n = \mu^*$, if C is provable in F then $K_v \supset C_v$ is provable without axioms (11). Therefore $K_v' \supset A_v'$ is also probable in F.

This completes the proof of lemma 10.1.

It is immediate from (iii) and (iv) that if C is provable in F, then $\mathfrak{a}$ is provable in $\mathfrak{F}$; i. e. our interpretation is complete in the sense of theorem 5.

We shall use the deduction given by (iii) to find a counter-example for (10) if (1) is refutable, in analogy with lemma 4.1, but the process will be more complex. By (iii), if $-\mathfrak{a}'$ is provable in $\mathfrak{F}$ the negation of (1) is also provable, and we can therefore prove

$$(Ec_1) \dots (Ec_\mu)[K_1' \mathbin{\&} -A_1' .v \dots v. K_u' \mathbin{\&} -A_u']$$

where $u = 2^{\mu^*}$ and the C of lemma 10.1 is an arbitrary A_n. Then by Herbrand's theorem we can prove in F

$$K_{11} \mathbin{\&} -A_{11}.v \dots v.K_{u1} \mathbin{\&} -A_{u1}. v \dots$$
$$v .K_{1h'} \mathbin{\&} -A_{1h'}.v \dots v.K_{uh'} \mathbin{\&} -A_{uh'} \qquad (15)$$

where for $j = 1 \dots h'$, $v = 1 \dots u$, $K_{vj} \mathbin{\&} -A_{vj}$ is a substitution-case pf $K_v' \mathbin{\&} - A_v'$ by terms of F.

We can suppose that (15) is closed and therefore that each alternand is decidable.[5] At least one, say K_{vh} & A_{vh}, must be provable in F and numerically true.

We seek a counter-example to A_n. We suppose that A_n satisfies the condition that if $r_{i_1}' \dots r_{i_q}'$ are all the terms occurring in A_n in place of existentially quantified variables of (1) (and (3)), then <u>every</u> k -tuple of these terms occurs in some alternand of A_n in place of $y_1 \dots y_k$. If this does not hold, then in view of the ordering of k -tuples used in the proof of lemma 4.2, it does hold for some larger n such that a counterexample to this A_n will also serve as a counterexample to the original one.

For each j, $1 < j \leq k$, let a_j^* be the function described as follows:

If $v_1 \dots v_{j-1}$ are the values of the terms replacing $y_1 \dots y_{j-1}$ in (say) the p th alternand of A_{vh}, then $a_j^*(v_1 \dots v_{j-1})$ is the value of the term u_{pj} which replaces x_j in this alternand.

If there is no such p, then $a_j^*(v_1 \dots v_{j-1}) = 0$.

In addition, we let x_1^* be the value of the term which replaces x_1 in each alternand of A_{vh}.

---

[5]The case where $\mathfrak{a}'$ and therefore (1) have function variables can be handled as in the proof of lemma 4.1; see p. 46. Or we can for each substitution for such variables and each $h \leq u$ find $x_{1h}^*, a_{2h}^* \dots a_{kh}^*$ such that the alternation of all these substitutions in $- A_n$ is false.

We need to show that

(vi) α_j^* is a single-valued function.

(vii) If x_1^*, α_2^* ... α_k^* are substituted for x_1, α_2 ... α_k in A_n, the result of the substitution has the same truth-value as A_{vh} and is therefore false.

(vi) Suppose s_{i1} ... $s_{i,j-1}$ are the terms replacing y_1 ... y_{j-1} in the i th alternand of A_{vh}. We must show that if for each $j' < j$ the values of $s_{ij'}$ and $s_{pj'}$ are the same, then the values of u_{ij} and u_{pj} are the same.

Let $\alpha_j(t_{i1} \ldots t_{i,j-1})$ be the term replacing x_j in the i th alternand of A_n (see (10), p. 81). Consider the axioms

$$t_{i1} = t_{p1} \supset \alpha_j(t_{i1} \ldots t_{i,j-1}) = \alpha_j(t_{p1}, t_{i2} \ldots t_{i,j-1})$$

$$\ldots$$

$$t_{i,j-1} = t_{p,j-1} \supset \alpha_j(t_{p1} \ldots t_{p,j-2}, t_{i,j-1}) = \alpha_j(t_{p1} \ldots t_{p,j-1}),$$

where the consequents change $\alpha_j(t_{i1} \ldots t_{i,j-1})$ into $\alpha_j(t_{p1} \ldots t_{p,j-1})$ one argument at a time. From them can be derived in F without further axioms (11)

$$t_{i1} = t_{p1} \,\&\, \ldots \,\&\, t_{i,j-1} = t_{p,j-1}. \supset \alpha_j(t_{i1} \ldots t_{i,j-1}) = \alpha_j(t_{p1} \ldots t_{p,j-1}). \quad (16)$$

If we subject this derivation to the same transformations as those which yield C_v in the proof of lemma 10.1, then by the same argument as that for (v) we obtain a derivation of the formula into which (16) is transformed, without axioms of form (11). This derivation remains one if we replace the terms r_q' by variables σ_i and then carry out the substitution by which A_{vh} was obtained from A_v'. Then we have a derivation in F of the formula

$$K_{vh} \supset : s_{11} = s_{p1} \& \dots s_{1,j-1} = s_{p,j-1} . \supset u_{pj} = u_{rj} .$$

This formula must therefore be numerically true. Since by hypothesis, its antecedents are true, its consequent must also be true; i. e. u_{pj} and u_{rj} have the same value, q. e. d.

(vii) It suffices to show that for each $j \leq k$, if t_{ij}^* is the result of substituting $x_1^*, \alpha_2^* \dots \alpha_k^*$ for $x_1, \alpha_2 \dots \alpha_k$ in t_{ij} [cf. (10), (16)], then t_{ij}^* has the same numerical value as the term s_{ij} which replaces y_j in A_{vh}.

Suppose this is true for each $j' < j$. Then by the definition of α_j^*, the term u_{ij}, which replaces x_j in A_{vh} will have the same value as $\alpha_j(s_{11} \dots s_{1,j-1})$, and therefore the same as $\alpha_j^*(t_{11}^* \dots t_{1,j-1}^*)$, which is the result of substituting α_j^* for α_j (all j) in $\alpha_j(t_{11} \dots t_{1,j-1})$. Therefore for each i, the two formulae will have terms of the same value substituted for the variables of (1). Therefore the corresponding alternands will have the same truth-value, and so will the formulae as a whole.

The claim in the first paragraph is proved by induction on the construction of t_{ij}.

We note that by the construction of lemma 4.2 and our assumption about A_n, if r_q occurs as a proper part of t_{ij}, then for some i', j' it is $t_{i'j'}$; in fact for any $j' \leq k$, any j'-tuple of proper parts of t_{ij} is $t_{i'1} \ldots t_{i'j'}$ for some $i' \leq n$.

Then we prove the following: If r_q occurs as t_{ij}, then the result of substituting $x_1^*, a_2^* \ldots a_k^*$ for $x_1, a_2 \ldots a_k$ in r_q, which we call r_q^*, has the same value as s_{ij}.

1. t_{ij} (r_q) is a constant of (1). Then s_{ij} is the same term.

2. r_q is x_1. Then s_{ij} is the term which replaces x_1 in A_{vh}, and therefore has the value x_1^*.

3. r_q is $f(r_{i_1} \ldots r_{i_w})$, where f is a function symbol of (1). By our remark above, each term r_{i_m} is $t_{i'j'}$ for some i', j', and by the hypothesis of induction $r_{i_m}^*$ has the same value as $s_{i'j'}$. If r_q is t_{ij}, then s_{ij} is obtained from t_{ij} by the same transformations as those by which $t_{i'j'}$ yielded $s_{i'j'}$. Therefore s_{ij} is $f(\ldots s_{i'j'} \ldots)$. Since r_q^* is $f(r_{i_1}^* \ldots r_{i_m}^*)$, it follows that these have the same value.

4. r_q is $a_j(r_{i_1} \ldots r_{i_{j-1}})$. Then if r_q is t_{ij}, we can find i' such that $r_{i_1} \ldots r_{i_{j-1}}$ are $t_{i'1} \ldots t_{i',j-1}$. By the hypothesis of induction, $r_{i_m}^*$ has the

same value as $s_{1'm}$. But then $a_j^*(r_{1_1}^* \ldots r_{1_{j-1}}^*)$, i. e. t_{1j}^* , has the same value as $u_{1'j}$. But $u_{1'j}$ is the term which in A_{vh} supplants $a_j(t_{1'1} \ldots t_{1',j-1})$. Therefore t_{1j} is supplanted in A_{vh} by $u_{1'j}$; i. e. $u_{1'j}$ is s_{1j} . Therefore r_q^*, i. e. t_{1j}^*, and s_{1j} have the same value, q. e. d.

Thus we have found functions such that if $- \mathcal{A}'$ is provable in $\mathcal{F}$, then the result of substituting these functions in A_n is numerically false. It will be refutable in F if F contains each function which is 0 except for finitely many arguments. This proves (b) of def. 1.

Finally, we show that the no-counter-example interpretation of $\mathcal{F}$ is strong. Suppose $\mathcal{B}$ is deduced from $\mathcal{A}$ in $\mathcal{F}$, and let A_n be the alternation (10) associated with $\mathcal{A}$. We gave a procedure (lemma 10.1, (iii) and (iv)), which gives for any proof of A_n a proof of $\mathcal{A}$. Using the deduction of $\mathcal{B}$ from $\mathcal{A}$, we can then find a provable formula associated with $\mathcal{B}$.

In fact, we need assume only that A_n is verifiable; then the formula B_n associated with $\mathcal{B}$ can be proved from verifiable axioms. For $\mathcal{B}$ can, by its deducibility from $\mathcal{A}$ and lemma 10.1 (iii), be deduced from the conjunction of the formulae $K_v' \supset A_v'$ in $\mathcal{F}$. Therefore so can the formula B obtained from $\mathcal{B}$ as (3) was obtained from

$\mathfrak{a}'$. Therefore by Herbrand's theorem we can obtain an Herbrand alternation of B which is deducible in the elementary calculus with free variables from the conjunction of $K_v' \supset A_v'$. By lemma 4.2 and the construction of the interpretation, this alternation is a subalternation of some B_m , which is therefore also so provable.

Hence it suffices to show that if A_n is verifiable, so is each of the formulae $K_v' \supset A_v'$. Consider any substitution of numerals for the variables c_q . Let the resulting formula be $K_v^* \supset A_v^*$. If K_v^* is true, then by the method of pp. 89-90, we can find substitutions x_1^*, a_2^* ... a_k^* for which A_n has the same truth-value as A_v^* , namely truth. Therefore $K_v^* \supset A_v^*$ is true.

This completes the proof of theorem 10.

3. No-counter-example interpretation, 1*-consistency, and external consistency.

We have pointed out that if a system is uniformly 1*-consistent, we can describe a putative no-counter-example interpretation which satisfies (a) of def. 1. The main result of this section, theorem 12, willshow that if a system with induction is uniformly 1*-consistent, then it has a no-counter-example interpretation, i. e. which also satisfies (b) [and (c)].

First we shall discuss the relations of 1*-consistency with Hilbert and Bernays' concept of external consistency

(HB II, 282-3).

<u>Definition 24</u>. An extension $\mathcal{F}$ of a system of elementary number theory is <u>externally consistent</u> if it is consistent and remains so if a verifiable axiom is added, even if new function symbols are involved.

<u>Theorem 11</u> (cf. Kreisel [3]). (a) If $\mathcal{F}$ is 1*-consistent, and contains quantifier-free expressions for Kleene's predicates T_n and function U (IM, p. 281), then $\mathcal{F}$ is externally consistent. (The "verifiable axiom" is taken to be a formula of recursive number theory.)

(b) If $\mathcal{F}$ is externally consistent, then $\mathcal{F}$ is 1*-consistent.

<u>Proof</u>. (a) Let A be a formula of recursive number theory. Let A' be the conjunction of A with the verifiable formulae

$$T_m(e, a_1 \ldots a_m, y) \;\&\; T_m(e, a_1 \ldots a_m, z) \;.\supset y = z \quad (17)$$

for each m for which A' contains a new function symbol with m arguments.

If, say, 0 = 1 is deducible in $\mathcal{F}$ from A , it is deducible from A' , and we can by the deduction theorem prove in

$$(Ex_1) \ldots (Ex_k)\, A''$$

where A" is the disjunctive normal form of A' . This deduction may contain identity axioms with new symbols.

For each new symbol f , let e_f be a Gödel number

of f . We replace f by a representing predicate, using $(Ey)[T_m(0^{(e_f)}, t_1 \ldots t_m, y) \& U(y) = t]$ if the context $f(t_1 \ldots t_m) = t$ is a non-negated prime formula in A" (at each step of the elimination, we transform into prenex and disjunctive normal form) and $(y)[T_m(0^{(e_f)}, t_1 \ldots t_m, y) \supset U(y) = t]$ if $f(t_1 \ldots t_m) = t$ is a negated prime formula. Then the axioms of identity with the new symbols can be <u>proved</u> from (17). The final result is a deduction from (17) of a formula

$$(Ez_1) \ldots (Ez_p)\ A^*$$

from which we obtain a proof in $\mathcal{F}$ of

$$(Ez_1) \ldots (Ez_q)[A^* \vee - 17] \qquad (18)$$

where we have added more variables to quantify the free variables of (17). Then since $\mathcal{F}$ is 1*-consistent, we can find numbers $n_1 \ldots n_q$ such that the result of substituting $0^{(n_1)} \ldots 0^{(n_q)}$ in (18) for $z_1 \ldots z_q$ is true. Since (17) is verifiable, the result of substituting them in A^* must be true and must therefore have a true alternand. Each prime formula $T_m(0^{(e_f)}, s_1 \ldots s_m, s)$ occurs without negation and is therefore true, from which it follows that the value of $U(s)$ is the value of f for arguments the values of $s_1 \ldots s_m$. Hence we can reverse the elimination of f , and replace

$$T_m(0^{(e_f)}, s_1 \ldots s_m, s) \& U(s) = s'$$

by $f(s_1 \ldots s_m) = s'$, and similarly if $U(s) = s'$ is negated.

The resulting formula is a counter-instance to A .
Hence if A is verifiable, $0 = 1$ cannot be deduced from it in $\mathfrak{F}$.

(b) Suppose we have a proof of

$$(Ex_1) \ldots (Ex_k)A(x_1 \ldots x_k)$$

in $\mathfrak{F}$. Then $\mathfrak{F}$ becomes inconsistent if

$$- A(a_1 \ldots a_k) \qquad (19)$$

is added as an axiom. Therefore (19) is not verifiable, and there must be $0^{(n_1)} \ldots 0^{(n_k)}$ such that

$$A(0^{(n_1)} \ldots 0^{(n_k)})$$

is true.

If the external consistency of $\mathfrak{F}$ has been constructively proved, then $n_1 \ldots n_k$ can be found effectively.

We remark that if $\mathfrak{F}$ is <u>uniformly</u> 1*-consistent, then (a) holds if we assume that the functions represented by the symbols of A are recursive relative to given functions. (We use Kleene's normal form applied to relative recursiveness; IM, pp. 290-5; we must suppose $\mathfrak{F}$ contains enough apparatus to define course-of-values functions). That is, we can admit functional symbols into the "verifiable formula", but use them in such a way that the function variables are parameters, i. e. not substituted for.

Theorem 12 justifies us in thinking of uniform 1*-consistency and the existence of a no-counter-example interpretation as generalizations of external consistency.

<u>Theorem 12</u> (Kreisel [3]). Suppose $\mathfrak{F}$ is an extension of an elementary number theory with induction for which we have for each k a functional $H(x_1, \alpha_2 \ldots \alpha_k, p)$ such that if p is the number of a proof of a closed prenex formula of elementary number theory

$$(x_1)(Ey_1) \ldots (x_k)(Ey_k)A(x_1 \ldots x_k, y_1 \ldots y_k) \qquad (20)$$

then

$$A[x_1, \alpha_2(Y_{p1}) \ldots \alpha_k(Y_{p1} \ldots Y_{p,k-1}), Y_{p1} \ldots Y_{pk}] \qquad (21)$$

is verifiable, where for $i = 1 \ldots k$

$$Y_{pi} = \nu_k^i[H(x_1, \alpha_2 \ldots \alpha_k, p)] \,.$$

Then the subsytem of $\mathfrak{F}$ consisting of theorems which are formulae of elementary number theory without free function variables has a no-counter-example interpretation.

The hypothesis holds if $\mathfrak{F}$ is uniformly 1*-consistent. In this case, the interpretation extends to formulae with free function variables, provided refutation is understood as proof of the negation with the free variables.[6]

<u>Proof</u>. <u>Definition 25</u>. A functional $Y(x_1, \alpha_2 \ldots \alpha_k)$ (where α_{i+1} has i arguments, but cf. note 1) is <u>simply representable</u> in $\mathfrak{F}$ if there is a formula

$$(z_1)(Ew_1) \ldots (z_k)(Ew_k)B(z_1 \ldots z_k, w_1 \ldots w_k) \qquad (22)$$

where $B(z_1 \ldots z_k, w_1 \ldots w_k)$ has no quantifiers or other free variables, which is provable in $\mathfrak{F}$, and there is

[6] We could probably weaken this to proof of the negation with terms of $\mathfrak{F}$, or even ε-terms, substituted for the free function variables. To establish this would be very complex and tedious.

a (recursive) term $t(a)$ of $\mathcal{F}$ such that

$$Y(x_1, \alpha_2 \dots \alpha_k) =$$
$$t\,[\mu w B\{x_1, \alpha_2[\nu_k^1(w)] \dots \alpha_k[\nu_k^1(w) \dots \nu_k^{k-1}(w)], \nu_k^1(w) \dots \nu_k^k(w)\}] .$$

We say that Y is represented in $\mathcal{F}$ by the formula (22). and the term $t(a)$. (In the case where x_1 is missing, (z_1) is also missing.)

Let $t_1(a)$, $t_2(a) \dots$ be an enumeration of all the terms of $\mathcal{F}$ with one free variable a. We can enumerate all functionals with arguments $x_1, \alpha_2 \dots \alpha_k$ as follows: If $\nu_2^1(n)$ is the number of a proof of a formula of the form (22), then Y_n is the functional represented by the formula (22) and the term $t_{\nu_2^2(n)}$; otherwise Y_n is identically 0.

Now we set $Y_n^i = \nu_k^i(Y_n)$. This functional is in fact $Y_{\varphi(i,\, n)}$ for a certain function φ, where $\nu_2^1[\varphi(i, n)] = \nu_2^1(n)$ and $\nu_2^2[\varphi(i, n)]$ is the number in the above enumeration of terms of the term $\nu_k^i[t_{\nu_2^2(n)}(a)]$. Clearly φ is primitive recursive if the enumeration is reasonable.

Given a formula $\mathcal{A}$, of elementary number theory without free function variables, let (20) be a standard prenex equivalent of $\mathcal{A}$. Then we associate with it the sequence of formulae

$$A[x_1, \alpha_2(Y_n^1) \dots \alpha_k(Y_n^1 \dots Y_n^{k-1}), Y_n^1 \dots Y_n^k] . \qquad (23)$$

Suppose $t_1(a)$ is the term a. Then if p is the number

of a proof of $(\mathfrak{A})$ (which can be obtained effectively from a proof of $\mathfrak{A}$, then (23) is verifiable for $n = \nu_2(p, 1)$. This can be seen from the hypothesis, for

$$Y_n = \mu y \{ y \leq H(x_1, \alpha_2 \ldots \alpha_k, p) \ \& \ A(x_1, \alpha_2[\nu_k^1(y)] \ldots \alpha_k[\nu_k^1(y) \ldots \nu_k^{k-1}(y)], \nu_k^1(y) \ldots \nu_k^k(y)) \}$$

We have assumed that $\mathfrak{F}$ contains the n -tuple functions, and to prove (b), we shall assume that $\mathfrak{F}$ contains the exponential function, the product with a variable number of factors, and the exponent function $(x)_y$. Since these functions are all primitive recursive (IM pp. 222, 223,224, 230), if $\mathfrak{F}$ contains Z , then an inessential extension of $\mathfrak{F}$ satisfies our condition, which by lemma 3.1 is 1*-consistent if $\mathfrak{F}$ is externally consistent.

We have proved (a) of def. 1. The idea of the proof of (b) is as follows. If (23) is true for all functions, we might expect to deduce (20) from it, in view of theorem 9. Thus if $\mathfrak{A}$ and therefore (20) are refutable, we could prove

$$(Ex_1)(E\alpha_2) \ldots (E\alpha_k) - 23 .$$

However, we should have no way of effectively finding substitutions for the bound variables to make (23) false. However, we note that if (23) is false for someset of values of the function variables, then it is false for a set of functions zero except for finitely many arguments. Any such function can be represented by a term $(0^{(1)})_{\nu_j}(a_1 \ldots a_j)$

and <u>all</u> such functions can be enumerated by the term $(w)\nu_j(a_1 \dots a_j)$ (see page 15). Therefore we can hope to prove

$$(Ex_1) \dots (Ex_k) \underset{-}{A}[x_1,\ (x_2)Y^1_n(Y^1 .\ (x_k)\nu_k(Y^1_n \dots Y^{k-1}_n),\ Y^1_n \dots Y^k_n] .$$

This will be, in effect, the conclusion of lemma 12.3.

<u>Lemma 12.1</u>. Let $\mathcal{A}$ be the prenex formula (20). Then if

$$(Ey_1)(x_1) \dots (Ey_k)(x_k)(Ey_{k+1})B_i(x_1 \dots x_k,\ y_1 \dots y_{k+1}) \tag{24}$$

is provable for $i = 1 \dots k$, then we can prove

$$\begin{aligned}(Ep_1) \dots (Ep_k)(Ex_1) \dots (Ex_k) \Big[\mathcal{A} \supset \underset{-}{A}[t_1(x_1) \dots t_k(x_k),\ (p_1)t_1(x_1) \dots (p_k)\nu_k[t_1(x_1) \dots t_{k-1}(x_{k-1})]] . \\ \& \bigwedge_{i=1}^{k}\{\underset{-}{B_i}[(p_1)x_{i1}{*} \dots (p_k)\nu_k(x_{i1}{*} \dots x_{ik}{*}),\ x_{i1}{*} \dots x_{i,k+1}{*}] \\ \& (w)(w < x_i \supset -\underset{-}{B_i}[(p_1)w_1{*} \dots (p_k)\nu_k(w_1{*} \dots w_k{*}),\ w_1{*} \dots w_{k+1}{*}])\}\Big]\end{aligned} \tag{25}$$

where $a_i{*}$ abbreviates $\nu^i_{k+1}(a)$.

This formula says that if functionals X_i are represented in $\mathcal{F}$ by formulae (24) and terms $t_i(a)$, then there are numbers $x_1 \dots x_k$ and functions $\beta_1 \dots \beta_k$, zero except for finitely many arguments, such that if $\mathcal{A}$ holds then so does

$$\underset{-}{A}[x_1 \dots x_k,\ \beta_1(x_1) \dots \beta_k(x_1 \dots x_k)]$$

and x_i is the value of X_i for the arguments $\beta_1 \dots \beta_k$.

Proof. A. First we derive

$$(x)[x \leq w \supset (Ey)\mathcal{A}(x, y)] \supset (Ep)(x)\{x \leq w \supset \mathcal{A}[x, (p)_x]\}$$

where $\mathcal{A}(x, y)$ is any formula with the indicated free variables.

1. $\mathcal{A}(0, y) \supset \mathcal{A}[0, (2^y)_0]$

$$\supset (x)\{x \leq 0 \supset \mathcal{A}[x, (2^y)_x]\}$$

$$\supset (Ep)(x)\{x \leq 0 \supset \mathcal{A}[x, (p)_x]\} \qquad (26)$$

whence $(Ey)\mathcal{A}(0, y) \supset R26$

$$(x)[x \leq 0 \supset (Ey)\mathcal{A}(x, y)] \supset R26 .$$

Let the formula be $\mathcal{C}(w)$. Then we have derived $\mathcal{C}(0)$.

2. Assume $\mathcal{C}(w)$. Then first we have

$$(x)[x \leq Sw \supset (Ey)\mathcal{A}(x, y)]$$

$$\supset . (x)[x \leq w \supset (Ey)\mathcal{A}(x, y)] \; \& \; (Ey)\mathcal{A}(Sw, y)$$

$$\supset . (Ep)(x)\{x \leq w \supset \mathcal{A}[x, (p)_x]\} \; \& \; (Ey)\mathcal{A}(Sw, y) \qquad (27)$$

by $\mathcal{C}(w)$.

We have also

$a \leq w \supset (p)_a = (p_{w+1}{}^b \cdot \prod_{1 \leq w} p_1{}^{(p)_1})_a$, whence

$$(x)\{x \leq w \supset \mathcal{A}[x, (p)_x]\}$$

$$\supset (x)\{x \leq w \supset \mathcal{A}[x, (p_{w+1}{}^b \cdot \prod_{1 \leq w} p_1{}^{(p)_1})_x]\} \qquad (28)$$

Moreover, since

$$(p_{w+1}{}^b \cdot \prod_{1 \leq w} p_1{}^{(p)_1})_{Sw} = b$$

$$\mathcal{A}(Sw, b) \supset \mathcal{A}[Sw, (p_{w+1}{}^b \cdot \prod_{1 \leq w} p_1{}^{(p)_1})_{Sw}]$$

$$\supset (x)\{x = Sw \supset \mathcal{A}[x, (p_{w+1}{}^b \cdot \prod_{1 \leq w} p_1{}^{(p)_1})_x]\} \qquad (29)$$

by (28)

$$L28 \;\&\; L29 . \supset (x)\{x \leq Sw \supset \mathcal{A}[x, (p_{w+1}{}^{b} \cdot \prod_{i \leq w} p_i{}^{(p)_i})_x]\}$$

$$\supset (Ep)(x)\{x \leq Sw \supset \mathcal{A}[x, (p)_x]\} \qquad (30)$$

from which follows

$$(Ep)L28 \;\&\; (Eb)L29 . \supset R30 ,$$

from which by (27) follows

$(x)[x \leq Sw \supset (Ey)\mathcal{A}(x, y)] \supset R30$, i. e. $\mathcal{C}(Sw)$.

Then by the deduction theorem we have

$$\mathcal{C}(w) \supset \mathcal{C}(Sw)$$

and by $\mathcal{C}(0)$ and induction, we have $\mathcal{C}(w)$.

3. Given a formula $\mathcal{A}(x_1 \ldots x_n, y)$, from $\mathcal{C}(w)$ with $\mathcal{A}[\nu_n^1(x) \ldots \nu_n^n(x), y]$ for $\mathcal{A}(x, y)$, we can deduce with the help of the formulae

$$\nu_n^i[\nu_n(x_1 \ldots x_n)] = x_i ,$$

the formula

$$(x_1) \ldots (x_n)[\nu_n(x_1 \ldots x_n) \leq w \supset (Ey)\mathcal{A}(x_1 \ldots x_n, y)]$$

$$\supset (Ep)(x_1) \ldots (x_n)\{\nu_n(x_1 \ldots x_n) \leq w$$

$$\supset \mathcal{A}[x_1 \ldots x_n, (p)_{\nu_n(x_1 \ldots x_n)}]\} \qquad (31)$$

B. Let $A_i(a_1 \ldots a_i, b_1 \ldots b_i)$ be the formula $(i = 0 \ldots k)$

$$(x_{i+1})(Ey_{i+1}) \ldots (x_k)(Ey_k)[\mathcal{A} \supset A(a_1 \ldots a_i, x_{i+1} \ldots x_k, b_1 \ldots b_i, y_{i+1} \ldots y_k)]$$

Then for $i = 1 \ldots k$, let $A_i{}^*(a_1 \ldots a_i, b_1 \ldots b_i)$ be

$$A_i(a_1 \ldots a_i, b_1 \ldots b_i) \;\&\; (w)[w < b_i$$

$$\supset - A_i(a_1 \ldots a_i, b_1 \ldots b_{i-1}, w)]$$

Then we derive

$$(Ep_1)\ \ldots\ (Ep_k)\ \bigwedge_{i=1}^{k} (x_1)\ \ldots\ (x_i)\{\nu_i(x_1\ \ldots\ x_i) \leq w$$
$$\supset A_i{*}[x_1\ \ldots\ x_i,\ (p_1)_{x_1}\ \ldots\ (p_i)_{\nu_i(x_1 \ldots x_i)}]\}$$

i. $(x_1)(Ey_1)\ \ldots\ (x_k)(Ey_k) \bigwedge_{i=1}^{k} A_i{*}(x_1\ \ldots\ x_i,\ y_1\ \ldots\ y_i)$ (32)

By the least-number principle

$$A_i(a_1\ \ldots\ a_i,\ b_1\ \ldots\ b_i) \supset (Ey_i)A_i{*}(a_1\ \ldots\ a_i,\ b_1\ \ldots\ b_{i-1},\ y_i)$$

from which follows

$$(x_i)(Ey_i)A_i(a_1\ \ldots\ a_{i-1},\ x_i,\ b_1\ \ldots\ b_{i-1},\ y_i)$$
$$\supset (x_i)(Ey_i)A_i{*}(a_1\ \ldots\ a_{i-1},\ x_i,\ b_1\ \ldots\ b_{i-1},\ y_i)\ , \quad (33)$$

i. e.

$$A_{i-1}(a_1\ \ldots\ a_{i-1},\ b_1\ \ldots\ b_{i-1}) \supset R33\ . \qquad (34)$$

But evidently

$$A_{i-1}{*}(a_1\ \ldots\ a_{i-1},\ b_1\ \ldots\ b_{i-1}) \supset L34$$
$$\supset R33 \text{ by } (34).$$

from which follows

$$\bigwedge_{j=1}^{i-1} A_j{*}(a_1\ \ldots\ a_j,\ b_1\ \ldots\ b_j) \supset$$
$$(x_i)(Ey_i)[\bigwedge_{j=1}^{i-1} A_j{*}(a_1\ \ldots\ a_j,\ b_1\ \ldots\ b_j)\ \& \quad (35)$$
$$A_i{*}(a_1\ \ldots\ a_{i-1},\ x_i,\ b_1\ \ldots\ b_{i-1},\ y_i)]$$

from which we infer

$$(x_1)(Ey_1)\ \ldots\ (x_{i-1})(Ey_{i-1}) \bigwedge_{j=1}^{i-1} A_j{*}(x_1\ \ldots\ x_j,\ y_1\ \ldots\ y_j)$$
$$(x_1)(Ey_1)\ \ldots\ (x_i)(Ey_i) \bigwedge_{j=1}^{i} A_j{*}(x_1\ \ldots\ x_j,\ y_1\ \ldots\ y_j)$$

Let this formula be $E_{i-1} \supset E_i$. Then (32) is E_k . By an obvious induction we have E_1 . E_k ; i. e.

$$(x_1)(Ey_1)A_1{*}(x_1, y_1) \supset 32$$

from which by (34)

$$A_0 \supset 32 .$$

A_0 is provable, for it is obtainable from $\mathfrak{a} \supset \mathfrak{a}$ by moving out the quantifiers in the consequent to govern the whole formula. Therefore (32) is provable.

2. Let $A_i'(a_1 \ldots a_i, b_{1} \ldots b_i)$ be the formula

$$(x_{i+1})(Ey_{i+1}) \ldots (x_k)(Ey_k) \bigwedge_{j=i+1}^{k} A_j{*}(a_1 \ldots a_i, x_{i+1} \ldots x_j, b_1 \ldots b_i, y_{i+1} \ldots y_j)$$

Then clearly

$$A_{i-1}'(a_1 \ldots a_{i-1}, b_1 \ldots b_{i-1}) \\ (x)[x_i \leq w \supset (Ey_i)A_i'(a_1 \ldots a_{i-1}, x_i, b_1 \ldots b_{i-1}, y_i)] \qquad (37)$$

hence by the formula (which follows from defs. 9 & 10)

$$\nu_i(x_1 \ldots x_i) \leq w \supset . \nu_{i-1}(x_1 \ldots x_{i-1}) \leq w \;\&\; x_i \leq w$$

we have

$$(x_1) \ldots (x_{i-1})[\nu_{i-1}(x_1 \ldots x_{i-1}) \supset A_{i-1}'(x_1 \ldots x_{i-1}, (p_1)_{x_1} \ldots (p_{i-1})_{\nu_{i-1}(x_1 \ldots x_{i-1})})]$$

$$\supset (x_1) \ldots (x_i)[\nu_i(x_1 \ldots x_i) \leq w \supset (Ey_i)A_i'(x_1 \ldots x_i, (p_1)_{x_1} \ldots (p_{i-1})_{\nu_{i-1}(x_1 \ldots x_{i-1})}, y_i)]$$

by (31)

$$\supset (Ep_i)(x_1) \ldots (x_i)[\nu_i(x_1 \ldots x_i) \leq w \supset A_i'(x_1 \ldots x_i, (p_1)_{x_1} \ldots (p_i)_{\nu_i(x_1 \ldots x_i)})] \qquad (38)$$

But from

$$A_{i-1}'(a_1 \ldots a_{i-1}, b_1 \ldots b_{i-1}) \supset A_{i-1}^*(a_1 \ldots a_{i-1}, b_1 \ldots b_{i-1}) \quad (39)$$

we have

$$L38 \supset (x_1) \ldots (x_{i-1})\{\nu_{i-1}(x_1 \ldots x_{i-1}) \leq w \supset A_{i-1}^*[\underline{x}_1 \ldots x_{i-1}, (p_1)_{x_1} \ldots (p_{i-1})_{\nu_{i-1}(x_1 \ldots x_{i-1})}]\}$$

Let the consequent of this formula be D_{i-1} Then with (38)

$$\bigwedge_{j=1}^{i-2} D_j \;\&\; L38. \supset \bigwedge_{j=1}^{i-1} D_j \;\&\; R38 .$$

Let L38 be C_{i-1}. Then the above implies

$$\bigwedge_{j=1}^{i-2} D_j \;\&\; C_{i-1}. \supset (Ep_i)[\bigwedge_{\underline{j}=1}^{i-1} D_j \;\&\; C_i]$$

from which follows

$$(Ep_1) \ldots (Ep_{i-1})[\bigwedge_{\underline{j}=1}^{i-2} D_j \;\&\; C_{i-1}] \supset (Ep_1) \ldots (Ep_i)[\bigwedge_{\underline{j}=1}^{i-1} D_j \;\&\; C_i]$$

Hence by a chain of inferences

$$(Ep_1)C_1 \supset (Ep_1) \ldots (Ep_k)[\bigwedge_{\underline{j}=1}^{k-1} D_j \;\&\; C_k] \quad (40)$$

But C_k is

$$(x_1) \ldots (x_k)[\underline{\nu}_k(x_1 \ldots x_k) \leq w \supset A_k'(x_1 \ldots x_k, (p_1)_{x_1} \ldots (p_k)_{\nu_k(x_1 \ldots x_k)})]$$

which by (39) implies

$$(x_1) \ldots (x_k)[\underline{\nu}_k(x_1 \ldots x_k) \leq w \supset A_k^*(x_1 \ldots x_k) (p_1)_{x_1} \ldots (p_k)_{\nu_k(x_1 \ldots x_k)})] ,$$

i. e. D_k . By (40)

$$(Ep_1)C_1 \supset (Ep_1) \ldots (Ep_k) \bigwedge_{j=1}^{k} D_j . \quad (41)$$

the consequent of which is (B).

Now A_0' is the provable formula (32). By (37)

$$A_0' \supset (x_1)[x_1 \leq w \supset (Ey_1)A_1'(x_1, y_1)]$$
$$\supset (Ep_1)C_1 \quad \text{by (30)}$$

and therefore (B) follows by (41).

C. For $i = 1 \ldots k$ we can derive

$$(Ey)(Ez_1) \ldots (Ez_k)[B_1(z_1 \ldots z_k, y_1^* \ldots y_{k+1}^*) \\ \& \bigwedge_{j=1}^{k} A_j^*(y_1^* \ldots y_j^*, z_1 \ldots z_j)]$$

Let $B_{1r}(a_1 \ldots a_r, b_1 \ldots b_{r+1})$ be the formula

$$(x_{r+1})(Ey_{r+2}) \ldots (x_k)(Ey_{k+1}) \\ B_1(a_1 \ldots a_r, x_{r+1} \ldots x_k, b_1 \ldots b_{r+1}, y_{r+2} \ldots y_{k+1})$$

so that (24) (more fully, (24_1)) is $(Ey_1)B_{1o}(y_1)$.

The formula

$$B_{1r}(z_1 \ldots z_r, y_1 \ldots y_{r+1}) \& (x_{r+1})(Ez_{r+1}) \ldots (x_k)(Ez_k) \\ \bigwedge_{j=1}^{k} A_j^*(y_1 \ldots y_r, x_{r+1} \ldots x_k, z_1 \ldots z_k). \\ \supset (Ez_{r+1})[B_{1r}(z_1 \ldots z_r, y_1 \ldots y_{r+1}) \& (x_{r+2})(Ez_{r+2}) \\ \ldots (x_k)(Ez_k) \bigwedge_{j=1}^{k} A_j^*(y_1 \ldots y_{r+1}, x_{r+2} \ldots x_k, z_1 \ldots z_k)] \qquad (42)$$

is provable in the predicate calculus. By the formula

$$B_{1r}(z_1 \ldots z_r, y_1 \ldots y_{r+1}) \\ \supset (Ey_{r+2})B_{1,r+1}(z_1 \ldots z_{r+1}, y_1 \ldots y_{r+2})$$

we have

$$142 \supset (Ez_{r+1})(Ey_{r+2})[B_{1,r+1}(z_1 \ldots z_{r+1}, y_1 \ldots y_{r+2}) \\ \& (x_{r+2})(Ez_{r+2}) \ldots (x_k)(Ez_k) \bigwedge_{j=1}^{k} A_j^*(y_1 \ldots y_{r+1},$$

$$x_{r+2} \ldots x_k,\ z_1 \ldots z_k)] \qquad (43)$$

from which follows

$$(Ez_1)(Ey_2) \ldots (Ez_r)(Ey_{r+1})L42$$
$$\supset (Ez_1)(Ey_2) \ldots (Ez_r)(Ey_{r+1})R43, \qquad (4$$

which is of the form $E_i \supset E_{i+1}$. Therefore we have $E_o \supset E_k$, i. e.

$$B_{1o}(y_1)\ \&\ (x_1)(Ez_1) \ldots (x_k)(Ez_k) \bigwedge_{j=1}^{k} A_j{}^*(x_1 \ldots x_j,$$
$$z_1 \ldots z_j). \supset (Ez_1)(Ey_2) \ldots (Ez_k)(Ey_{k+1})$$
$$[B_1(z_1 \ldots z_k,\ y_1 \ldots y_{k+1})\ \&$$
$$\bigwedge_{j=1}^{k} A_j{}^*(y_1 \ldots y_j,\ z_1 \ldots z_j)] . \qquad (44)$$

The second conjunct of the antecedent is the provable formula (32). Therefore we have

$$(Ey_1)B_{1o}(y_1) \supset (Ey_1)(Ez_1) \ldots (Ey_k)(Ez_k)(Ey_{k+1})$$
$$[\text{scope of } \bar{R}44]$$
$$\supset (Ey_1) \ldots (Ey_{k+1})(Ez_1) \ldots (Ez_k)$$
$$[\text{scope of } \bar{R}44] , \qquad (45)$$

where the antecedent is the provable formula (24_1). For any formula $C(y_1 \ldots y_{k+1})$ we have

$$(Ey_1) \ldots (Ey_{k+1})C(y_1 \ldots y_{k+1})$$
$$\supset (Ey)C[\nu_{k+1}^{1}(y) \ldots \nu_{k+1}^{k+1}(y)]$$

(cf. lemma 3.2), and so (R45) implies

$$(Ey)(Ez_1) \ldots (Ez_k)[B(z_1 \ldots z_k,\ y_1{}^* \ldots y_{k+1}{}^*)\ \&$$
$$\bigwedge_{j=1}^{k} A_j{}^*(y_1{}^* \ldots y_j{}^*,\ z_1 \ldots z_j)],$$ q. e. d.

D. Let $C_1(y)$ be the formula

$$(Ez_1) \ldots (Ez_k)[B_1(z_1 \ldots z_k, y_1^* \ldots y_{k+1}^*) \bigwedge_{j=1}^{k} A_j^*(y_1^* \ldots y_j^*, z_1 \ldots z_j)] .$$

Let $D_1(y)$ be the formula

$$C_1(y) \ \& \ (w)[w < y \supset - C_1(w)] .$$

By the least number principle

$$C_1(y) \supset (Ey_1)D_1(y_1)$$

and therefore by (C)

$$(Ey_1)D_1(y_1) . \tag{46}$$

By (B)

$$(Ey_1) \ldots (Ey_k)(Ep_1) \ldots (Ep_k)\{\bigwedge_{i=1}^{k} D_i(y_i) \ \&$$

$$\bigwedge_{j=1}^{k} (x_1) \ldots (x_j) (\nu_j(x_1 \ldots x_j) \leq \nu_k(t \ldots t) A_j^*[x_1 \ldots x_j, (p_1)_{x_1} \ldots (p_j)_{\nu_j(x_1 \ldots x_j)}])\} \tag{47}$$

where t is $\max_{i \leq k}[y_i, t_i(y_i)]$ (so that $\nu_i(y_1 \ldots y_i) \leq \nu_k(t \ldots t)$). Let the scope of (47) be $H(y_1 \ldots y_k, p_1 \ldots p_k)$.

Since we have $\nu_i[t_1(y_1) \ldots t_i(y_i)] \leq \nu_k(t \ldots t)$,

$$H(y_1 \ldots y_k, p_1 \ldots p_k) \supset \bigwedge_{j=1}^{k} A_j^*[t_1(y_1) \ldots t_j(y_j), (p_1)_{t_1(y_1)} \ldots (p_j)_{\nu_j[t_1(y_1) \ldots t_j(y_j)]}]$$

$$\supset . \mathcal{A} \supset A[t_1(y_1) \ldots t_k(y_k), (p_1)_{t_1(y_1)} \ldots (p_k)_{k[\ldots t_k(y_k)]}] \tag{48}$$

using the case $j = k$.

By the uniqueness of the least number

$$A_1{*}[a_1,\ (p_1)_{a_1}]\ \&\ A_1{*}[a_1,\ z_1].\supset z_1 = (p_1)_{a_1}$$

$$A_j{*}[a_1 \ldots a_j,\ (p_1)_{a_1} \ldots (p_j)_{\nu_j(a_1 \ldots a_j)}]\ \&$$

$$A_j{*}(a_1 \ldots a_j,\ z_1 \ldots z_j)\ \&\ z_1 = (p_1)_{a_1}\ \&\ \ldots\ \&$$

$$z_{j-1} = (p_{j-1})_{\nu_{j-1}(a_1 \ldots a_{j-1})}.\supset z_j = (p_j)_{\nu_j(a_1 \ldots a_j)}$$

so that by a chain of inferences

$$\bigwedge_{j=1}^{k} A_j{*}[a_1 \ldots a_j,\ (p_1)_{a_1} \ldots (p_j)_{\nu_j(a_1 \ldots a_j)}]\ \&$$

$$A_j{*}(a_1 \ldots a_j,\ z_1 \ldots z_j).\supset \bigwedge_{j=1}^{k} z_j = (p_j)_{\ j(a_1 \ldots a_j)}$$

$$\supset.\ B_1(z_1 \ldots z_k,\ a_1 \ldots a_{k+1})$$

$$\equiv B_1[(p_1)_{a_1} \ldots (p_k)_{\ k(a_1 \ldots a_k)},\ a_1 \ldots a_{k+1}]$$

from which follows

$$D_1(a)\ \&\ \bigwedge_{j=1}^{k} A_j{*}[a_1{*} \ldots a_j{*},\ (p_1)_{a_1{*}} \ldots (p_j)_{\nu_j(a_1^{*} \ldots a_j^{*})}].$$

$$\supset B_1[(p_1)_{a_1{*}} \ldots (p_k)_{\nu_k(a_1^{*} \ldots a_k^{*})},\ a_1{*} \ldots a_{k+1}{*}] \quad (49)$$

Now for $r \leq k$

$$y_{1r}{*} = \nu_{k+1}^{r}(y_1) \leq y_1 \leq t$$

and so for any $j \leq k$

$$\nu_j(y_{11}{*} \ldots y_{1j}{*}) \leq \nu_j(t \ldots t) \leq \nu_k(t \ldots t)$$

from which follows

$$H(y_1 \ldots y_k,\ p_1 \ldots p_k)\supset.D_1(y_1)\ \&\ \bigwedge_{j=1}^{k} A_j{*}[y_{11}{*} \ldots y_{1j}{*},$$

$$(p_1)_{y_{11}{*}} \ldots (p_j)_{\nu_j(y_{11}{*} \ldots y_{1j}{*})}]$$

$$\text{by (49)} \supset B_1[(p_1)_{y_{11}{*}} \ldots (p_k)_{\ k(y_{11}{*} \ldots y_{1k}{*})},\ y_{11}{*} \ldots y_{1,k+1}{*}] \quad (50)$$

Evidently

$$w < y_1 \supset \nu^{r}_{k+1}(w) < y_1 \leq t$$

so that as above for each $j \leq k$

$$w < y_1 \supset \nu_j(w_1^* \ldots w_j^*) \leq {}_k(t \ldots t)$$

from which follows

$$H(y_1 \ldots y_k, p_1 \ldots p_k) \;\&\; w < y_1 \,.$$

$$\supset \bigwedge_{j=1}^{k} A_j^*[w_1^* \ldots w_j^*, (p_1)_{w_1^*} \ldots (p_j)_{\nu_j(w_1^* \ldots w_j^*)}] \qquad (51)$$

$$\supset :B_1[(p_1)_{w_1^*} \ldots (p_k)_{\nu_k(w_1^* \ldots w_k^*)}, w_1^* \ldots w_{k+1}^*]$$

$$\supset . B_1[(p_1)_{w_1^*} \ldots (p_k)_{\nu_k(w_1^* \ldots w_k^*)}, w_1^* \ldots w_{k+1}^*] \;\&\; R51 \qquad (52)$$

$$\supset . IR52 \supset (Ez_1) \ldots (Ez_k)[B_1(z_1 \ldots z_k, w_1^* \ldots w_{k+1}^*]$$

$$\& \bigwedge_{j=1}^{k} A_j^*(w_1^* \ldots w_j^*, z_1 \ldots z_j)], \text{ i. e.} \qquad (53)$$

$$\supset . IR52 \supset C_1(w)$$

But $H(y_1 \ldots y_k, p_1 \ldots p_k) \supset D_1(y_1)$

$$\supset . w < y_1 \supset -\, C_1(w)$$

Therefore by (53)

$$H(y_1 \ldots y_k, p_1 \ldots p_k) \supset . w < y_1 \supset -\, IR52$$

$$H(y_1 \ldots y_k, p_1 \ldots p_k) \supset (w)(w < y_1 \supset -\, IR52)$$

Combining with (48) and (50) we have

$$H(y_1 \ldots y_k, p_1 \ldots p_k) \supset : \alpha \supset A[t_1(y_1) \ldots t_k(y_k),$$

$$(p_1)_{t_1(y_1)} \ldots (p_k)_{\nu_k[t_1(y_1) \ldots t_k(y_k)]}] \;\&$$

$$\bigwedge_{j=1}^{k} B_1[(p_1)_{y_{11}^*} \ldots (p_k)_{\nu_k(y_{11}^* \ldots y_{1k}^*)}, y_{11}^* \ldots y_{1,k+1}^*]$$

$$\& \ (w)(w < y_i \supset - B_i[(p_1)_{w_1*} \ldots (p_k)_{\nu_k(w_1* \ldots w_k*)}, \; w_1* \ldots w_{k+1}*]) \tag{54}$$

$$(Ey_1) \ldots (Ey_k)(Ep_1) \ldots (Ep_k)H(y_1 \ldots y_k, p_1 \ldots p_k) \supset (Ey_1) \ldots (Ey_k)(Ep_1) \ldots (Ep_k)R54 .$$

The consequent is (25), and the antecedent is the provable formula (47). Therefore (25) is provable, q. e. d.

<u>Lemma 12.2</u>. If the hypotheses of lemma 12.1 hold, and for $i = 1 \ldots k$ the formulae

$$(x_1)(Ey_1) \ldots (x_k)(Ey_k)C_i(x_1 \ldots x_k, y_1 \ldots y_k) \tag{55_i}$$

are provable, then we can derive

$$(Ey_1) \ldots (Ey_k)(Ep_1) \ldots (Ep_k)(Ex_1) \ldots (Ex_k)(Eq_1) \ldots (Eq_k)$$
$$\{- A[q_1, (q_2)_{s_1(x_1)} \ldots (q_k)_{\nu_{k-1}[s_1(x_1) \ldots s_{k-1}(x_{k-1})]}, s_1(x_1) \ldots s_k(x_k)] \vee A[t_1(y_1) \ldots t_k(y_k), (p_1)_{t_1(y_1)} \ldots$$
$$(p_k)_{\nu_k[t_1(y_1) \ldots t_k(y_k)]}]. \ \& \bigwedge_{j=1}^{k} \Big(C_i[q_1, (q_2)_{x_{i1}''} \ldots (q_k)_{\nu_{k-1}[x_{i1}'' \ldots x_{i,k-1}'']}, x_{i1}'' \ldots x_{ik}''] \ \& \ (w)(w < x_i \supset$$
$$- C_i[q_1, (q_2)_{w_1''} \ldots (q_k)_{w_k(w_1'' \ldots w_{k-1}'')}, w_1'' \ldots w_k''])$$
$$\& \ B_i[(p_1)_{y_{i1}*} \ldots (p_k)_{\nu_k(y_{i1}* \ldots y_{ik}*)}, y_{i1}* \ldots y_{i,k+1}*]$$
$$\& \ (w)(w < y_i \supset - B_i[(p_1)_{w_1*} \ldots (p_k)_{\nu_k(w_1* \ldots w_k*)}, \; w_1* \ldots w_{k+1}*])\Big)\} \tag{56}$$

<u>Proof.</u> Let $H'(y_1 \ldots y_k, p_1 \ldots p_k)$ be the scope of (22). By lemma 12.1 with the prenex of $-\mathfrak{a}$ replacing $\mathfrak{a}$ and (55_i) replacing (24_i), we can derive

$$(Ex_1) \ldots (Ex_k)(Eq_1) \ldots (Eq_k)\{-\mathfrak{a} \supset - A[q_1, (q_2)_{s_1(x_1)}$$

$$\ldots (q_k)\ {}_{k-1}[s_1(x_1) \ldots s_{k-1}(x_{k-1})],\ s_1(x_1) \ldots s_k(x_k)]. \&$$

$$\bigwedge_{j=1}^{k} \Big(C_1[q_1,\ (q_2)_{x_{11}}{}'' \ldots (q_k)_{\nu_{k-1}}[x_{11}{}'' \ldots x_{1,k-1}{}''],$$

$$x_{11}{}'' \ldots x_{1k}{}''] \ \&\ (w)(w < x_1 \supset -C_1[q_1,\ (q_2)_{x_1}{}'' \ldots$$

$$(q_k)_{\nu_{k-1}}[w_1{}'' \ldots w_{k-1}{}''],\ w_1{}'' \ldots w_k{}'']) \Big) \Big\} \qquad (57)$$

where a_1'' abbreviates $\nu_k^1(a)$. Let the scope of (57) be $K(x_1 \ldots x_k,\ q_1 \ldots q_k)$. If we call the first conjunct $-\mathcal{A} \supset -A_2$, and the first conjunct of $H'(y_1 \ldots y_k,\ p_1 \ldots p_k)$ $\mathcal{A} \supset A_1$, then the first conjunct, of the scope of (56) is $-A_2 \vee A_1$. Therefore

$$H'(y_1 \ldots y_k,\ p_1 \ldots p_k) \ \&\ K(x_1 \ldots x_k,\ q_1 \ldots q_k)\ .$$
$$\supset \text{scope of } (56)$$

from which follows

$$(Ey_1) \ldots (Ey_k)(Ep_1) \ldots (Ep_k)(Ex_1) \ldots (Ex_k)(Eq_1) \ldots (Eq_k)$$
$$[H'(y_1 \ldots y_k,\ p_1 \ldots p_k) \ \&\ K(x_1 \ldots x_k,\ q_1 \ldots q_k)] \supset 56$$

i. e.

$$(Ey_1) \ldots (Ey_k)(Ep_1) \ldots (Ep_k)H'(y_1 \ldots y_k,\ p_1 \ldots p_k) \ \&$$
$$(Ex_1) \ldots (Ex_k)(Eq_1) \ldots (Eq_k)K(x_1 \ldots x_k,\ q_1 \ldots q_k).$$
$$\supset 56\ ;$$

so that (56) follows by (57) and (22).

<u>Lemma 12.3</u>. If with the formula $\mathcal{A}$ are associated formulae (23), where the functionals Y_n^i are simply representable in $\mathcal{F}$, then we can find numbers $q_1 \ldots q_k$ such that if $-\mathcal{A}$ is provable, then (23) is false when $0^{(q_1)}$ is

substituted for x_1 , and $\lambda y_1 \ldots y_{i-1}(0^{(q_i)})_{\nu_i}(y_1 \ldots y_{i-1})$ is substituted for α_i , $1 < i \leq k$.

Proof. Suppose the functional Y_n^1 is represented in by the provable formula (55_1) and the term $s_1(a)$. Now since $-\mathcal{A}$ is provable, then so is the prenex formula

$$(Ex_1)(y_1) \ldots (Ex_k)(y_k) - A(x_1 \ldots x_k, y_1 \ldots y_k) .$$

Then by (a), we can find functionals X_i , $i = 1 \ldots k$, simply representable in $\mathcal{F}$, such that the formula

$$- A[X_1 \ldots X_k, \beta_1(X_1) \ldots \beta_k(X_1 \ldots X_k)] \qquad (58)$$

is verifiable.

Now we can suppose that X_i is represented in by the formula (24_i) and the term $t_i(a)$. Then by lemma 12.2, the formula (56) is provable in $\mathcal{F}$. Since $\mathcal{F}$ is 1*-consistent (this follows from (a)), we can find numbers $\mathfrak{x}_1 \ldots \mathfrak{x}_k$, $p_1 \ldots p_k$, $x_1 \ldots x_k$, $q_1 \ldots q_k$, og which the scoper of (56) is true. It follows that

$$x_i = \mu x C_i[q_1, (q_2)_{x_1''} \ldots (q_k)_{\nu_{k-1}(x_1'' \ldots x_{k-1}'')}, x_1'' \ldots x_k'']$$

$$y_i = \mu y B_i[(p_1)_{y_1^*} \ldots (p_k)_{\nu_k(y_1^* \ldots y_k^*)}, y_1^* \ldots y_{k+1}^*]$$

which implies that

$t_i(\mathfrak{x}_i)$ is the value of X_i for the arguments $\lambda y_1 (p_1)_{y_1} \ldots \lambda y_1 \ldots y_k (p_k)_{\nu_k(y_1 \ldots y_k)}$.

$s_1(x_1)$ is the value of Y_n^1 for the arguments q_1, $\lambda x_1 (q_2)_{x_1} \ldots \lambda x_1 \ldots x_{k-1} (q_k)_{\nu_{k-1}(x_1 \ldots x_k)}$.

It follows that if

$$A[t_1(y_1) \ldots t_k(y_k), (p_1)_{t_1(y_1)} \ldots (p_k)_{\nu_k[t_1(y_1)\ldots t_k(y_k)]}]$$

holds, then (58) is false with

$\lambda y_1 \ldots y_j(p_j)_{\nu_j(y_1 \ldots y_j)}$ for β_j. Therefore it does not hold. It follows that

$$- A[q_1, (q_2)_{s_1(x_1)} \ldots (q_k)_{\nu_{k-1}[s_1(x_1)\ldots s_{k-1}(x_{k-1})]}, s_1(x_1) \ldots s_k(x_k)]$$

holds. Since for each i $s_i(y_i)$ is the value of Y_n^i for $q_1, \lambda x_1(q_2)_{x_1} \ldots \lambda x_1 \ldots x_{k-1}(q_k)_{k-1(y_1 \ldots y_{k-1})}$, it follows that $q_1 \ldots q_k$ are the required numbers.

Lemma 12.3 proves (b) of def. 1.

We show that our interpretation is strong. Suppose $\mathcal{B}$ is derived from $\mathcal{A}$ in $\mathcal{F}$; let the prenex of $\mathcal{A}$ be (20); let the prenex of $\mathcal{B}$ be

$$(z_1)(Ew_1) \ldots (z_h)(Ew_h)D(z_1 \ldots z_h, w_1 \ldots w_h). \quad (59)$$

First we prove

<u>Lemma 12.4</u> (cf. Kreisel [1], p. 51). If the formulae (55_i) are provable, then we can derive

$$(z_1)(Ew_1) \ldots (z_h)(Ew_h)(Ex_1) \ldots (Ex_k)(Eq_1) \ldots (Eq_k)$$
$$[- A[q_1, (q_2)_{s_1(x_1)} \ldots (q_k)_{\nu_{k-1}[s_1(x_1)\ldots s_{k-1}(x_{k-1})]},$$
$$s_1(x_1) \ldots s_k(x_k) \vee B(z_1 \ldots z_h, w_1 \ldots w_h). \;\&$$
$$\bigwedge_{i=1}^{k}\{C_i[q_1, (q_2)_{x_{i1}''} \ldots (q_k)_{\nu_{k-1}(x_{i1}'' \ldots x_{i,k-1}'')}, x_{i1}''$$
$$\ldots x_{ik}''] \;\&\; (w)(w < x_i \supset - C_i[q_1, (q_2)_{w_1''} \ldots$$

$$(q_k)\nu_{k-1}(w_1'' \ldots w_{k-1}''),\ w_1'' \ldots w_k''])\}] \qquad (60)$$

on the assumption that $\mathcal{B}$ is derivable from $\mathcal{A}$.

Proof. The proof of lemma 12.1 for $-\mathcal{A}$ replacing $\mathcal{A}$ goes through if the formula $A_i(a_1 \ldots a_i, b_0 \ldots b_i)$, defined on page 103, is defined as

$$(y_{i+1})(Ex_{i+2}) \ldots (y_k)[-\mathcal{B} \supset -A(b_0 \ldots b_i, x_{i+2} \ldots x_k, a_1 \ldots a_i, y_{i+1} \ldots y_k)]$$

for by the deduction theorem, $-\mathcal{B} \supset -\mathcal{A}$ is provable in $\mathcal{F}$, and $(Ex_1)A_0(x_1)$ is the result of bringing quantifiers of the consequent into the prefix of this formula, and is therefore provable.[7] This is the only use made in the proof of the form of the antecedent of the conditional in the first conjunct of the scope of (57) (cf. (22)).

Therefore what we obtain instead of (22) or (57) is

$$(Ex_1) \ldots (Ex_k)(Eq_1) \ldots (Eq_k)\Big[-\mathcal{B} \supset -A[q_1, \text{etc.}]. \&\ \bigwedge_{i=1}^{k}\{C_i[\ ] \ \&\ (w)(w < x_i \supset -C_i[\ ])\}\Big] \qquad \text{(cf. (57))},$$

which is equivalent to

$$(Ex_1) \ldots (Ex_k)(Eq_1) \ldots (Eq_k)(z_1)(Ew_1) \ldots (z_h)(Ew_h)\Big[D(z_1 \ldots z_h, w_1 \ldots w_h) \vee -A[q_1, \text{etc.}]. \&\ \bigwedge_{i=1}^{k}\{C_i[\ ] \ \&\ (w)(w < x_i \supset -C_i[\ ])\}\Big]$$

which implies (60).

---

[7]The modification of the proof of lemma 12.1 where the initial quantifier is existential consists in carrying the argument through with a free variable and then using the provability of $(Ex_1)A_0(x_1)$ instead of that of A_0. This accounts for the presence of q_1 in (57).

Now by (a), lemma 12.4 implies that we can find a functional $W(z_1, \gamma_2 \ldots \gamma_h)$ such that

$$- \underset{-}{A}[W_{h+k+1}, (W_{h+k+2})_{s_1(W_{h+1})} \ldots (W_{h+2k})_{\nu_{k-1}[s_1(W_{h+1}) \ldots , s_{k-1}(W_{h+k-1})]}$$

$$s_1(W_{h+1}) \ldots s_k(W_{h+k})] \vee \underset{-}{D}[z_1, \gamma_2(W_1) \ldots \gamma_h(W_1 \ldots W_{h-1}), W_1 \ldots W_h] \qquad (61)$$

is verifiable, where

$$W_i = \nu_h^i(W) \qquad \text{if} \quad i < h$$

$$= \nu_{2k+1}^{i-h+1}[\nu_h^h(W)] \quad \text{if} \quad h \leq i \leq h + 2k$$

(This is based on the assumption that we collapse the last existential quantifiers of (60) into one.)

Moreover

$$W_{h+i} = \mu x C_i[W_{h+k+1}, (W_{h+k+2})_{x_1}" \ldots (W_{h+2k})_{\nu_{k-1}(x_1" \ldots x_{k-1}")}, x_1" \ldots x_k"] \qquad (1 \leq i \leq k)$$

so that $s_i(W_{h+i})$ is the value of the functional represented by (55_i) for the arguments $W_{h+k+1}, \lambda x_1(W_{h+k+2})_{x_1} \ldots \lambda x_1 \ldots x_{k-1}(W_{h+2k})_{\nu_{k-1}(x_1 \ldots x_{k-1})}$.

Now suppose that (55_i) and $s_i(a)$ are so chosen as to represent the functional Y_n^i where (23) is verifiable. Then clearly the first alternand of (61) is false for any $z_1, \gamma_2 \ldots \gamma_h$, and therefore

$$\underset{-}{B}[z_1, \gamma_2(W_1) \ldots \gamma_h(W_1 \ldots W_{h-1}), W_1 \ldots W_h] \qquad (62)$$

is verifiable.

Let $t(a) = \nu_h\{\nu_h^1(a) \ldots \nu_h^{h-1}(a), \nu_{2k+1}^1[\nu_h^h(a)]\}$.

Then $\nu^1_h[t(W)] = W_1$ for $1 \leq h$. Suppose that $t(a)$ is $t_q(a)$ in the enumeration of terms mentioned on page 99, and suppose p is the number of a proof of the formula obtained from (60) by collapsing the final existential quantifiers. Then $t(W)$ is the $\nu_2(p, q)$ th of the functionals corresponding to $\mathcal{B}$ (by way of (59)), and since $W_1 = \nu^1_h[t(W)]$, (62) is equivalent to the $\nu_2(p, q)$ th formula associated with $\mathcal{B}$ under the interpretation. Therefore the latter formula is verifiable, proving (c).

The proof of theorem 12 is now complete except for the remarks concerning formulae with free function variables. All the above arguments go through for such formulae except that at certain points uniform 1*-consistency must be appealed to, and a simply representable functional may have certain "hidden" arguments, corresponding to the free variables of the interpreted formula $\mathcal{A}$.[8]

4. Ordinal recursive functionals. 1*-consistency of number theory with induction.

Our next task will be to show that elementary number

---

[8]The limitation of our procedure is as follows: We do not include among the Y_n functionals represented by formulae

$$(Ey_1) \ldots (Ey_k)C(x_1, a_2 \ldots a_k, y_1 \ldots y_k)$$

where the free variables occur in quite arbitrary ways. In order to refute (23) in the case where a substitution-case of $-\mathcal{A}$ has been proved, we should have to include these functionals and lemmas 12.1 and 12.2 would have to be replaced by something much more complex.

theories with induction are uniformly 1*-consistent. In the light of theorem 12, we shall then have shown how to construct no-counter-example interpretations of such systems. In the process, we shall obtain a characterization in terms of recursive function theory of the functionals representable in such systems, in a more general sen se of "representable" which we shall define.

Defintion 26. A primitive recursive functional is a functional which can be defined by applications of the schemata defining primitive recursive functions, with function vatiables as parameters, and the schema

$$F(f_1 \ldots f_k, a_1 \ldots a_m) = f_i[G_1(f_1 \ldots f_k, a_1 \ldots a_m) \ldots G_{r_i}(f_1 \ldots f_k, a_1 \ldots a_m)] \quad (1)$$

(f_j has r_j arguments.) (Cf pp. 16-18 above. This definition agrees with that of Kleene [10], p. 3, when the types of the arguments are the same.)

We notethat we have no notation for the substitution for function variables in the course of a definition; this accounts for the fact that if $f_1 \ldots f_k$ are primitive recursive functions, then $\lambda a_1 \ldots a_m F(f_1 \ldots f_k, a_1 \ldots a_m)$ is a primitive recursive function.[9]

[9] Thus such definitions as that of Peter, p. 128, which defines a non-primitive recursive function by means of primitive recursions of higher type, are inadmissible. Our class of primitive recursive functionals is thus narrower than the class of objects of these types which are primitive recursive functionals in the sense of Gödel [2].

In order togive the general definition of representable functional, we generalize Kleene's notions of numeralwise expression (IM, p. 197) and numeralwide representation (IM, p. 200).

<u>Definition 27</u>. Let $A(a_1 \ldots a_k)$ be a formula of a system $\mathcal{F}$ which is an elementary number theory or enlargement of such a theory by symbols for functionals. Then A <u>numeralwise expresses</u> the predicate $\mathcal{A}(a_1 \ldots a_k)$ if

(i) If $\mathcal{A}(a_1 \ldots a_k)$, then $A(a_1 \ldots a_k)$ is deducible from all (and therefore from a finite number of) true formulae of the form $a_1(0^{(n_1)} \ldots 0^{(n_{r_1})}) = 0^{(m)}$, where r_1 is the number of arguments of a_1 (if a_1 is a number variable, $r_1 = 0$ and the formula is $a_1 = 0^{(m)}$).

(ii) If $- \mathcal{A}(a_1 \ldots a_k)$, then $- A(a_1 \ldots a_k)$ is deducible from such formulae.

<u>Definition 28</u>. Let $A(a_1 \ldots a_k, y)$ be a formula of the system $\mathcal{F}$ of def. 27. Then A <u>numeralwise represents</u> the functional $F(a_1 \ldots a_k)$ if

(i) If $F(a_1 \ldots a_k) = n$, then $A(a_1 \ldots a_k, 0^{(n)})$ is deducible from true formulae of the form $a_1(0^{(n_1)} \ldots 0^{(n_{r_1})}) = 0^{(m)}$.

(ii) $(Ex)\{A(a_1 \ldots a_k, x) \; \& \; (y)[A(a_1 \ldots a_k, y) \supset y = x]\}$ is deducible from such formulae.

<u>Definition 29</u>. Let $\mathcal{F}$ be as in def. 27. Then the

formula $A(a_1 \ldots a_k, y)$ and the term $t(a)$ of strongly represent the functional $F(a_1 \ldots a_k)$ if

(i) $(Ez)[A(a_1 \ldots a_k, z) \& t(z) = y]$ numeralwise represents $F(a_1 \ldots a_k)$ in $\mathcal{F}$.

(ii) $(Ey)A(a_1 \ldots a_k, y)$ is provable in $\mathcal{F}$.

[The term $t(a)$ is supposed not to have any other free variables and therefore has no functional symbols.]

Definition 30. Suppose a recursive functional is defined by means of recursion equations involving symbols $F_1 \ldots F_n$, where the last is the symbol for the functional defined, F. Then we say that F is provably (general) recursive in a system $\mathcal{F}$ if $\mathcal{F}$ contains terms $F_1^o \ldots F_n^o$ such that the results of substituting them for $F_1 \ldots F_n$ in the recursion equations are provable formulae.

Then the formula $F_n^o = y$ will strongly represent F, so that if a functional is provably recursive, then it is strongly representable.

We shall now define a class of functionals such that if Z_o is an elementary number theory with induction whose predicate and function symbols have primitive recursive valuations, then the strongly representable functionals of Z_o are of this class. In the next section we shall show that every functional of this class is provably recursive in Z_μ, and strongly representable in Z.

The functionals in question will be those ordinal recursive on a particular sequence of "natural" primitive recursive well-orderings of the natural numbers.

<u>Definition 31</u>. Let $<_1$ be any primitive recursive well-ordering of the natural numbers. Then we define

$$a <_{p+1} b \equiv :a = 0 \;\&\; b \neq 0.\vee (Ex)\{x \leq \ln(b) \;\&\; (y)[y \leq \ln(b) \;\&\; x <_p y .\supset (a)_y = (b)_y] \;\&\; (a)_x < (b)_x\}$$

where $\ln(b)$ is the greatest i for which $(b)_i \neq 0$.
$\ln(b) = \mu x\{x \leq b \;\&\; (b)_x \neq 0 \;\&\; (y)[x < y \leq b \supset (b)_y = 0]\}$
and is therefore primitive recursive. If $b \neq 0$, then
$b = \prod_{i \leq \ln(b)} p_i^{(b)_i}$.

It follows that the three-place predicate $a <_p b$ is primitive recursive.

Suppose $a = p_{a_1} \cdot \ldots \cdot p_{a_k}$, where $a_k \leq_p \ldots \leq_p a_1$, $b = p_{b_1} \cdot \ldots \cdot p_{b_m}$, where $b_m \leq_p \ldots \leq_p b_1$; then $a <_{p+1} b$, holds if $k \leq m$ and for all $i \leq k$, $a_i = b_i$, or if there is an $i < k$ for which $a_{i+1} <_p b_{i+1}$ while for each $j \leq i$, $a_j = b_j$. For in the former case, $(a)_y = (b)_y$ whenever $a_k \leq_p y$, but if $y <_p a_k$, then $(a)_y$ is always 0 but $(b)_y$ is sometimes $\neq 0$. In the latter case, if $b_{i+1} <_p y$, then $(a)_y = (b)_y$, but $(a)_{b_{i+1}} < (b)_{b_{i+1}}$, for if $b_{i+1} = a_i$, then $p_{b_{i+1}}$ contributes to $(b)_{a_i}$ but

$a_{i+1} \underset{p}{<} a_i$ and therefore $\varphi_{a_{i+1}}$ does not contribute to $(a)_{b_{i+1}}$. If $b_{i+1} \neq a_i$, then $(a)_{b_{i+1}} = 0$, but $1 \leq (b)_{b_{i+1}}$.

It follows that $\underset{p+1}{<}$ is isomorphic to the lexicographic ordering of finite sequences of numbers ordered according to $\underset{p}{<}$. Therefore if $\underset{p}{<}$ is of type α, then $\underset{p+1}{<}$ is of type ω^{α}. If $\omega_0(\alpha) = \alpha$, $\omega_{n+1}(\alpha) = \omega^{\omega_n(\alpha)}$, then it follows that if $\underset{1}{<}$ is of type α, then $\underset{p}{<}$ will be of type $\omega_{p-1}(\alpha)$, and the limit of these order typeswill be the first ε-number $\geq \alpha$.

Definition 32. The ordinal recursive functionals of degree p on a given well-ordering $\underset{1}{<}$ are defined as follows:[10]

A. Therordinal recursive functionals of degree 0 are the primitive recursive functionals (def. 26).

B. 1. If F is ordinal recursive of degree p, then F is ordinal recursive of degree p + 1.

2. If G, $H_1 \ldots H_r$ are ordinal recursive functionals wihh the same function arguments, of r, n ... n number variables respectively, and

$$F(\bar{f}, a_1 \ldots a_n) = G[H_1(\bar{f}, a_1 \ldots a_n) \ldots H_r(\bar{f}, a_1 \ldots a_n)] \quad (2)$$

then F is an ordinal recursive functional of degree p + 1

[10] Kreisel uses the phrase "order p", but "degree" fits better with the terminology we use below.

if $G, H_1 \ldots H_r$ are. ($\bar{f}$ refers to the sequence of function parameters)

3. If $G_1 \ldots G_{r_1}$ are ordinal recursive functionals of degree $p + 1$, and F is defined from them by the schema (1) (page 119), then F is ordinal recursive of degree $p + 1$.

4. Let $K, G, G_1 \ldots G_r$ be ordinal recursive functionals of degree $p + 1$ with the same function arguments and of $n - 1$, $n+1$, $n_1 \ldots n_r$ number variables respectively. Given a term $t(a)$, let $t^*(a) = t(a) \cdot o'[p + 1, t(a), a]$, where $o'(p, n, m) = 1$ if $n \underset{p}{<} m$; 0 otherwise. Given F of the same function arguments as K, etc., and n number arguments, we define an <u>admissible term</u> as follows:

a. $x_1 \ldots x_{n-1}$, a) are admissible terms.

b. If $\mathcal{B}(x_1 \ldots x_{n-1}, a)$ is an admissible term, so is $F[\bar{f}, x_1 \ldots x_{n-1}, \mathcal{B}^*(x_1 \ldots x_{n-1}, a)]$.

c. If $\mathcal{H}_1 \ldots \mathcal{H}_{n_j}$ are admissible terms, so is $G_j(\bar{f}, \mathcal{H}_1 \ldots \mathcal{H}_{n_j})$.

Now if $\mathcal{H}(a)$ is an admissible term and

$$F(\bar{f}, x_1 \ldots x_{n-1}, 0) = K(\bar{f}, x_1 \ldots x_{n-1})$$

$$F(\bar{f}, x_1 \ldots x_{n-1}, Sa) = G[\bar{f}, x_1 \ldots x_{n-1}, a, F(\bar{f}, x_1 \ldots x_{n-1}, \mathcal{H}^*(Sa))], \quad (3)$$

then F is ordinal recursive of degree $p + 1$.

The reason for this somewhat elaborate ordinal recursion step is to allow for interlocked recursions. This is not done by Kreisel in [1]. He claims (in correspondence) that interlocked recursions on $<_p$ can be reduced to simple recursions on $<_{p+2}$, if $<_1$ is the ordering

$$a <_1 b \equiv : \nu_2^1(a) < \nu_2^1(b) \ \mathrm{v}. \nu_2^1(a) = \nu_2^1(b) \ \& \ \nu_2^2(a) < \nu_2^2(b) \ .$$

I have not been able to determine whether this claim is true or false. In this case, it follows from Peter, §6, that if interlocked recursions are not admitted, then the ordinal recursive functionals of order 1 are all primitive recursive.

Unless we indicate the contrary, the ordering $<_1$ will be the one defined above. It is clearly of type ω^2 ; so that in this case the ordering $<_p$ will be of type $\omega_{p-1}(\omega^2)$. Therefore the limit of their order types is ε_0 .[11]

Before stating the main theorem, we need one more definition

Definition 33. If A is a first order formula, its binding degree is defined inductively as follows:

1. If A is prime, its binding degree is 0 .

2. If B has binding degree p , and A is - B , then A has binding degree p .

3. If B has degree p and C has binding degree

[11] These orderings are isomorphic to those of Ackermann [2], although the induction step in the definition is that of HB II, 361. It follows that analysis of Ackermann's consistency proof would also yield theorem 13.

q , and A is $B \vee C$, $B \& C$, $B \supset C$, or $B \equiv C$, then A has binding degree $\max(p, q)$.

4. If $B(x)$ has binding degree p , and A is $(x)B(x)$ or $(Ex)B(x)$, then A has binding degree $p + 1$.

Therefore the binding degree of a formula is the maximum length of a sequence of nested quantifiers, so that a prenex formula with k quantifiers has binding degree k .

<u>Theorem 13</u> (Kreisel [1]). If Z_0 is any elementary number theory with induction, then Z_0 is uniformly 1*-consistent.

Let Z_0^p be the subsystem of Z_0 obtained by restricting the application of the induction rule to formulae of binding degree $\leq p$. Then given formulae

$$(Ex)A(f_1 \ldots f_k, a_1 \ldots a_m, x) \tag{4}$$

a functional ordinal recursive of degree $p + 1$ in a function which enumerates the functions expressed by function symbols of Z_0 will enumerate all functionals

$$F(\overline{f}, \overline{a}) = \mu x A(\overline{f}, \overline{a}, x)$$

for which (4) is provable in Z_0^p , and a fortiori such a functional will enumerate all functionals representable in Z_0^p , for which the formula A of def. 29 is quantifier-free.

Given a proof of (4) in Z_0 , we can (primitiver recursively) find numbers p, q such that, with respect to an initial ordering of type $\omega \cdot q$, F is ordinal recursive of degree $p + 1$ in functions expressed by symbols of Z_0 . Thus if these are primitive recursive, then F

is ordinal recursive of degree $p + 1$ with respect to an ordering of type $\omega \cdot q < \omega^2$.

Proof. This result is, as Kreisel noticed, a corollary of the methods used to prove the consistency of elementary number theory. Thus our proof implicitly contains a proof of the consistency of Z_0. (If we apply our reductions to a variable-free formula, the result will be a proof of it in the underlying numerical system. Therefore it must be true, so that it is not, say, $0 \neq 0$.) Most of the major consistency proofs of sufficiently constructive character yield results of this type.[12]

---

[12]From the proof of Ackermann [2], see Kreisel [1], [3]. From the proof by Gödel's interpretation of intuitionism, see Kreisel [7]. Our treatment is based on Schütte's proof by infinite induction ([2], ch. 6 of [4]), whose applicability to the no-counter-example interpretation was announced in Shoenfield [2]. I have worked out his brief explanation (given in correspondence) in a way which may differ from his (see below, note 16).

1*-consistency can also be obtained from Schütte's other proof ([4], pp. 158-67). The procedure is as follows: The endpiece (Endstück, p. 154) is enlarged so that bindings (S 3') are included within it. The predicate-logical reduction (pp. 161-66) is practiced on Quantorenbünde for which a generalization is an initial formula of the endpiece, a binding within it. The grosser Formelbund of the last line of the proof does not intersect any Quantorenbund (this cannot be taken for granted, since we allow the last line to be of the form (4)), so the last line is unaltered. In the sentential-logical reduction (pp. 166-67), formulae of the grosser Formelbund of the last line are exempted from the substitution of $0 = 0$ or $0 = S0$. From the final result of the reductions we can easily construct a proof of (4) from true numerical formulae. Of course, this depends on initially chosen values of the free variables, including function variables.

This proof is methodologically more satisfactory than

The proof we give is based on Schütte's consistency proof of [2], which is in a sense a generalization of Gentzen's normal form theorem (IM, p. 453). It therefore requires a special formulation of the logic, which we shall now describe. Schütte's formulation avoids Gentzen's device of sequents, used in Kleene's treatment of Gentzen's theorem.

We suppose (only in order to avoid multiplication of cases) that - and v are the only propositional connectives in the formulae of our system. However, we do keep both types of quantifiers.[13] Then we suppose that the logical axioms and rules of the system are as follows:

I. Axioms: All formulae P v - P , where P is a prime

---

the one we give, since it avoids infinite induction. This might be regarded as a matter only of appearance, since examination of what our use of it actually amounts to shows that it assumes no more than what is assumed in verifying the transfinite inductions assumed in all the proofs, namely the repeated use of universal quantification in the antecedents of conditionals, which are applied in particular cases only where the antecedents are seen to be true (see pp. 22-5 above).

A disadvantage which seems to me more important is that it gives for proofs in Z_0^p an enumerating functional on orderings of type $\omega_p(\omega^\omega)$, i. e. $\omega_{p+1}(\omega)$, which is a weaker result than we give. I think both of these might be improved on by closer analysis of the recursions. I conjecture that the best possible result is $\omega_p(\omega)$. This holds in the case p = 0 , since quantifier-free inductions can be dealt with by Herbrand-type methods (see pp. 73-5).

[13] This is a departure from Schütte's papers. In other respects we follow these rather than [4], which uses an apparatus too involved for us to explain here.

formula.

II. Rules of inference

A. Rearrangements (Umformende Schlüsse)

1. $$\frac{\mathfrak{M} \vee (\mathfrak{A} \vee (\mathfrak{B} \vee \mathfrak{N}))}{\mathfrak{M} \vee (\mathfrak{B} \vee (\mathfrak{A} \vee \mathfrak{N}))}$$ (Interchange)

2. $$\frac{\mathfrak{A} \vee (\mathfrak{A} \vee \mathfrak{N})}{\mathfrak{A} \vee \mathfrak{N}}$$ (Contraction)

B. Constructional inferences (aufbauende Schlüsse)

1. $$\frac{\mathfrak{N}}{\mathfrak{A} \vee \mathfrak{N}}$$ (Weakening)

2. $$\frac{\mathfrak{A} \vee \mathfrak{N}}{--\mathfrak{A} \vee \mathfrak{N}}$$ (Negation)

3. $$\frac{-\mathfrak{A} \vee \mathfrak{N} \qquad -\mathfrak{B} \vee \mathfrak{N}}{-(\mathfrak{A} \vee \mathfrak{B}) \vee \mathfrak{N}}$$ (Composition)

4. If $\mathfrak{A}(t)$ contains free occurrences of the term t wherever $\mathfrak{A}(x)$ contains free occurrences of the variable x , then

$$\frac{\mathfrak{A}(t) \vee \mathfrak{N}}{(Ex)\,\mathfrak{A}(x) \vee \mathfrak{N}}$$

$$\frac{-\mathfrak{A}(t) \vee \mathfrak{N}}{-(x)\,\mathfrak{A}(x) \vee \mathfrak{N}}$$ (Bindings)

5. If $\mathfrak{A}(a)$ contains free occurrences of the variable a where and only where $\mathfrak{A}(x)$ contains free occurrences of x , and contains no free occurrences of a , then

$$\text{(i)}\quad \frac{\mathcal{A}(a) \vee \mathcal{N}}{(x)\mathcal{A}(x) \vee \mathcal{N}}$$

$$\text{(ii)}\quad \frac{-\mathcal{A}(a) \vee}{-(\exists x)\mathcal{A}(x) \vee \mathcal{N}} \qquad \text{(Generalizations)}$$

C. Cut $\dfrac{\mathcal{M} \vee \mathcal{A} \qquad -\mathcal{A} \vee \mathcal{N}}{\mathcal{M} \vee \mathcal{N}}$

The statements are intended to cover the cases where one (or both of) the formula(e) $\mathcal{M}, \mathcal{N}$ is (are) missing, unless this would make either premiss or conclusion empty.

Definition 34. The first alternands of constructional inferences [$- - \mathcal{A}$, $(x)\mathcal{A}(x)$, etc.] are called the principal formulae of the inferences. In II B 2-6, the first alternands of the premisses ($\mathcal{A}$, $-\mathcal{A}$, etc.) are called side formulae of the inferences. The formulae $\mathcal{M}$, $\mathcal{N}$ are called secondary formulae of the inferences. The term t of the bindings is called the principal term. The variable a of the generalizations is called the principal variable. $\mathcal{A}$ is the cut formula of II C .

For our systems, the non-logical axioms will of course be quantifier-free. It is convenient to have them primary formulae, i. e. alternations of prime formulae and their negations (since any formula is truth-functionally equivalent to a conjunction of primary formulae, any system of axioms may be replaced by an equivalent system of primary axioms). Moreover, we suppose that the axioms are closed under substitution for free (number) variables. This obviates a substitution rule. Clearly any axiom added to obtain such closure is provable with the substitution rule. That the substitution rule is eliminable once the new axioms are added can be shown by the method of pushing substitutions back to the axioms. (Ruckverlegung der Einsetzungen in die Ausgangsformeln, HB I, 225 ff.).

Induction in this formulation takes the form

$$\frac{\mathfrak{A}(0) \qquad - \mathfrak{A}(a) \vee \mathfrak{A}(Sa)}{\mathfrak{A}(t)}$$

where a does not occur in $\mathfrak{A}(0)$.

We take for granted Schütte's version of the normal form theorem: If a system $\mathfrak{F}$ is formalized with quantifier-free axioms, and no rules except under (II) above, and the axioms are primary formulae and closed under cuts and rearrangements, then from any proof in $\mathfrak{F}$ we can effectively obtain a proof without cuts. All cuts except on prime formulae can be eliminated without the condition on the axioms. The arithmetization of the procedure is by a primitive recursive function (cf. appendix I).

This theorem is proved in Schütte [1], by much the same method as in the proof of the normal form theorem for Gentzen's systems (IM, pp. 448-460, Gentzen [1]). Although it is more normally used in order to prove Herbrand's theorem, it follows from it, for the bindings, rearrangements, and generalizations are sufficient to duplicate derivations in Dreben's Herbrand normal form.

We note that for all this discussion we regard equality axioms as non-logical.

Proofs will be pictured (and, in appendix I, numbered) as finite trees with the last line at the base.

Definition 35. Let $\mathcal{A}$ be a line of a proof in Schütte's logic. Let $\mathcal{B}_0$ be an occurrence of a formula as an alternand of $\mathcal{A}$, not itself an alternation. Then we define the kleiner Formelbund of $\mathcal{B}_0$ as a tree extracted from the proof as follows:

1. $\mathcal{B}_0$ is at the base of the kleiner Formelbund.

2. Suppose $\mathcal{C}$ is the conclusion of an inference, and $\mathcal{D}_0$ is an occurrence of an alternand of $\mathcal{C}$, not an alternation, which belongs to the kleiner Formelbund of $\mathcal{B}_0$. Then if $\mathcal{D}_0$ is not in the principal formula of a constructional inference, it matches an occurrence in a premiss (if in the secondary formula of II B 3, in each premiss). This corresponding occurrence (these occurrences) belong to the Formelbund.

For example, given the inference

$$\frac{A(t) \vee [(Ex)A(x) \vee B]}{(Ex)A(x) \vee [(Ex)A(x) \vee B]} \qquad (5)$$

if both the occurrences of (Ex)A(x) belong to the Formelbund, then the branch of the left one ends, the one corresponding to the occurrence on the right is the only member of the

Formelbund of the premiss.

If the $\mathcal{A}$ of II A 1 belongs to the <u>Formelbund</u>, in the conclusion, then it is the $\mathcal{A}$ which belongs in the premiss. In the case of II A 2, <u>both</u> occurrences of $\mathcal{A}$ belong to the <u>Formelbund</u> if the $\mathcal{A}$ of the conclusion does.

It is plain by induction that every formula of the <u>Formelbund</u> of an occurrence of $\mathcal{B}$ is also an occurrence of $\mathcal{B}$.

<u>Definition 36</u>. The <u>grosser Formelbund</u> of an occurrence is defined similarly, except that at constructional inferences where the principal formula belongs to the Formelbund, then so do[es] the side formula(e).

The end of any branch of a kleiner Formelbund is either in a principal term of a weakening (II B 1) or in an axiom, or in a constructional inference whose form is determined by that of $\mathcal{B}$ as follows:

1. If $\mathcal{B}$ is a double negation, it must be II B 2.
2. If $\mathcal{B}$ is $-(\mathcal{C} \vee \mathcal{D})$, it must be II B 3.
3. If $\mathcal{B}$ is $-(x)\mathcal{C}(x)$, it must be II B 4 (ii).
4. If $\mathcal{B}$ is $-(Ex)\mathcal{C}(x)$, it must be II B 5 (ii).
5. If $\mathcal{B}$ is a negated prime formula, it must be II B 1.
6. If $\mathcal{B}$ is $(x)\mathcal{C}(x)$, it must be II B 5 (i).
7. If $\mathcal{B}$ is $(Ex)\mathcal{C}(x)$, it must be II B 4 (i).

We are now ready to begin the proof proper. We asume that Z_0 is formalized in Schütte's logic. After a preliminary reduction, we transform a given proof in Z_0 into a proof in a system in which induction has been replaced by an effective <u>infinite induction</u>, so that the system is no longer properly formal. Then for proofs in <u>this</u> system, it is possible to eliminate cuts. If the last line is of the form (4), then we can reduce the cut-free proof to a proof consisting essentially of numerical computation and existential generalization, and from this final proof, we can effectively recover an x such that $A(\bar{f}, \bar{a}, a^{(x)})$. Throughout the work in the informal system, we assume a particular substitution for $f_1 \ldots f_k$, $a_1 \ldots a_k$.

The preliminary reduction is

<u>Lemma 13.1</u>. Suppose we have a formula C provable in Z_0^p. Then from a given proof of C we can effectively obtain a proof which has no cuts except on subformulae of induction formulae (provided that the axioms of Z_0 satisfy the conditions for the normal form theorem, see p. 131; in any case the only other cuts remaining will be on prime formulae). This proof is given primitive recursively from the original proof.

<u>Proof</u>. Let B be either the last line, or one of the premisses of an induction in the given proof. Let $A_1(a_1 \ldots a_k)$

... $A_r(a_1 \ldots a_k)$ be the lowest conclusions of inductions in the proof of B ; i. e. consider the tree obtained by branching upward from B , stopping either at initial formulae of the proof or at the conclusions of inductions; $A_1 \ldots A_r$ are all the conclusions of inductions at the tops of this tree; $a_1 \ldots a_k$ are all the free variables of $A_1 \ldots A_r$ which are generalized within the tree.

We show that if $A_1 \ldots A_r$ have proofs satisfying the condition of the lemma, then so has B . It will follow by induction that C has such a proof.

By the deduction theorem

$$(x_1) \ldots (x_k)[A_1(x_1 \ldots x_k) \mathbin{\&} \ldots \mathbin{\&} A_r(a_1 \ldots a_k)] \supset B$$

and therefore

$$(Ex_1) \ldots (Ex_k) - A_1(x_1 \ldots x_k) \vee \ldots \vee (Ex_1) \ldots (Ex_k) \overline{A}_r(x_1 \ldots x_k) \vee B \qquad (6)$$

are provable in Z_0 without induction. By the normal form theorem, it is provable <u>without cuts</u>. In this proof, consider the tops of the <u>Formelbünde</u>[14] of the alternands

$$(Ex_1) \ldots (Ex_k) - A(x_1 \ldots x_k) \,. \qquad (7)$$

These must be either at weakenings or at the conclusions of bindings (by no. 7, p. 133)

$$\frac{(Ex_2) \ldots (Ex_k) - A_1(t_1, x_2 \ldots x_k) \vee \mathcal{N}}{(Ex_1) \ldots (Ex_k) - A_1(x_1 \ldots x_k) \vee \mathcal{N}}$$

[14] When we speak of a <u>Formelbund</u> without qualification, we refer to a <u>kleiner Formelbund</u>.

If we consider the Formelbünde of the first alternands of these premisses, we can trace them to further bindings until we eventually reach bindings

$$\frac{-A_1(t_1 \dots t_k) \vee \mathcal{M}}{(Ex_k) - A_1(t_1 \dots t_{k-1}, x_k) \vee \mathcal{M}} \qquad (8)$$

Now we can from the given proof of $A_1(a_1 \dots a_k)$, which we assume to have no cuts except on subformulae of induction formulae, obtain a proof of $A_1(t_1 \dots t_k)$ which is essentially obtained by substitution in the given one, and in particular contains no more complex cuts. We replace (8) by a cut

$$\frac{A_1(t_1 \dots t_k) \qquad - A_1(t_1 \dots t_k) \vee \mathcal{M}}{\mathcal{M}}$$

and drop the entire grosser Formelbund of (7) from this point down to the point where it merges with another, or failing that to its place in (6). Since we can perform this reduction on every branch of the grosser Formelbund, we can in fact eliminate all the alternands (7) to obtain a proof of B .

The cuts introduced are all on subformulae of $A_1(a_1 \dots a_k)$, so that the proof of B satisfies the condition. [We must regard A(t) as a subformula of A(a) . In substituting $t_1 \dots t_k$ in the proof of $A_1(a_1 \dots a_k)$, it can also happen that cuts on formulae $D(a_1 \dots a_k)$ become cuts on formulae $D(t_1 \dots t_k)$, so that this meaning of "subformula" is necessary here also. What is necessary to our later work is that the degree of the cut formula should not be increased. In a proof transformed by this procedure, the degree of the formula $\mathcal{A}$ of any cut $\leq$ the maximum degree of induction formulae, and the binding degree of $\mathcal{A} \leq p$.]

If a is the number of the given proof of C , the number rp(a) of the reduced proof is given by a function which it is mechanical to verify is primitive recursive, given that the cut-elimination function of the normal form theorem is such.

<u>Lemma 13.2</u>. Let S_0 be an informal system in which the induction schema of Z_0 is replaced by the rule of "effective infinite induction":

InI. If an effective method is given which yields proofs of the formulae $\mathcal{A}(0^{(n_1)} \ldots 0^{(n_k)})$ for all $n_1 \ldots n_k$, then $\mathcal{A}(a_1 \ldots a_k)$ is a theorem of S_0 .

This is made more precise as follows: We assign numbers to the proofs of S_0 and interpret InI by defining a certain primitive recursive function In(e, b) so that if e is such that for each n , e(n) (i. e. $U[\mu y T_1(e, n, y)]$; IM p. 340) is the number of a proof of $\mathcal{A}[0^{((n)_0)} \ldots 0^{((n)_{k-1})}]$, where b is the number of $\mathcal{A}(a_1 \ldots a_k)$, then In(e, b) is the number of a proof in S_o of $\mathfrak{A}(a_1 \ldots a_k)$.

Otherwise, the rules of S_o are the same as those of Z_o , with the exception that we make the convention that if C is an axiom of S_o , and C' is obtained from C by replacing certain occurences of a closed numerical term in C by occurences of another term of the same numerical value, then C' is an axiom of S_o .

This is intended to be relative in the following sense: We pick out certain number and function variables of Z_o , say $f_1 \ldots f_k, a_1 \ldots a_m$. Then a term is called closed if it has no free variables not among these, and in speaking of the "numerical value" of a term we assume a choice of a substitution for these variables.

The recursive function in the statement of the rule of infinite induction must also be relative to $f_1 \ldots f_k$, $a_1 \ldots a_m$; i.e. it is a recursive functional of those arguments and n.

Then there is a <u>primitive recursive functional</u> $Sp(\overline{f}, \overline{a}, b)$ such that if b is the number of a proof in Z_o of a formula whose free variables are among $f_1 \ldots f_k$, $a_1 \ldots a_m$, then $Sp(\overline{f}, \overline{a}, b)$ is the number of a proof in S_o of the same formula, which has cuts only on subformulae of cut formulae and induction formulae of the given proof.

<u>Proof.</u> For this argument we regard <u>all</u> function symbols of

the proof, except S , as variables. The point of this is that then the functional which gives the numerical value of a term is primitive recursive (appendix I, def. 28). This has the consequence that the functionals which we define apply to the class of proofs having a certain finite set of function symbols. To give the enumerating functional of theorem 13, we assume that one of our function variables stands for a function which enumerates all the functions represented by symbols of Z_0. If this variable is $f(n, a)$, then before beginning the transformation we replace each functional symbol $f_n(b_1 \ldots b_r)$ by $f[0^{(n)}, 2^{b_1} \ldots p_{r-1}{}^{b_r}]$. (We assume the enumerating function φ is such that for each n, a for which there is a symbol f_n, $\varphi[n, a] = f_n[(a)_0 \ldots (a)_{r-1}]$; cf. Kleene [6]).

What is important is that the axioms of S_0 should be true for the given substitution for $\bar{f}$, $\bar{a}$ and for any substitution for other (number) variables which occur in them.

Hereafter when we refer to the "free variables" of a term or a formula we shall exempt $f_1 \ldots f_k$, $a_1 \ldots a_k$ [so that if n is the chosen value of a_1, a proof of $C(a_1)$ can be obtained from one of $C(0^{(n)})$ by replacement, without infinite induction].

Any axiom of Z_0 is an axiom of S_0 ; any inference of Z_0, except induction, is mapped onto an inference of S_0.

Suppose we have proofs in Z_0 of $\mathcal{A}(0)$ and $-\mathcal{A}(a) \vee \mathcal{A}(Sa)$. Then we can obtain by a primitive recursive function proofs of $-\mathfrak{A}(0^{(n)}) \vee \mathfrak{A}(0^{(n+1)})$ for each n, of no greater length than the given proof of $-\mathfrak{A}(a) \vee \mathfrak{A}(Sa)$. Then by the hypothesis of induction, we obtain proofs of $\mathfrak{A}(0)$ and $-\mathfrak{A}(0^{(n)}) \vee \mathfrak{A}(0^{(n+1)})$ in S_0; then by cut we obtain one of $\mathfrak{A}(0^{(n+1)})$. By induction, we have a proof in S_0 of $\mathfrak{A}(0^{(n)})$ for each n. Then if $b_1 \ldots b_r$ are the free variables of t, for each $m_1 \ldots m_k$, if n_0 is the numerical value of $t(0^{(m_1)} \ldots 0^{(m_k)})$, we have by replacement of terms in the proof of $\mathfrak{A}(0^{(n_0)})$ a proof of $\mathfrak{A}[t(0^{(m_1)} \ldots 0^{(m_k)})]$, from which we obtain a proof of $\mathfrak{A}(t)$ by infinite induction.

The details of arithmetization are given in appendix I. The full definition of Sp is definition 41. It will follow in particular that the numbers e of the functions at infinite inductions of the proofs we obtain by lemma 13.2 are numbers of primitive recursive functionals.

We can assign ordinal numbers called <u>orders</u> to the lines in the proof such that the order of an axiom is 0, of the conclusion of a structural inference the same as that of its premiss, that of the conclusion of any other inference greater than that of any of its premisses. The order of the last line of the proof is called the order of the proof.

It is clear that a proof without induction is mapped by the procedure of lemma 13.2 into a proof of finite order. It follows that the proof of the conclusion of an induction with none above it can be mapped into one in S_0 with order

$\leq \omega$.. By induction, the proof of the conclusion of an induction with no more than n above it can be mapped into one with order $\leq \omega \cdot (n+1)$.[15]

It follows that if n is the maximum number of inductions in any branch of the given proof, it can be mapped onto a proof in S_0 of order $< \omega \cdot (n + 1)$.

Since we assume throughout one substitution for $f_1 \ldots f_k$, $a_1 \ldots a_m$, from now on we suppress these arguments. We can think of ourselves as defining functions recursive relative to $f_1 \ldots f_k.\ a_1 \ldots a_m$.

Lemma 13.3. There is a primitive recursive functional $\sigma_1(a, b)$ such that if a is the number of a proof in S_0 in which no cut has logical degree more than b, then $\sigma_1(a, b)$ is the number of a proof of the same formula, in which every cut has a truth-functionally simple cut formula. If α is the order of the given proof, then the order of the new proof $\leq \alpha \cdot 2^b$.

If b is an upper bound on the logical degrees of the cut formulae in the proof, then we say the proof has degree b ; if p is an upper bound on the binding degrees of the cut formulae in the proof, we say it has binding degree, p.

Then the binding degree of the proof is not increased.

---

[15]At the price of more quantifiers in the cuts, this bound can be decreased to $\omega + 1$, but not to ω, for in the latter case one could obtain a cut-free proof of order $\leq \omega$, which as we shall see would be contrary to Gödel's second undecidability theorem.

Definition 37. If A is a first order formula, its truth-functional degree (tf-degree) is defined inductively as follows:

1. If A is prime or $(x)B(x)$ or $(Ex)B(x)$, its tf-degree is 0.

2. If A is $-B$ and that of B is p , that of A is $p + 1$.

3. If A is $B \vee C$ and those of B, C are p, q that of A is $\max(p, q) + 1$.

The concepts of Formelbund given by definitions 35 and 36 apply only to proofs without induction, but they can be extended to proofs with infinite induction. Then every occurrence in a Formelbund of a formula in the conclusion of an infinite induction corresponds to an occurrence in each premiss of a formula obtained from it by substitution of numerals for free variables. This occurrence is to belong to the kleiner Formelbund, and a fortiori to the grosser Formelbund. Thus the Formelbund, like the proof itself, is now a tree which at certain points can have infinite branchings.

By induction on the construction of the given proof, we define a functional $\rho_1(a)$ such that if a is the number of a proof of order α in S_0 of a formula C where the cuts in the proof have truth-functional degree $\leq r$, then $\rho_1(a)$ is the number of a proof of C of order $\leq \alpha \cdot 2$

where the cuts have truth-functional degree $\leq r \dot{-} 1$.

1. C is an axiom. Then $\rho_1(a) = a$.

2. C is the conclusion of a structural inference. Then the proof of the premiss has order α and tf-degree $\leq r$. By hypothesis of induction we have a proof of the premiss with order $\leq \alpha \cdot 2$ and tf-degree $\leq r \dot{-} 1$. The same inference yields a proof of C with these properties.

3. C is the conclusion of a constructional inference or an infinite induction. The proofs of the premisses have orders $< \alpha$ and tf-degree $\leq r$, by hypothesis of induction we can obtain proofs of the premisses with orders $< \alpha \cdot 2$ and tf-degrees $\leq r \dot{-} 1$. The same inference yields C with order $\alpha \cdot 2$ and tf-degree $\leq r \dot{-} 1$.

4. C is the conclusion of a cut, i.e. C is $\mathcal{R} \vee \mathcal{S}$ and the premisses are $\mathcal{R} \vee \mathcal{A}$ and $-\mathcal{A} \vee \mathcal{S}$, where $\mathcal{R}$ or $\mathcal{S}$ may be missing.

a. $\mathcal{A}$ is truth-functionally simple. Then the argument is the same as no. 3.

b. $\mathcal{A}$ is $-\mathcal{B}$. Then the right premiss is $- -\mathcal{B} \vee \mathcal{S}$. If the orders of the proofs of $\mathcal{R} \vee -\mathcal{B}$ and $- -\mathcal{B} \vee \mathcal{S}$ are β_1 and β_2 respectively, then by the hypothesis of induction we can obtain proofs of orders $\leq \beta_1 \cdot 2$ and $\beta_2 \cdot 2$ respectively, whose cut formulae have tf-degree $\leq r \dot{-} 1$. Then from the reduced proof of $- -\mathcal{B} \vee \mathcal{S}$ we can obtain one of $\mathcal{B} \vee \mathcal{S}$ with order $\leq \beta_2 \cdot 2$ and tf-degree $\leq r \dot{-} 1$. For if we consider the tops of the Formelbund of $- - \mathcal{B}$ in the reduced proof of $- - \mathcal{B} \vee \mathcal{S}$, we see that they are in principal formulae of weakenings or are principal formulae of inferences

$$\frac{\mathcal{B}^* \vee \mathcal{N}}{- - \mathcal{B}^* \vee \mathcal{N}}$$

where $\mathcal{B}^*$ is obtained from $\mathcal{B}$ by substituting numbrals for free variables. By dropping the double negations and the above inferences, we obtain a proof of $\mathcal{B} \vee \mathcal{S}$, which has no more complex cuts than the given proof of $- - \mathcal{B} \vee \mathcal{S}$. That the function giving this proof is primitive recursive is shown by the definition of φ_1 (appendix I, def. 30). Then we obtain $\mathcal{R} \vee \mathcal{S}$ by the figure

$$\frac{\begin{matrix} \mathcal{B} \vee \mathcal{S} & \mathcal{R} \vee - \mathcal{B} \\ \mathcal{S} \vee \mathcal{B} & - \mathcal{B} \vee \mathcal{R} \end{matrix}}{\begin{matrix} \mathcal{S} \vee \mathcal{R} \\ \mathcal{R} \vee \mathcal{S} \end{matrix}} \qquad \frac{\begin{matrix} \beta_2 \cdot 2 & \beta_1 \cdot 2 \\ \beta_2 \cdot 2 & \beta_1 \cdot 2 \end{matrix}}{\begin{matrix} \alpha \cdot 2 \\ \alpha \cdot 2 \end{matrix}}$$

where the tree at the right gives the orders. If the tf-degree of $\mathcal{A}$ is $d \leq r$, then that of $\mathcal{B}$ is $d - 1 \leq r - 1$, and therefore the new proof has degree $\leq r - 1$.

c. $\mathcal{A}$ is $\mathcal{B} \vee \mathcal{B}'$; i. e. we have

$$\frac{\mathcal{R} \vee (\mathcal{B} \vee \mathcal{B}') \qquad - (\mathcal{B} \vee \mathcal{B}') \vee \mathcal{S}}{\mathcal{R} \vee \mathcal{S}}$$

where the proofs of the premisses have orders $\beta_1, \beta_2 < \alpha$. Then by the hypothesis of the induction we have proofs of the premisses of orders $\beta_1 \cdot 2$ and $\beta_2 \cdot 2$ and tf-degrees $\leq r - 1$. By a similar method to case 4b, we can obtain proofs of $-\mathfrak{B} \vee \mathfrak{S}$ and $-\mathfrak{B}' \vee \mathfrak{S}$ of order $\leq \beta_2 \cdot 2$ and tf-degrees $\leq r - 1$. [I. e., we replace the Formelbund of $-(\mathfrak{B} \vee \mathfrak{B}')$ in the reduced proof of the right premiss by $-\mathfrak{B}$ (and the corresponding numerical instances) or $-\mathfrak{B}'$.] Then we obtain $\mathfrak{R} \vee \mathfrak{S}$ by the figure

$$\mathfrak{R} \vee (\mathfrak{B} \vee \mathfrak{B}') \qquad\qquad \beta_1 \cdot 2$$

$$\mathfrak{B} \vee (\mathfrak{R} \vee \mathfrak{B}')$$

$$\frac{(\mathfrak{R} \vee \mathfrak{B}') \vee \mathfrak{B} \qquad -\mathfrak{B} \vee \mathfrak{S}}{(\mathfrak{R} \vee \mathfrak{B}') \vee \mathfrak{S}} \qquad\qquad \frac{\beta_1 \cdot 2 \qquad \beta_2 \cdot 2}{[\max(\beta_1, \beta_2)] \cdot 2 + 1}$$

$$\mathfrak{S} \vee (\mathfrak{R} \vee \mathfrak{B}') \qquad\qquad 〃$$

$$\mathfrak{S} \vee (\mathfrak{B}' \vee \mathfrak{R}) \qquad\qquad 〃$$

$$\mathfrak{B}' \vee (\mathfrak{S} \vee \mathfrak{R}) \qquad\qquad 〃$$

$$\frac{(\mathfrak{S} \vee \mathfrak{R}) \vee \mathfrak{B}' \qquad -\mathfrak{B}' \vee \mathfrak{S}}{(\mathfrak{S} \vee \mathfrak{R}) \vee \mathfrak{S}} \qquad\qquad \frac{[\max()] \cdot 2 + 1 \qquad \beta_2 \cdot 2}{\alpha \cdot 2}$$

$$\mathfrak{S} \vee (\mathfrak{S} \vee \mathfrak{R}) \qquad\qquad 〃$$

$$\mathfrak{S} \vee \mathfrak{R} \qquad\qquad 〃$$

$$\mathfrak{R} \vee \mathfrak{S} \qquad\qquad \alpha \cdot 2$$

where the tree on the right again gives the orders; since $\beta_2 < \alpha$, $\beta_2 \cdot 2 < \alpha \cdot 2$; $\max(\beta_1, \beta_2) \cdot 2 + 1 < \max(\beta_1, \beta_2) \cdot 2 + 2 = [\max(\beta_2, \beta_2) + 1] \cdot 2 \leq \alpha \cdot 2$. Again, if the tf-degree of $\mathfrak{A}$ is $d \leq r$, then those of $\mathfrak{B}$ and $\mathfrak{B}'$ are $\leq d - 1 \leq r - 1$, so that the tf-degree of the new proof $\leq r - 1$.

The numerical definition of ρ_1 is given in appendix I, def. 42. It is clear that the maximum degree and binding degree of the cut formulae in the proof are not increased by the transformation.

Now we set $\sigma_1(a, 0) = a$

$\sigma_1(a, p + 1) = \rho_1[\sigma_1(a, p)]$;

then evidently the tf-degree of the proof number $\sigma_1(a, p)$ $\leq r \dot{-} p$. Since $r \leq b$, the cuts in the proof number $_1(a, b)$ are truth-functionally simple. By an obvious induction, the order of $\sigma_1(a, p) \leq \alpha \cdot 2^b$.

Lemma 13.4. There is a primitive recursive functional $\sigma_2(a, b)$ such that if a is the number of a proof in S_o of a formula C , with binding degree d and degree b , then $\sigma_2(a, b)$ is the number of a proof of C of binding degree $d \dot{-} 1$, degree b , and order $\leq 2^{\alpha : 2^b}$ ($= \omega^{\alpha \cdot 2^b}$ if α is infinite).

Proof. We define a functional $\rho_2(a)$ such that if a is the number of a proof of C of order α , then $\rho_2(a)$ is the number of a proof of C in which the binding degree of every truth-functionally simple cut (not on a prime formula) has been reduced by one, of order 2^α .

By induction on the construction of the proof. The steps are the same as in lemma 13.3 except in the case where the last inference is a cut, with of course 2^α replacing $\alpha \cdot 2$.

4. C is theconclusion of a cut

$$\frac{\mathcal{R} \vee \mathcal{A} \qquad -\mathcal{A} \vee \mathcal{S}}{\mathcal{R} \vee \mathcal{S}}$$

where theorders of the proofs of $\mathcal{R} \vee \mathcal{A}$ and $-\mathcal{A} \vee \mathcal{S}$ are β_1 and β_2 respectively, $< \alpha$.

a. $\mathcal{A}$ is a prime formula, of the form $-\mathcal{B}$, or of the form $-(\mathcal{B} \vee \mathcal{B}')$. Then the argument is the same as case 3.

b. $\mathcal{A}$ is of the form $(x)\mathcal{B}(x)$. Now consider the Formelbund of $-(x)\mathcal{B}(x)$ in the proof which, by hypothesis of the induction, we obtain from the given one of the right premiss of the cut. The highest formulae in it are either in the principal formulae of weakenings or are principal formulae of bindings

$$\frac{-\mathcal{B}^*(t) \vee \mathcal{N}}{-(x)\mathcal{B}^*(x) \vee \mathcal{N}} \tag{9}$$

where $\mathcal{B}^*(x)$ is a numerical instance of $\mathcal{B}(x)$.

From the given proof of $\mathcal{R} \vee (x)\mathcal{B}(x)$, of order β_1, we obtain by hypothesis of the induction a reduced proof of order $\leq 2^{\beta_1}$. From this we can obtain a proof of order $\leq 2^{\beta_1}$, with no more complex cuts, of $\mathcal{R}^* \vee \mathcal{B}^*(t)$. This proof is obtained by the same devices as before: The tops of the Formelbund of $(x)\mathcal{B}(x)$ are in the principal formulae of weakenings or in generalizations

$$\frac{\mathcal{B}^{**}(a) \vee \mathcal{M}}{(x)\mathcal{B}^{**}(x) \vee \mathcal{M}}$$

where $\mathfrak{B}^{**}(a)$ is obtained from $\mathfrak{B}(a)$ by substituting numerals for variables. From the premiss we obtain a proof of $\mathfrak{B}^{***}(t)$, where $\mathfrak{B}^{***}(a)$ is obtained by substituting in $\mathfrak{B}^{**}(a)$ the same numerals for the same variables as in passing from $\mathfrak{B}(a)$ to $\mathfrak{B}^{*}(a)$. Then below this we replace $(x)\mathfrak{B}^{**}(x)$ by $\mathfrak{B}^{***}(t)$, but introduce the same variables at infinite inductions as were introduced at the infinite inductions in the reduced proof of $\mathfrak{R} \vee (x)\mathfrak{B}(x)$. Then the result will be $\mathfrak{R}^{*} \vee \mathfrak{B}^{*}(t)$. The function φ_8 which accomplishes this is described in appendix I, def. 37.

Then we replace (9) by

$$\frac{\mathfrak{R}^{*} \vee \mathfrak{B}^{*}(t) \qquad -\mathfrak{B}^{*}(t) \vee \mathfrak{N}}{\mathfrak{R}^{*} \vee \mathfrak{N}} \tag{10}$$

and in the proof below it leading to $-\mathfrak{A} \vee \mathfrak{S}$, replace the formulae of the Formelbund of $-\mathfrak{A}$ by the corresponding numerical instance of $\mathfrak{R}$. The result is a proof of $\mathfrak{R} \vee \mathfrak{S}$. If the conclusion of (9) has order γ, we give the conclusion of (10) the order $2^{\beta}1 + \gamma$, and add $2^{\beta}1$ to the order of all succeeding lines. Then the cuts (10) satisfy the condition that the order of their conclusions should be greater than those of their premisses. If there are inferences (9) above theone with which we are operating, then the right premiss of (10) will have order $< 2^{\beta}1 + \gamma$, the left order $\leq 2^{\beta}1$; since $\gamma > 0$, $2^{\beta}1 + \gamma$, the order of the conclusion, is greater than that of either premiss.

Then the order of the last line $\mathcal{R} \vee \mathcal{S} = 2^{\beta_1} + 2^{\beta_2} \leq 2^{\max(\beta_1, \beta_2)} + 2^{\max(\beta_1, \beta_2)} = 2^{\max(\beta_1, \beta_2)+1} \leq 2^{\alpha}$.

c. $\mathcal{A}$ is of the form $(Ex)\mathcal{B}(x)$. Similarly. We consider the Formelbund of $(Ex)\mathcal{B}(x)$ in the reduced proof of the left premiss, and from the proof of $-(Ex)\mathcal{B}(x) \vee \mathcal{S}$ we obtain proofs of formulae $-\mathcal{B}^*(t) \vee \mathcal{S}$.

For the arithmetical details of the definition of ρ_2, see appendix I, def. 43.

Now let $\sigma_2(a, b) = \rho_2[\sigma_1(a, b)]$. Since the proof obtained by applying σ_1 has only truth-functionally simple cut formulae which are subformulae of the original cut formulae, and ρ_2 removes the outermost quantifier from any cut formula of the form of a quantification, the effect of σ_2 is to remove all the truth-functional complexity and then the outermost quantifiers from each cut formula, i. e. to replace each cut by cuts on subformulae of the outermost quantifications in the cut formula. It follows that if the proof has degree b and binding degree p , then the new proof has degree $\leq b$ and binding degree $p \dot{-} 1$.

The order condition follows from those of σ_1 and ρ_2.

Lemma 13.5. There is a primitive recursive functional $\sigma(a, b, p)$ such that if a is the number of a proof in S_0 of a formula C , of order α , degree b , binding degree p , then $\sigma(a, b, p)$ is the number of a proof of C with cuts only on prime formulae of order $\leq \omega_p(\alpha \cdot 2^{b+1})$.

<u>Proof.</u>[16] Let $\sigma(a, b, 0) = \sigma_1(a, b)$

$$\sigma(a, b, p + 1) = \sigma[\sigma_2(a, b), b, p] .$$

Then the result is proved by induction on p . If $p = 0$, then by lemma 13.3 σ_1 gives a proof in which every cut formula is prime, of order $\alpha \cdot 2^b \leq \alpha \cdot 2^{b+1}$.

By lemma 13.4, if a is the number of a proof of binding degree $p + 1$ and satisfying the other above conditions, then $\sigma_2(a, b)$ is the number of a proof of C of binding degree $\leq p$ and degree $\leq b$, of order $2^{\alpha \cdot 2^b}$. Then by the hypothesis of induction, $\sigma[\sigma_2(a, b), b, p]$ is the number of a proof of C with cuts only on prime formulae, of order $\leq \omega_p(2^{\alpha \cdot 2^b} \cdot 2^{b+1}) \leq \omega_p(\omega^{\alpha \cdot 2^b} \cdot 2^{b+1})$

$$\leq \omega_p(\omega^{\alpha \cdot 2^b} \cdot \omega) \leq {}_p(\omega^{\alpha \cdot 2^b+1}) \leq \omega_p(\omega^{\alpha \cdot 2^{b+1}}) \leq \omega_{p+1}(\alpha \cdot 2^{b+1}).$$

Since $\sigma(a, b, p + 1) = \sigma[\sigma_2(a, b), b, p]$, our claim

---

[16] Lemma 13.5 may seem impossible for the following reasons: Suppose we start with a proof in Z_o of a numerical formula E . Then by lemmas 13.2 and 13.5 we arrive by a <u>primitive</u> <u>recursive</u> functional at a proof of E in S_o with cuts only on prime formulae. It might seem that this is essentially a numerical computation, for quantificational steps are clearly excluded, and that we ought to be able to arrive in this way at a proof that E must be true which could be formalized in Z , contrary to Gödel's second undecidability theorem. The reason why this does not happen is that the proof obtained by lemma 13.5 can contain infinite inductions which, since eventhe cuts on prime formulae can be eliminated primitive recursively, may be allvacuous, i. e. such that the formula $A(a_1 \ldots a_k)$ does not actually contain any of $a_1 \ldots a_k$. To obtain the calculation one has to "unpack" these infinite inductions, a step which will involve a transfinite induction on the order, which, if arbitrary proofs in Z_o are considered, is bounded by ε_o .

holds for $p + 1$.

<u>Lemma 13.6</u>. There is a functional $\Gamma_p(a, b, r)$ such that if a is the number of a proof in S_o with primitive recursive functionals at infinite inductions, of degree b , binding degree p , and order $\leq \omega \cdot r$, of a formula of form (4), then $\Gamma_p(a, b, r)$ is the number of a cut-free deduction of (4) in Schütte's quantification theory from formulae true for the given subsitution for $f_1 \ldots f_k$, $a_1 \ldots a_m$. Γ_p is ordinal recursive of order $p + 1$.
<u>Proof</u>. If a satisfies the conditions, then $\sigma(a, b, p)$ is the number of a proof of (4) of order $\leq \omega_p(\omega \cdot 2^{b+1} \cdot r)$ with no cuts except on prime formulae. In fact (see appendix II) we have a primitive recursive function $wor(p, b, r)$ which gives a notation for $\omega_p(\omega \cdot 2^{b+1} \cdot r)$ in the ordering $<_{p+1}$, and our function $\sigma(a, b, p)$ can be so defined that its value encodes the order of the reduced proof (indeed this follows from the way proofs are numbered in appendix I); in particular, so $(\sigma(a, b, p))_1 <_{p+1} wor(p, b, r)$ and is the order of the reduced proof (see appendix II).

Now given a proof of (4) with cuts only on prime formulae, we obtain <u>by induction on its order</u> a deduction from true numerical formulae of (4) without cuts ["numerical" is relative to $f_1 \ldots f_k$, $a_1 \ldots a_m$].

We note that since (4) is (relatively) closed, so is every formula in its grosser Formelbund. Evary other formula in the proof is in the grosser Formelbund of a formula which is the cut formula of some cut, and which is therefore a prime formula. It follows that there are no generalizations in the proof, and that the proof connection is preserved by, at any infinite induction with conclusion $A(a_1 \ldots a_k)$, dropping the infinite induction and carrying on from theproof of $A(0 \ldots 0)$. Moreover, throughout the proof we can substitute 0 for any other free variable. The resulting proof has no free variables and no infinite inductions. To describe more exactly how to obtain this proof and eliminate the cuts at the same time, consider any proof of a formula C which contains no generalizations and cuts only on prime formulae. We obtain a proof of C* , the result of substituting 0 for each free variable of C , which contains neither free variables, infinite inductions, nor cuts, but which may have arbitrary true numerical formulae as initial formulae.

1. C is an initial formula. Then C is verifiable, so C* is admissible as an initial formula.

2. C is theconclusion of astructural or constructional inference, with premiss(es) B (and D). Then since the inference is not a generalization, the same inference leads from B* (and D*) to C* .

3. C is the conclusion of an infinite induction; i. e. C is $C(a_1 \ldots a_k)$, and if a is the number of the given proof, then $(a)_4$ is the number of a recursive functional such that $(a)_4(n)$ is the number of a proof of $C[0^{((n)_0)} \ldots 0^{((n)_{k-1})}]$ (see appendix I, def. 28), when $(a)_4(1)$ is the number of a proof of $C(0 \ldots 0)$, for $(1)_i = 0$ for each i , which has order less than that of C ; i. e. $((a)_4(1))_1 \underset{p+1}{<} (a)_1$. Then by the hypothesis of induction we can find from this a proof of $[C(0 \ldots 0)]^*$, i. e. C^* , which has no free variables, infinite inductions, or cuts. (This step involves the use of a functional which enumerates all the functionals generating proofs of the premisses of infinite inductions. Since these functionals are all primitive recursive, they can be enumerated by a functional which is double recursive, i. e. ordinal recursive of degree 1 .)

4. C is the conclusion of a cut

$$\frac{\mathfrak{R} \vee P \qquad -P \vee \mathfrak{S}}{\mathfrak{R} \vee \mathfrak{S}}$$

where P is a prime formula. Then we can obtain reduced proofs of $\mathfrak{R}^* \vee P^*$ and $-P^* \vee \mathfrak{S}^*$.

a. P^* is true. Then the proof connection is preserved by omitting the Formelbund of $-P^*$, from the proof of $-P^* \vee \mathfrak{S}^*$, for it could be affected only in initial formulae of which $-P^*$ is an alternand, which are still true if it is omitted. Thus we have a proof of $\mathcal{S}^*$ which has the properties of a reduced proof, and $\mathcal{R}^* \vee \mathcal{S}^*$ can be obtained by weakening.

b. P* is false. A similar operation performed on the proof of $\mathcal{R}^* \vee P^*$ to obtain one of $\mathcal{R}^*$ will then, by weakening, yield the reduced proof of $\mathcal{R}^* \vee \mathcal{S}^*$.

This completes the proof of lemma 13.6. Although numerical details are given in appendix I, it is well to comment here on why this functional is of a different character from thefunctions of lemmas 13.3-5. The point is that in the inductions on the constructions of proofs in these definitions, at all inferences other than infinite inductions the functional was given in terms of its value for proofs with numbers <u>less</u> than that of the proof of the conclusion of the inference. (There are exceptions for which some simple function of the number of the proof is less, e. g. def. 33 of appendix I). In some cases, e. g. 4b and 4c, pp.143-5, this required auxiliary functionals.

In the case of infinite inductions, there is a primitive recursive function which gives, from the number of a functional giving th e preofs of the numbrical instances, and from certain other parameters (including the number of the functional being defined, so that there is an appeal to the recursion theorem), the number of a functional, primitive recursive in the first one, which gives reduced proofs of the numerical instances of the formula of which we want the transformation to produce a proof. It follows from the recursion theorem that the functional defined is primitive recursive, since it is the fixed point of a primitive recursive function of a Gödel number (or index) and parameters. (For a proof of the recursion theorem, see IM §66; the form we use is the corollary to theorem XXVII, pp. 353-4.)

In case 3 of the present lemma, infinite induction must be handled differently, since we cannot transform an infinite induction into another but must actually find the proof of an instance, whose number is now not nedessarily smaller than that of the conclusion, but only of lesser order. Then we apply the reduction to this proof. It follows that all we can say about the reduction function is that it is ordinal recursive on the ordering in terms of which the orders of the class of proofs are determined, viz. $<_{p+1}$.

<u>Completion of the proof of theorem 13</u>. Lemma 13.6 obtains for us a proof of (4) in a system to which Herbrand's theorem applies. It follows from that result that given the proof a of (4) satisfying the hypotheses of lemma 13.6, then from the proof number $\Gamma_p(a, b, r)$ we can primitive recursively obtain terms $t_1 \ldots t_q$, composed of 0 , S , $f_1 \ldots f_k$, $a_1 \ldots a_m$, such that

$$A(\bar{f}, \bar{a}, t_1) \vee \ldots \vee A(\bar{f}, \bar{a}, t_q) \tag{11}$$

is true for the given substitution. Indeed, since the proof number $\Gamma_p(a, b, r)$ is already without cuts, we do not need to use the full force of Herbrand's theorem. (11) can be obtained by the method of permuting bindings with other constructional inferences so that there comes to be a point below which there are only bindings and structural inferences.[17]

If c is the number of (4), and d is the number of a proof of (4) without cuts, from (relatively) closed quantifier-free formulae, let r* be a primitive recursive function which carries out this transformation and searches the proof to produce a number r*(c, d) such that if $i < q$ (q is obviously a primitive recursive function of the number of the proof obtained by the transformation), then $(r^*(c, d))_i$ is the number of the term t_{i+1} of (11), where (11) is provable in the propositional calculus from initial formulae of the proof number d .

Then if the initial formulae of the proof number d are all true,

$$\mu x\Big(x \le \max_{i \le \ln[r^*(c,d)]}[\mathrm{val}\{(r^*(c, d))_i\}] \;\&\; A(\bar{f}, \bar{a}, x)\Big) \tag{12}$$

[17] In the Gentzen route to Herbrand's theorem, this is the step from the normal form theorem (Hauptsatz, IM p. 453, to the extended normal form theorem (erweiterter Hauptsatz, IM p. 460). Then Herbrand's theorem follows by examining the "midsequent" or "midformula" of the second normal proof.

is a functional satisfying (4), where val(m) is the functional which gives the numerical value of the (relatively) closed term number m (appendix I, def. 26).

Let p*(a) be a primitive recursive function such that if a is the number of a proof in Z_0, then p*(a) is one greater than the greatest number of inductions in each branch. Let d*(a) be the maximum degree of induction formulae (and a fortiori, of cut formulae) of the proof number rp(a) obtained by lemma 13.1.

If a is the number of a proof in Z_0^p of (4), then by lemmas 13.1 and 13.2 $Sp[\overline{f}, \overline{a}, rp(a)]$ is the number of a proof in S_0 of (4), of binding degree p, degree $\leq$ d*(a), and order $\leq \omega \cdot$ p*(a). Then by lemma 13.6, $\Gamma_p\{Sp[\overline{f}, \overline{a}, rp(a)], d^*(a), p^*(a)\}$ is the number of a cut-free deduction from true formulae of (4). Then in view of the fact that $(a)_0$ is the number of the last line of the proof number a (see appendix I, def. 25), the substitution of $\Gamma_p\{Sp[f, a, rp(a)], d^*(a), p^*(a)\}$ for d and $(a)_0$ for c results in a functional satisfying (4).

Let ex(a, n) be a primitive recursive function such that if c is the number of a formula (Ex)B(x), then ex(c, n) is the number of $B(0^{(n)})$. Let $Tr(\overline{f}, \overline{a}, c)$ be the predicate which is true of $\overline{f}, \overline{a}$, c if c is the number of a true formula (for the given substitution for $\overline{f}, \overline{a}$), which is readily definable from val (appendix I, def. 26). Of course Tr applies only to (relatively) numerical formulae. Consider the functional

$$\mu x\Big(x \leq \max\Big[\mathrm{val}\Big\{\bar{f}, \bar{a}, (r^* [\Gamma_p\{\mathrm{Sp}[\bar{f}, \bar{a}, \mathrm{rp}(a)], d^*(a)\}]_{i}, p^*(a)\}, \; i \leq \ln[r^*(\Gamma_p\{\}, (a)_o)] \; (a)_o\Big])_i^-\Big\}\Big] \;\&\; \mathrm{Tr}(\bar{f}, \bar{a}, \mathrm{ex}[(a)_o, x])\Big) \tag{13}$$

If we adopt the procedure described under lemma 13.2, of making one of the function variables represent a function enumerating all the functions expressed by symbols of Z_o, then the functional obtained by adding the recursion equations for this enumerating function to those of (13) will be a functional which enumerates all the functionals F (see p. 126) corresponding to provable formulae (4) of Z_o^p. It follows that Z_o^p is uniformly 1*-consistent. This functional is ordinal recursive of degree $p + 1$ relative to the enumerating function. If the given functions of Z_o are all primitive recursive, this function is of degree 1, so that the functional (which we shall call H_p) is of degree $p + 1$ absolutely.

If the argument is carried out using an ordering of type ε_o to serve as orders for proofs in S_o, then the resulting functional H is ordinal recursive on this ordering (relative to the enumerating function) and enumerates all functionals F corresponding to provable formulae (4) of Z_o. Equivalently, such a functional can be defined if we have a function which enumerates all functionals ordinal recursive of all degrees p relative to the function enumerating the given functions of Z_0'. This proves the uniform 1*-consistency of Z_0.

The functional $\lambda a \Gamma_p(a, b, r)$ for fixed p, b, r, which we call $\Gamma_p^{b,r}$, can be defined by an ordinal recursion on an ordering of the natural numbers of type $\omega_p(\omega \cdot 2^{b+1} \cdot r)$ by starting with an ordering $\underset{1}{<}$ of type $\omega \cdot 2^{b+1} \cdot r$; thus $\Gamma_p^{b,r}$ is ordinal recursive of degree $p + 1$ with respect to that ordering as $\underset{1}{<}$. Suppose that for each function symbol of Z_0 which occurs in a given proof in Z_0 of (4), we have a variable representing it. Then if we add to the recursion equations for the functional

$$\mu x\left\{x \leq \max_{i \leq \underline{l}n[r*(\Gamma_p^{br}(\lambda (a)_0)]}\left[\text{val}\{f, a, (r*[\Gamma_p^{b,r}(\underline{S}p[f, a, \underline{r}p(a)])], (a)_0)_i\}\right] \;\&\; \text{Tr}(f, a, \underline{e}x[(a)_0, x])\right\} \tag{14}$$

the recursion equations for each of these given functions with the chosen variable as principal function letter, then if a is the number of a proof of (4) in Z_0^p with no function symbols except these, of degree b, and $p*(a) = r$, then the resulting functional satisfies (4) and is ordinal recursive of degree $p + 1$ with respect to the ordering $\underset{1}{\leq}$ of type $\omega \cdot 2^{b+1} \cdot r$ in given functions of Z_0.

To complete the proof of theorem 13, we need only consider the matter of representable functionals.

If a functional $G(a_1 \dots a_k)$ is strongly represented in Z_0^p by the quantifier-free formula $A(a_1 \dots a_k, y)$ and the term $t(a)$, then consider the formula

$$(Ey)\{A[a_1 \dots a_k, \nu_2^1(y)] \ \& \ t[\nu_2^1(y)] = \nu_2^2(y)\} \tag{15}$$

which, since it follows in the predicate calculus from $(Ey)A(a_1 \dots a_k, y)$ and $\nu_2[\nu_2^1(a), \nu_2^2(a)] = a$, is provable in Z_0^p (or by the extension by the last formula as axiom; but since we assumed earlier that these formulae were provable in our systems, we might as well assume that they are provable in Z_0). It follows that

$$H_p(a_1 \dots a_k, a) = \mu y\{A[a_1 \dots a_k, \nu_2^1(y)] \ \& \ t[\nu_2^1(y)] = \nu_2^2(y)\} \tag{16}$$

if a is the number of a proof in Z_0^p of (15). It follows that

$$G(a_1 \dots a_k) = \nu_2^2[H_p(a_1 \dots a_k, a)] \,. \tag{17}$$

For it follows from (i) of def. 29, with def. 28, that if $G(a_1 \dots a_k) = w$, then we can prove in Z_0^p from true formulae $a_i(0^{(n_1)} \dots 0^{(n_{r_i})}) = 0^{(m)}$, the formula

$$(Ey)[A(a_1 \dots a_k, y) \ \& \ t(y) = 0^{(w)} \ \& \ (z)((Ex)[A(a_1 \dots a_k, x) \ \& \ t(x) = z] \supset z = 0^{(w)})]$$

from which follows

$$(Ey)\Big[A(a_1 \dots a_k, y) \ \& \ t(y) = 0^{(w)} \ \& \ (z)(x)\{\nu_2(z, x) < \nu_2(y, 0^{(w)}) \supset -[A(a_1 \dots a_k, x) \ \& \ t(x) = z]\}\Big].$$

By the 1*-consistency of Z_0^p, we can find from the proof of the last formula a number n such that

$$A(a_1 \ldots a_k, 0^{(n)}) \ \& \ t(0^{(n)}) = 0^{(w)} \ \& \ (z)(x)\{\nu_2(\bar{z}, x) < \nu_2(0^{(n)}, 0^{(w)}) \supset - [A(a_1 \ldots a_k, x) \ \& \ t(x) = z]\}$$

is true. It follows that $\nu_2(n, w)$ is the value of the term on the right of (16) and therefore of $H_p(a_1 \ldots a_k, a)$. Therefore (17)holds.[18]

It follows that for variable a, the functional on the right of (17) enumerates all functionals representable in Z_o^p by quantifier-free formulae.

---

[18] It is necessary for this to enlarge the argument of theorem 13 to allow bounded quantifiers in theformula A of (4). This does not affect the argument until lemma 13.6. We combine lemma 13.6 and the final step by using the lemma: If C is a closed formula with only bounded quantifiers, then from a proof of $C \vee \mathcal{N}$ in S_o from true axioms, we can obtain a proof in S_o from such axioms of $\mathcal{N}$, which has no greater order than the given one, and no more complex cuts, if C is numerically false. (Proved by induction on the construction of C.)

Given the proof obtained first by lemma 13.5 and then by eliminating cuts on prime formulae, any generalizations and non-vacuous infinite inductions must be in the grosse Formelbünde of subformulae of $A(\bar{f}, \bar{a}, y)$. The last constructional inference must be a binding

$$\frac{A(\bar{f}, \bar{a}, t) \vee \mathcal{M}}{(Ex)A(f, a, t) \vee \mathcal{M}} \qquad (A)$$

where we can suppose t is closed. If $A(\bar{f}, \bar{a}, t)$ is false, we apply the lemma; cannot be empty and is an alternation of (4)'s, so (4) follows by contractions, with decreased order. By transfinite induction, we can find a binding (A) such that $A(\bar{f}, \bar{a}, t)$ is true. (To find these bindings, we must evaluate the functions at infinite inductions, as in lemma 13.6.)

We have not shown, although we probably could, that the order estimates of lemmas 13.3-5 still hold if bounded quantifiers do not contribute to the binding degree. This is, however, not necessary for the argument here. We point out that this note is necessary only for the effectiveness of the proof of (17); it follows from (16) and the intuitive meaning of the formulae of Z_o.

If instead of using H_p we use $H_p^{b,r}$ where $b = d^*(a)$ and $r = p^*(a)$, we obtain a proof that every functional representable in Z_o^p by a quantifire-free formula is ordinal recursive of degree $p + 1$ in given functions of Z_o, with respect to an ordering of type $\omega \cdot 2^{b+1} \cdot r$ as $\underset{1}{<}$.

This completes the proof of theorem 13.

Corollary 13.1. If Z_o is an elementary number theory with induction, then Z_o is externally consistent.

Proof. By definition 15, Z_o is still an elementary number theory with induction if a verifiable axiom, even with new function symbols, is added to it. By theorem 13, the extension is 1*-consistent and therefore consistent.

Corollary 13.2. If Z_o is an elementary number theory with induction, then Z_o has a no-counter-example interpretation by ordinal recursive functions of finite degree in the given functions of Z_o.

Proof. By theorems 12 and 13.

Corollary 13.3. Z is consistent, uniformly 1*-consistent, externally consistent, and has a no-counter-example interpretation by ordinal recursive functionals of finite degree. The same is true of Z_μ. (HB I, 371; II, 293.)

5. Representation of ordinal recursive functionals in elementary number theory

We conclude this chapter by showing that every ordinal recursive functional of degree p is provably recursive, and therefore strongly representable, in a certain extension $Z_{1\mu}^{p+1}$ of Z_{μ}^{p+1} ; in fact strongly representable in a similar extension of Z^{p+1} . These extensions will be inessential extensions of Z in such a way that every ordinal recursive functional of finite degree is provably recursive in Z_{μ} and strongly representable in the (inessential) extension of Z by the function U or the pairing functions. These results will follow from theorem 15 below.

First we shall discuss the formalization of transfinite induction

Definition 38. Let $<^*$ be any primitive recursive linear ordering of the natural numbers. By (formal) transfinite induction with respect to $<^*$ we mean the schema

$$\frac{(x)[x <^* a \supset \mathfrak{A}(x)] \qquad \mathfrak{A}(a)}{\mathfrak{A}(t)} \tag{1}$$

Theorem 14 (cf. HB II, 361 ff., Schütte [2], [4] ch. VII, Gentzen [4]). Let $\mathfrak{A}(a)$ be a formula of binding degree d of a system Z_2 obtained from Z by adding symbols for all primitive recursive functions and their recursion equations. Then if $p > 0$, transfinite induction with respect to $<_p$ on the formula $\mathfrak{A}(a)$ can be derived in Z_2^{p+d} .

Proof. We can prove in Z_2^0

$$x <_1 y \equiv : \nu_2^1(x) \ll \nu_2^1(y) \;.\mathrm{v}.\; \nu_2^1(x) = \nu_2^1(y) \;\&\; \nu_2^2(x) < \nu_2^2(y)$$

from which follows

from which follows

$$(x)[x \underset{1}{<} a \supset \mathfrak{a}(x)] \supset . (x)(y)[x < \nu_2^1(a) \supset \mathfrak{a}(\nu_2(x, y))] \ \& \ (y)[y < \nu_2^2(a) \supset \mathfrak{a}\{\nu_2[\nu_2^1(a), y]\}] . \quad (2)$$

Clearly we have

$$(x)[\nu_2^1(x) < 0 \supset \mathfrak{a}(x)] . \quad (3)$$

Suppose we have proved

$$(x)[\nu_2^1(x) < a \supset \mathfrak{a}(x)] ; \quad (4)$$

then by substituting $\nu_2(x, y)$ for x and using $\nu_2^1[\nu_2(x, y)] = x$, we obtain

$$(x)(y)[x < a \supset \mathfrak{a}(\nu_2(x, y))] .$$

Substituting $\nu_2(a, b)$ for a in (2), using $\nu_2^1[\nu_2(a, b)] = a$ and $\nu_2^2[\nu_2(a, b)] = b$, we obtain by (4)

$$(y)(y < b \supset \mathfrak{a}[\nu_2(a, y)]) \supset (x)[x \underset{1}{<} \nu_2(a, b) \supset \mathfrak{a}(x)] \supset \mathfrak{a}[\nu_2(a, b)]$$

if we assume the premiss of (1) with $\underset{1}{<}$ as $<^*$; next we infer

$$(y)(y < b \supset \mathfrak{a}[\nu_2(a, y)]) \supset (y)(y < Sb \supset \mathfrak{a}[\nu_2(a, y)]) . \quad (5)$$

Since clearly we have

$$(y)(y < 0 \supset \mathfrak{a}[\nu_2(a, y)])$$

we infer by induction (in Z_2^{d+1}) (R5) and therefore

$$\mathfrak{a}[\nu_2(a, b)]$$

$$c = \nu_2(a, b) \supset \mathfrak{a}(c)$$

$$(Ey)[c = \nu_2(a, y)] \supset \mathfrak{a}(c) . \quad (6)$$

Since (L6) is equivalent to $\nu_2^1(c) = a$, (6) implies

$$\nu_2^1(c) = a \supset \mathfrak{a}(c) .$$

By generalization and (4) we obtain

$$(x)[\nu_2^1(x) < Sa \supset \mathcal{A}(x)] ,$$

and by the deduction theorem[19]

$$(x)[\nu_2^1(x) < a \supset \mathcal{A}(x)] \supset (x)[\nu_2^1(x) < Sa \supset \mathcal{A}(x)] . \qquad (7)$$

By (3) and induction we obtain

$$(x)[\nu_2^1(x) < \nu_2^1(t) + 1 \supset \mathcal{A}(x)] ,$$

and therefore by $\nu_2^1(a) < \nu_2^1(a) + 1$, we obtain

$$\mathcal{A}(t)$$

the conclusion of (1). Therefore (1) is a derived rule. Our induction formulae have binding degree $d + 1$. This proves theorem 14 for the case where $p = 1$.

$p = q + 1$, where $1 \leq q$. In HB II, 361 ff., it is shown that if $<_{q+1}$ is defined from $<_q$ by the induction step of our definition 31, then transfinite induction on $<_{q+1}$ is derivable by means of trandfinite induction on $<_q$ with the formula $\mathcal{B}(\ell)$:

$$(x)\{C_q(x, \ell) \ \& \ (y)[y <_{q+1} x \supset \mathcal{A}(y)] .$$
$$(y)[y <_{q+1} x \cdot p_\ell \supset \mathcal{A}(y)]\} .$$

Now we note that the innermost quantifiers of the last induction derivation were universal. (If $1 < q$, this

---

[19] We note that in the proofs of the deduction theorem, induction on the formula B(a) in the deduction from a formula C is replaced by induction on $C \supset B(a)$. Since in our case C and B(a) both have binding degree $d + 1$, the proof of (7) obtained is also in Σ_2^{d+1} .

follows by inspection of the formula with $q - 1$ replacing q ; if $q = 1$, this follows from the above derivation.) It follows that by use of pairing functions, these innermost quantifiers can be merged with the outer universal quantifier of $\mathcal{B}(\ell)$, so that although $\mathcal{B}(\ell)$ has binding degree $d + 2$, introducing it in the last induction derivation involves ordinary induction on formulae of binding degree only one more than for the earlier one. I. e., transfinite induction on $<_q$ with a predicate variable $A(a)$ can, by hypothesis of induction, be carried out in Z_2^q ; substituting $\mathcal{B}(a)$ for $A(a)$ in this derivation, we obtain a proof in Z_2^{q+d+2} which can be replaced by one in Z_2^{q+d+1} (i. e. Z_2^{p+d}) by replacing formulae of the form

$$(z)[z <^* s \supset \mathcal{B}(t)] \tag{8}$$

first by

$$(z)(x)\{z <^* s \supset [C_q(x, t) \;\&\; \text{etc.} \;\ldots\;]\}$$

and then by

$$(z)\{\nu_2^1(z) <^* s^* \supset . C_q[\nu_2^2(z), t^*] \;\&\; \text{etc.} \;\ldots\} \tag{9}$$

where s^*, t^* are obtained from s, t by replacing z by $\nu_2^1(z)$, x by $\nu_2^2(z)$. If (8) is of binding degree $q + d + 2$, then (9) is of binding degree $q + d + 1$, q. e. d.

<u>Theorem 15</u>. Let Z_1 be the system obtained by adding to Z free function variables, a symbol for each primitive recursive function with its recursion equations as axioms,

and a symbol and recursion equations for the course-of-values functional described below. Then if F is an ordinal recursive functional of degree p, then F is representable in Z_1^{p+1}, and there is a term F^o, of the system $Z_{1\mu}^{p+1}$ obtained by adding the least number operator, of which the recursion equations of F are provable.

Proof. If F has k function and m number arguments, then the idea of the proof is to take F^o as the Kleene normal form $U[\mu y T_n^{f_1 \ldots f_k}(0^{(e)}, a_1 \ldots a_n, y)]$, if e is a Gödel number of F.

Given $f_1 \ldots f_k$ of $m_1 \ldots m_k$ arguments, Kleene defines course-of-values functions $\tilde{f}_1 \ldots \tilde{f}_k$. To introduce these into the system without quantifiers for variable f_1, we need for each m a functional $\prod_{i<y} p_i^{f[\nu_m^1(i) \ldots \nu_m^m(i)]}$; it would suffice to have one such functional if we allow subsitution for function variables, for then we can obtain the above for any m by substitution in $\prod_{i<y} p_i^{f(i)}$. (This definition departs inessentially from Kleene.)

Then he defines a primitive recursive predicate $T_m^{m_1 \ldots m_k}(w_1 \ldots w_k, z, a_1 \ldots a_m, y)$ such that $T_m^{f_1 \ldots f_k}(z, a_1 \ldots a_m, y)$ is defined as

$$T_m^{m_1 \ldots m_k}[\tilde{f}_1(y \ldots y) \ldots \tilde{f}_k(y \ldots y), z, a_1 \ldots a_m, y] .$$

Then for any general recursive functional F there is a number e such that

(i) $(x_1)\ldots(x_m)(Ey)T_m^{\bar{f}}(e, x_1 \ldots x_m, y)$

(ii) $(x_1) \ldots (x_m)(y)[T_m^{\bar{f}}(e, x_1 \ldots x_m, y)$

$$U(y) = F(f_1 \ldots f_k, x_1 \ldots x_m)]$$

where $\bar{f}$ abbreviates $f_1 \ldots f_k$. Therefore

(iii) $F(f_1 \ldots f_k, a_1 \ldots a_m) =$

$$U[\mu y T_m^{\bar{f}}(e, a_1 \ldots a_m, y)] .$$ (See IM pp. 290-2.)

It follows from the hypothesis of the theorem that U and the characteristic function of $T_m^{m_1 \ldots m_k}(w_1 \ldots w_k, a_1 \ldots a_m, y)$ are represented by terms of Z_1 for which the recursive relations are provable in Z_1^o. It follows from the presence of the course-of-values functionals that $T_m^{\bar{f}}(e, a_1 \ldots a_m, y)$ is expressed by a quantifier-free formula of which the appropriate recursive relations can be proved in Z_1^o.

<u>Lemma 15.1</u>. If e is the Gödel number of the defining equations of a general recursive functional with arguments $f_1 \ldots f_k, a_1 \ldots a_m$, then

$$(Ey)T_m^{\bar{f}}(0^{(e)}, a_1 \ldots a_m, y) \ \& \ U(y) = z]$$

numeralwise represents F in Z_1^o.

<u>Proof</u>. We note that if $w_1 \ldots w_k$ are values for sufficiently large arguments of the course-of-values functions of $f_1 \ldots f_k$, then $T_m^{m_1 \ldots m_k}(w_1 \ldots w_k, e, a_1 \ldots a_m, y)$ holds if and only if y is the number of the first deduction of an equation $f(0^{(a_1)} \ldots 0^{(a_m)}) = 0^{(z)}$ from form-

$$f_1(0^{(n_1)} \ldots 0^{(n_{m_1})}) = 0^{(r)} \tag{10}$$

which, in view of the assumption about w_1, are true. It follows that if $T_m^{m_1 \ldots m_k}(w_1 \ldots w_k, e, a_1 \ldots a_m, y)$ holds, then $U(y)$ is the value of $F(\bar{f}, a_1 \ldots a_m)$ if e is the Gödel number of its defining equations.[20]

Therefore if F is general recursive

(a) If $F(f_1 \ldots f_k, a_1 \ldots a_m) = z$, then $T_m^{m_1 \ldots m_k}(w_1 \ldots w_k, e, a_1 \ldots a_m, y) \& U(y) = z$ holds.

(b) We can now choose new w_1 so that

$$\tilde{f}_1(y \ldots y) = w_1 ,$$

since any argument of f_1 involved in the computation must be less than the Gödel number of the computation; (a) will still hold.

(c) $T_m^{m_1 \ldots m_k}(0^{(w_1)} \ldots 0^{(w_k)}, 0^{(e)}, 0^{(a_1)} \ldots 0^{(a_m)}, 0^{(y)}) \& U(0^{(y)}) = 0^{(z)}$ (11)

is provable in Z_1^0.

(d) By (b), from sufficiently many true equations of the form (10), we can deduce by a primitive recursive computation which can be carried out in Z_1^0,

$$\tilde{f}_1(0^{(y)} \ldots 0^{(y)}) = 0^{(w_1)}$$

and therefore by (11) and the definition of $T_m^{\bar{f}}$

$$T_m^{\bar{f}}(0^{(e)}, 0^{(a_1)} \ldots 0^{(a_m)}, 0^{(y)}) \& U(0^{(y)}) = 0^{(z)}$$

---

[20] We observe that the Kleene formalism for recursive functionals is the same as that for uniform relative recursiveness, so that the principal function letter (in our case f) does not have function arguments. See IM, pp. 290-5.

whence

$$(Ey)[T^{\bar{f}}_m(0^{(e)}, 0^{(a_1)} \ldots 0^{(a_m)}, y) \ \& \ U(y) = 0^{(z)}] \tag{12}$$

is provable in Z^0_1 from equations (10).

(e) Since F is general recursive, for each $f_1 \ldots f_k$, $a_1 \ldots a_m$ we can find a y such that

$$T^{\bar{f}}_m(0^{(e)}, 0^{(a_1)} \ldots 0^{(a_m)}, 0^{(y)}) \ \& \ U(0^{(y)}) = U(0^{(y)}) \tag{13}$$

is deducible in Z^0_1 from equations (10) which are true of $\bar{f}$ (cf. (a)-(c)). Immediately from the definition of $T^{\bar{f}}_m$ we have

$$T^{\bar{f}}_m(e, a_1 \ldots a_m, y) \ \& \ T^{\bar{f}}_m(e, a_1 \ldots a_m, z). \supset y = z \tag{14}$$

from which with (13) we infer

$$(Ez) \Big[(Ey)[T^{\bar{f}}_m(0^{(e)}, 0^{(a_1)} \ldots 0^{(a_m)}, y) \ \& \ U(y) = z] \ \& \ (w)\{(Ey)[T^{\bar{f}}_m(0^{(e)}, 0^{(a_1)} \ldots 0^{(a_m)}, y) \& \ U(y) = w] \supset z = w\}\Big].$$

Lemma 15.1 now follows by (d), (e), and def. 29.

To prove theorem 15, we show of any ordinal recursive functional F of degree p whose Gödel number is e

(i) $(x_1) \ldots (x_m)(Ey)T^{\bar{f}}_m(0^{(e)}, x_1 \ldots x_m, y)$ (15)

is provable in Z^{p+1}_1.

(ii) The recursion equations for F are provable of the term $F^0(\bar{f}, a_1 \ldots a_m)$, i. e.

$$U[\mu y T^{\bar{f}}_m(0^{(e)}, a_1 \ldots a_m, y)] ,$$

in $Z^{p+1}_{1\mu}$.

Then that F is strongly representable in Z^{p+1}_1 follows from (i) by lemma 15.1.

(15) is simply the arithmetization of the statement that F is general recursive. We shall carry out the argument that F is general recursive in such a way that it will be plain that working out the details of its arithmetization and formalization would yield a proof in Z_1^{p+1}.

The proof is by induction on p, and we assume as hypothesis of induction that (i) and (ii) hold for all F ordinal recursive of degree $q < p$. If we suppose F is of degree p, then there are five cases.

1. F is of order $< p$. By hypothesis of induction.

2. F is an initial primitive recursive function, say a_1. Then it is plain that for any $x_1 \ldots x_m$, the single equation $f(0^{(x_1)} \ldots 0^{(x_m)}) = 0^{(x_1)}$ is an evaluation of F for $\bar{f}, x_1 \ldots x_m$; so that since the arithmetization of this is a truth of primitive recursive number theory, it is provable in Z_1^0. Therefore (15) is provable in Z_1^0.

For (ii), we note that the formula

$$T_m^{\bar{f}}(0^{(e)}, a_1 \ldots a_m, y) \supset U(y) = a_1$$

is also a truth of primitive recursive number theory, for any derivation from $f(a_1 \ldots a_m) = a_1$ must be simply a substitution of numerals for the variables. Substituting $\mu y T_m^{\bar{f}}(0^{(e)}, \bar{a}, y)$ for y, we infer

$$T_m^{\bar{f}}[0^{(e)}, \bar{a}, \mu y T_m^{\bar{f}}[0^{(e)}, \bar{a}, y)] \supset F^0(\bar{f}, \bar{a}) = a_1$$

and since the antecedent is provable by (15) and the least-number principle, in $Z_{1\mu}^1$, the consequent, q. e. d.

The other subcases (constant and successor; IM p. 219) are similar.

3. $F(f_1 \ldots f_k, a_1 \ldots a_m) = f_1(F_1 \ldots F_{m_1})$, where we have numbers $e_1 \ldots e_{m_1}$ such that we can derive

$$(x_1) \ldots (x_m)(Ey)T_m^{\bar{f}}(0^{(e_j)}, x_1 \ldots x_m, y) \qquad (16)$$

in Z_1^{p+1} for $j = 1 \ldots m_1$, and such that the recursion equations for F_j are provable in $Z_{1\mu}^{p+1}$ of F_j^o .

Now a computation of F for the arguments $\bar{f}, \bar{x}$ consists of a deduction in the formalism of recursive functions from true equations (10) of an equation

$$f(0^{(x_1)} \ldots 0^{(x_m)}) = 0^{(s)}$$

where f is the principal function letter of the set number e defining F . If y is the number of the computation, then $s = U(y)$.

Let g_j be the principal function letter of the equations number e_j . Then (16) says that for any (consistent) set of equations (10), and any $x_1 \ldots x_m$, there is a deduction from the equations (10) of a formula

$$g_j(0^{(x_1)} \ldots 0^{(x_m)}) = 0^{(r_j)} . \qquad (17)$$

Let e be the number of the set of equations obtained by adding to all the equations number e_j the equation

$$f(a_1 \ldots a_m) = f_1[g_1(a_1 \ldots a_m) \ldots g_{m_1}(a_1 \ldots a_m)]. \qquad (18)$$

Then from any equation of the form

$$f_1(0^{(r_1)} \ldots 0^{(r_{m_1})}) = 0^{(s)}$$

and (18), we can derive, first by substituting $0^{(x_1)}$ for

a_1 and then by replacing the left side of (17) by the right, the equation

$$f(0^{(x_1)} \ldots 0^{(x_m)}) = f_1(0^{(r_1)} \ldots 0^{(r_{m_1})}) ,$$

whence

$$f(0^{(x_1)} \ldots 0^{(x_m)}) = 0^{(s)} . \tag{19}$$

Thus we have produced a derivation of (19) from the equations number e and equations of form (10).

We have made the assumptions that

(a) If G is a subset of a set E of equations, then a derivation of an equation from G is a derivation of the same equation from E .

(b) Given a derivation of the equations E_1 (and E_2) in the formalism from the equations E , if E_3 follows from E_1 by the substitution rule R1 (from E_1 and E_2 by the replacement rule R2), then we have a derivation of E_3 from E . (See IM, p. 264.)

Since (a) and (b) go by arithmetization into elementary truths of primitive recursive number theory, it is a mechanical matter to formalize in Z_1^0 the proof of

$$\bigwedge_{j=1}^{m_1} T_m^{\bar{f}}(0^{(e_j)}, x_1 \ldots x_m, y_j).$$
$$\supset T_m^{\bar{f}}[0^{(e)}, x_1 \ldots x_m, \varphi(y_1 \ldots y_{m_1})] \tag{20}$$

for a suitable primitive recursive term φ of Z_1 . Then by (16), (15) follows.

We have not made quite clear the role of the function

variables in the derivation of (20) and (15). The derivation will refer syntactically to equations of the form (10) which are represented by numbers which, in effect, encode values of the course-of-values function of f_1. The variable f_1 will enter into the derivation only through substitution for variables representing these numbers, in keeping with Kleene's definition of $T_m^{\bar{f}}$ referred to on page 167 above.

The situation differs from that with respect to numeralwise representation (lemma 15.1) in that in this case the w_i appear in the proof as variables, so that terms $\tilde{f}_1(y \ldots y)$ can be substituted for them; therefore no equations of form (10) are necessary as premisses in the proof.

We can also formalize in $Z_{1\mu}^{p+1}$ the proof of

$$T_m^{\bar{f}}(0^{(e)}, a_1 \ldots a_m, y) \supset U(y) = f_1(F_1^o \ldots F_{m_1}^o) . \qquad (21)$$

We assume that the recursion equations for F_j are provable in $Z_{1\mu}^{p+1}$ of F_j^o.

For consider a deduction from equations (10) and the equations number e of an equation (19). Since (18) is the only one of the initial equations in which the letter f appears, (19) must have been derived by evaluating the right side of the appropriate numerical instance of (18). But then the deduction number y must include deductions numbered $y_1 \ldots y_{m_1}$ of formulae (17); i. e.

$$T_m^{\bar{f}}(0^{(e)}, a_1 \ldots a_m, y) \supset \bigwedge_{j=1}^{m_1} T_m^{\bar{f}}[0^{(e_j)}, a_1 \ldots a_m, y_j]$$

but since by (14) we have (using (16))

$$T_m^{\bar{f}}(0^{(e_j)}, a_1 \dots a_m, y_j) \supset y_j = \mu y T_m^{\bar{f}}(0^{(e_j)}, a_1 \dots a_m, y)$$

we infer

$$T_m^{\bar{f}}(0^{(e)}, a_1 \dots a_m, y) \supset \bigwedge_{j=1}^{m_1} U(y_j) = F_j^o . \qquad (22)$$

Now (22) says that the value $0^{(r_j)}$ (see (17)) obtained in the deduction number y_j is unique; it follows that the deduction of (19) must have proceeded by replacing $g_j(0^{(x_1)} \dots 0^{(x_m)})$ by this value; that is, (21) holds.

Substituting $\mu y T_m^{\bar{f}}(0^{(e)}, a_1 \dots a_m, y)$ for y in (21), the antecedent becomes provable by (15) and the least number principle, in $Z_{1\mu}^{p+1}$. Therefore

$$F^o = f_1(F_1^o \dots F_{m_1}^o)$$

is provable. The other equations for F are simply the equations for F_j . Since by hypothesis of induction these are provable in $Z_{1\mu}^{p+1}$ of F_j^o , it follows that all the equations for F are provable of F^o in $Z_{1\mu}^{p+1}$, q. e. d.

4. $F(\bar{f}, \bar{a}) = G[H_1(\bar{f}, \bar{a}) \dots H_r(\bar{f}, \bar{a})]$. If e_j is the number of H_j , we assume that (16) is provable for $j = 1 \dots r$ and if d is the number of G , we assume that

$$(x_1) \dots (x_r)(Ey)T_r^{\bar{f}}(0^{(d)}, x_1 \dots x_r, y) \qquad (23)$$

is provable, all in Z_1^{p+1} . We also assume that the recursion equations for H_j and G are provable in $Z_{1\mu}^{p+1}$ of H_j^o and G^o respectively.

Let e be the number of the set of equations obtained by combining the equations numbered $e_1 \ldots e_r$, d and the equation

$$f(a_1 \ldots a_m) = g[h_1(a_1 \ldots a_m) \ldots h_r(a_1 \ldots a_m)] , \quad (24)$$

where g is the principal function letter of the set number d , and h_j is the principal function letter of the set number e_j .

Then from the set number e_j and equations (10) we can deduce

$$h_j(0^{(x_1)} \ldots 0^{(x_m)}) = 0^{(r_j)} \quad (25)$$

for each $x_1 \ldots x_m$ and some r_j . Then for some s we can deduce from d , and therefore from (the set number) e

$$g(0^{(r_1)} \ldots 0^{(r_r)}) = 0^{(s)} \quad (26)$$

and therefore by subsitution of $0^{(x_i)}$ for a_i in (24) followed by replacements of the left side of (25) by the right, followed by replacement of the left side of (26) by the right, we infer

$$f(0^{(x_1)} \ldots 0^{(x_m)}) = 0^{(s)} . \quad (27)$$

In other words, we could find a primitive recursive term $\eta(y_1 \ldots y_r, z)$ such that

$$\bigwedge_{j=1}^{r} T_n^{\bar{f}}(0^{(e_j)}, x_1 \ldots x_m, y_j). \;\&\; T_r^{\bar{f}}[0^{(d)}, U(y_1) \ldots U(y_r), z]:$$
$$\supset T_m^{\bar{f}}[0^{(e)}, x_1 \ldots x_m, \eta(y_1 \ldots y_r, z)]$$

is provable in Z_1^0 . Then by (16) and (23), (15) follows in Z_1^{p+1} .

Conversely, any deduction of an equation (27) for some

s must proceed in the above-described way, so that we can obtain primitive recursive terms $\eta_0(y) \ldots \eta_r(y)$ such that

$$T_m^{\bar{f}}(0^{(e)}, a_1 \ldots a_m, y) \supset . \bigwedge_{j=1}^{r} T_m^{\bar{f}}[0^{(e_j)}, a_1 \ldots a_m, \eta_j(y)]$$
$$\& \; T_r^{\bar{f}}\{0^{(d)}, U[\eta_1(y)] \ldots U[\eta_r(y)], \eta_0(y)\} \;\&\; U(y) = U[\eta_0(y)] \quad (28)$$

But then (as above) by (14) and (16)

$$T_m^{\bar{f}}[0^{(e_j)}, a_1 \ldots a_m, \eta_j(y)] \supset U[\eta_j(y)] = H_j^0$$

and likewise by (14) and (23)

$$T_r^{\bar{f}}\{0^{(d)}, U[\eta_1(y)] \ldots U[\eta_r(y)], \eta_0(y)\}$$
$$\supset U[\eta_0(y)] = G^0\{\bar{f}, U[\eta_1(y)] \ldots U[\eta_r(y)]\} .$$

From these two formulae we infer

$$R28 \supset U[\eta_0(y)] = G^0(\bar{f}, H_1^0 \ldots H_r^0)$$

and therefore by (28)

$$T_m^{\bar{f}}(0^{(e)}, a_1 \ldots a_m, y) \supset U(y) = G^0(\bar{f}, H_1^0 \ldots H_r^0)$$

Again, substituting $\mu y T_m^{\bar{f}}(0^{(e)}, a_1 \ldots a_m, y)$ for y, we obtain by (15) and the least number principle

$$F^0 = G^0(\bar{f}, H_1^0 \ldots H_r^0)$$

in $Z_{1\mu}^{p+1}$. Since the other equations for F are those for $G, H_1 \ldots H_r$, it follows that all the equations of F are provable, q. e. d.

5. $F(\bar{f}, a_1 \ldots a_{m-1}, 0) = K(\bar{f}, a_1 \ldots a_{m-1})$

$$F(\bar{f}, a_1 \ldots a_{m-1}, Sa) = G(\bar{f}, a_1 \ldots a_{m-1}, Sa,$$
$$F[f, a_1 \ldots a_{m-1}, \mathcal{H}^*(Sa)])$$

where $\mathcal{H}^*$ (which may contain $a_1 \ldots a_{m-1}$) is an admissible term (see page 124), and $p \neq 0$. (For the case $p = 0$, see below.)

Let d be the Gödel number of K, e_j be the Gödel number of G_j which occurs in $\mathcal{H}$ (see p. 124), e_o be the number of G, and e' be the number of the function o' (p. 124), and m' be the number of multiplication. We assume that

$$(x_1) \ldots (x_{m-1})(Ey)T^{\bar{f}}_{m-1}(0^{(d)}, x_1 \ldots x_{m-1}, y) \qquad (29)$$

$$(x_1) \ldots (x_{n_j})(Ey)T^{\bar{f}}_{n_j}(0^{(e_j)}, x_1 \ldots x_{n_j}, y) \qquad (30)$$

for $j = 0 \ldots r$ $(n_o = n+1)$ are provable in Z_1^{p+1}, and

$$(v)(w)(x)(Ey)T_3(0^{(e')}, v, w, x, y) \qquad (31)$$

$$(w)(x)(Ey)T_2(0^{(m')}, w, x, y) \qquad (32)$$

are provable in Z_1^1, while in each case the recursion equations are provable of the terms K^o, G^o, $G_1^o \ldots G_r^o$, o', and the notation for multiplication. From (31) and (32) we can derive

$$T_3(0^{(e')}, p, a, b, c) \supset U(c) = o'(p, a, b) \qquad (33)$$

$$T_2(0^{(m')}, a, b, c) \supset U(c) = a \cdot b \qquad (34)$$

Let e be the number of the set of equations consisting of the sets number d, $e_o \ldots e_r$, e', m', and the equations

$$f(a_1 \ldots a_{m-1}, 0) = k(a_1 \ldots a_{m-1}) \qquad (35)$$

$$f(a_1 \ldots a_{m-1}, Sa) = g(a_1 \ldots a_{m-1}, a, f[a_1 \ldots a_{m-1}, \hbar^*(Sa)]) \qquad (36)$$

where $\hbar^*(Sa)$ is $h[\hbar(Sa), f'(0^{(p)}, \hbar(Sa), Sa)]$, where h is the principal function letter of the set number m' and f' is the principal function letter of the set number e', while $\mathcal{k}(a)$ is constructed from f, $g_1 \dots g_r$, h, f' in the same way as $\mathcal{H}(a)$ was constructed from F, $G_1 \dots G_r$, ' , and o' .

(a) Clearly for any $x_1 \dots x_{m-1}$, to a derivation from the set number d and equations (10) of an equation

$$k(0^{(x_1)} \dots 0^{(x_{m-1})}) = 0^{(z_0)}$$

we can, by substitution of $0^{(x_1)}$ for a_1 in (35) and replacement, obtain a derivation of

$$f(0^{(x_1)} \dots 0^{(x_{n-1})}, 0) = 0^{(z_0)} \; ; \tag{37}$$

i. e. there is a primitive recursive term $t_o(y)$ of Z_1 such that

$$T^{\bar{f}}_{m-1}(0^{(d)}, x_1 \dots x_{m-1}, y)$$
$$\supset . T^{\bar{f}}_m[0^{(e)}, x_1 \dots x_{m-1}, 0, t_o(y)]$$
$$\& \; U[t_o(y)] = U(y) \; . \tag{38}$$

Moreover, since this is the only way to obtain (37), there is a primitive recursive term $t^o(y)$ such that

$$T^{\bar{f}}_m(0^{(e)}, a_1 \dots a_m, y)$$
$$\supset . T^{\bar{f}}_{m-1}[a_1 \dots a_{m-1}, t^o(y)] \; \& \; U[t^o(y)] = U(y). \tag{39}$$

(b) Given a closed term T of the formalism of recursive functions, we define an evaluation of T , relative to a number e and a set of equations (10), as follows: Consider those terms which are parts of T and are of the form $h'(0^{(s_1)} \dots 0^{(s_q)})$, where h' is any function letter. Then an evaluation of T consists of a derivation from the set of equations number e and the given equations (10) of an equation $h'(0^{(s_1)} \ldots 0^{(s_q)}) = 0^{(s)}$ for each such term, followed by an evaluation of the term T' which results from replacing each $h(0^{(s_1)} \ldots 0^{(s_q)}) = 0^{(s)}$. This is a proper recursive definition since the term T' has nesting of function letters of degree one less than T.

It follows by induction on this degree of T that from an equation $h''(0^{(x_1)} \ldots 0^{(x_m)}) = T$ and an evaluation of T, we can obtain a derivation from the set number e and the equations (10) of an equation

$$h''(0^{(x_1)} \ldots 0^{(x_m)}) = 0^{(z)} .$$

(c) We wish to show that if

$$(x_1) \ldots (x_m)[o'(0^{(p)}, x_m, Sa) = 1 \supset (Ey)T_m^{\bar{f}}(0^{(e)}, x_1 \ldots x_m, y)] \quad (40)$$

holds, then we can carry out an evaluation of the right hand side of (36) relative to e and true equations (10) for $\bar{f}$. Then this will result in a numeral $e^{(s)}$ such that we shall have a derivation of

$$f(0^{(x_1)} \ldots 0^{(x_{n-1})}, 0^{(a+1)}) = 0^{(s)}$$

from the defining equations number e and the given equations (10). I. e., we shall have proved

$$(Ey)T_m^{\bar{f}}(0^{(e)}, x_1 \ldots x_{m-1}, Sa, y) . \quad (41)$$

(d) Clearly we have in Z_1^0

$$b \cdot o'(0^{(p)}, b, Sa) = 0 \ \vee \ o'[0^{(p)}, b \cdot o'(0^{(p)}, b, Sa), Sa] = 1$$

and therefore by (29) and (38)

$$40 \supset (Ey)T_{\underline{m}}^{\overline{f}}[0^{(e)}, x_1 \ldots x_{m-1}, b \cdot o'(0^{(p)}, b, Sa), y] . \tag{42}$$

(e) By induction on the definition of admissible term (p. 12$\frac{4}{5}$) we prove that if $\mathscr{g}(x_1 \ldots x_{m-1}, Sa)$ is an admissible term, then we can find an evaluation of

$$\mathscr{g}(0^{(x_1)} \ldots 0^{(x_{m-1})}, 0^{(a+1)}) \tag{43}$$

relative to e and given equations (10), if (40) holds.

1. $\mathscr{g}$ is an x_i or Sa. Then we have an "empty" evaluation by giving the numeral, $0^{(x_i)}$ or $0^{(a+1)}$.

2. $\mathscr{g}$ is $f[x_1 \ldots x_{\underline{m}-1}, \mathscr{g}'*(a_1 \ldots a_{m-1}, Sa)]$. Then by (31) and (32) we can obtain an evaluation of

$$h[\mathscr{g}'(0^{(x_1)} \ldots 0^{(x_{m-1})}, 0^{(a+1)}), f'(0^{(p)}, \mathscr{g}'(\ ), 0^{(a+1)})]$$

if we assume, as hypothesis of induction, that we have an evaluation of (43′). By (33) and (34) the numeral obtained will be $0^{(r \cdot o'(p,r,a+1))}$, if r is the value obtained for (43′). If (40) holds, then by (42) we can obtain a deduction from the equations number e and the given equations (10) of

$$f(0^{(x_1)} \ldots 0^{(x_{m-1})}, 0^{(r \cdot o'(p,r,a+1))}) = 0^{(s)}$$

for some s, and we can therefore find an evaluation of

$$f[0^{(x_1)} \ldots 0^{(x_{m-1})}, \mathscr{g}'*(0^{(x_1)} \ldots 0^{(x_{m-1})}, 0^{(a+1)})] .$$

3. $\mathscr{g}$ is $g_j(\mathscr{h}_1 \ldots \mathscr{h}_{n_j})$. If $0^{(r_1)} \ldots 0^{(r_{n_j})}$ are the numerals obtained (by hypothesis of induction) for $\mathscr{h}_1 \ldots \mathscr{h}_{n_j}$, then by (30) we can obtain a deduction of

$$g_j(o^{(r_1)} \ldots o^{(r_{n_j})}) = o^{(s')}$$

for some s', and therefore an evaluation of $\mathscr{g}$.

Under case 3, we could have allowed $j = 0$. It follows that we can obtain an evaluation of

$$g(o^{(x_1)} \ldots o^{(x_{m-1})}, o^{(a)}, f[o^{(x_1)} \ldots o^{(x_{m-1})}, \mathfrak{p}*(o^{(a+1)})])$$

and therefore by (b), we can obtain a deduction from the equations number e and the given equations (10) of

$$f(o^{(x_1)} \ldots o^{(x_{m-1})}, o^{(a+1)}) = o^{(s)} .$$

That is, (41) holds.

If we formalize this argument, then we have in Z_1^{p+1}

$$b = Sa \supset . (x_m)[o'(o^{(p)}, x_m, b) = 1 \supset T_m^{\bar{f}}(o^{(e)}, x_1 \ldots x_m, y)]$$
$$\supset (Ey)T_m^{\bar{f}}(o^{(e)}, x_1 \ldots x_{m-1}, b, y) . \qquad (44)$$

and by (29) and (38)

$$b = 0 \supset (Ey)T_m^{\bar{f}}(o^{(e)}, x_1 \ldots x_{m-1}, b, y)$$

from which we deduce by (44)

$$LR44 \supset (Ey)T_m^{\bar{f}}(o^{(e)}, x_1 \ldots x_{m-1}, y) .$$

Since we can take $o'(p, a, b) = 1$ as the expression in Z_1 for $a \underset{p}{<} b$, by transfinite induction on $\underset{p}{<}$, we have (by theorem 14) in Z_1^{p+1}

$$(Ey)T_m^{\bar{f}}(o^{(e)}, x_1 \ldots x_m, y) . \qquad (45)$$

This proves (i).

(ii) is proved in the same way as before. By (45) with 0 for x_m and (39) with $\mu y T_m^{\bar{f}}(o^{(e)}, x_1 \ldots x_{m-1}, 0, y) = Y$ for y, we have

$$T_m^{\bar{f}}(0^{(d)}, a_1 \ldots a_{m-1}, t^{\circ}(Y)) \; \& \; F^{\circ}(\bar{f}, a_1 \ldots a_{m-1}, 0) = U[t^{\circ}(Y)] \, . \quad (46)$$

But by (14) and (29) we have

$$t^{\circ}(Y) = \mu y T_{m-1}^{\bar{f}}(0^{(d)}, a_1 \ldots a_{m-1}, y)$$

from which follows by (46)

$$F^{\circ}(\bar{f}, a_1 \ldots a_{m-1}, 0) = K^{\circ}(\bar{f}, a_1 \ldots a_{m-1}) \, . \quad (47)$$

To prove the second equation, we argue as follows: Any derivation of an equation

$$f(0^{(x_1)} \ldots 0^{(x_{m-1})}, 0^{(a+1)}) = 0^{(s)}$$

from the equations e and equations (10) must use (36) and therefore contain a derivation of

$$g(0^{(x_1)} \ldots 0^{(x_{m-1})}, 0^{(a)}, 0^{(q)}) = 0^{(s)} \quad (48)$$

for some q.

But then (by (14)) s is $F^{\circ}(x_1 \ldots x_{m-1}, Sa)$ and also $G^{\circ}(x_1 \ldots x_{m-1}, a, q)$. Hence we have

$$(Eq)[F^{\circ}(a_1 \ldots a_{m-1}, Sa) = G^{\circ}(a_1 \ldots a_{m-1}, a, q)] \quad (49)$$

But then $0^{(q)}$ could only have been substituted in (48) on the basis of a derivation of

$$f(0^{(x_1)} \ldots 0^{(x_{m-1})}, 0^{(q_1)}) = 0^{(q)}$$

for some q_1; i. e. (49) can be strengthened to

$$(Eq_1)(Eq)[F^{\circ}(a_1 \ldots a_{m-1}, Sa) = G^{\circ}(a_1 \ldots a_{m-1}, a, q) \; \& \; q = F^{\circ}(a_1 \ldots a_{m-1}, q_1)] \, . \quad (50)$$

Now $0^{(q_1)}$ could only have been put in on the basis of an evaluation of $h^*(Sa)$. Then by (33) and (34)

$$q_1 = q_2 \cdot o'(0^{(p)}, q_2, Sa)$$

Now $\mathcal{L}(Sa)$ is an admissible term with one less nesting of f than on the right of (36); hence we can suppose, as the hypothesis of a metamathematical induction, that

$$q_2 = \mathcal{H}^{o}(Sa) \ ;$$

that is, that (50) can be strengthened to

$$(Eq_2)(Eq_1)(Eq)[F^{o}(\ ) = G^{o}(\ ) \ \& \ q = F^{o}(a_1 \ldots a_{m-1}, q_1)$$
$$\& \ q_1 = q_2 \cdot o'(0^{(p)}, q_2, Sa) \ \& \ q_2 = \mathcal{H}^{o}(Sa)] \ ; \text{ i. e.}$$
$$F^{o}(a_1 \ldots a_{m-1}, Sa) = G^{o}(a_1 \ldots a_{m-1}, a,$$
$$F^{o}(a_1 \ldots a_{m-1}, \mathcal{H}^{o}(Sa) \cdot o'[0^{(p)}, \mathcal{H}^{o}(Sa), Sa]) \ ,$$

the second equation. (We have suppressed function arguments.)

Thus by (47) and the fact that the rest of the equations for F are those for K, G, $G_1 \ldots G_r$, o', and $\cdot$, we have with F^{o} the equations for F.

Since the argument rests only on (45), (29)-(34), and searching the computation of $F(\bar{f}, a_1 \ldots a_m)$, it can be formalized in $Z^{p+1}_{1\mu}$. This completes the proof of (ii).

$p = 0$. Then F is defined by a primitive recursion

$$F(\bar{f}, a_1 \ldots a_{m-1}, 0) = K(\bar{f}, a_1 \ldots a_{m-1}, 0)$$
$$F(\bar{f}, a_1 \ldots a_{m-1}, Sa) = G[\bar{f}, a_1 \ldots a_{m-1}, a,$$
$$F(\bar{f}, a_1 \ldots a_{m-1}, a)] \ .$$

where we assume (29), (30) with $j = 0$, and that the recursion equations for K and G are provable in $Z^{1}_{1\mu}$ of K^{o} and G^{o}. Then the proofs of (38) and (39) go through as before, so that we have again

$$(Ey)T_m^{\bar{f}}(0^{(e)}, x_1 \ldots x_{m-1}, 0, y) \qquad (51)$$

$$F^0(\bar{f}, a_1 \ldots a_{m-1}, 0) = K^0(\bar{f}, a_1 \ldots a_{m-1}) .$$

By an argument like that of case 4 we have in Z_1^1 (using (30))

$$(\hat{E}y)T_m^{\bar{f}}(0^{(e)}, x_1 \ldots x_{m-1}, a, y) \supset (Ey)T_m^{\bar{f}}(0^{(e)}, x_1 \ldots x_{m-1}, Sa, y)$$

so that by (51) and induction, we have (15) in Z_1^1.

The proof of the second equation is similar to previous cases, especially case 4.

This completes the proof of theorem 15.

Corollary 15.1. Any ordinal recursive functional of finite degree is provably recursive in Z_μ with free function variables. Any ordinal recursive function of finite degree is provably recursive in Z_μ without function variables.

Proof. In HB I, 401-421, it is shown that every primitive recursive function is represented in Z by an ι-term of which the recursion equations of the function are provable. Then the equations are provable in Z_μ of the corresponding μ-terms. The same Gödel method (see also IM §41) will obtain a representing formulate for each course-of-values functional, of which the recursion equations are provable of the corresponding μ-term. It follows that the proofs in Z_1 obtained from theorems 14 and 15 can be mapped into proofs in Z_μ. The same is true of Z if we admit ι-terms;

otherwise, we can still prove (15) with a suitable formula to express $T_m^{\bar{f}}$, and by lemma 15.1, if we have a term for the function U, every ordinal recursive functional is strongly representable. Or if we use for the A of def. 29 the formula

$$(Ey)[T_m^{\bar{f}}(0^{(e)}, a_1 \ldots a_m, \nu_2^1(y)) \,\&\, U(\nu_2^1(y)) = \nu_2^2(y)],$$

the functions within the quantifier can be expressed by predicates, and in order strongly to represent F it will suffice to add a term $\nu_2^2(a)$ to Z.

CHAPTER V

RAMIFIED ANALYSIS

1. Description of systems

By ramified analysis we mean an extension of elementary number theory obtained by adding bound variables ranging over classes, relations, predicates, or functions of natural numbers, which are assigned ordinal numbers as levels, so that (say) a class is of level $\alpha + 1$ if its defining formula contains bound variables of level α.

We shall consider formal systems in which bound class variables of arbitrary finite levels are admitted, but the principles of the investigation would be the same if infinite levels (indexed by constructive ordinals) were admitted, or if higher types were admitted. It is true, however, that the ordinal recursions and transfinite inductions involved in the metamathematical study of systems with infinite levels are more complex than in our investigation. (Cf. Schütte [4] ch. IX, esp. pp. 264-5.)

Definition 39. Let $\mathfrak{F}$ be an elementary number theory whose quantification theory is our version of Schütte's calculus. Then the ramified analysis of $\mathfrak{F}$ (of level ω), which we call RA($\mathfrak{F}$), is the system obtained by the following additions to the formation and transformation rules (cf. Schütte [3], [4] ch. IX):

I/ Formation

A. For each natural number n we admit a sequence

$X_1, X_2, \ldots$ of class variables of level n. These variables count as <u>class terms</u> of $RA(\mathfrak{F})$.

B. If t is a (numerical) term of $\mathfrak{F}$, and T is a class term of $RA(\mathfrak{F})$ of level n, then $t \varepsilon T$ is a formula of $RA(\mathfrak{F})$ of level n, prime if T is a variable.

C. If $\mathfrak{A}$ is a formula of $RA(\mathfrak{F})$ of level p, and X is a class variable of level n, then $(X)\mathfrak{A}$ and $(EX)\mathfrak{A}$ are formulae of $RA(\mathfrak{F})$ of level $\max(p, n+1)$.

D. If $\mathfrak{A}$ is a formula of $RA(\mathfrak{F})$ of level p, and x is a (number) variable of $\mathfrak{F}$, then $\hat{x}\mathfrak{A}$ is a class term of $RA(\mathfrak{F})$ of level p.

The old formation processes of $\mathfrak{F}$ are of course still in force, but it is necessary to explain how levels are assigned by them.

E. 1. A prime formula of $\mathfrak{F}$ has level 0.

2. If B has level p, and C has level q, then $B \vee C$ has level $\max(p, q)$, and $-B$ has level p.

3. If $\mathfrak{A}$ is of level p, then $(x)\mathfrak{A}$ and $(Ex)\mathfrak{A}$ are of level p.

We note that we can obtain the effect of relation variables by the abbreviations

$$t_1 \ldots t_n \varepsilon X \quad \text{for} \quad \nu_n(t_1 \ldots t_n) \varepsilon X$$

$$\hat{x}_1 \ldots \hat{x}_n \mathfrak{A}(x_1 \ldots x_n) \quad \text{for} \quad \hat{x}\mathfrak{A}[\nu_n^1(x) \ldots \nu_n^n(x)]$$

provided $\mathfrak{F}$ contains symbols for the functions ν_n, ν_n^i and the axioms $\nu_n[\nu_n^1(a) \ldots \nu_n^n(a)] = a$ and $\nu_n^i[\nu_n(a_1 \ldots a_n)] = a_i$.

For this reason we do not follow Schütte in taking relation variables as primitive. For other purposes (cf. ch. IV), we shall need the n-tuple functions anyway.

II/ Transformation

A. Axioms: Add all formulae $t \notin X \vee t \in X$, where X is a class variable and t is a term of

B. Constructional inferences (continuing from p. 130)

6. If $\mathfrak{A}(T)$ contains free occurrences of the class term T wherever $\mathfrak{A}(X)$ has free occurrences of the class variable X, and the level of $T \leq$ level of X,

$$\text{(i)}\quad \frac{\mathfrak{A}(T) \vee \mathfrak{N}}{(EX)\mathfrak{A}(X) \vee \mathfrak{N}} \qquad \text{(ii)}\quad \frac{-\mathfrak{A}(T) \vee \mathfrak{N}}{-(X)\mathfrak{A}(X) \vee \mathfrak{N}} \qquad \text{(Bindings)}$$

7. If $\mathfrak{A}(Y)$ is as above, but Y does not occur free in the conclusion, and the levels of X and Y are the same,

$$\text{(i)}\quad \frac{\mathfrak{A}(Y) \vee \mathfrak{N}}{(X)\mathfrak{A}(X) \vee \mathfrak{N}} \qquad \text{(ii)}\quad \frac{-\mathfrak{A}(Y) \vee \mathfrak{N}}{-(EX)\mathfrak{A}(X) \vee \mathfrak{N}} \qquad \text{(Generalizations)}$$

8. If $\mathfrak{A}(t)$ contains free occurrences of the term t of $\mathfrak{F}$ wherever $\mathfrak{A}(x)$ contains free occurrences of x,

$$\text{(i)}\quad \frac{\mathcal{A}(t) \vee \mathcal{N}}{t \varepsilon \hat{x}\mathcal{A}(x) \vee \mathcal{N}} \qquad \text{(ii)}\quad \frac{-\mathcal{A}(t) \vee \mathcal{N}}{t \not\varepsilon \hat{x}\mathcal{A}(x) \vee \mathcal{N}} \qquad \text{(Abstractions)}$$

Of course the original inference schemata of $\mathcal{F}$ are in fact extended, in that instances which are formulae of RA($\mathcal{F}$) but not of $\mathcal{F}$ are now admitted. In particular this is true of cuts and inductions. The level of a cut is the level of the cut formula; the level of an induction is the level of the induction formula.

We point out that the terms principal formula, side formula, and secondary formula extend in obvious ways to the new constructional inferences (see def. 34).

2. Ramified analysis without induction

We consider first RA($\mathcal{F}$) where $\mathcal{F}$ is an elementary number theory without induction. We show that Schütte's version of Gentzen's normal form theorem holds for such systems.

Theorem 16. If $\mathcal{F}$ is a system formalized in Schütte's predicate calculus with quantifier-free axioms, then any proof in RA($\mathcal{F}$) can be (primitive recursively) transformed into a proof in which cuts occur only on prime formulae. If the axioms of $\mathcal{F}$ are primary formulae and closed under cuts, then the proof can be primitive recursively transformed into one without cuts.

proof. The key to the proof is that, as in the first-order theorem (Schütte [1]; IM pp. 453 ff.), cuts on logically complex formulae can be replaced by cuts on subformulae which are logically simpler. In the present case, however, these concepts are more complex and depend on the hierarchy of levels.

Definition 40. The top degree of a formula of ramified analysis is defined as follows:

1. The top degree of a prime formula is 0 .

2. If the top degree of A is p , then the top degree of - A is p + 1 .

3. If the top degree of B is p , and the top degree of C is q , and B and C are of the same level, then the top degree of B v C is max(p, q) + 1 . Otherwise, it is one more than the top degree of the alternand of higher level.

4. If the top degree of A(x) is p , then the top degree of (x)A(x) or (Ex)A(x) is p + 1 .

5. If X is of level m , and A(X) is of level n and top degree p , then the top degree of (X)A(X) or (EX)A(X) is

a. p + 1 , if m < n .

b. 0 otherwise.

6. If A(a) is of top degree p , then t ε $\hat{x}$A(x) is of top degree p + 1 .

Definition 41. The binding degree of a formula of ramified analysis is defined as follows:

1. The binding degree of a prime formula is 0 .

2. If the binding degree of A is p , then so is that of - A .

3. If the binding degree of B is p , and that of C is q , then if B and C are of the same level, then the binding degree of B v C is max(p, q) ; otherwise it is the binding degree of the alternand of higher level.

4, 5. Like definition 40.

6. If A(a) is of binding degree p , then t ε x̂A(x) is of binding degree p .

The top degree and the binding degree arelike the logical degree and binding degree of first-order formulae (defs. 22 and 33) except that they measure complexity only at the highest level; if the level of a formula is increased by adding a quantifier (case 5b, where the level of A(X) is ≤ m , but that of (X)A(X) is m + 1), then the top degree and binding degree both drop to 0 . It follows that the binding degree is the maximum number of nested quantifiers whose scopes are of the same level as the formula as a whole.

Definition 42. An immediate subformula of a formula A is defined as follows:

1. If A is a prime formula, then it has no immediate

subformulae.

2. The only immediate subformula of $-B$ is B.

3. The immediate subformulae of $B \vee C$ are B and C.

4. The immediate subformulae of $(x)A(x)$ are all formulae $A(t)$, where t is a numerical term. Likewise $(Ex)A(x)$.

5. The immediate subformulae of $(X)A(X)$ and $(EX)A(X)$, where X is a class variable of level n, are all formulae $A(T)$, where T is a class term of level $\leq n$.

6. The only immediate subformula of $t \in \hat{x}A(x)$ is $A(t)$.

Lemma 16.1. If B is an immediate subformula of A, then either B is of lesser level than A, or it is of the same level and lesser binding degree, or it is of the same level and binding degree and of lesser top degree.

Proof. 1. A is prime. Vacuous.

2. A is $-B$. Then by case 2 of def. 40, B is of lesser top degree.

3. A is $B \vee C$ or $C \vee B$. If B and C are of the same level, and therefore of the same level as A, then B is of the same level and binding degree and of lesser top degree. The same holds if the level of B is greater than that of C. Otherwise, the level of B < the level of C = level of A.

4. A is (x)C(x) or (Ex)C(x) and B is C(t). Then by case 4 of def. 41, B is of the same levelas A and lesser binding degree.

5. A is (X)C(X) or (EX)C(X), where X is of level m. Then the level of A is at least m + 1. If B is C(T), then either the level of B $\leq$ m, or the level of T, which $\leq$ m, is less than that of B. In that case the quantifiers of T do not contribute to the binding degree of B, which must be one less than that of A.

6. A is t ε x̂A(x) and B is A(t). Then clearly B is of the same level and binding degree and lesser top degree than that of A.

<u>Definition 43</u>. B is a <u>(proper) subformula</u> of A if it is an immediate subformula of A or a proper subformula of an immediate subformula of A.

This inductive definition is shown by lemma 16.1 to be well-founded.

<u>Proof of theorem 16</u>. The fact that it is possible to give a definition of subformula such that the side formula of any constructional inference in the logic of RA($\mathfrak{T}$) is a subformula of the principal formula is the key to the applicability of the Gentzen-Schütte procedure. If there were no level restrictions on the bindings, then we might have a binding where the principal term T already contained the

formula $(EX)\mathfrak{A}(X)$, so that to replace a cut on $(EX)\mathfrak{A}(X)$ by one on $\mathfrak{A}(T)$ would be no advance. This situation can arise in impredicative analysis.

The replacement of cuts by simpler ones proceeds exactly as in Schütte [1]; we have two additional cases to consider. We note that, by induction on the construction of the proof, we replace the given proof by a proof in which the cuts are either of lesser level, or of the same level and lesser binding degree, or of the same leveland binding degree and lesser degree.[1]

All cases are handled in [1] (cf. lemmas 13.3 and 13.4 above) except two where the last inference is a cut

$$\frac{\mathfrak{R} \vee \mathfrak{A} \qquad -\mathfrak{A} \vee \mathfrak{S}}{\mathfrak{R} \vee \mathfrak{S}}$$

4c. $\mathfrak{R}$ is $(X)\mathfrak{B}(X)$, where X is a class variable. Then we can obtain a proof of $\mathfrak{R} \vee \mathfrak{B}(X)$ whose cuts are no more complex than those of the reduced proof of the left premiss (by a less complex version of the method of case 4b, lemma 13.4, pp. 146-7 above). By substitution of T for

[1]One might suppose that this process would involve us in a triple recursion or transfinite recursion of type ω^3. Such a recursion can be eliminated because there is no interlocking (as with degree and binding degree in lemmas 13.3-4). We can define a primitive recursive function which reduces the top degree of certain cuts and replaces each one by a cut whose cut formula is of the form of a class quantification; a second p.r. function replaces each class quantification which is not the innermost of highest level by a subformula; and a third which replaces the innermost. One applies a function only when the previous ones have been exhausted.

X in this proof we obtain such a proof of $\mathfrak{R} \vee \mathfrak{B}(T)$ for any class term T of level $\leq$ that of X .[2]

The procedure is exactly like that of lemma 15.4. The highest term of the Formelbund of $-\mathfrak{A}$ in the proof of the right premiss are in principal formulae of weakenings or are principal formulae of bindings.

$$\frac{-\mathfrak{B}(T) \vee \mathfrak{N}_1}{-(X)\mathfrak{B}(X) \vee \mathfrak{N}_1}$$

(where in this case there are only a finite number of these, a primitive recursive function of the number of the proof.

We replace the bindin g by a cut

$$\frac{\mathfrak{R} \vee \mathfrak{B}(T) \qquad -\mathfrak{B}(T) \vee \mathfrak{N}_1}{\mathfrak{R} \vee \mathfrak{N}_1}$$

and in the subsequent development, replace the occurrences of $-(X)\mathfrak{B}(X)$ in the Formelbund of $-\mathfrak{A}$ by occurrences of $\mathfrak{R}$.

It follows by lemma 16.1 that the cut has been replaced by on either of lesser level or of the same level and lesser binding degree.

4d. $\mathfrak{A}$ is $(EX)\mathfrak{B}(X)$. Similarly.

5. $\mathfrak{A}$ is $t \varepsilon \hat{x}\mathfrak{B}(x)$. Then from the proof of the left premiss we obtain a proof of $\mathfrak{R} \vee \mathfrak{B}(t)$, and from

---

[2]The axioms $t \notin X \vee t \varepsilon X$ are replaced by formulae $t \notin T \vee t \varepsilon T$, which are in general not axioms and of which proofs must be appended. The method of obtaining such proofs is given in appendix I, def. 29.

the reduced proof of the right premiss we obtain a proof of $- \mathcal{B}(t) \vee \mathcal{S}$;[3] the cuts in both proofs are notmore complex than those in the reduced proofs of the original premisses. The method is the same as usual: the highest terms in the Formelbünde of $t \in \hat{x}\mathcal{B}(x)$ and $t \notin \hat{x}\mathcal{B}(x)$ are in the principal formulae of weakenings or are the principal formulae of abstractions where the side formulae are $\mathcal{B}(t)$ and $- \mathcal{B}(t)$ respectively, so that we can omit the abstractions and replace the Formelbünde by occurrences of $\mathcal{B}(t)$ and $- \mathcal{B}(t)$ respectively.

Then by a cut on $\mathcal{B}(t)$ we immediately obtain $\mathcal{R} \vee \mathcal{S}$ In this case the original cut is replaced by one of the same level and binding degree and lesser top degree.

The procedure for dealing with cuts on prime formulae. is exactly the same as that of Schütte [1].

The functionals ρ_1, ρ_2, and ρ_3 of appendix I (defs. 42-44) can be used for these reductions by dropping the clauses referring to infinite inductions and dropping the exponent of ω_3 which refers to the order. Cf. theorem 17 below.

This completes the proof of theorem 16.

---

[3]It could be that t contains a free variable which would be captured by a quantifier in $\mathcal{B}(x)$. In this case, one must rename the bound variables throughout the proofs of both premisses, so that $\mathcal{B}(x)$ is replaced by a formula $\mathcal{B}'(x)$ for which this does not happen. It is clear that this does not affect the conclusion.

The effect of eliminating cuts from a proof in RA($\mathfrak{F}$) is to produce a proof in which every line is an alternation of subformulae of the alternands of the last line. Therefore we have

Corollary 16.1. If E is a quantifier-free formula provable in RA($\mathfrak{F}$), then E can be proved in RA($\mathfrak{F}$) without quantifiers. Therefore RA($\mathfrak{F}$) is consistent if the axioms of $\mathfrak{F}$ are verifiable.

Corollary 16.2. If C is a formula without bound class variables, then C is provable without bound class variables. If C is a formula of $\mathfrak{F}$, then C is provable in $\mathfrak{F}$. Therefore the Herbrand interpretation of $\mathfrak{F}$ covers formulae of $\mathfrak{F}$ provable in RA($\mathfrak{F}$); in fact, it also covers formulae with free class variables (for in Herbrand's theorem, expressions ' ε X ' can be treated as predicate symbols).

Corollary 16.3. If the axioms of $\mathfrak{F}$ are verifiable, then RA($\mathfrak{F}$) is 1*-consistent.

3. Recursive well-orderings and ordinal recursive functionals

Before discussing ramified analysis with induction, for whose number-theoretic theorems we shall prove results corresponding to those of the last chapter, we shall describe a sequence of well-orderings of much higher type than were considered in the last chapter, and then a class of functionals ordinal recursive on these well-orderings, in terms of which, in the next section, we shall characterize the functionals representable (by quantifier-free formulae) in ramified analysis with induction.

As one would expect, the situation is considerably more complicated than for elementary number theory. Given an ordinal α, we shall define a sequence of orderings of types $\varepsilon^n(\alpha)$, where

$$\varepsilon^0(\alpha) = \alpha$$
$$\varepsilon^{n+1}(\alpha) = \varepsilon_{\varepsilon^n(\alpha)},$$

where ε_β is the β th ε-number. The limit of the sequence $\varepsilon^n(\alpha)$ is clearly the first critical ε-number after α. (α is a critical ε-number if $\alpha = \varepsilon_\alpha$.)

We assume that $<_0$ is a given primitive recursive well-ordering of type α. Moreover, we assume we have defined the ordering $<_n$, and the predicates and functions

$Suc_n(i)$	i is a successor element in $<_n$
$pred_n(i)$	if $Suc_n(i)$, the predecessor of i
$sc_n(i)$	the successor of i
$Lim_n(i)$	i is a limit element in the ordering
$lim_n(m, i)$	the m th element of a sequence whose limit is i, if $Lim_n(i)$
$ub_n(m)$	the m th element of an unbounded sequence in $<_n$

The orderings will be so defined that the initial element of each one will be 0 .

Now for each i we shall define by simultaneous recursion predicates and functions

$L(n, a, b, i)$	which will be an ordering
$Suc(n, a, i)$	a is a successor element in the ordering $L(n, a, b, i)$
$sc(n, a, i)$	the successor of a in $L(n, a, b, i)$
$pred(n, a, i)$	the predecessor of a, if $Suc(n, a, i)$
$Lim(n, a, i)$	a is a limit element in $L(n, a, b, i)$
$lim(n, m, a, i)$	if $Lim(n, a, i)$, the m th element of a sequence whose limit is a
$ub(n, m, i)$	an unbounded sequence in $L(n, a, b, i)$

For each i , $L(n, a, b, i)$ is to be a primitive recursive well-ordering; if $i = sc_n(j)$, then the type of $L(n, a, b, i)$ is the next ε-number after the type of $L(n, a, b, j)$; if i is a limit element in $<_n$, then the type of $L(n, a, b, i)$ is the limit of the types of $L[n, a, b, lim_n(m, i)]$. If $L(n, a, b, 0)$ is so chosen as to be of type ε_0 , then it will follow by transifinite induction that if i is a notation in $<_n$ for α , then the type of $L(n, a, b, i)$ is ε_α . If the type of $<_n$

is a limit number α_0 , then it will follow that the upper bound of the types of $L(n, a, b, i)$ will be ε_{α_0} . We shall define $<_{n+1}$ so that its type will be this upper bound. Therefore if the type of $<_n$ is $\varepsilon^n(\alpha)$, then the type of $<_{n+1}$ will be $\varepsilon^{n+1}(\alpha)$.

We shall assume that α , the type of $<_0$, is a limit number; and we shall regard the functions and predicates of page 199 as given for $n = 0$.

Definition 44a.

$L(n, a, b, i) \equiv : a = 0 \ \& \ b \neq 0 . \vee (Ex)\{x \leq ln(a) \ \& \ (a)_x < (b)_x$
$\& \ (y)[y \leq ln(a) \ \& \ L(n, x, y, i) . \supset (a)_y = (b)_y]\}$
if $i = 0$,
$\equiv : a = 0 \ \& \ b \neq 0 . \vee (Ex)\{x \leq ln(a) \ \&$
$L[n, (a)_x, (b)_x, pred_n(i)]$
$\& \ (y)[y \leq ln(a) \ \& \ L(n, x, y, i) . \supset (a)_y = (b)_y]\}$
if $Suc_n(i)$
$: \nu_2^1(a) < \nu_2^1(b) \ \vee . \ \nu_2^1(a) = \nu_2^1(b) \ \&$
$L[n, \nu_2^2(a), \nu_2^2(b), lim_n(\nu_2^1(a), i)]$
if $Lim_n(i)$.

If we set $dp(a) = 0$ if $a = 0$, $= 1$ if $a = 2^{(a)_0}$, $= \max_{(a)_i \neq 0} dp(i)$ otherwise, then we observe that

(i) If $(a)_i \neq 0$, then $dp(i) < dp(a)$.

(ii) If $L(n, a, b, 0)$, then $dp(a) \leq dp(b)$. This is seen by induction on $dp(b)$. If $dp(b) = 1$, then

$L(n, a, b, 0)$ only if $a = 0$ or $a = 2^{(a)_0}$ with $(a)_0 < (b)_0$, i. e. $dp(a) \leq 1$. If $dp(b) = n + 2$, let $r = \mu x\{x \leq ln(b)\ \&\ (a)_x < (b)_x\ \&\ (y)[y \leq ln(b)\ \&\ L(n, x, y, 0). \supset (a)_y = (b)_y]\}$. If $(a)_i \neq 0$, then if $L(n, r, i, 0) \vee r = i$, $(b)_i \neq 0$ also; if $L(n, i, r, 0)$, then since by (i) $dp(r) \leq n + 1$, by the hypothesis of induction, $dp(i) \leq dp(r) < dp(b)$. Hence if $(a)_i \neq 0$, $dp(i) < dp(b)$, and $dp(a) \leq dp(b)$, q. e. d.

(iii) $L(n, a, b, 0)$ orders $\hat{y}[dp(y) \leq n + 1]$ with type $\omega_{n+1}(0)$.

It is obvious that $\hat{y}[dp(y) \leq 1]$ is ordered with type ω. The ordering of $\hat{y}[dp(y) \leq n + 2]$ is obtained from that of $\hat{y}[dp(y) \leq n + 1]$ as $\underset{n+2}{<}$ is obtained from $\underset{n+1}{<}$ (see definition 31); hence if (iii) holds for n, the ordering of $\hat{y}[dp(y) \leq n + 2]$ is of type $\omega^{\omega_{n+1}(0)} = \omega_{n+2}(0)$, and (iii) follows by induction.

It follows that $L(n, a, b, 0)$ is of type ε_0.

Suppose $/i/$ is the ordinal represented by i in $<_n$. Given β, let $\varepsilon(\beta, 0) = \varepsilon_\beta$; $\varepsilon(\beta, n + 1) = \varepsilon_\beta^{\varepsilon(\beta,n)}$. The limit of this sequence is $\varepsilon_{\beta+1}$.

(iv) If $i = sc_n(j)$, and $L(n, a, b, j)$ has type $\varepsilon_{/j/}$, then $L(n, a, b, i)$ orders $\hat{y}[dp(y) \leq n + 1]$ with type $\varepsilon(/j/, n)$.

Since $L(n, 2^a, 2^b, i)$ if and only if $L(n, a, b, j)$, the numbers y with $dp(y) \leq 1$ are ordered by $L(n, a, b, i)$

with type $\varepsilon_{/j/}$.

If $dp(a) \leq n + 2$, consider the function $\lambda x\ (a)_x$, with domain restricted to $\hat{y}[dp(y) \leq n + 1]$. These functions are in one-to-one correspondence with $\hat{z}[z \neq 0\ \&\ dp(z) \leq n + 2]$, and are zero except for finitely many arguments. If we take the values to be ordered by $L(n, a, b, j)$, then they correspond, by hypothesis of induction, to functions whose domain consists of ordinals $< \varepsilon(/j/, n)$ and whose range consists of ordinals $< \varepsilon_{/j/}$. Two functions f and g are so ordered that f precedes g if and only if there is an ordinal β such that $f(\beta') = g(\beta')$ for every β' with $\beta < \beta' < \varepsilon(/j/, n)$ and $f(\beta) < g(\beta)$. By the definition of ordinal exponentiation, the ordering of these functions is of type $\varepsilon_{/j/}{}^{\varepsilon(/j/,n)} = \varepsilon(/j/, n + 1)$. It is isomorphic to the ordering of $\hat{z}[z \neq 0\ \&\ dp(z) \leq n + 2]$ by $L(n, a, b, i)$. Therefore the ordering of $\hat{y}[dp(y) \leq n + 2]$ isof type $\varepsilon(/j/, n + 1)$.

(iv) follows by induction. Therefore we infer

(v) If $i = sc_n(j)$, and $L(n, a, b, j)$ has type $\varepsilon_{/j/}$, then $L(n, a, b, i)$ has type $\varepsilon_{/i/}$.

(vi) If $Lim_n(i)$, and for each m $L[n, a, b, lim_n(m, i)]$ is of type $\varepsilon_{/lim_n(m,i)/}$, then $L(n, a, b, i)$ is of type $\varepsilon_{/i/}$.

For $L(n, a, b, i)$ is so constructed that its type will be the limit of $\sum_{i=0}^{m} \varepsilon_{/lim_n(m,i)/}$. Since if $\alpha < \beta$,

$\varepsilon_\alpha + \varepsilon_\beta = \varepsilon_\beta$, it follows that the type of L(n, a, b, i) is $\lim_m \varepsilon_{/\lim_n(m,i)/} = \varepsilon_{\lim_m/\lim_n(m,i)/} = \varepsilon_{/i/}$.

It follows by transfinite induction on $<_n$ that L(n, a, b, i) is of type $\varepsilon_{/i/}$ for every i.

We note that in spite ofthe reference in the defini-tion of L(n, a, b, i) to L(n, a, b, j) for numbers $j <_n i$, the definition of L(n, a, b, i) can be so reduced as to be primitive recursive in Suc_n, $pred_n$, Lim_n, and lim_n. For in view of the fact that $\nu_2^1(a)$, $\nu_2^2(a)$, $(a)_x$, and any x such that $(a)_x \neq 0$ are less than a (at least unless a = 0, 1), the determination of L(n, a, b, i) can be reduced to the determination of $L(n, a_m, b_m, j_m)$, where $a_m < a$, $b_m < b$, and a_m, b_m, j_m are given primitive recursively in Suc_n, etc. from a, b, i. Therefore def. 44a is a course-of-values recursion in which the para-meters are varied. If we combine the results of Péter §3 and §5, we see that this can be reduced to a primitive recursion.

<u>Definition 44b.</u> $a <_{n+1} b \equiv: \nu_2^1(a) <_n \nu_2^1(b) \vee.$ $\nu_2^1(a) = \nu_2^1(b) \;\&\; L[n, \nu_2^2(a), \nu_2^2(b), sc_n(\nu_2^1(a))]$.

By transfinite induction on $<_n$, we show that if the type of $a <_{n+1} b \;\&\; \nu_2^1(b) <_n i$ is $\varepsilon_{/i/}$.

If $Suc_n(i)$, then by (v) and the hypothesis of induction, it is $\varepsilon_{/pred_n(i)/} + \varepsilon_{/sc_n[pred_n(i)]/} = \varepsilon_{/i/}$.

If $Lim_n(i)$, the type of $a <_{n+1} b \,\&\, \nu_2^1(b) <_n lim_n(m, i)$ is, by hypothesis of induction, $\varepsilon_{/lim_n(m,i)/}$. The type of $a <_{n+1} b \,\&\, \nu_2^1(b) <_n i$ is the limit of this, namely $\varepsilon_{/i/}$.

Therefore the claim holds in general. It follows that if the type of $<_n$ is $\varepsilon^n(\alpha)$, then the type of $<_{n+1}$ is $\lim_{\beta<\varepsilon^n(\alpha)} \varepsilon_\beta = \varepsilon_{\varepsilon^n(\alpha)} = \varepsilon^{n+1}(\alpha)$. (We use the fact that $\varepsilon^n(\alpha)$ is a limit number.)

In order to complete the induction step, we must define $Suc_{n+1}(i)$, etc. This is done by the intermediacy of corresponding functions and predicates forthe orderings $L(n, a, b, i)$.

<u>Definition 44c</u>. $Suc(n, a, i) \equiv a = 1 \lor 2 \mid a$ if $i = 0$;

$\equiv a = 1 \lor Suc[n, (a)_0, pred_n(i)]$ if $Suc_n(i)$;

$\equiv Suc[n, \nu_2^2(a), lim_n(\nu_2^1(a), i)]$ if $Lim_n(i)$.

<u>Definition 44d</u>. $sc(n, a, i) = 1$ if $i = 0$, $a = 0$,

$= 2a$ if $i = 0$, $a \neq 0$;

$= \prod_{i \neq 0} \mathfrak{p}_i^{(a)_i} \cdot 2^{sc[n, (a)_0, pred_n(i)]}$ if $Suc_n(i)$ &

$a \neq 0$,

$= 1$ if $Suc_n(i)$ & $a = 0$;

$= \nu_2\{\nu_2^1(a),\ sc[n,\ \nu_2^2(a),\ lim_n(\nu_2^1(a),\ i)]\}$

if $Lim_n(i)$.

Definition 44e. $pred(n, a, i) = a/2$

if $i = 0$ & $2|a$,

$= 0$ if $i = 0 \vee Suc_n(i)$.& $a = 1$,

$= \prod_{i \neq 0} p_i^{(a)_i} \cdot 2^{pred[n, (a)_0, pred_n(i)]}$

if $Suc_n(i)$ & $a \neq 1$;

$= \nu_2\{\nu_2^1(a),\ pred[n,\ \nu_2^2(a),\ lim_n(\nu_2^1(a),\ i)]\}$ if $Lim_n(i)$.

Definition 44f. $Lim(n, a, i) \equiv . a \neq 0$ & $- Suc(n, a, i)$

Definition 44g. $lim(n, m, a, i) = \prod p_i^{h_o(n,m,a,i,j)}$

if $i = 0 \vee Suc_n(i)$, where if we set $r_{ni}(a) =$ $\mu x\{x \leq ln(a)$ & $(a)_x \neq 0$ & $(y)[y \leq ln(a)$ & $(a)_y \neq 0. \supset$ $L(n, x, y, i).\}$ $, x = y]\}$, then we have

$h_o(n, m, a, i, j) = (a)_j$ if $L[n, r_{ni}(a), j, i]$;

moreover if $i = 0$ then

$h_o(n, m, a, i, j) = (a)_j - 1$ if $r_{ni}(a) = j$

$= m$

if $Suc[n, r_{ni}(a), 0]$ & $j = pred[n, r_{ni}(a), 0]$,

$= 1$

if $Lim[n, r_{ni}(a), 0]$ & $i = lim[n, m, r_{ni}(a), 0]$ (we note that $r_{ni}(a) < a$);

$= 0$ otherwise;

if $Suc_n(i)$ then

$h_o(n, m, a, i, j) = \text{pred}[n, (a)_j, \text{pred}_n(i)]$

if $j = r_{ni}(a)$ & $\text{Suc}[n, (a)_j, \text{pred}_n(i)]$,

$= \lim[n, m, (a)_j, \text{pred}_n(i)]$,

if $j = r_{ni}(a)$ & $\text{Lim}[n, (a)_j, \text{pred}_n(i)]$,

$= \text{sc}[n, 0, \text{pred}_n(i)]$

if $\text{Suc}[n, (a)_{r_{ni}(a)}, \text{pred}_n(i)]$ & $\text{Lim}[n, r_{ni}(a), i]$ &
$j = \lim[n, m, r_{ni}(a), i]$,

$= \text{ub}[n, m, \text{pred}_n(i)]$

if $\text{Suc}[n, (a)_{r_{ni}(a)}, \text{pred}_n(i)]$ & $\text{Suc}[n, r_{ni}(a), i]$ &
$j = \text{pred}[n, r_{ni}(a), i]$,

$= 0$ otherwise;

if $\text{Lim}_n(i)$ then

$$\lim(n, m, a, i) = \nu_2\{\nu_2^1(a), \lim[n, m, \nu_2^2(a), \lim_n(\nu_2^1(a), i)]\}$$
$$\text{if } \nu_2^2(a) \neq 0 ,$$
$$= \nu_2\{\nu_2^1(a) - 1, \text{ub}[n, m, \lim_n(\nu_2^1(a) - 1, i)]\}$$
$$\text{if } \nu_2^1(a) \neq 0 \text{ \& } \nu_2^2(a) = 0 \text{ ..}$$

<u>Definition 44h</u>.. $\text{ub}(n, 0, 0) = 1$

$\text{ub}(n, m + 1, 0) = \varphi_{\text{ub}(n,m,0)}$;

$\text{ub}(n, 0, i) = 1$

$\text{ub}(n, m + 1, i) = \varphi_{\text{ub}(n,m,i)}^{\text{sc}[n, 0, \text{pred}_n(i)]}$

if $\text{Suc}_n(i)$;

$\text{ub}(n, m, i) = \nu_2(m, 0)$ if $\text{Lim}_n(i)$ ..

<u>Definition 44i</u>.. $sc_{n+1}(a) = \nu_2[\nu_2^1(a),\ sc(n, \nu_2^2(a), sc_n[\nu_2^1(a)])]$ ..

<u>Definition 44j</u>.. $Suc_{n+1}(a) \equiv Suc\{n, \nu_2^2(a),\ sc_n[\nu_2^1(a)]\}$

<u>Definition 44k</u>.. $pred_{n+1}(a) = pred\{n, \nu_2^2(a),\ sc_n[\nu_2^1(a)]\}$

<u>Definition 44</u>.. $Lim_{n+1}(a) \equiv : Lim\{n, \nu_2^2(a),\ sc_n[\nu_2^1(a)]\}$ v. . $\nu_2^1(a) \neq 0\ \&\ \nu_2^2(a) = 0$

<u>Definition 44m</u>.. $lim_{n+1}(m, a) = \nu_2\{\nu_2^1(a),$ $lim[n, m, \nu_2^2(a),\ sc_n(\nu_2^1(a))]\}$ if $\nu_2^2(a) \neq 0$,

$= \nu_2\{pred_n[\nu_2^1(a)],\ ub[n, m, pred_n(sc_n[\nu_2^1(a)])]\}$

if $\nu_2^2(a) = 0\ \&\ Suc_n[\nu_2^1(a)]$,

$= \nu_2\{lim_n[m, \nu_2^1(a)],\ 0\}$

if $\nu_2^2(a) = 0\ \&\ Lim_n[\nu_2^1(a)]$ ..

<u>Definition 44n</u>. $ub_{n+1}(m) = \nu_2[ub_n(m),\ 0]$

On the primitive recursiveness of $Suc(n, a, i)$, $Lim(n, a, i)$, $pred(n, a, i)$, $lim(n, m, a, i)$, and $sc(n, a, i)$, the same considerations apply as for $L(n, a, b, i)$; see above, page 204..

By induction on n , we have for each n an ordering $<_n$ such that $a = 0$ (in which case $a \leq_n b$ for all b) or $Suc_n(a)$, in which case if $b <_n a$, then $b \leq_n pred_n(a)$, or $Lim_n(a)$, in which case if $b <_n a$, then there is an m such that $b <_n lim_n(m, a)$. The proofs of these facts are more or less mechanical and will not be given. We observe that $<_n$ is primitive recursive also in n.

Definition 45. The ordinal recursive functionals of level n with respect to a given primitive recursive well-ordering $<_0$ are the functionals defined from initial primitive recursive functions by the schemata of explicit definition ((a), page 123), the schema (1) on page 119, the schema of primitive recursion, and the ordinal recursion schema of page 124 for each $p \leq n$, with $o'(p, n, m)$ replaced by the function

$$o''(p, n, m) = 1 \text{ if } n <_p m$$
$$= 0 \text{ otherwise.}$$

Definition 46. The ordinal recursive functionals of level n and degree p with respect to a given well-ordering $\underset{1}{<}$ are the ordinal recursive functionals of level n with respect to the ordering $\underset{p}{<}$ (of def. 31) on $\underset{1}{<}$.

If $\underset{1}{<}$ is unspecified, we assume it is the one defined on page 125, of type ω^2.

The ordinal recursive functionals of level n and degree ω are the ordinal recursive functionals of level n with respect to the ordering $L(n, a, b, 0)$ as $<_0$, of type ε_0.

3. Ramified analysis with induction

We now consider systems $RA(Z_0)$ where Z_0 is an elementary number theory with induction. Let $RA^n(Z_0)$ be the subsystem of $RA(Z_0)$ obtained by restricting the apllication of the induction rule to formulae of level $\leq n$. Let $RA^n_p(Z_0)$ be the subsystem (whose class of theorems is not closed under logical implication) obtained by restricting the application of both the induction rule and the cut to formulae of level $< n$ or level n and binding degree $\leq p$.

We now prove a theorem which gives, for formulae of number theory provable in $RA(Z_0)$, the information given for theorems of Z_0 by theorem 13.

Theorem 17. If Z_0 is any elementary number theory with induction, then $RA(Z_0)$ is uniformly 1*-consistent.

Given formulae

$$(Ex)A(f_1 \ldots f_k, a_1 \ldots a_m, x) \tag{1}$$

where $A(\overline{f}, \overline{a}, x)$ is a quantifier-free formula of Z_0, a functional ordinal recursive of level n and degree $q + 1$ in a function which enumerates the functions expressed by function symbols of Z_0 will enumerate all functionals

$$F(\overline{f}, \overline{a}) = \mu x A(\overline{f}, \overline{a}, x) \tag{2}$$

for which (1) is provable in $RA^n_q(Z_0)$. A functional of level n and degree ω in a function which enumerates the functions expressed by function symbols of Z_0 will enumerate all functionals (2) for which (1) is provable in $RA^n(Z_0)$.

Given a proof of (1) in $RA(Z_0)$, we can effectively find numbers n, q, r such that F isordinal recursive of level n and degree q with respect to an ordering $<_1$ of type $\omega_q(\omega \cdot r)$, in given functions of Z_0 .

Proof. The method is essentially the same as that of theorem 13.

Lemma 17.1. If C is a formula provable in $RA^n(Z_0)$, then it has a proof, given primitive recursively from the original proof, in which no cut has level more than n .

Proof. The argument forlemma 13.1 goes through with the variables and terms x_1, t_1 including class variables and class terms.

We note that if $B(a, \overline{X}, \overline{b})$ is an induction formula of the original proof, the cuts introduced by the transformation are on formulae of the form $B(a, \overline{T}, \overline{t})$ where class and number terms have been substituted for certainclass and number variables of the original induction formula. Although this formula has no greater level than the formula $B(a, \overline{X}, \overline{b})$, it may well have greater binding degree.

In order to apply the normal form theorem in the argument, we appeal to theorem 16.

We note finally that if q is the maximum binding degree of inductions and cuts of level n in the reduced proof, then the reduced proof is a proof in $RA^n_q(Z_0)$.
Thus we have

<u>Lemma 17.2</u>. Given a proof of a formula C in $RA(Z_o)$ with number a , we can primitive recursively find numbers n, q such that C is provable in $RA_q^n(Z_o)$.

Let $q = p^*(a)$ and let the number of the reduced proof be rp(a) .

The "system" $RA(S_o)$ is defined from $RA(Z_o)$ in the same way as S_o was defined from Z_o by adding infinite induction in place of ordinary induction and the conven tion that replacing closed numerical terms in axioms by other such terms yields new axioms. As before, we carry out our discussion relative to a given substitution for $f_1 \ldots f_k$, $a_1 \ldots a_m$, and adopt the same way of treating the function symbols of Z_o (see above, pp. 137-9).

Then we have

<u>Lemma 17.3</u>. There is a primitive recursive functional $Sp(\bar{f}, \bar{a}, b)$ which gives for each proof in $RA(Z_o)$ with number b of a formula C , a proof in $RA(S_o)$ of C with cuts only on formulae of level and binding degree no greater than those of cut formulae and induction formulae ofthe given proof.

<u>Proof</u>. Same as that of lemma 13.2.

The assignment of orders to the lines of the "proofs" in $RA(S_o)$ is handled in the same way as in S_o (we note that the class bindings and generalizations and the abstractions count as constructional inferences, so that the order of their conclusions will be greater than that of their premisses). If n is the maximum number of inductions in any branch of a given proof in $RA(Z_0)$, then the proof can be mapped into a proof in $RA(S_0)$ of order $< \omega \cdot (n + 1)$.

<u>Lemma 17.4</u>. There is a functional $\sigma_1(a, b, n)$, primitive recursive in the function which represents addition in whatever numerical representation of the orders we use, such that if a is the number of a proof in $RA(S_0)$ of a formula C , in which no cut has level more than n and no cut of level n has top degree more than b , then $\sigma_1(a, b, n)$ is the number of a proof of C in which no cut formula of level n is a negation, an alternation, or of the form $t \varepsilon \hat{x}A(x)$. If α is the order of the given proof, then the order of the new proof is $\leq \alpha \cdot 2^b$.

<u>Proof</u>. We define the functional ρ_1 as in the proof of lemma 13.3, except that r is now like the top degree except that it is 0 for any quantification, so that it increases with negations, alternations, and formulae $t \varepsilon \hat{x}A(x)$. Cases 4b and 4c (pp. 143-5) are taken only if the cut formula is of level n . We add the case

5. $\mathcal{A}$ is $t \varepsilon \hat{x}\mathcal{B}(x)$. Let $\beta_1, \beta_2 < \alpha$ be the orders of the proofs of the premisses of the cut, $\mathcal{R} \vee t \varepsilon \hat{x}\mathcal{B}(x)$ and $t \not\varepsilon \hat{x}\mathcal{B}(x) \vee \mathcal{S}$ respectively. By hypothesis of induction, we obtain reduced proofs of these formulae of orders $\leq \beta_1 \cdot 2, \beta_2 \cdot 2$ respectively.

Then we can obtain proofs of $\mathcal{R} \vee \mathcal{B}(t)$ and $-\mathcal{B}(t) \vee \mathcal{S}$ with these orders and the properties of reduced proofs. (See above, p. 197; the transformation is accomplished by the functionals φ_{11} and φ_{12} of appendix I, def. 40.) In order to avoid the possibility that a free variable of t should be captured by a quantifier of $\mathcal{B}(x)$, we need the devide, adopted in appendix I, of making the classes of free and bound variables disjoint; see below, pp. 264-6.

Finally we set

$$\sigma_1(a, 0, n) = a$$

$$\sigma_1(a, c + 1, n) = \rho_1[\sigma_1(a, c, n)] .$$

Then if the above-mentioned degree outside the outermost qunatifier in cuts of level n in a is r, in $\sigma_1(a, c, n)$ it is $r \dot{-} c$, and the order of $\sigma_1(a, c, n)$ is $\leq \alpha \cdot 2^c$. Then clearly the cuts of level n in $\sigma_1(a, b, n)$ have the required property.

We note that addition ($\beta \cdot 2 = \beta + \beta$) and the obviously primitive recursive maximum function are the only ordinal operations used in defining the function ρ_1. See appendix I, def. 42.

<u>Lemma 17.5</u>. There is a functional $\sigma_2(a, n, b)$ such that if a is the number of a proof in $RA(S_0)$ of a formula C, with no cuts of level more than n, or of level n

and binding degree more than q or top degree more than b (if these hold, we say that the proof is of level n, binding degree q, and top degree b), then $\sigma_2(a, b, n)$ is the number of a proof of C of level $\leq n \dot{-} 1$ or of or of level n and binding degree $< q$ (and top degree $< b$), in both cases of order $\leq \omega^{\alpha \cdot 2^b}$.

σ_2 is primitive recursive in the functions which represent ordinal addition and $\lambda \alpha\, \omega^\alpha$.

Proof. Similar to lemma 13.4. We define a function $\rho_2(a, n)$ such that if a is the number of a proof of C of order α, then $\rho_2(a, n)$ is the number of a proof of C in which the outermost quantifier of every truth-functionally simple cut formula of level n has been pared off, of order ω^α.

The induction on the construction of the proof is the same as in the proof of lemma 13.4, except for case 4.

4. C is the conclusion of a cut

$$\frac{\mathcal{R} \vee \mathcal{A} \qquad -\mathcal{A} \vee \mathcal{S}}{\mathcal{R} \vee \mathcal{S}}$$

where the orders of the proofs of $\mathcal{R} \vee \mathcal{A}$ and $-\mathcal{A} \vee \mathcal{S}$ are β_1 and β_2 respectively, $< \alpha$.

a. $\mathcal{A}$ is of level $< n$, or a numerical prime formula, or of the form $-\mathcal{B}$, or of the form $\mathcal{B} \vee \mathcal{B}'$. Then the argument is the same as case 3.

b. $\mathcal{A}$ is of level n and of the form $(x)\mathcal{B}(x)$.

The argument is the same as for case 4b of lemma 13.4, except that in computing the orders $\lambda\alpha\, 2^{\alpha}_{c}$ is replaced by $\lambda\alpha\, \omega^{\alpha}$. By definitions 40 and 41, the binding degree and top degree are reduced.

c. $\mathcal{A}$ is of the form $(Ex)\mathcal{B}(x)$. The same change from case 4c of lemma 13.4.

d. $\mathcal{A}$ is of the form $(X)\mathcal{B}(X)$. By the hypothesis of induction, we obtain from the given proof of $-\mathcal{A} \vee \mathcal{S}$ a reduced proof of it of order β_2. Consider the <u>Formelbund</u> of $-(X)\mathcal{B}(X)$ in this proof. The highest formulae in it are either the principal formulae of weakenings or are principal formulae of bindings

$$\frac{-\mathcal{B}^*(T) \vee \mathcal{N}}{-(X)\mathcal{B}^*(X) \vee \mathcal{N}} \tag{3}$$

From the given proof of $\mathcal{R} \vee (X)\mathcal{B}(X)$, of order β_1, we obtain the reduced proof of order $\leq \omega^{\beta_1}$. From this we can obtain a proof of order $\leq z + \omega^{\beta_1}$, for some finite z, of $\mathcal{R} \vee \mathcal{B}^*(T)$ (see appendix I, def. 37; the reason for the addition of z is that substitution of T for a variable in the proof means that axioms $s \notin Y \vee s \in Y$ are replaced by formulae $s \notin T^* \vee s \in T^*$, to which proofs (of bounded finite order) have to be appended). Since $\mathcal{R} \vee (X)\mathcal{B}(X)$ is not an axiom, $\beta_1 \neq 0$, and therefore ω^{β_1} is infinite. Therefore $z + \omega^{\beta_1} = \omega^{\beta_1}$, and our proof is of the latter order. We replace (3) by

$$\frac{\mathcal{R} \vee \mathcal{B}*(T) \qquad - \mathcal{B}*(T) \vee \mathcal{N}}{\mathcal{R} \vee \mathcal{N}} \qquad (4)$$

and in the proof below it leading to $-\mathcal{A} \vee \mathcal{S}$, replace the formulae of the Formelbund of $-\mathcal{A}$ by $\mathcal{R}$. The result is a proof of $\mathcal{R} \vee \mathcal{S}$. If the conclusion of (3) has order γ, we give to the conclusion of (4) the order $\omega^{\beta_1} + \gamma$, and add ω^{β_1} to the order of all succeeding lines. Then the cuts (4) satisfy the condition that the order of their conclusions should be greater than those of their premisses. If there are inferences (4) above the one at which we are operating, then the right premiss of (4) will have order $< \omega^{\beta_1} + \gamma$, the left order ω^{β_1} ; since $\gamma > 0$, $\omega^{\beta_1} + \gamma$ is greater than the order of either premiss.

Then the order of the last line $\mathcal{R} \vee \mathcal{S}$ is $\omega^{\beta_1} + \omega^{\beta_2} \leq \omega^{\max(\beta_1,\beta_2)} + \omega^{\max(\beta_1,\beta_2)} \leq \omega^{\max(\beta_1,\beta_2)+1} \leq \omega^{\alpha}$.

It follows from lemma 16.1 that either the levels of the cuts introduced are all less than that of the one removed, or their levels are the same and their binding degrees are less. In the latter case, the proof of lemma 16.1 shows that the top degrees are also less.

e. $\mathcal{A}$ is of the form $(EX)\mathcal{B}(X)$. Similarly. We consider the Formelbund of $(EX)\mathcal{B}(X)$ in the reduced proof of the left premiss, and from the proof of $-(EX)\mathcal{B}(X) \vee$ we obtain proofs of formulae $-\mathcal{B}*(T) \vee \mathcal{S}$.

f. $\mathcal{A}$ is of the form $t \varepsilon \hat{x}\,\mathcal{B}(x)$. The argument is the same as case 3.

g. $\mathcal{A}$ is a prime formula $t \varepsilon Y$, where Y is of level n. By hypothesis of induction, we have a reduced proof of $t \notin Y \vee \mathcal{S}$ of order $\omega^{\beta}2$. The tops of the Formelbund of $t \notin Y$ are either in principal formulae of weakenings or inaxioms. Axioms of the form

$$t^* \notin Y \vee s \varepsilon Y \qquad (5)$$

where s and t^* have the same numerical value, suffice to deduce all the other axioms in volving Y. For these are formulae obtained by replacing numerical terms by others of the same value from

$$s \notin Y \vee s \varepsilon Y$$

$$s \neq t \vee s \notin Y \vee r \varepsilon Y$$

The cases of the second for closed terms can be deduced with order 1 from axioms (5) or true formulae $s \neq r$, which we can also add as axioms. Therefore we can obtain any such axiom from axioms (5) with order 2, by a single infinite induction. Hence we can eliminate them.

In the cases of (5) in which $t^* \notin Y$ is in the Formelbund of $t \notin Y$, t^* is obtained from t by substituting numerals for variables. By the hypothesis of induction, we obtain a reduced proof of $\mathcal{R} \vee t^* \varepsilon Y$ and can from this obtain one of $\mathcal{R}^* \vee t^* \varepsilon Y$ (see appendix I, def. 34), and therefore one of $\mathcal{R}^* \vee s \varepsilon Y$ by replacement (appendix I, def. 32). If we use this formula with its proof in place of (5), and replace each formula of the Formelbund of $t \notin Y$ by the corresponding substitution-case of $\mathcal{R}$, we obtain a proof of $\mathcal{R} \vee \mathcal{S}$ from which the cut has been eliminated.

We assign to each line into which a case of $\mathcal{R}$ has been introduced in this way the order $\omega^{\beta_1} + 2 + \gamma$, if it original order was γ. By the same argument as in case 4b, we see that the rules for orders are obeyed, and that the order of $\mathcal{R} \vee \mathcal{S}$ in the new proof is $\omega^{\beta_1} + 2 + \omega^{\beta_2}$. If $-\mathcal{A} \vee \mathcal{S}$ is not an axiom, then, this is $\omega^{\beta_1} + \omega^{\beta_2}$ since $\beta_2 \neq 0$ and ω^{β_2} is infinite. If $\beta_2 = 0$ and $\beta_1 \neq 0$, then $\omega^{\beta_1} + 2 + \omega^{\beta_2} = \omega^{\beta_1} + 3 < \omega^{\beta_1 + 1} = \omega^{\max(\beta_1, \beta_2) + 1} = \omega^{\alpha}$.

For the arithmetical details of the definition of ρ_2, see appendix I, def. 43.

Now let $\sigma_2(a, b, n) = \rho_2[\sigma_1(a, b, n), n]$. The proof obtained by applying σ_1 is such that a cut of level n in it is on a formula which is truth-functionally simple and is not of the form $t \varepsilon \hat{x} \mathcal{B}(x)$, and is a proper sub-formula (or obtained from one by replacement of numerical terms) of a cut formula of the original proof. Then ρ_2 removes theoutermost quantifier of any cut formula of level n which is of the form of a quantification and again introduces cuts on proper subformulae. Thus by lemma 16.1, if the binding degree is $\neq 0$, then either it is reduced without increasing the level, or the level is reduced. If the binding degree is 0 and the level $\neq 0$, then by lemma 16.1 and the fact that σ_2 also eliminates cuts on formulae $t \varepsilon Y$ of level n, the level is reduced. If the binding degree and level are both 0, then neither is increased; in fact it is plain that the only cuts remaining in this case are on numerical prime formulae.

The order condition follows from those on σ_1 and ρ_2.

Lemma 17.6. There is a functional $\sigma_3(a, b, n, q)$ such that if a is the number of a proof in $RA(S_0)$ of a formula C, of order α, level n, binding degree q, and top degree b, then $\sigma_3(a, b, n, q)$ is the number of a proof of C of level $< n$ if $n \neq 0$, and with cuts only on numerical prime formulae if $p = 0$, of order $\leq \omega_q(\alpha \cdot 2^{b+1})$.

Proof. This is proved by induction on q. If $q = 0$, then by lemma 17.5, $\sigma_2(a, b, n)$ is the number of a proof of C of level $< n$ if $n \neq 0$; if $n = 0$, the cuts remaining are all on numerical prime formulae. The order is $\omega^{\alpha \cdot 2^b} = \omega_1(\alpha \cdot 2^b) < \omega_1(\alpha \cdot 2^{b+1})$.

Suppose that $q = p + 1$. Then by lemma 17.5 $\sigma_2(a, b, n)$ is the number of a proof of order $\leq \omega^{\alpha \cdot 2^b}$ of level $< n$ or of level n and binding degree p. By the hypothesis of induction, $\sigma_3[\sigma_2(a, b, n), n, b, p]$ is the number of a proof of C of level $< p$ (or if $n = 0$, wiht cuts only on numerical prime formulae) and order $\omega_p(\omega^{\alpha \cdot 2^b} \cdot 2^{b+1}) \leq \omega_p(\omega^{\alpha \cdot 2^{b+1}}) = \omega_{p+1}(\alpha \cdot 2^{b+1})$ (cf. lemma 13.5).

Then the lemma will hold if we set

$\sigma_3(a, b, n, 0) = \sigma_2(a, b, n)$

$\sigma_3(a, b, n, p + 1) = \sigma_3[\sigma_2(a, b, n), b, n, p]$.

Since it is primitive recursive in σ_2, σ_3 is, by lemma 17.5, primitive recursive in the functions representing ordinal addition and $\lambda\alpha\, \omega^\alpha$.

<u>Lemma 17.7</u>. There is a functional $\sigma_4(a, n)$ such that if a is the number of a proof of a formula C in $RA(S_0)$, of order $\leq \alpha$ and level n (the binding degrees and top degrees of cuts of level n may in this case be unbounded), then $\sigma_4(a, n)$ is the number of a proof of C of level $< n$ if $n \neq 0$, and with cuts only on numerical prime formulae if $n = 0$, of order $\leq \varepsilon_\alpha$.

σ_4 is primitive recursive in the functions representing ordinal addition and $\lambda\alpha\, \omega^\alpha$, and $\lambda\alpha\, \varepsilon_\alpha$.

<u>Proof</u>. By induction on the construction of the proof.

1. C is an axiom. Then $\sigma_4(a, n) = a$.

2. C is the conclusion of a structural inference. Then the proof of the premiss has order α and level n. By the hypothesis of the induction we obtain a reduced

proof of the premiss of order $\leq \varepsilon_\alpha$ and satisfying the conditions on the level. The same inference yields a proof of C satisfying these conditions.

3. C is the condlusion of a constructional inference, infinite induction, cut of level $< n$, or cut on a numerical prime formula. Then by the hypothesis of induction, if $\beta < \alpha$ is the order of the given proof of some premiss, we can obtain a reduced proof of the same premiss with order $\leq \varepsilon_\beta < \varepsilon_\alpha$. Then the same inference yields a reduced proof of C of order $\leq \varepsilon_\alpha$.

4. C is the conclusion of a cut of level n. Suppose the top degree of this cut is b and its binding degree is q ($\leq b$). If the orders of the proofs of the premkses are α_1, α_2, then by the hypothesis of induction we can obtain reduced proofs of these premisses with orders $\leq \varepsilon_{\alpha_1}$ and ε_{α_2} respectively. If $n = 0$, these proofs have binding and top degrees 0; if $n \neq 0$, they have no cuts of level n.

In either case, the proof of C obtained by appending the given cut to the reduced proofs of the premisses has level n, <u>finite</u> binding degree q and top degree b. It can be assigned the order $\varepsilon_\mu + 1$, where $\mu = \max(\alpha_1, \alpha_2)$. If a_1 is the number of this proof, then $\sigma_4(a, n) = \sigma_3(a_1, b, n, q)$; i. e. we apply lemma 17.6 to obtaina proof of C of level $< p$ and order $\leq \omega_q[(\varepsilon_\mu + 1) \cdot 2^{b+1}] <$

$\varepsilon_{q+1}(\varepsilon_\mu + 1) < \varepsilon_{\mu+1} \leq \varepsilon_\alpha$, since $\mu + 1 \leq \alpha$.

It is clear that σ_4 is primitive recursive in σ_3 and the functions representing addition, $\lambda\alpha\, \omega^\alpha$, and $\lambda\alpha\, \varepsilon_\alpha$, and is therefore primitive recursive in the mentioned functions.

Lemma 17.8. There is a functional $\sigma_5(a, b, n, q)$ such that if a is the number of a proof of a formula C in $RA(S_0)$ of order α , level n , binding degree q , and top degree b , then $\sigma_5(a, b, n, q)$ is the number of a proof of C with cuts only on numerical prime formulae, of order $\leq \varepsilon^n[\omega_q(\alpha \cdot 2^{b+1})]$.

Proof. By lemma 17.6, if $n = 0$ the claim holds if we set $\sigma_5(a, b, 0, q) = \sigma_3(a, b, 0, q)$.

If $n = m + 1$, then by lemma 17.6, $\sigma_3(a, b, n, q)$ is the number of a proof of C of level $\leq m$, of order $\omega_q(\alpha \cdot 2^{b+1})$. If we apply σ_4 n times, then we shall by lemma 17.7 obtain a proof of C with cuts only on numerical prime formulae and order $\leq \varepsilon^n[\omega_q(\alpha \cdot 2^{b+1})]$; i. e. we set

$$\sigma_4'(a, 0) = \sigma_4(a, 0)$$

$$\sigma_4'(a, m + 1) = \sigma_4'[\sigma_4(a, m + 1), m]$$

Then if a is the number of a proof of order β and level 0 , then $\sigma_4'(a, 0)$ has order $\leq \varepsilon_\beta$ and cuts only on numerical prime formulae; if a is the number of a proof of order β and level $m + 1$, then $\sigma_4(a, m + 1)$ has order

ε_β and level $\leq m$; we can suppose that $\sigma_4'[\sigma_4(a, m+1), m]$ has order $\leq \varepsilon^{m+1}(\varepsilon_\beta) = \varepsilon^{m+2}(\beta)$ and cuts only on numerical prime formulae.

Finally we set

$$\sigma_5(a, b, 0, q) = \sigma_3(a, b, 0, q)$$

$$\sigma_5(a, b, m+1, q) = \sigma_4'[\sigma_3(a, b, m+1, q), m] .$$

In the case $n = m + 1$, $\sigma_3(a, b, m+1, q)$ has level $\leq m$ and order $\leq \omega_q(\alpha \cdot 2^{b+1})$; by the last paragraph, $\sigma_5(a, b, m+1, q)$ has cuts only on numerical prime formulae and order $\leq \varepsilon^{m+1}[\omega_q(\alpha \cdot 2^{b+1})] = \varepsilon^n[\omega_q(\alpha \cdot 2^{b+1})]$. By induction, σ_5 satisfies the conditions of the lemma.

σ_5 is clearly primitive recursive in σ_3 and σ_4 and is therefore primitive recursive in the functions representing ordinal addition, $\lambda\alpha\, \omega^\alpha$, and $\lambda\alpha\, \varepsilon_\alpha$.

Lemma 17.9. There is a functional $\Gamma_{nq}(a, b, r)$ such that if a is the number of a proof in $RA(S_0)$ with primitive recursive functionals at infinite inductions of the formula (1), of order $\leq \omega \cdot r$, level $\leq n$, binding degree $\leq q$, and top degree $\leq b$, then $\Gamma_{nq}(a, b, r)$ is the number of a cut-free deduction of (1) from true closed numerical formulae in Schütte's predicate calculus (of first order). If (1) has free class variables, the same holds with additional initial formulae $t \notin Y \vee s \in Y$, where s and t are closed terms with the same numerical value, for the free class variables Y occurring in (1).

Γ_{nq} is ordinal recursive of level n and degree $q + 1$ relative to the functions representing ordinal addition, $\lambda\alpha\, \omega^{\alpha}$, and $\lambda\alpha\, \varepsilon_{\alpha}$ in the ordering $<_n$ with $\underset{q+1}{<}$ as initial ordering $<_o$.

<u>Proof</u>. From lemma 17.7 as lemma 13.6 was obtained from lemma 13.5.

By lemma 17.8, the order of the proof given by $\sigma_5(a, b, n, q)$, from which the elimination of infinite inductions and cuts on numerical prime formulae starts, is $\varepsilon^n[\omega_q(\omega \cdot 2^{b+1} r)] < \varepsilon^n[\omega_q(\omega^2)]$. It follows that the orders in terms of which the transformations of lemmas 17.4-7 are carried out, and in terms of which the transfinite induction of the present transformation are carried out, can be represented by natural numbers ordered according to the ordering $<_n$ with $\underset{q+1}{<}$ (of type $\omega_q(\omega^2)$) as the base ordering $<_o$. Therefore the final claim of the lemma follows from the corresponding property of σ_5. See appendix I, def. 46.

<u>Completion of the proof of theorem 17</u>. The deduction obtained by lemma 17.9 does not differ from that obtained by lemma 13.6; hence the rest of the proof is essentially the same as that of theorem 13.

Again by Herbrand's theorem, we can primitive recursively obtain from the proof number $\Gamma_{nq}(a, b, r)$ terms

$t_1 \ldots t_p$, composed of $0, S, f_1 \ldots f_k, a_1 \ldots a_m$, such that

$$A(\bar{f}, \bar{a}, t_1) \vee \ldots \vee A(\bar{f}, \bar{a}, t_p) \qquad (6)$$

is true for the given substitution.

If a is the number of a proof of (1) in $RA^n_q(Z_o)$, let $d^*(a)$ be the maximum top degree of cuts and inductions in the proof; let $q^*(a)$ be the maximum number of inductions in each branch of the proof.

Then by lemma 17.9, $\Gamma_{nq}[Sp[\bar{f}, \bar{a}, a), d^*(a), q^*(a)]$ is the number of a cut-free deduction of (1) from true numerical formulae. Consider the functional

$$\mu x\left\{x \le \max_{1 \le ln[r^*(\Gamma_{nq}[], (a)_o)]}\left(val\left[\bar{f}, \bar{a}, (r^*\{\Gamma_{nq}[Sp(\bar{f}, \bar{a}, a), d^*(a), q^*(a)], (a)_o\})_i\right]\right) \;\&\; Tr(\bar{f}, \bar{a}, ex[(a)_o, x])\right\} \qquad (7)$$

where $val(\bar{f}, \bar{a}, b)$ is the numerical value of the term number b, r^* is a primitive recursive function which searches a cut-free proof from true numerical formulae to find terms $t_1 \ldots t_p$ so (6) is true, $Tr(\bar{f}, \bar{a}, b)$ holds if b is the number of a true numerical formula, and if b is the number of $(Ex)B(x)$, $ex(b, m)$ is the number of $B(0^{(n)})$.

Then as on pp. 156-8, if we add the recursion equations for a function enumerating the given functions of Z_o to the recursion equations for the functional (7), with the variable we have chosen to represent it (see lemma 13.2) as principal function letter, we obtain a definition, ordinal recursive of level n and degree $q + 1$ in the enumerating function and the representations in $<^{n}_{q+1}$ of $\lambda\alpha\beta(\alpha + \beta)$, $\lambda\alpha\, \omega^{\alpha}$, and $\lambda\alpha\, \varepsilon_{\alpha}$, of a functional which enumerates the functionals F satisfying formulae (1) provable in $RA^{n}_{q}(Z_{o})$. We call this H_{nq}.

In appendix II, we prove that if the ordinal operations and certain other functions on $<_{o}$ are primitive recursive, then those on $<_{n+1}$ are ordinal recursive of level n. It follows that H_{nq} is ordinal recursive of level n and degree $q + 1$ in the enumerating function.

If, in the proof of lemma 17.9, we represent the orders of proofs in $RA(S_{o})$ by numbers ordered according to $<_{n}$ for the $<_{o}$ of type ε_{o}, defined $L(n, a, b, Q)$9, then we obtain a functional $\Gamma_{n}(a, b, r, q)$, ordinal recursive of level n and degree ω (simply in view of the last paragraph), of which the claims of lemma 17.9 are now true for variable q.

If a is the number of a proof of (1) in $RA^{n}(Z_{o})$, then $rp(a)$ is, by lemmas 17.1-2, the number of a proof of (1) in $RA^{n}_{p*(a)}(Z_{o})$. Then by lemma 17.3, $Sp[\bar{f}, \bar{a}, rp(a)]$ is the number of a proof of (1) in $RA(S_{o})$ of level n, binding degree $p*(a)$, top degree $d*[rp(a)]$, and order $< \omega \cdot q*[rp(a)]$. Then if in the definition of H_{nq} we replace a by $rp(a)$ [but note that $(a)_{o} = (rp(a))_{o}$]

and Γ_{nq} by $\lambda abr\Gamma_n[a, b, r, p^*(a)]$, we obtain a functional H_q which enumerates all functionals F satisfying formulae (1) provable in $RA^n(Z_o)$. H_q is ordinal recursive of level n and degree ω. Thus $RA^n(Z_o)$ is 1*-consistent, in fact uniformly 1*-consistent.

If the argument is carried out by representing the orders in the ordering

$$a <_\omega b \equiv: \nu_2^1(a) < \nu_2^1(b) \text{ v. } \nu_2^1(a) = \nu_2^1(b) \text{ \& } \nu_2^2(a) <_{\nu_2^1(a)} \nu_2^2(b) ,$$

Then the proof of lemma 17.9 yields a functional $\Gamma(a, b, r, p, n)$, ordinal recursive on this ordering, and the subsequent argument yields a functional H , ordinal recursive on this ordering in the enumerating function, which enumerates the functionals F satisfying formulae (1) prpvable in $RA(Z_o)$. Therefore $RA(Z_o)$ is uniformly 1*-consistent.

Let Γ_{nq}^{br} be the functional $\lambda a\Gamma_{nq}(a, b, r)$. It can be defined by representing the orders in the ordering $<_n$ where now the ordering $<_o$ is the ordering $\underset{q+1}{<}$ for an ordering of type $\omega\cdot 2^{b+1}r$ as $\underset{1}{<}$, so that it is ordinal recursive of level n and degree q + 1 with respect to this ordering. Suppose now that for each function symbol of Z_o which occurs in a given proof in $RA(Z_o)$ of (1), we have a variable representing it. Then if we add to the recursion equations for the functional

$$\mu x\left\{x \leq \max_{i \leq \ln[r^*(\Gamma^{br}_{nq}(), (a)_o)]}\left(\mathrm{val}\left[f, a, (r^*\{\Gamma^{br}_{nq}(\mathrm{Sp}[f, a, \mathrm{rp}(a)]), (a)_o\})_i\right]\right) \;\&\; \mathrm{Tr}(f, a, \mathrm{ex}[(a)_o, x])\right\}$$

(cf. (14), p. 159) the recursion equations for each of these given functions with the chosen variable as principal function letter, then if a is the number of a proof of (1) in $RA^n(Z_o)$ such that $p^*(a) \leq q$, $d^*[\mathrm{rp}(a)] \leq b$, and $q^*[\mathrm{rp}(a)] \leq r$, then the resulting functional satisfies (1) and is ordinal recursive of level n and degree $q + 1$ with respect to the above-mentioned ordering of type $\omega \cdot 2^{b+1}r$, in the given functions of Z_o .

The claims of theorem 17 about representable functionals are provedfrom the above in the same way as were proved the corresponding claims of theorem 13 (see pp. 159-62). This completes the proof of theorem 17.

Suppose now that (1) contains free class variables and perhaps abstraction, but no bound class variables or number quantifiers. Let $A'(f, a, x)$ be the formula obtained from $A(f, a, x)$ by first, for any free class variable X_1 , substituting $\hat{x}[g_1(x) = 0]$, where g_1 is a new free function variable.

Then by lemma 17.9, we can obtain the cut-free proof from true numerical formulae and formulae $t \notin X_1 \vee s \in X_1$ of (1), and by Herbrand's theorem (to which, in view of theorem 16, the presence of free class variables and abstracts is no bar), a cut-free proof in the propositional calculus of §6). By substituting $\hat{x}[g_1(x) = 0]$ for X_1 in this proof, we obtain such a proof of

$$A'(\bar{f}, \bar{a}, t_1) \vee \ldots \vee A'(\bar{f}, \bar{a}, t_p) .$$

Therefore the same types of functionals satisfy

$$(Ex)A'(\bar{f}, \bar{a}, x)$$

as in the case without free class variables and abstracts, given a proof of (1).

By the same arguments as for corollaries 13.1-3 we have

Corollary 17.1. If Z_o is an elementary number theory with induction, then $RA(Z_o)$ is externally consistent.

Corollary 17.2. If Z_o is an elementary number theory with induction, then the system of theorems of $RA(Z_o)$ which are formulae of Z_o has a no-counter-example interpretation by ordinal recursive functionals of finite level and degree in the given functions of Z_o .

Corollary 17.3. RA(Z) is consistent, uniformly 1*-consistent, externally consistent, and its theorems which are formulae of Z have a no-counter-example interpretation by ordinal recursive functionals of finite level and degree.

Finally, we note that if Z_o contains a function which enumerates all functions ordinal recursive of level n and degree q , so that every such function is representable in Z_o^o by a quantifier-free formula, then no new functions are representable by such formulae in $RA^n(Z_o)$ without cuts or inductions of level n and binding degree at least q .

5. Representation of ordinal recursive functionals in ramified analysis

We complete our discussion of the metamathematics of ramified analysis by proving that every ordinal recursive functional of finite level and degree $\leq \omega$ is representable in RA(Z) and provably recursive in $RA(Z_\mu)$. The proof is essentially the same as that of theorem 15, except that the preliminary theorem about the derivability of transfinite inductions is somewhat more complex.

Theorem 18 (cf. Schütte [4], §29). Let $\underset{q}{<}_n$ be the well-ordering $<_n$ on $\underset{q}{<}$ as $<_o$ $(q \neq 0)$; let $<_n$ be the well-ordering $<_n$ with the ordering $<_o$ of p. 209 as $<_o$. Then transfinite induction on a formula of level r and binding degree s with respect to the ordering $\underset{q}{<}_n$ is derivable in $RA^{n+r}(Z_2)$; the same induction with respect to the ordering $<_n$ is derivable in $RA^{n+r+1}(Z_2)$.

Z_2 is the extension of Z of theorem 14, by a symbol and the recursion equations for each primitive recursive function.

Proof. If n = 0 , the claims for $\underset{q}{<}_n$ (in this case

$<_q$) follow from the proof of theorem 14. For regarding the $\mathcal{A}(a)$ of those derivations as a schematic letter, we noted that induction on $<_q$ on $\mathcal{A}(a)$ can be carried out in Z_2^q ; i. e. the most complex induction in the proof is of level 0 and binding degree q . Then substituting $\mathcal{B}(a)$ for $\mathcal{A}(a)$, where $\mathcal{B}(a)$ is a formula of level r and binding degree s , will increase the level to r and the binding degree to $q + s$, since the quantifiers of the schematic derivation will be on the outside of the formula.

We consider an axiom schema of transfinite induction, namely

$$(x)\{(y)[y <^* x \supset A(y)] \supset A(x)\} \supset (x)A(x)$$

which we shall write as $I_{\underline{x}}[A(x), <^*]$. By a generalization on a , the antededent of $I_{\underline{x}}[A(x), <^*]$ is obtainable from the premiss of

$$\frac{(x)[y <^* x \supset A(x)] \supset A(a)}{A(t)} \qquad (8)$$

(cf. def. 38), and therefore from $I_{\underline{x}}[A(x), <^*]$ and the premiss of (8), the conclusion, A(t) , is obtainable by cuts. Therefore with the axiom schema, the rule is a derived rule. In fact, with any given instance of the schema, that instance of the rule is derivable. It follows that it will be sufficient to derive instances of the axiom schema. If X is a class variable of level r , then if we can prove $I_{\underline{x}}[x \in X, <^*]$, we can infer $(X)I_{\underline{x}}[x \in X, <^*]$, which we shall abbreviate as $I_r(<^*)$. Clearly we can derive

$$- I_r(<^*) \vee I_{\underline{x}}[x \varepsilon \hat{y}\mathfrak{A}(y), <^*]$$

and hence $- I_r(<^*) \vee I_{\underline{x}}[\mathfrak{A}(x), <^*]$,[4]

for any formula $\mathfrak{A}(a)$ of level $\leq r$. It follows that if $\mathfrak{A}(a)$ is a formula of level r , then transfinite induction with respect to $<^*$ and $\mathfrak{A}(a)$ is derivable in $RA(Z_0)$ with no more complex inductions than it takes to prove $I_r(<^*)$.

Lemma 18.1. In $RA^{r+1}(Z_2)$ we can derive

$$I_{\underline{r}}[\hat{x}\hat{y}L(n, x, y, 0)] .$$

Proof. If $\underset{1}{<}$ is the ordering $<$ of type ω , then the argument of HB II 361 ff. in effect proves

$$I_{\underline{x}}[B(x), \underset{p+1}{<}] \supset I_{\underline{x}}[A(x), \underset{p+2}{<}] \tag{9}$$

where $B(x)$ is the formula $\mathfrak{B}(x)$ (see p. 165) with the scheamtic formula $A(a)$ for $\mathfrak{A}(a)$. Let $B(X, x)$ be the same formula with $a \varepsilon X$ replacing $\mathfrak{A}(a)$. This formula is of the same level as X , say r . Therefore by (9)

$$I_{\underline{x}}[B(X, x), \underset{p+1}{<}] \supset I_{\underline{x}}[x \varepsilon X, \underset{p+2}{<}]$$

$$I_{\underline{x}}[x \varepsilon \hat{y}B(X, y), \underset{p+1}{<}] \supset I_{\underline{x}}[x \varepsilon X, \underset{p+2}{<}]$$

$$(X)I_{\underline{x}}[x \varepsilon X, \underset{p+1}{<}] \supset (X)I_{\underline{x}}[x \varepsilon X, \underset{p+2}{<}] . \tag{10}$$

All this holds in $RA^r(Z_2)$ with variable p . We can easily derive $I_r(<)$ in $RA^r(Z_2)$. Therefore by (10) and induction we have $I_r(\underset{p}{\leq})$ in $RA^{r+1}(Z_2)$ with variable p .

---

[4] By the two abstraction inferences, $x \notin \hat{y}\mathfrak{A}(y) \vee \mathfrak{A}(x)$ and $- \mathfrak{A}(x) \vee x \varepsilon \hat{y}\mathfrak{A}(y)$ are both derivable, and the interchangeability of $\mathfrak{A}(x)$ and $x \varepsilon \hat{y}\mathfrak{A}(y)$ is therefore provable without induction.

Next we note that if $dp(b) \leq p$, then $L(n, a, b, 0)$ (which we shall write as $a <_o b$) holds if and only if $a \underset{p+2}{<} b$. If $p = 0$, this follows from $0 <_o b \equiv 0 \underset{2}{<} b \equiv b \neq 0$. If $dp(b) \leq p + 1$, then if $(b)_x \neq 0$, $dp(x) \leq p$.

If $a <_o b$, then by (11), p. 201, $dp(a) \leq p + 1$. Let $r = \mu x\{x \leq ln(b) \,\&\, (a)_x < (b)_x \,\&\, (y)[y \leq ln(a) \,\&\, x <_o y. \supset (a)_y = (b)_y]\}$. If $r \underset{p+2}{<} y$, then either $(a)_y = (b)_y = 0$ or $dp(y) \leq p$. In the second case, by hypothesis of induction $r <_o y$, whence $(a)_y = (b)_y$. Therefore $a \underset{p+3}{<} b$.

If $a \underset{p+3}{<} b$ and $dp(b) \leq p + 1$, let $s = \mu x\{x \leq ln(b) \,\&\, (a)_x < (b)_x \,\&\, (y)[y \leq ln(a) \,\&\, x \underset{p+2}{<} y. \supset (a)_y = (b)_y]\}$. By the same argument as for (11) p. 201, $dp(a) \leq p + 1$. Then if $r <_o y$, either $(a)_y = (b)_y = 0$ or $dp(y) \leq p$, in which case by hypothesis of induction $r \underset{p+2}{<} y$, whence $(a)_y = (b)_y$. Therefore $a <_o b$.

The conclusion follows by induction. We can formalize in Z_2 the proof of

$$dp(b) \leq p \supset. a <_o b \supset a \underset{p+2}{<} b . \tag{11}$$

From the forward implication we infer

$$(y)[y \underset{p+2}{<} x \supset. dp(y) \leq p \supset y \varepsilon X] \supset$$
$$(y)[y <_o x \supset. dp(y) \leq p \supset y \varepsilon X] . \tag{12}$$

By (11), p. 201

$$dp(x) \leq p \supset. y <_o x \supset dp(y) \leq p$$

$\supset . R12 \supset (y)[y \mathrel{\underset{-}{<_o}} x \supset y \in X]$

$\supset :(x)\ (y)[y <_o x \supset y \in X] \supset x \in X$

$\supset . R12 \supset x \in X$

$\supset . L12 \supset x \in X$, i. e.

$(x)\{(y)[y \mathrel{\underset{-}{<_o}} x \supset y \in X] \supset x \in X\}$

$$\supset :L12 \supset . dp(x) \leq p \supset x \in X \qquad (13)$$

$L13 \supset (x)[L12 \supset . dp(x) \leq p \supset x \in X]$

from which follows by $I_r(\underset{p}{<})$

$\supset (x)[dp(x) \leq p \supset x \in X]$

$L13 \supset (p)(x)[dp(x) \leq p \supset x \in X]$

$\supset (x)(x \in X)$, i. e. $I_{\underset{-}{x}}[x \in X, <_o]$.

We infer $I_r(<_o)$ by generalization.

Lemma 18.2. In $RA^{r+1}(Z_2)$ we can derive

$$Suc_n(i) \ \& \ I_r\{\hat{x}\hat{y}L[n, x, y, pred_n(i)]\} . \supset I_r[\hat{x}\hat{y}L(n, x, y, i)]$$

Proof. Suppose we let $L[n, a, b, pred_n(i)]$ be $\underset{o}{\leq^*}$ and let $\underset{p+1}{<^*}$ be defined by

$$a \underset{p+1}{<^*} b \equiv : a = 0 \ \& \ b \neq 0 \ .v\ (Ex)\{x \leq ln(b) \ \&$$
$$L[n, (a)_x, (b)_x, pred_n(i)] \ \& \ (y)[y \leq ln(a) \ \& \ x \underset{p}{\leq^*} y \ .$$
$$\supset (a)_y = (b)_y]\} \ .$$

Then by the same argument as in the proof of lemma 18.1 we can show (assuming $Suc_n(i)$, as we shall throughout the proof of this lemma; since Suc_n is primitive recursive, the application of the deduction theorem cannot increase the level of any induction)

$$dp(b) \leq p \supset . L(n, a, b, i) \equiv a \underset{p+1}{<^*} b$$

and then derive $I_r[\hat{x}\hat{y}L(n, x, y, i)]$ from $I_r(\underset{p+1}{<^*})$ with variable p. Then we have in $RA^0(Z_2)$

$$(p)I_r(\underset{p}{<^*}) \supset I_r[\hat{x}\hat{y}L(n, x, y, i)] \qquad (14)$$

$I_r(\underset{p+1}{<^*})$ is derived from $I_r(\underset{0}{\leq^*})$ by an argument similar to that of HB II 361 ff. Let $C(p, x, k)$ be

$$x \neq 0 \;\&\; (y)[y \leq \ln(x) \;\&\; (x)_y \neq 0. \supset \; k \underset{p}{<^*} y] ,$$

and then (cf. HB II 363) let $B(X, k, a)$ be the formula

$$(x)\; C(p, x, k) \;\&\; (y)[y \underset{p+1}{<^*} x \supset y \in X]. \supset (y)[y \underset{p+1}{<^*} x \cdot p_k{}^a \supset y \in X] .$$

Following HB, we say that a is <u>accessible</u> if $(y)[y \underset{p+1}{<^*} a \supset y \in X]$ holds. Then $B(X, k, a)$ says that for any x if all m such that $(x)_m \neq 0$ satisfy $k \underset{p}{<^*} m$, then $x \cdot p_k{}^a$ is accessible. We hope to derive

$$I_r(\underset{0}{\leq^*}) \;\&\; I_r(\underset{p}{\leq^*}) \;\&\; (x)\{(y)[y \underset{p+1}{<^*} x \supset y \in X] \supset x \in X\}. \supset (w)(z)B(X, w, z). \qquad (15)$$

The argument is essentially the same as in HB except that $I_r(\underset{0}{<^*})$ is needed instead of an (implicit) ordinary induction on the exponent a in $B(X, k, a)$.

(i) If m, q are such that for any s, if $(q)_s \neq 0$ then $(z)B(X, s, z)$ holds, and if further $(m)_r \neq 0$, then $s \underset{p}{<^*} r$, then if m is accessible, then mq is accessible.

For if $s_k \underset{p}{<^*} s_{k-1} \underset{p}{<^*} \dots \underset{p}{<^*} s_1$ are the numbers s such that $(q)_s \neq 0$, then since $(z)B(X, s_1, z)$ holds, if m is accessible, then $m \cdot \varphi_{s_1}{}^{(q)}{}_{s_1}$ is accessible (for $C(p, m, s_1)$ follows from the hypothesis). If $i < k$, then clearly if $(m \cdot \prod_{j \leq i} \varphi_{s_j}{}^{(q)}{}_{s_j})_r \neq 0$, then $s_{i+1} \underset{p}{<*} r$. Therefore since $(z)B(s_{i+1}, z)$ holds, if $m \cdot \prod_{j \leq i} \varphi_{s_j}{}^{(q)}{}_{s_j}$ is accessible, then so is $m \cdot \prod_{j \leq i+1} \varphi_{s_j}{}^{(q)}{}_{s_j}$. By induction on i, $m \cdot \prod_{j \leq k} \varphi_{s_j}{}^{(q)}{}_{s_j} = m \cdot q$ is accessible.[5]

(ii) It follows that if $0 \varepsilon X$ and $B(X, k, a)$ holds for every k, a, then every number q is accessible. Since $(1)_r \neq 0$ for no r, the conditions of (i) are satsified for any q. Therefore $1q = q$ is accessible.

(iii) If

$$(x)\{(y)[y \underset{p+1}{\underset{-}{<*}} x \supset y \varepsilon X] \supset x \varepsilon X\} \tag{16}$$

holds, then so does $0 \varepsilon X$. Therefore we have by (ii)

$$(w)(z)B(X, w, z) \supset .16 \supset (x)(y)(y \underset{p+1}{<*} x \supset y \varepsilon X)$$
$$\supset (x)(x \varepsilon X)$$
$$\supset I_{\underset{-}{x}}[x \varepsilon X, \underset{p+1}{<*}] .$$

Hence if we have derived (15), then we have

$$I_r(\underset{o}{\leq*}) \ \& \ I_r(\underset{p}{\leq*}) . \supset I_{\underset{-}{x}}[x \varepsilon X, \underset{p+1}{<*}]$$

$$I_r(\underset{o}{<*}) \supset I_r(\underset{p}{<*}) . \supset . I_r(\underset{o}{<*}) \supset I_r(\underset{p+1}{<*})$$

and therefore by induction and generalization, we have in $RA^{r+1}(Z_2)$

---

[5]The formal induction will be on a formula like $B(X,k,a)$, containing free X but no class quantifiers. It is therefore of level r.

$$I_r(\underset{o}{<^*}) \supset (p)I_r(\underset{p}{<^*}) .$$

Then the conclusion of the lemma follows by (14).

(iv) It remains only to derive (15). We prove

$$16 \ \& \ (w)[w \underset{\bar{p}}{<^*} k \supset (z)B(X, w, z)].$$

$$\supset .(z)[z \underset{o}{\leq^*} a \supset B(X, k, z)] \supset B(X, k, a) . \qquad (17)$$

Suppose x is accessible and if $(x)_j \neq 0$, then $k \underset{p}{<^*} j$. Then if $y \underset{p+1}{<^*} x \cdot p_k{}^a$, then either $y \underset{p+1}{<^*} x$, in which case $y \in X$, or $x \underset{\bar{p}+1}{\leq^*} y \underset{p+1}{<^*} x \cdot p_k{}^a$, in which case $y = x \cdot p_k{}^b \cdot q$, for some q, b such that $b \underset{o}{\leq^*} a$ and if $(q)_m, (x)_j \neq 0$, $m \underset{p}{<^*} j, k$. Clearly $C(p, x, m)$ holds for all such m.

By IR17, i. e. the fact that $B(X, k, z)$ holds for $z \underset{o}{\leq^*} a$, $x \cdot p_k{}^b$ is accessible. Since $(z)B(X, m, z)$ holds for each $m \underset{p}{<^*} k$, by (i) and the last paragraph, it follows that $x \cdot p_k{}^b \cdot q = y$ is accessible, i. e. $(w)[w \underset{\bar{p}+1}{<^*} y \supset w \in X]$. By (16), $y \in X$. Thus we have $(y)[y \underset{p+1}{<^*} x \cdot p_k{}^a \supset y \in X]$ on the assumption of $C(p, x, k)$ and the accessibility of x, i. e. $B(X, k, a)$ holds. This proves (17). Since induction is involved only in the appeal to (i), this proof can be formalized in $RA^r(Z_2)$.

This completes the proof of lemma 18.2.

<u>Lemma 18.6</u>. In $RA^{r+1}(Z_2)$ we can derive

$$Lim_n(i) \ \& \ (u)I_{\bar{r}} \, xyL[n, x, y, lim_n(i)] .$$

$$\supset I_{\bar{r}}[xyL(n, x, y, i)] .$$

Proof. We assume $\text{Lim}_n(1)$. We write $L(n, a, b, 1)$ as $a <^* b$ and $L[n, a, b, \text{lim}_n(m, 1)]$ as $a <^m b$. Then by definition 44a and elementary properties of the pairing functions we have

$$(x)\{(y)[y <^* x \supset y \in X] \supset x \in X\}$$
$$\supset :(y)[\nu_2^1(y) < a \supset y \in X] \qquad (18)$$
$$\supset .(y)[y <^a b \supset \nu_2(a, y) \in X] \supset \nu_2(a, b) \in X .$$

Now evidently

$$I_x[\nu_2(a, x) \in X, <^a] \supset .RR18 \supset RRR18 \qquad (19)$$

so that by (18)

$$L19 \ \& \ L18. \supset .LR18 \supset \nu_2(a, b) \in X$$
$$\supset :LR18 \supset .c = \nu_2(a, b) \supset c \in X$$
$$L19 \ \& \ L18. \supset :LR18 \supset .(Ew)[c = \nu_2(a, w)] \supset c \in X$$
$$\supset .\nu_2^1(c) = a \supset c \in X$$

from which follows

$$L19 \ \& \ L18.$$
$$\supset .(y)[\nu_2^1(y) < a \supset y \in X] \supset (y)[\nu_2^1(y) < Sa \supset y \in X]$$

Since $(y)[\nu_2^1(y) < 0 \supset y \in X]$ is evidently provable, we have by induction on L19 & L18. LR18

$$L19 \ \& \ L18. \supset (y)[\nu_2^1(y) < Sa \supset y \in X]$$
$$\supset \nu_2(a, b) \in X . \qquad (20)$$

The induction formula is clearly of level r . Since $\nu_2(a, x) \in X$ is of level r we have

$I_r(<^a) \supset I_x[\nu_2(a, x) \in X, <^a]$, whence by (20)

$$(u)I_r(<^u) \supset .L18 \supset \nu_2(a, b) \in X$$

from which follows

$$(u)I_r(<^u) \supset .L18 \supset (x)(x \varepsilon \underline{X})\ ,\ \text{i. e.}\ I_x(x \varepsilon X, <*)\ .$$

The conclusion follows by generalization and application of the deduction theorem to remove the premiss $Lim_n(i)$.

Lemma 18.4. In $RA^{r+1}(Z_2)$ we can derive

$$(y)(y <_n i \supset I_{\underline{r}}[\hat{z}\hat{w}L(n, z, w, y)]) \supset I_{\underline{r}}[\hat{z}\hat{w}L(n, z, w, i)]$$

($<_n$ can be relative toany $<_o$). (21)

Proof. From $Suc_n(i) \supset pred_n(i) <_n i$ we infer

$$Suc_n(i) \supset .L21 \supset I_{\underline{r}}\{\hat{z}\hat{w}L[n, z, w, pred_n(i)]\}$$

and then by lemma 18.2

$$\supset .L21 \supset I_{\underline{r}}[\hat{z}\hat{w}L(n, z, w, i)]\ . \qquad (22)$$

From $Lim_n(i) \supset lim_n(m, i) <_n i$ we infer

$$Lim_n(i) \supset .L21 \supset I_{\underline{r}}\{\hat{z}\hat{w}L[n, z, w, lim_n(m, i)]\}$$

from which we infer

$$Lim_n(i) \supset .L21 \supset (u)I_{\underline{r}}\{\hat{z}\hat{w}L[n, z, w, lim_n(u, i)]\}$$

and then by lemma 18.3

$$Lim_n(i) \supset 21\ .$$

Then (21) follows by (22), lemma 18.1, and

$$i = 0 \vee Suc_n(i) \vee Lim_n(i)\ .$$

Lemma 18.5. We can prove without induction

$$I_r(<_n)\ \&\ (u)I_{\underline{r}}[\hat{x}\hat{y}L(n, x, y, u)]. \supset I_r(<_{n+1})\ .$$

Proof. We write $L[n, a, b, sc_n(i)]$ as $a <^i b$. Then by definition 44b and elementary properties of the pairing functions we have

$$(x)\{(y)[y <_{n+1} x \supset y \varepsilon X] \supset x \varepsilon X\} \supset$$

$:(y)[\nu_2^1(y) <_n a \supset y \in X]$ (23)

$\supset.(y)[y <^a b \supset \nu_2(a, y) \in X] \supset \nu_2(a, b) \in X$.

Clearly we have

$(u)I_r(<^u) \supset I_{\underset{-}{x}}[\nu_2(a, x) \in X, <^a]$

so that by cut with (23) we have

$(u)I_r(<^u)$ & L23. $\supset$ .LR23 $\supset \nu_2(a, b) \in X$. (24)

From the properties of the pairing functions we have

LR23 $\supset (y)[y <_n a \supset (w)(\nu_2(y, w) \in X)]$ (25)

and therefore by (24)

L24 $\supset$ .R25 $\supset \nu_2(a, b) \in X$

L24 $\supset$ .R25 $\supset (w)[\nu_2(a, w) \in X]$. (26)

Now since $(w)[\nu_2(x, w) \in X]$ is of level r ,

$I_r(<_n) \supset I_{\underset{-}{x}}[(w)(\nu_2(x, w) \in X), <_n]$

and by cut with (26)

$I_r(<_n)$ & $(u)I_r(<^u)$ & L23. $\supset (w)(\nu_2(a, w) \in X)$

from which we readily obtain

$I_r(<_n)$ & $(u)I_r(<^u)$. $\supset$ .L23 $\supset (x)(x \in X)$, i. e.

$\supset .I_{\dot{x}}[x \in X, <_{n+1}]$.

The conclusion follows by generalization.

Proof of theorem 18. We showed (p. 231) that the rule of transfinite induction on $<_{\underset{-}{q}}{}^{o}$ with a formula of level r is obtainable in $RA^r(Z_2)$. It follows by the deduction theorem that the axiom $I_{\underset{-}{x}}[x \in X, <_{q}{}_{o}]$ is so obtainable, and theorefore that $I_r(<_{q}{}_{o})$ is so obtainable. By lemma 18.1,

$I_r(<_0)$ (i. e. $I_r[\hat{x}\hat{y}L(n, x, y, 0)])$ is obtainable in $RA^{r+1}(Z_2)$.

Now suppose we have derived $I_r(\underset{q}{<}_n)$ in $RA^{n+r}(Z_2)$ and $I_r(<_n)$ in $RA^{n+r+1}(Z_2)$. It follows (see p. 231) that the rule of trnasfinite induction on the ordering with formulae of level r is a derived rule of the system in question.

Then by lemma 18.4, $I_r[\hat{z}\hat{w}L(0^{(n)}, z, w, 1)]$ is derivable in $RA^{n+r+1}(Z_2)$. Then by genaralization

$$(u)I_r[\hat{z}\hat{w}L(0^{(n)}, z, w, 1)] \tag{27}$$

is also so derivable, for the case of $\underset{q}{<}_n$. For the case $<_n$, the system is $RA^{n+r+2}(Z_2)$.

Then by (27) and lemma 18.5, it follows that $I_r(\underset{q}{<}_{n+1})$ is derivable in $RA^{n+r+1}(Z_2)$, and that $I_r(<_{n+1})$ is derivable in $RA^{n+r+2}(Z_2)$.

It follows by induction on n that $I_r(\underset{q}{<}_n)$ is derivable in $RA^{n+r}(Z_2)$, and that $I_r(<_n)$ is derivable in $RA^{n+r+1}(Z_2)$, for every n . Then any case of the rule with a formula of level $\leq r$ is obtainable in the corresponding subsystem, q. e. d.

We note that we have derived induction on $<_n$ only for fixed n , although the predicate is primitive recursive with variable n . From $I_r(<_n)$ with variable n , we could derive $I_r(<_\omega)$, where $<_\omega$ is the ordering, of type $\aleph_0$, defined on page 227. Then (see below) we could represent by a quantifier-free formula in Z_2 the functional H which is such that $\nu_2^2(H)$ enumerates all functionals repeesentable by a quantifier-free formula in $RA(Z_2)$. By a diagonal argument, this can be seen to be impossible.

Theorem 19. If F is an ordinal recursive functional of level n and degree q, then F is representable in $RA^n(Z_1)$ and provably recursive in $RA^n(Z_{1\mu})$. If F is an ordinal recursive functional of level n and degree ω, then F is representable in $RA^{n+1}(Z_1)$ and provably recursive in $RA^{n+1}(Z_{1\mu})$. Z_1 is the system of theorem 15.

Proof. By cases according to the definition of ordinal recursive functional of finite level, def. 45.

1. F is an initial primitive recursive function. By case 2 of theorem 15 (pp. 171-2).

2. $F(\bar{f}, \bar{a}) = f_1[F_1(\bar{f}, \bar{a}) \ldots F_{m_1}(\bar{f}, \bar{a})]$. The argument of case 3, theorem 15 (pp. 172-5), deduces

$$(x_1) \ldots (x_m)(Ey)T_m^{\bar{f}}(0^{(e)}, x_1 \ldots x_m, y) \qquad (31)$$

where e is a Gödel number of F, from the formulae

$$(x_1) \ldots (x_m)(Ey)T_m^{\bar{f}}(0^{(e_j)}, x_1 \ldots x_m, y) \qquad (32)$$

in Z_1^0. Suppose, as hypothesis of induction, that each functional presupposed in the definition of F is representable in $RA^n(Z_1)$ [for the case of degree q] or in $RA^{n+1}(Z_1)$ [for the case of degree ω]. Then each formula (32) is provable in $RA^n(Z_1)$ or $RA^{n+1}(Z_1)$ respectively.

By lemma 15.1, F is representable in $RA^n(Z_1)$ or $RA^{n+1}(Z_1)$ respectively, since (31) is now provable.

Likewise, the argument of case 3 deduces

$$F_0^0(\bar{f}, \bar{a}) = f_1[F_1^0(\bar{f}, \bar{a}) \ldots F_{m_1}^0(\bar{f}, \bar{a})]$$

from (31) and the other recursion equations for F , in $Z_{1\mu}^0$. Therefore if the other recursion equations for F are provable in $RA^n(Z_{1\mu})$ or $RA^{n+1}(Z_{1\mu})$, then all the equations are provable in $RA^n(Z_{1\mu})$ or $RA^{n+1}(Z_{1\mu})$ respectively.

3. F is explicitly defined from G, $H_1 \ldots H_r$ Similarly.

4. F is defined from K and G by primitive recursion. Then by the case 5, p = 0 of theorem 15 (pp. 184-5), we can deduce (31) from

$$(x_1) \ldots (x_{m-1})(\exists y)T_{m-1}^{\bar{f}}(0^{(d)}, x_1 \ldots x_{m-1}, y)$$

$$(x_1) \ldots (x_{m+1})(Ey)T_{m+1}^{\bar{f}}(0^{(e_0)}, x_1 \ldots x_{m+1}, y) ,$$

where d is a Gödel number of K and e_0 of G , in Z_1^1 . It follows that if K and G are representable in $RA^n(Z_1)$ then F is representable in $RA^n(Z_1)$, and likewise for $RA^{n+1}(Z_1)$.

The same situation as in case 3 obtains for the recursion equations.

5. F is defined from K, G, $G_1 \ldots G_r$ by an interlocked ordinal recursion on $<_p$, for some $p \leq n$. Then as in the other cases, the argument of case 5 with $p \neq 0$ de-

duces the representability of F from that of K, G, G_1 ... G_r, this time from apparatus of Z_1^o plus transfinite induction on $<_p$ with a formula of level 0. By theorem 18, this is obtainable in $RA^{p+1}(Z_1)$ if $<_o$ is the ordering of L(n;a;b;0), in $RA^p(Z_1)$ if $<_o$ is a $\underset{q}{<}$.

By the hypothesis of induction, if K, G, G_1 ... G_r are ordinal recursive of level n and degree q and $<_p$ is $\underset{q}{<}\,p$, then F is representable in $RA^n(Z_1)$ since $p \leq n$.

Likewise, if K, G, G_1 ... G_r are ordinal recursive of level n and degree ω and $<_p$ is the ordering L(n;a;b,0), then F is representable in $RA^{n+1}(Z_1)$ since $p + 1 \leq n + 1$.

The same considerations apply to the provability of recursion equations in $RA^n(Z_{1\mu})$ of $RA^{n+1}(Z_{1\mu})$.

<u>Corollary 19.1</u>. Any ordinal recursive functional of finite level and degree $\leq \omega$ is provably recursive in $RA(Z_\mu)$ with free function variables. Any ordinal recursive <u>function</u> of finite level and degree $\leq \omega$ is provably recursive in $RA(Z_\mu)$ without free function variables.

<u>Proof</u>. From theorem 19, as corollary 15.1 was obtained from theorem 15.

CHAPTER VI

Ω-CONSISTENCY

1. Critique of the concept of ω-consistency

The standard definition of ω-consistency has been as follows: A system $\mathfrak{F}$ containing an elementary number theory is ω-consistent if whenever a formula $-(x)\mathfrak{A}(x)$ is provable in $\mathfrak{F}$, then it is not the case that every formula $\mathfrak{A}(0^{(n)})$ is provable. Kreisel (e. g. [1], p. 245) has pointed out that this definition is not satisfactory from the point of view of constructive metamathematics. For suppose we formalize it: let $s^*(a, n)$ be the function which gives the number of $\mathfrak{A}(0^{(n)})$ from the number a of $(x)\mathfrak{A}(x)$; let neg be the negation function; let $Pr(a, b)$ be the proof predicate of $\mathfrak{F}$. Then $\mathfrak{F}$ is ω-consistent if

$$(Ez)Pr[z, neg(a)] \supset -(y)(Ez)Pr[z, s^*(a, y)]$$

holds for all a , i. e. if

$$(x)(Ey)(z)\{Pr[\nu_2^2(z), neg(x)] \supset -Pr[\nu_2^1(z), s^*(x, y)]\}, \quad (1)$$

a formula of a form which theorem 2 shows not always to be recursively satisfiable. It follows that the constructive interpretation of ω-consistency cannot be taken for granted.

In fact (1) is <u>not</u> recursively satisfiable if $\mathfrak{F}$ satisfies the conditions of theorem 2. Let $A(x, y, z)$ be the formula of which theorem 2 shows that $(x)(Ey)(z)A(x, y, z)$ is provable in $\mathfrak{F}$ but not recursively satisfiable. Let a_0 be the number of the formula $(y)(Ez) - A(b, y, z)$. Let

f be the function purporting to satisfy (1). If it does, then

$$Pr(b, \underline{neg}[s(a_o, n)]) \supset - Pr\left[c, s^*\{s(a_o, n), \underline{f}[s(a_o, n)]\}\right] \quad (2)$$

is verifiable, where $s(a_o, n)$ is the number of $(y)(Ez) - A(0^{(n)}, y, z)$.

Now clearly $- (y)(Ez) - A(0^{(n)}, y, z)$, whose number is $neg[s(a_o, n)]$, is provable, for it is equivalent to $(Ey)(z)\bar{A}(0^{(n)}, y, z)$. Therefore by (2)

$$(Ez) - \underline{A}[0^{(n)}, 0^{(\underline{f}[s(a_o, n)])}, z] \quad (3)$$

is unprovable. Now for any m, if

$$A[0^{(n)}, 0^{(f[s(a_o,n)])}, 0^{(m)}] \quad (4)$$

is false, then its negation is provable; and by existential generalization, (3) is provable. Therefore (4) is true for every m. Since this argument holds for every n, it follows that

$$A\{n, \underline{f}[s(a_o, n)], m\}$$

is verifiable, contrary to the assertion of theorem 2 that $(x)(Ey)(z)A(x, y, z)$ is not recursively satisfiable. Therefore f does not satisfy (1); and (1) is not recursively satisfiable, q. e. d.

It follows that we shall have to find some other concept of ω-consistency or acknowledge that the interesting systems are all not ω-consistent. We should, however, only call a system <u>ω-inconsistent</u> if we could actually produce, for some formula $\mathfrak{a}(a)$, proofs of $\mathfrak{a}(0^{(n)})$ for each n and a proof of $-(x)\mathfrak{a}(x)$. For this to be impossible, it suffices that the <u>no-counter-example</u> interpretation of (1) should hold: that is, given a proof of $-(x)\mathfrak{a}(x)$ and a function $f(n)$ (which purports to generate a sequence of proofs of $\mathfrak{a}(0^{(n)})$), we can effectively find a number m such that $f(m)$ is <u>not</u> the number of a proof of $\mathfrak{a}(0^{(m)})$. We shall say that a system is ω-consistent if this holds.

<u>Definition 47.</u>[1] An extension $\mathfrak{F}$ of a system of elementary number theory is <u>ω-consistent</u> if we have a functional $K(f, a)$, where f has one argument place, such that if a is the number of a proof in $\mathfrak{F}$ of $-(x)\mathfrak{a}(x)$, then if $m = K(f, a)$, then $f(m)$ is not the number of a proof in $\mathfrak{F}$ of $\mathfrak{a}(0^{(m)})$.

We note that if $\mathfrak{F}$ is ω-consistent, then from a proof of $(Ex)\mathfrak{a}(x)$ and a function f we can effectively find an m such that $f(m)$ is not the number of a proof of $-\mathfrak{a}(0^{(m)})$, for from the given proof of $(Ex)\mathfrak{a}(x)$ we can obtain a proof of $-(x)-\mathfrak{a}(x)$.

---

[1] In Kreisel [3], p. 3, called <u>weak</u> ω-consistency. $\mathfrak{F}$ is <u>strongly ω-consistent</u> according to [3] if whenever $(Ex)\mathfrak{a}(x)$ is provable, an m can be effectively found such that $\mathfrak{a}(0^{(m)})$ is provable. This clearly implies that if the system is consistent, then every prenex theorem is recursively satisfiable. Therefore it does not hold if every recursive function is numeralwise representable in $\mathfrak{F}$.

2. Ω-consistency, external consistency, and 1*-consistency

In this section, we show that ω-consistency is an essentially stronger condition on a system than either external consistency or 1*-consistency.

Theorem 20 (cf. Kreisel [3]). If $\mathcal{F}$ is ω-consistent, then $\mathcal{F}$ is 1-consistent. Then if $\mathcal{F}$ contains symbols for ν_m, ν_m^1, and the formulae (1_{1m}) of page 34 are theorems, then $\mathcal{F}$ is 1*-consistent. If in the latter case $\mathcal{F}$ contains formulae which numeralwise express the Kleene Predicates T_m and one which numeralwise represents the Kleene function U, then $\mathcal{F}$ is externally consistent.

Proof. Let $A(x)$ be a quantifier-free formula of $\mathcal{F}$. For any n, the formula $A(0^{(n)})$ can be effectively decided in $\mathcal{F}$ by proofs which are essentially numerical computations; it follows that the function $f(n) = \mu x[x$ is the number of a computational proof, i. e. without quantifiers, of $A(0^{(n)})$ v x is the number of a computational proof of $- A(0^{(n)})$] is everywhere defined (and recursive). If $\mathcal{F}$ is ω-consistent, then from f and a proof of $(Ex)A(x)$ we can find an m such that $f(m)$ is not the number of a proof of $- A(0^{(m)})$. By the definition of f, $f(m)$ must be the number of a computational proof of $A(0^{(m)})$ Therefore $A(0^{(m)})$ is true, and $\mathcal{F}$ is 1-consistent.

Then the 1*-consistency of $\mathcal{F}$ under the given hypothesis follows by lemma 3.2.

We note that by essentially the same argument as in passing from ω-consistency to 1-consistency, $\mathfrak{F}$ is also 1*-consistent if it is what we might call ω*-consistent: that is, if from a proof of a formula $(Ex_1) \ldots (Ex_k)$ $\mathcal{A}(x_1 \ldots x_k)$ and a function f of k variables, we can effectively find $m_1 \ldots m_k$ such that $f(m_1 \ldots m_k)$ is not the number of a proof of $-\ \mathcal{A}(0^{(m_1)} \ldots 0^{(m_k)})$. Then by the proof of lemma 3.2, if $\mathfrak{F}$ satisfies the conditions of that lemma and is ω-consistent, then it is ω*-consistent.

We note that if $\mathfrak{F}$ is ω-consistent, it remains so if symbols are introduced by explicit definition (cf. note 5, page 39). For let g be a recursive function such that if b is the number of a proof involving the explicit definitions of a formula $\mathcal{B}$, then g(b) is the number of a proof not containing the explicit definitions of the formula $\mathcal{B}'$ obtained by eliminating the <u>definienda</u> in favor of their <u>definientia</u>. Given a proof perhaps with explcit definitions of a formula $-\ (x)\mathcal{A}(x)$, with number a, then g(a) is the number of a proof without the definitions of $-\ (x)[\mathcal{A}(x)]'$. If $\mathfrak{F}$ is ω-consistent and K is the functional of def. 47, then if $K[\lambda x g(f(x)), g(a)] = m$, then g(f(m)) is not the number of a proof in $\mathfrak{F}$ of $[\mathcal{A}(0^{(m)})]'$. It follows that f(m) is not the number of a proof of $\mathcal{A}(0^{(m)})$ in the extension by the explicit definitions. Therefore the extension is ω-consistent.

Then if $\mathfrak{F}$ contains formulae which express the predicate T_m and represent the function U, $\mathfrak{F}$ remains ω-consistent if we introduce symbols by explicit definition for T_m and $U(a) = b$. Then by the second claim of the theorem, the extension is 1*-consistent. By theorem 11, it is externally consistent. Therefore so is $\mathfrak{F}$, q. e. d.

Theorem 21 (Kreisel [3]). By adding a single axiom to Z, we can obtain a system which is 1*-consistent and externally consistent but ω-inconsistent.

Proof. Let Z_2 be the extension of Z by adding symbols for each recursive function with its recursion equations. Let $N(p)$ be a primitive recursive function which gives for each p the number of the formula of Z_2

$$(Ey)(Ex)[T_1(0^{(p)}, y, z) \& U(z) = 0],$$

where T_1 and U are the normal form predicate and function of IM p. 281, as before.

Let $Dd(a, b, c)$ be the primitive recursive predicate ' b is the number of a deduction in Z_2 of the formula number c from the formula number a '. Now consider the formula of Z_2

$$(Eu)(Ep)(v)(Ew)\{T_1(p, v, w) \& U(w) \neq 0 \& Dd[s(b, b), u, N(p)]\}, \quad (1)$$

where s is the Gödel substitution function for formulae of Z_2 (see theorem 2).

Let p_o be the number of (1), and let s_o be the term $s(0^{(p_o)}, 0^{(p_o)})$.

Then we add to Z_2 as axiom the formula

$$(Eu)(Ep)(v)(Ew)\{T_1(p, v, w) \& U(w) \neq 0 \& Dd[s_o, u, N(p)]\} \quad (2)$$

Now let $A(x)$ be a quantifier-free formula of this system, where in fact $A(x)$ expresses a primitive recursive predicate. Let e_o be a Gödel number of the characteristic function of $\hat{x}A(x)$. Then by theorem 15 one can prove in Z_2 (the functional added to get Z_1 from Z_2 is used only in the representation of proper functionals)

$$(x)(Ey)[T_1(0^{(e_o)}, x, y) \&: U(y) = 0 \& A(x) .v. U(y) = 1 \& - A(x)] . \quad (3)$$

First we show that Z_2 with (2) added is 1-consistent. By (3) we have in Z_2

$$(Ex)A(x) \supset (Ey)(Ez)[T_1(0^{(e_o)}, y, z) \& U(y) = 0] , \quad (4)$$

so that if $(Ex)A(x)$ is provable in the extension, then (R4) is deducible in Z_2 from (2). Let u_o be the number of this deduction. We note that the number of (2) is $s(p_o, p_o)$, and the number of (R4) is $N(e_o)$.

By the deduction theorem, we have $2 \supset R4$ in Z_2, from which follows

$$(v)(Ew)\{T_1(0^{(e_o)}, v, w) \& U(w) \neq 0 \& Dd[s_o, 0^{(u_o)}, N(0^{(e_o)})]\} \supset (Ey)(Ez)[T_1(0^{(e_o)}, y, z) \& U(y) = 0] . \quad (5)$$

From available proofs of

$$0^{(s(p_o,p_o))} = s(0^{(p_o)}, 0^{(p_o)})$$

$$0^{(n_o)} = N(0^{(e_o)})$$

$$Dd(0^{(s(p_o,p_o))}, 0^{(u_o)}, 0^{(n_o)}) ,$$

where $n_o = N(e_o)$, we infer

$$Dd[s_o, 0^{(u_o)}, N(0^{(e_o)})] ;$$

and therefore (5) implies

$$(v)(Ew)[T_1(0^{(e_o)}, v, w) \& U(w) = 0] \supset R5$$

in Z_2 , i. e.

$$(Ey)(Ez)(Ev)\{(w)[- T_1(0^{(e_o)}, v, w) \vee U(w) = 0] \quad \dot{v}. T_1(0^{(e_o)}, y, z) \& U(z) = 0\} \tag{6}$$

But we have

$$(w)[- T_1(0^{(e_o)}, v, w) \vee U(w) = 0] \& (Ew)T_1(0^{(e_o)}, v, w). \quad \supset (Ew)[T_1(0^{(e_o)}, v, w) \& U(w) = 0] ,$$

so that since $(Ew)T_1(0^{(e_o)}, v, w)$ is provable by (3), (6) implies

$$(Ey)(Ez)(Ev)(Ew)[T_1(0^{(e_o)}, v, w) \& U(w) = 0 . \quad \dot{v}. T_1(0^{(e_o)}, y, z) \& U(z) = 0]$$

which implies (R4). It follows that (R4) is already provable in Z_2 , and by the 1*-consistency of that system (theorem 13), we can find n, m such that

$$T_1(e_o, n, m) \& U(m) = 0 .$$

From the choice of e_o , it is plain that $A(0^{(n)})$ is true. This proves that Z_2 with (2) as additional axiom is 1-consistent. By lemma 3.2, it is 1*-consistent. By theorem

11, it is externally consistent.

We now show that Z_2 with (2) is ω-inconsistent. Consider any numbers u_o and e_o. The formula

$$Dd[s_o, 0^{(u_o)}, N(0^{(e_o)})] \tag{6a}$$

is decidable in Z_2. If it is refutable, then one can prove

$$-(v)(Ew)\{T_1(0^{(e_o)}, v, w) \ \& \ U(w) \neq 0 \ \& \ Dd[s_o, 0^{(u_o)}, N(0^{(e_o)})]\}$$

in Z_2. (7)

If it is provable, one can prove

$$(v)(Ew)[T_1(0^{(e_o)}, v, w) \ \& \ U(w) \neq 0] \supset 2 . \tag{8}$$

However, u_o must be the number of a deduction in Z_2 from (2) of (R4), and so by the deduction theorem we have in Z_2

$$2 \supset (Ey)(Ez)[T_1(0^{(e_o)}, y, z) \ \& \ U(z) = 0]$$

and therefore by (8)

$$L8 \supset (Ey)(Ez)[T_1(0^{(e_o)}, y, z) \ \& \ U(z) = 0] . \tag{9}$$

By the formula

$$T_1(e, y, z) \ \& \ U(z) = 0 \ \& \ T_1(e, y, w) . \supset z = w$$

from which follows

$$(Ez)[T_1(e, y, z) \ \& \ U(z) = 0] \supset -(Ew)[T_1(e, y, w) \ \& \ U(w) \neq 0]$$

$$\supset -(v)(Ew)[T_1(e, v, w) \ \& \ U(w) \neq 0]$$

from which we infer $R9 \supset -L8$, and hence by (9), $-L8$. Then by (6a), (7) again follows.

Thus (7) is provable in Z_2 for each u_o, p_o. Let

the scope of (Ep) in (2) be $\mathcal{C}(u, p)$. Then from (2) we can deduce in Z_2

$$(Eu)\mathcal{C}[\nu_2^1(u), \nu_2^2(u)]$$

Then by taking $u_o = \bar{\nu}_2^1(n)$, $p_o = \nu_2^2(n)$, we see that for each n , $-\mathcal{C}[\nu_2^1(0^{(n)}), \nu_2^2(0^{(n)})]$ is provable, for it is equivalent to (7), and therefore that Z_2 with (2) as added axiom is ω-inconsistent.

This proves theorem 21 with Z_2 replacing Z . Consider the formula obtained from (2) by replacing $T_1(p, v, w)$, $U(w) = 0$, and $Dd[s(b, b), u, N(p)]$ by their numeralwise expressions under Gödel's method. By HB I, 401-21, the recursion equations for these predicates are provable in Z , and therefore the resulting formula $\mathfrak{a}$ is provable in Z_2 from (2), for the uniqueness of the solution of a set of recursion equations is easily provable. Therefore the system obtained by adding $\mathfrak{a}$ to Z is a subsystem of Z_2 plus (2), and is therefore 1*-consistent and externally consistent.

But by the same argument as that for explicit definitions on pp. 248-9, the ω-inconsistency of this system follows from that of Z_2 plus (2). This proves theorem 21.

3. Ω-consistency of ramified analysis

Theorem 22 (Parsons [2]). Let Z_o be an elementary number theory with induction. Then $RA(Z_o)$, and a fortiori Z_o , are ω-consistent.

Proof.[2] Suppose we are given a function f and a proof in $RA(Z_0)$ of $(Ex)\mathcal{A}(x)$. Then by lemma 17.3 we can primitive recursively obtain a proof of this formula in the system $RA(S_0)$ with effective infinite induction. By lemma 17.8, we can obtain a proof in $RA(S_0)$ with cuts only on numerical prime formulae, which we can also eliminate, by the proofs of lemmas 13.6 and 17.9.

The procedure of the proof will be to transformthis cut-free "proof" $\mathcal{P}$ into another one $\mathcal{Q}$ which we can "search" to find an m such that $f(m)$ is not the number of a proof in $RA(Z_0)$ of $-\mathcal{A}(0^{(m)})$. The main step is .

Lemma 22.1. Let $\mathcal{B}$ be any cut-free proof in $RA(S_0)$. Then $\mathcal{B}$ can be effectibely replaced by a proof $\mathcal{B}'$ (which will in general contain cuts) which has the same last line and which has the following two properties

(i) If a binding

$$\frac{\mathcal{C}(t) \vee \mathcal{N}}{(Ex)\mathcal{C}(x) \vee \mathcal{N}} \tag{1}$$

occurs in $\mathcal{B}'$, where $\mathcal{C}(x)$ can be obtained from $\mathcal{A}(x)$ by replacing free variables other than x by numerals, then t is closed, and $f(\text{val } t)$ is not the number of

---

[2]Kreisel proves the ω-consistency of Z in [5], and has sent me another proof based on the interpretation of Heyting's arithmetic in Gödel [2].

a proof in $RA(Z_0)$ of $-\mathcal{A}(0^{(\text{val } t)})$.

(ii) Any cut in $\mathcal{D}'$ is on a <u>proper</u> subformula of a numerical instance of $(Ex)\mathcal{A}(x)$.

<u>Proof</u>. By induction on the construction of $\mathcal{D}$.

1. If $\mathcal{D}$ consists only of an axiom, then (i) and (ii) are vacuous; let $\mathcal{D}' = \mathcal{D}$.

2. If the last inference of $\mathcal{D}$ is not of the form (1), then to the derivation(s) of the premiss(es) obtained by the hypothesis of induction, we add the same inference as ended $\mathcal{D}$. Since it is not a cut, (i) and (ii) are preserved.

3. If the last inference of $\mathcal{D}$ is of the form (1), then by the hypothesis of induction we have a proof satisfying (i) and (ii) of its premiss. Let

$$\mathcal{C}^*(t^*) \vee \mathcal{N}^* \tag{2}$$

be the result of substituting in the premiss of (1) arbitrary numerals for the free number variables of t. Then by substitution in the assumed derivation (cf. appendix I, def. 34), we obtain a derivation of (2) which can be seen also to satisfy (i) and (ii).

If $f(\text{val } t^*)$ is not the number of a proof in $RA(Z_0)$ of $-\mathcal{A}(0^{(\text{val } t^*)})$, then we infer $(Ex)\mathcal{C}^*(x) \vee$ * by binding.

If $f(\text{val } t^*)$ <u>is</u> the number of a proof in $RA(Z_0)$ of $-\mathcal{A}(0^{(\text{val } t^*)})$, then we can obtain from this a derivation of $- \mathcal{C}^*(t^*)$, first by substituting numerals for free variables in $- \mathcal{A}(0^{(\text{val } t^*)})$ and then using the provable formula $t^* -= 0^{(\text{val } t^*)}$. Then by lemmas 17.3 and 17.8 and the proof of lemma 17.9 we again obtain a cut-free proof in $RA(S_0)$ of $- \mathcal{C}^*(t^*)$. By cut with (2), we obtain a derivation of $\mathcal{N}^*$, and infer $(Ex)\mathcal{C}^*(x) \vee \mathcal{N}^*$ by weakening.

Then by infinite induction we have a derivation of $(Ex)\mathcal{C}(x) \vee \mathcal{N}$ from which every inference which might have violated (i) or (ii) has been eliminated. Let this be $\mathcal{D}'$

This completes the proof of lemma 22.1

Let $\mathcal{Q}$ be the derivation of $(Ex)\mathcal{A}(x)$ which we obtain from $\mathcal{P}$ by lemma 22.1. Then we can obtain a derivation $\mathcal{R}$ of $(Ex)\mathcal{A}(x)$ by eliminating the cuts from $\mathcal{Q}$. Inspection of the procedure (esp. lemmas 13.3, 13.4, 17.5) shows that (ii) implies that any new inference introduced in the course of it has as principal formula a proper subformula of a numerical instance of $(Ex)\mathcal{A}(x)$. It follows that no new inferences of the form (i) are introduced, and therefore that $\mathcal{R}$ satisfies (i).[3]

---

[3]Since the upper bound on the order of the cut-free proof of $- \mathcal{C}^*(t^*)$ is κ_0, by an induction parallel to the proof of lemma 22.1, if α is the order of $\mathcal{P}$, the order of $\mathcal{Q}$ is $\leq \kappa_0 + \alpha \cdot 2 < \kappa_0 \cdot 3$. It follows that the order of $\mathcal{R} < \kappa_1$, the second critical ε-number. It follows that our proof implicitly involves transfinite induction up to that number. With only number variables, the numbers

By the subformula property, the last inference of not an infinite induction must be of the form (1), where by (i), t is closed and f(val t) is not the number of a proof in $RA(Z_0)$ of $-\mathcal{a}(0^{(\text{val } t)})$. If we meet an infinite induction, we can take any brandh. Since at each such point the order decreases, we must eventually find an inference (1). Thus we find an m such that f(m) is not the number of a proof of $-\mathcal{a}(0^{(m)})$, proving theorem 22.

We conclude with a theoremwhich establishes an analogue of ω-consistency for formulae $(EX)\mathcal{a}(X)$, where X is a class variable.

<u>Theorem 23</u> (Parsons [2]). Given any n, let $T_0, T_1, T_2,$ ... be an effective enumeration of the class terms without free number variables, of level $\leq n$. Then given any proof in $RA(Z_0)$ of a formula $(EX)\mathcal{a}(X)$, where X is of level n, and any function f, an m can be found such that f(m) is not the number of a proof in $RA(Z_0)$ of $-\mathcal{a}(T_m)$, where T_m contains no free variable not

---

are ε_1 and ε_0 respectively. Since Kreisel's proof in [5] uses induction only to $\varepsilon_0{}^2$, it appears that our method is not the most ecohomical possible.

In the final elimination of cuts, the principal and side formulae of existing inferences (1) may be altered by replacing numerical terms by others of the same value. By this (i) does not cease to hold. The inferences (1) where $(Ex)\mathcal{C}(x)$ is in the <u>Formelbund</u> of $(Ex)\mathcal{a}(x)$, which are the only ones which count, cannot be altered in any other way.

free in $(EX)\mathcal{A}(X)$.

Proof. The idea of the proof is the same as that of the proof of theorem 22. As before, we obtain from the proof $(EX)\mathcal{A}(X)$ a cut-free proof $\mathcal{P}$ in $RA(S_0)$. We can suppose that any free variable in $\mathcal{P}$ is either a free variable of $(EX)\mathcal{A}(X)$ or the principal variable of some generalization. The rest can be subsituted out insome arbitrary way (those other than induction variables already in the proof in $RA(Z_0)$). The role of lemma 22.1 is played by

Lemma 23.1. Any cut-free proof $\mathcal{D}$ in $RA(S_0)$ can be effectively replaced by a derivation $\mathcal{D}'$, with cuts, of the same formula satisfying (ii) and

(i') If an inference of the form

$$\frac{\mathcal{C}(T) \vee \mathcal{N}}{(EX)\mathcal{C}(X) \vee \mathcal{N}} \tag{3}$$

occurs in $\mathcal{D}'$, where $\mathcal{C}(X)$ can be obtained from $\mathcal{A}(X)$ by substituting numerals for free number variables, and if $T = T_m$ (for T is of level $\leq n$), then $f(m)$ is not the number of a proof in $RA(Z_0)$ of $-\mathcal{A}(T)$.

Proof. Like lemma 22.1, except for case 3.

3. If the last inference of $\mathcal{D}$ is of the form (3), then as with lemma 22.1 we obtain a derivation of

$$\mathcal{C}^*(T^*) \vee \mathcal{N}^* \tag{4}$$

satisfying (i') and (ii). What we can now say about T^*

is that it has no free number variables. Suppose T^* is T_m.

If $f(m)$ is not the number of a proof in $RA(Z_o)$ of $-\mathcal{A}(T_m)$, we infer $(EX)\mathcal{C}^*(X) \vee \mathcal{N}^*$ by binding.

If $f(m)$ is the number of a proof in $RA(Z_o)$ of $-\mathcal{A}(T_m)$, then we obtain from this a proof in $RA(Z_o)$ of $-\mathcal{C}^*(T^*)$, and then a cut-free proof in $RA(S_o)$ of the same. By the subformula property, this contains no inference of form (3). By cut with (4), we obtain a derivation of $\mathcal{N}^*$, and infer $(EX)\mathcal{C}^*(X) \vee \mathcal{N}^*$ by weakening.

Then we infer the conclusion of (3) by infinite induction. (i') and (ii) are satisfied.

Let $\mathcal{R}$ be the cut-free proof of $(EX)\mathcal{A}(X)$ obtained from the one provided from $\mathcal{P}$ by lemma 23.1; as before, it satisfies (i'). By the subformula property, the last inference not an infinite induction must be of the form (3), where by (i') $T = T_m$ for some m such that $f(m)$ is not the number of a proof in $RA(Z_o)$ of $-\mathcal{A}(T_m)$. Since there is no generalization below, T contains no free variable not free in $(EX)\mathcal{A}(X)$, q. e. d.

It is plain that by the same use of the recursion theorem as in the proof of theorem 17 (see appendix I), we could give an explicit expression for the functional which, in lemmas 22.1 and 23.1, gives the number of $\mathcal{A}'$ as a function of f and the number of the given proof of $(EX)\mathfrak{A}(X)$ or $(Ex)\mathfrak{A}(x)$. It would turn out to be ordinal recursive on an ordering of type κ_1.

APPENDIX I

Arithmetization of Schütte's Cut-elimination Theorems

The purpose of this appendix is to give full recursive definitions for certain functionals used in the proofs of theorems 13 and 17, whose definitions depend on an arithmetization of the syntax of the systems we consider, including those with effective infinite induction. We adopt an extension to formulae of ramified analysis of a variant of the Gödel numbering given in HB II, 207 ff.

Definition 1. 1. The symbol 0 receives the number 2.

2. If a term t has the number n, then St has the number $3 \cdot n$.

3. With each function symbol with k arguments we associate a number $r > 2$ such that if the terms $t_1 \ldots t_k$ have numbers $n_1 \ldots n_k$, then the term $f(t_1 \ldots t_k)$ has number $5 \cdot p_r^{n_1} \cdot \ldots \cdot p_{r+k-1}^{n_k}$.

4. Since we do not yet follow HB in using different symbols for free and bound variables, we represent all number variables by primed ≥ 7.

5. If t_1 and t_2 have numbers m and n respectively, then the formula $t_1 = t_2$ has the number $20 \cdot 11^m \cdot 13^n$. We have assumed that the system Z_0 of theorems 13 and 17 has no other predicate symbols.

6. If A has the number a, B has the number b, then $A \vee B$ has the number $40 \cdot 7^a \cdot 11^b$.

7. If A has number a, then $-A$ has number $3a$.

8. If A has number a, and the variable x has the (prime) number p, then $(x)A$ has the number $50 \cdot p^a$.

9. Likewise, $(Ex)A$ has number $100 \cdot p^a$.

(Contrary to HB, we do not care whether x is free in A.)

The primitive recursive predicates $Tm(a)$ ' a is the number of a term ' and $Fl(a)$ ' a is the number of a formula ' are defined by obvious course-of-values recursions.

We shall now enlarge the numbering to cover formulae with bound class variables of finite levels.

Definition 2. 10. A class variable X of level k has a number $2^{k+1}p$ for some prime number p, $7 \leq p$.

11. If the number term t has number a and the class term T has number c, then the formula $t \varepsilon T$ has number $70 \cdot \wp_c{}^a$.

12. If the variable x has number $\wp_r$, and the formula A has number b, and is of level k, then the class term $\hat{x}A(x)$ has number $5^{k+1} \cdot \wp_r{}^b$.

13. If the variable X has number $2^{k+1}p$, and the formula A has number a, then $(X)A$ has number $2^{k+1}5^3p^a$.

14. Likewise, $(EX)A$ has number $2^{k+1}5^4p^a$.

These arrangements preserve the HB property that the number of a term is not divisible by 10 while that of a formula is. Term and formula are defined by simultaneous recursion, whose elimination is simpler because of this (see HB II, 301-2).

<u>Definition 3.</u> $\mathrm{CT}(k, a) \equiv : a = 2^{k+1} \cdot \wp_{\ln(a)} \;\&\; 2 \leq \ln(a)$

$\mathrm{v}. a = 5^{k+1} \cdot \wp_{\ln(a)}{}^{(a)_{\ln(a)}} \;\&\; \mathrm{Fla}[k, (a)_{\ln(a)}]$

$\mathrm{Fla}(0, a) \equiv :. a = 70 \cdot 11^{(a)_4} \cdot 13^{(a)_5} \;\&\; \mathrm{Tm}[(a)_4]$

$\&\; \mathrm{Tm}[(a)_5] : \mathrm{v} : a = 70 \cdot \wp_{\ln(a)}{}^{(a)_{\ln(a)}} \;\&\; \mathrm{CT}[0, (a)_{\ln a}].$

$\mathrm{v}.\; 3 | a \;\&\; \mathrm{Fla}(0, a/3).$

$\mathrm{v}.\; a = 40 \cdot 7^{(a)_3} \cdot 11^{(a)_4} \;\&\; \mathrm{Fla}[0, (a)_3] \;\&\; \mathrm{Fla}[0, (a)_4].$

$\mathrm{v}.\; a = 50 \cdot \wp_{\ln a}{}^{(a)_{\ln a}} \;\&\; \mathrm{Fla}[0, (a)_{\ln a}] \;\&\; 2 \leq \ln a\,.$

$\mathrm{v}.\; a = 100 \cdot \wp_{\ln a}{}^{(a)_{\ln a}} \;\&$ " "

$\mathrm{Fla}(k + 1, a) \equiv :: a = 70 \cdot \wp_{\ln a}{}^{(a)_{\ln a}} \;\&\; \mathrm{CT}[k + 1, (a)_{\ln a}].$

$\mathrm{v}.\; 3 | a \;\&\; \mathrm{Fla}(k + 1, a/3)$

$\mathrm{v}. : a = 40 \cdot 7^{(a)_3} \cdot 11^{(a)_4} \;\&: \mathrm{Fla}[k + 1, (a)_3] \;\&$
$(Ey)(y \leq k + 1 \;\&\; \mathrm{Fla}[y, (a)_4]).\mathrm{v}.\mathrm{Fla}[k + 1, (a)_4] \;\&$
$(Ey)(y \leq k + 1 \;\&\; \mathrm{Fla}[y, (a)_3]) :.$

$\mathrm{v}. : a = 2^{(a)_0} \cdot 5^{(a)_2} \cdot \wp_{\ln a}{}^{(a)_{\ln a}} \;\&: 0 < (a)_0 \leq 2 \;\&$
$(a)_2 = 2 \;\&\; \mathrm{Fla}[k + 1, (a)_{\ln a}].\mathrm{v}.\; 0 < (a)_0 \leq k + 1 \;\&_2 \leq 4$
$2 < (a)_2 \leq 4 \;\&\; \mathrm{Fla}[k + 1, (a)_{\ln a}] \;.\mathrm{v}.\; (a)_0 = k + 1 \;\&$
$2 < (a)_2 \leq 4 \;\&\; (Ey)(y \leq k \;\&\; \mathrm{Fla}[y, (a)_{\ln a}])$

Def. 3 defined by simultaneous recursion the predicates ' a is the number of a class term of level k ' and ' a is the number of a formula of level k '.

<u>Definition 4a.</u> $\mathrm{Of}(k, n, a) \equiv a \neq a$ if $a = 2$,

$\equiv . k = (a)_o$ & $\ln(a) = n$ if $a = 2^{(a)_o} \cdot p_{\ln a}$ & $2 < \ln a$,

$\equiv \mathrm{Of}(k, n, a/3)$ if $3 | a$,

$\equiv (Ez)(2 < z \leq \ln(a)$ & $\mathrm{Of}[k, n, (a)_z])$

if $a = 5 \cdot \prod_{2<i\leq \ln a} p_i^{(a)_1}$,

$\equiv . \mathrm{Of}[k, n, (a)_4] \vee \mathrm{Of}[k, n, (a)_5]$

if $a = 70 \cdot 11^{(a)_4} \cdot 13^{(a)_5}$,

$\equiv . \mathrm{Of}[k, n, \ln(a)] \vee \mathrm{Of}[k, n, (a)_{\ln a}]$

if $a = 70 \cdot p_{\ln a}^{(a)_{\ln a}}$,

$\equiv . \mathrm{Of}[k, n, (a)_3] \vee \mathrm{Of}[k, n, (a)_4]$

if $a = 40 \cdot 7^{(a)_3} \cdot 11^{(a)_4}$,

$\equiv . \mathrm{Of}[k, n, (a)_{\ln a}]$ & $- [k = (a)_o$ & $\ln(a) = n]$

if $a = 2^{(a)_o} \cdot 5^{(a)_2} \cdot p_{\ln a}^{(a)_{\ln a}}$ &: $(a)_o = 0 \vee .$ $(a)_o \neq 0$ & $2 < (a)_2 \leq 4$,

$\equiv . \mathrm{Of}[k, n, (a)_{\ln a}]$ & $- [k = 0$ & $\ln(a) = n]$

if $a = 50 \cdot p_{\ln a}^{(a)_{\ln a}} \vee a = 100 \cdot p_{\ln a}^{(a)_{\ln a}}$.

$\equiv a \neq a$ otherwise.

If a is the number of a formula of $RA(Z_o)$, then $\mathrm{Of}(k, n, a)$ holds if and only if the variable number $2^k \cdot p_n$ occurs free in the formula.

<u>Definition 4b.</u> $\mathrm{Ob}(k, n, a) \equiv a \neq a$

if $a = 2 \vee . a = 2^{(a)_o} \cdot p_{\ln a}$ & $2 < \ln a . \vee$ $a = 70 \cdot 11^{(a)_4} \cdot 13^{(a)_5} \vee a = 5 \cdot \prod_{2<i\leq \ln a} p_i^{(a)_1}$,

$\equiv \mathrm{Ob}(k, n, a/3)$ if $3 | a$,

$Ob(k, n, a) \equiv Ob[k, n, ln(a)]$ if $a = 70 \cdot \mathscr{P}_{ln\ a}{}^{(a)_{ln\ a}}$,

$\equiv . Ob[k, n, (a)_3] \vee Ob[k, n, (a)_4]$

if $a = 40 \cdot 7^{(a)_3} \cdot 11^{(a)_4}$,

$\equiv : Ob[k, n, (a)_{ln\ a}] \ v.\ k = (a)_o \ \&\ ln(a) = n$

if $a = 2^{(a)_o} \cdot 5^{(a)_2} \cdot \mathscr{P}_{ln\ a}{}^{(a)_{ln\ a}}$ &:

$(a)_o = 0 \ v.\ (a)_o \neq 0 \ \&\ 2 < (a)_2 \leq 4$,

$\equiv : Ob[k, n, (a)_{ln\ a}] \ v.\ k = 0 \ \&\ ln(a) = n$

if $a = 50 \cdot \mathscr{P}_{ln\ a}{}^{(a)_{ln\ a}} \vee a = 100 \cdot \mathscr{P}_{ln\ a}{}^{(a)_{ln\ a}}$,

$\equiv a \neq a$ otherwise.

If a is the number of a formula of $RA(Z_o)$, then $Ob(k, n, a)$ holds if and only if the variable number $2^k \cdot \mathscr{P}_n$ occurs bound in the formula; similarly if a is the number of a class term.

In order to avoid certain technical difficulties, we shall use, instead of the terms and formulae defined by def. 3, a subclass for which the classes of admissible free and bound variables are disjoint. Let n be called the <u>index</u> of the variable number $2^k \cdot \mathscr{P}_n$; we admit a variable as free if its index is odd, as bound if its index is even.

<u>Definition 5</u>. $WF(a) \equiv (x)(k)[x < a \ \&\ k < a . \supset .$

$Of(k, x, a) \supset -(2|x) .\&.\ Ob(k, x, a) \supset 2|x]$

$Wftm(a) \equiv . Tm(a) \ \&\ WF(a)$

$WFCT(k, a) . \equiv . CT(k, a) \ \&\ WF(a)$

$WFF(k, a) . \equiv . Fla(k, a) \ \&\ WF(a)$

I. e., those terms and formulae are (strongly) well-formed in which each free variable has odd index and each bound variable has even index.

<u>Definition 6.</u> $su(m, k, n, a) = m$ if $a = 2^k \cdot \mathcal{P}_n \ \& \ 2 < n$,

$= a$ if $a = 2^{(a)_0} \cdot \mathcal{P}_{\ln a} \ \& \ 2 < \ln a \ \& \ a \neq 2^k \cdot \mathcal{P}_n$,

$= a$ if $a = 2$,

$= 3 \cdot su[m, k, n, a/3]$ if $3 | a$,

$= 40 \cdot 7^{su[m,k,n,(a)_3]} \cdot 11^{su[m,k,n,(a)_4]}$

if $a = 40 \cdot 7^{(a)_3} \cdot 11^{(a)_4}$,

$= 5 \cdot \prod_{2<i\leq \ln a} \mathcal{P}_i^{\,su[m,k,n,(a)_i]}$

if $a = 5 \cdot \prod_{2<i\leq \ln a} \mathcal{P}_i^{\,(a)_i} \ \& \ (i)\{2 < i \leq \ln(a) \ \&$

$(a)_i \neq 0. \supset Tm[(a)_i]\}$,

$= 70 \cdot 11^{su[m,k,n,(a)_4]} \cdot 13^{su[m,k,n,(a)_5]}$

if $a = 70 \cdot 11^{(a)_4} \cdot 13^{(a)_5}$,

$= 70 \cdot \mathcal{P}_{su[m,k,n,\ln(a)]}^{\quad (a)} {}^{su[m,k,n,(a)_{\ln a}]}$

if $a = 70 \cdot \mathcal{P}_{\ln a}^{\,(a)_{\ln a}}$,

$= 5^{(a)_2} \cdot \mathcal{P}_{\ln a}^{\,su[m,k,n,(a)_{\ln a}]}$

if $a = 5^{(a)_2} \cdot \mathcal{P}_{\ln a}^{\,(a)_{\ln a}} \ \& \ Fla[(a)_2 \dot{-} 1, (a)_{\ln a}] \ \&$

$(a)_2 \neq 0 \ \& - [k = 0 \ \& \ \ln a = n]$,

$= 2^{(a)_0} \cdot 5^{(a)_2} \cdot \mathcal{P}_{\ln a}^{\,su[m,k,n,(a)_{\ln a}]}$

if $a = 2^{(a)_0} \cdot 5^{(a)_2} \cdot \mathcal{P}_{\ln a}^{\,(a)_{\ln a}} \ \& \ 0 < (a)_0 \leq 2 \ \&$

$(a)_2 = 2 \ \& - [k = 0 \ \& \ \ln(a) = n] \ \& - Of[0, \ln(a), m]$.

$v.(a)_0 \neq 0 \ \& \ 2 < (a)_2 \leq 4 \ \& - [k = (a)_0 \ \& \ \ln(a) = n] \ \&$

$- Of[(a)_0, \ln(a), m]$,

$= a$ otherwise.

Then if a is the number of a (number or class) term, or of a formula, and m is the number of a number term if $k = 0$, of a class term of level $< k$ if $k \neq 0$, then su(m, k, n, a) is the result of substituting in the object number a the term number m for each occurrence of the variable number $2^k \cdot p_n$; it is a term or a formula according as a is a term or a formula, and its level is no greater than that of a . If WF(a) and WF(m) both hold, then WF[su(m, k, n, a)] holds, and moreover no free variable in a can be captured by a quantifierin m , nor can any free variable in m be captured by a quantifier in a .

Note that we often omit the phrase "the term number ..." or "the formula number ..." and speak as if a formula or term and its number were identical.

We now consider the problem of numbering proofs in Z_0 and $RA(Z_0)$. We have the following predicates which correspond to the inferences of Schütte's logic. In most cases, we do not give the definition, which can be written down mechanically, and regard it as obvious that they are primitive recursive.

Def. 7. $Um_1(b, c) \equiv . b = 40 \cdot 7^{(b)_3} \cdot 11 \exp 40 \cdot 7^{(b)_{43}} \cdot 11^{40 \cdot 7^{(b)_{443}} \cdot 11^{(b)_{444}}}$ & $c = 40 \cdot 7^{(b)_3} \cdot 11 \exp 40 \cdot 7^{(b)_{443}} \cdot 11^{40 \cdot 7^{(b)_{43}} \cdot 11^{(b)_{444}}}$

$Um_1(b, c)$ holds if b is the number of a formula

$\mathfrak{M} \vee [\mathfrak{A} \vee (\mathfrak{B} \vee \mathfrak{N})]$ and c is the number of $\mathfrak{M} \vee [\mathfrak{B} \vee (\mathfrak{A} \vee \mathfrak{N})]$.

$Um_2(b, c)$ -- b is the number of $\mathfrak{A} \vee (\mathfrak{B} \vee \mathfrak{N})$, and c is the number of $\mathfrak{B} \vee (\mathfrak{A} \vee \mathfrak{N})$.

$Um_3(b, c)$ -- b is the number of $\mathfrak{M} \vee (\mathfrak{A} \vee \mathfrak{B})$, and c is the number of $\mathfrak{M} \vee (\mathfrak{B} \vee \mathfrak{A})$.

$Um_4(b, c)$ -- b is the number of $\mathfrak{A} \vee \mathfrak{B}$, and c is the number of $\mathfrak{B} \vee \mathfrak{A}$.

Um(b, c) -- b is obtained from c by interchange (II A 1, p. 129).

Ku(b, c) -- b is obtained from c by contraction

tion (II A 2).

Def. 8. Wk(b, c) -- b is obtained from c by weakening (II B 1).

Def. 9. Ne(b, c) -- b is obtained from c by negation (II B 2).

Def. 10. Cp(b, c, d) -- b is obtained from c and d by compositiont (II B 3).

Def. 11. $Bi_1(b, c)$ -- b is the number of a formula $(Ex)\mathfrak{A}(x) \vee \mathfrak{N}$, and c is the number of a formula $\mathfrak{A}(t) \vee \mathfrak{N}$, where may be missing.

$Bi_{11}(b, c)$ [$\mathfrak{N}$ present] ≡.

$b = 40 \cdot [7 \exp 100 \cdot p_{ln(b)_3}{}^{(b)_{3,ln(b)_3}}] \cdot 11^{(b)_4}$ &

$(Ey)\{y < (c)_3$ & $c = 40 \cdot 7 \exp su[y, 0, ln[(b)_3], (b)_{3,ln\,(b)_3}]$

$\cdot\, 11^{(b)_4}$ & $Tm(y)\}$

$Bi_{12}(b, c)$ ≡ the case with $\mathfrak{N}$ absent.

$Bi_1(b, c) \equiv . Bi_{11}(b, c) \vee Bi_{12}(b, c)$

Let bi(b, c) be the number of the term t, e. g.

$bi(b, c) = \mu y\{y < (c)_3$ & $c = 40 \cdot 7 \exp su[y, 0, ln((b)_3),$
$(b)_{3,ln\,(b)_3}] \cdot 11^{(b)_4}$ & $Tm(y)\}$ if $Bi_{11}(b, c)$

etc.

Def. 12. $Bi_2(b, c)$ -- b is the number of a formula $-(x)\mathfrak{A}(x) \vee \mathfrak{N}$, and c is the number of a formula $-\mathfrak{A}(t) \vee \mathfrak{N}$.

The definition of bi(b, c) should cover this case also.

Def. 13. $Ge_1(b, c)$ -- c is the number of $\mathfrak{A}(a) \vee \mathfrak{N}$, b is the number of a formula $(x)\mathcal{A}(x) \vee \mathcal{N}$, where a is not free in the conclusion

$Ge_{12}(b, c)$ [$\mathcal{N}$ missing] $\equiv . b = 50 \cdot \mathcal{P}_{ln\ b}{}^{(b)_{ln\ b}}$ & $(Ey)\{y < c$ & $c = su[\mathcal{P}_y, 0, ln(b), (b)_{ln\ b}]$ & $2 < y$ & $- Of[0, y, (b)_{ln\ b}]\}$

Then if $Ge_{11}(b, c)$ defines the case with present, $Ge_1(b, c) \equiv . Ge_{11}(b, c) \vee Ge_{12}(b, c)$.

Let $gev(b, c)$ be a primitive recursive function such that $\mathcal{P}_{gev(b,c)}$ is the number of the variable a .

Def. 14. $Ge_2(b, c)$ -- c is the number of a formula $- \mathcal{A}(a) \vee \mathcal{N}$, b is the number of $- (Ex)\mathcal{A}(x) \vee \mathcal{N}$, and the variable condition is satisfied.

The definition of $gev(b, c)$ should cover this case also.

Def. 15. $Cut(b, c, d)$ -- b is $\mathcal{M} \vee \mathcal{N}$, c is $\mathcal{M} \vee \mathcal{A}$ d is $- \mathcal{A} \vee \mathcal{N}$, where either $\mathcal{M}$ or $\mathcal{N}$, but not both, may be missing.

Let $cf(b, c, d)$ be the number of $\mathcal{A}$.

Def. 16. $Bi_3(b, c)$ -- b is the number of a formula $(EX)\mathcal{A}(X) \vee \mathcal{N}$, c is the number of a formula $\mathcal{A}(T) \vee \mathcal{N}$, where T is a class term whose level is not greater than that of X .

$Bi_{31}(b, c)$ [$\mathcal{N}$ present] $\equiv . b = 40 \cdot [7 \exp 2^{(b)_{30}} \cdot 5^4 \cdot \mathcal{P}_{ln\ (b)_3}{}^{(b)_{3, ln\ (b)_3}}] \cdot 11^{(b)_4}$ & $(b)_{30} \neq 0$

$\& \ (Ey)(Ex)\{y < (c)_3 \ \& \ x \leq (b)_{30} \dot{-} 1 \ \& \ CT(x, y) \ \&$

$c = 40 \cdot 7^{su[y, (b)_{30}, ln((b)_3), (b)_{3, ln(b)_3}]} \cdot 11^{(b)_4}\}$

Bi_3 similar to def. 13.

The definition of bi(b, c) should cover this case also.

Def. 17. $Bi_4(b, c)$ -- b is the number of a formula $-(X)\mathcal{A}(X) \vee \mathcal{N}$, c is the number of a formula $-\mathcal{A}(T) \vee \mathcal{N}$, with the same condition on T .

The definition of bi(b, c) should cover this case also.

Def. 18. $Ge_3(b, c)$ -- b is the number of a formula $\mathcal{A}(Y) \vee \mathcal{N}$, b is the number of a formula $(X)\mathcal{A}(X) \vee \mathcal{N}$, where the level of Y and the level of X are the same, and Y does not occur free in b .

Def. 19. $Ge_4(b, c)$ -- b is the number of a formula $-(EX)\mathcal{A}(X) \vee \mathcal{N}$, c is the number of a formula $-\mathcal{A}(Y) \vee \mathcal{N}$, and the other conditions of def. 18 hold.

The definition of gev(b, c) should cover these cases. If k is the level of X (i. e., in the case Ge_{31}, if $k + 1 = (b)_{30}$) then $2^{k+1} \cdot p_{gev(b, c)}$ should be the number of Y . Then set $k + 1 = gev_o(b, c)$.

Let $lv(b, c) = 0$ if $Ge_1(b, c) \vee Ge_2(b, c)$

$= (m)_o$, where m is the formula $(X)\mathcal{A}(X)$ or $(EX)\mathcal{A}(X)$, if $Ge_3(b, c) \vee Ge_4(b, c)$, so that in this case the level of X is $lv(b, c) \dot{-} 1$.

Def. 20. Abs(b, c) -- b is obtained from c by one of the two abstraction inferences (II B 8, pp. 189-90).

We now define proof predicates for systems without induction formalized in Schütte's logic. We assume that a primitive rexursive predicate Ax(a) , ' a is the number of a non-logical or equality axiom of $\mathfrak{F}'$ is given. We suppose the axioms are closed under substitution for number variables.

Def. 21. Prk(a, b) -- a is the number of a proof on the the formula number b from formulae satisfying Ax(a) in Schütte's first order predicate calculus.

$$\mathrm{Prk}(a, b) \equiv :: \mathrm{Fl}(b) \;\&:.$$

$$a = 2^b \;\&\; \mathrm{Ax}(b).$$

$$v.\; a = 2^b \;\&\; b = 40 \cdot 7^{3(b)_4} \cdot 11^{(b)_4}$$

$$\&\; (b)_4 = 70 \cdot 11^{(b)_{44}} \cdot 13^{(b)_{45}}.$$

$$v:\; a = 2^b \cdot 5^{(a)_2} \;\&\; \mathrm{Prk}[(a)_2, (a)_{20}] \;\&.\; \mathrm{Um}[b, (a)_{20}]$$

$$v\; \mathrm{Ku}[b, (a)_{20}]:$$

$$v.\; a = 2^b \cdot 5^{(a)_2} \cdot 7^{(a)_3} \;\&\; \mathrm{Prk}[(a)_2, (a)_{20}] \;\&$$

$$\mathrm{Prk}[(a)_3, (a)_{30}] \;\&\; \mathrm{Cut}[b, (a)_{20}, (a)_{30}].$$

$$v:\; a = 2^b \cdot 7^{(a)_3} \;\&\; \mathrm{Prk}[(a)_3, (a)_{30}] \;\&.\; \mathrm{Wk}[b, (a)_{30}]$$

$$v\; \mathrm{Ne}[b, (a)_{30}] \;v\; \mathrm{Bi}_1[b, (a)_{30}] \;v\; \mathrm{Bi}_2[b, (a)_{30}]$$

$$v\; \mathrm{Ge}_1[b, (a)_{30}] \;v\; \mathrm{Ge}_2[b, (a)_{30}]:$$

$$v.\; a = 2^b \cdot 7^{(a)_3} \cdot 11^{(a)_4} \;\&\; \mathrm{Cp}[b, (a)_{30}, (a)_{40}] \;\&$$

$$\mathrm{Prk}[(a)_{30}, (a)_{30}] \;\&\; \mathrm{Prk}[(a)_4, (a)_{40}] \;.$$

Def. 22. Prkr(a, b) -- a is the number of a proof of

the formula number b in Schütte's ramified second order predicate calculus. In def. 21, replace ' Fl(b) & WF(b) ' by ' (Ex)[x ≤ b & WFF(x, b)] ', and add the alternands

$$\text{v. } a = 2^b \ \& \ b = 40 \cdot 7^{3(b)_4} \cdot 11^{(b)_4} \ \&$$
$$(b)_4 = 70 \cdot \mathcal{P}_{\ln (b)_4}\ \exp (b)_{4,\ln (b)_4} \ \&$$
$$\ln[(b)_4] = 2^{(\ln[(b)_4])_0} \cdot \mathcal{P}_{\ln[\ln (b)_4]} \cdot$$
$$\text{v: } a = 2^b \cdot 13^{(a)_5} \ \& \ \text{Prkr}[(a)_5, (a)_{50}] \ \&. \ \text{Bi}_3[b, (a)_{50}]$$
$$\text{v Bi}_4[b, (a)_{50}] \text{ v Ge}_3[b, (a)_{50}] \text{ v Ge}_4[b, (a)_{50}] :$$
$$\text{v. } a = 2^b \cdot 17^{(a)_6} \ \& \ \text{Abs}[b, (a)_{60}] \ \& \ \text{Prkr}[(a)_6, (a)_{60}] ,$$

and of course change Prk to Prkr in the other alternands.

We now define proof predicates for systems with induction.

<u>Def. 23</u>. Prki(a, b) -- a is the number of a proof in Z_o of the formula number b , if Ax(a) is the predicate ' a is the number of an axiom of Z_o ' .

Add to the alternation of def. 21 the alternand

$$\text{v. } a = 2^b \cdot 5^{(a)_2} \cdot 11^{(a)_4} \ \& \ \text{Prki}[(a)_2, (a)_{20}] \ \&$$
$$\text{Prki}[(a)_4, (a)_{40}] \ \& \ (Ey)(Ez)\{y < b \ \& \ z < (a)_{403}/3$$
$$\& \ (a)_{20} = \text{su}[2, 0, z, (a)_{403}/3] \ \& \ (a)_{404} =$$
$$\text{su}[3z, 0, z, (a)_{403}/3] \ \& \ b = \text{su}[y, 0, z, (a)_{403}/3]$$
$$\& \ 2 < z \ \& \ (a)_{40} = 40 \cdot 7^{(a)_{403}} \cdot 11^{(a)_{404}} \ \& \ 3 | (a)_{403} \}$$

and change Prk to Prki in the others.

<u>Def. 24</u>. Prir(a, b) -- a is the number of a proof in $RA(Z_o)$ of the formula number b . The same change from

def. 22 as in def. 23 from def. 21.

Before introducing infinite induction and defining the functions used in the text, we define a multiple substitution function for number variables.

Def. 25. $\overline{st}(0, m, p, a) = a$

$\overline{st}(k + 1, m, p, a) = su\{(m)_k, 0, max(m, a) + 1, su[\mathscr{P}_{max(m,a)+1}, 0, (p)_k, \overline{st}(k, m, p, a)]\}$

Then if for each $i < k$, $(m)_i$ is the number of a numerical term and $2 < (p)_i$, then $\overline{st}(k, m, p, a)$ is the number of the result of simultaneous substitution of $(m)_0 \ldots (m)_{k-1}$ for the variables $\mathscr{P}_{(p)_0} \ldots \mathscr{P}_{(p)_{k-1}}$ respectively. At each stage, we first substitute the variable $\mathscr{P}_{max(m,a)+1}$, which is certain not to occur either in a or in any of the terms $(m)_i$.

We now define a valuation for numerical terms and formulae. This will be in the form of functionals whose arguments can be interpreted as the functions represented by the function symbols of the terms (either given functions of Z_0 or chosen substitutions for function variables). We shall also allow for a preassigned finite class of number variables.

Def. 26. Let $r_1 \ldots r_k$ be numbers such that the function symbol f_i is assigned the function $n_1 \ldots n_{m_i}$ $5 \cdot \mathscr{P}_{r_i}^{n_1} \cdot \ldots \cdot \mathscr{P}_{r_i+m_i-1}^{n_{m_i}}$, $i = 1 \ldots k$; let $s_1 \ldots$

s_m be the numbers of $a_1 \dots a_m$ respectively.

$$\begin{aligned} val(f_1 \dots f_k, a_1 \dots a_m, b) &= 0 \quad \text{if} \quad b = 2 , \\ &= val(f_1 \dots f_k, a_1 \dots a_m, b/3) \quad \text{if} \quad 3|b , \\ &= a_j \quad \text{if} \quad b = s_j \\ &= f_i\{val[\bar{f}, \bar{a}, (b)_{r_i}] \dots val[\bar{f}, \bar{a}, (b)_{r_i+m_i-1}]\} \\ &\quad \text{if} \quad b = 5 \cdot \prod_{j<m_i} p_{r_i+j}^{(b)_{r_i+j}} . \end{aligned}$$

Then if b is the number of a term whose only function symbols are S and $f_1 \dots f_k$ and whose only number variables are $a_1 \dots a_m$, then $val(\bar{f}, \bar{a}, b)$ is the numerical value of b for a given substitution for these symbols.

We also set

$$\begin{aligned} Val(\bar{f}, \bar{a}, c) &= 0 \quad \text{if} \quad c = 70 \cdot 11^{(c)_4} \cdot 13^{(c)_5} \ \& \\ &\qquad val[\bar{f}, \bar{a}, (c)_4] = val[\bar{f}, \bar{a}, (c)_5] , \\ &= 1 \quad \text{if} \quad c = 70 \cdot 11^{(c)_4} \cdot 13^{(c)_5} \ \& \\ &\qquad val[\bar{f}, \bar{a}, (c)_4] \neq val[\bar{f}, \bar{a}, (c)_5] \\ &= \overline{sg}[Val(\bar{f}, \bar{a}, c/3)] \quad \text{if} \quad 3|c , \\ &= Val[\bar{f}, \bar{a}, (c)_3] \cdot Val[\bar{f}, \bar{a}, (c)_4] \\ &\qquad \text{if} \quad c = 40 \cdot 7^{(c)_3} \cdot 11^{(c)_4} . \end{aligned}$$

Then if c is the number of a numerical formula composed of terms to which val applies by = and v and - , then $Val(\bar{f}, \bar{a}, c) = 0$ if c is true for the given substitution, and $Val(\bar{f}, \bar{a}, c) = 1$ if c is false. Then the predicate $Tr(\bar{f}, \bar{a}, c)$ of page 158 can be $Val(\bar{f}, \bar{a}, c) = 0$.

We now define a predicate which holds of two numbers

af and b iff b is the number of a formula obtained from the formula number a by replacing certain terms, closed relatively to $\overline{f}$, $\overline{a}$, by others of the same numerical value. We call two such formulae <u>equal-valued</u> (<u>gleichwertig</u>).

<u>Def. 27</u>. $Gw(a, b) \equiv :: Tm(a) \ \&\ Tm(b) \ \&\ (x)[2 < x < \max(a,b)$

$\&. Of(0, x, a) \vee Of(0, x, b) : \supset . \wp_x = s_1 \vee \ldots \vee$

$\wp_x = s_n] \ \&\ val(\overline{f}, \overline{a}, a) = val(\overline{f}, \overline{a}, b).$

$\vee.\ 3\ a \ \&\ 3\ b \ \&\ Gw[a/3, b/3]. \vee : a = b \ \&: a = 2 \vee . Pr(a) \ \&\ 7 \leq a :.$

$\vee. \bigvee_{1 \leq i \leq k} \quad a = 5 \cdot \prod_{j<m_i} \wp_{r_i+j}{}^{(a)_{r_i+j}} \ \&\ b = 5 \cdot \prod_{j<m_i} \wp_{r_i+j}{}^{(b)_{r_i+j}}$

$\&\ \bigwedge_{j<m_i} Gw[(a)_{r_i+j}, (b)_{r_i+j}]$

$\vee.\ a = 70 \cdot 11^{(a)_4} \cdot 13^{(a)_5} \ \&\ b = 70 \cdot 11^{(b)_4} \cdot 13^{(b)_5}$

$\&\ Gw[(a)_4, (b)_4] \ \&\ Gw[(a)_5, (b)_5]$, etc.

The rest of the cases are similar; at each stage of the inductive description of term-or-formula (cf. def. 3), $Gw(a, b)$ is asserted to hold if a and b have the same outermost form and Gw holds between the next inner components. For class variables we put in the clause

$\vee.\ a = b \ \&\ a = 2^{(a)_0} \cdot \wp_{\ln a} \ \&\ 2 < \ln(a).$

In this and in our subsequent exposition we shall consider a formula well-formed only if S , $f_1 \ldots f_k$ are its only function symbols. We do allow other number variables than $a_1 \ldots a_m$, but val is undefined for terms which contain such variables.

Now we are ready to give the proof predicate for systems with infinite induction. We set

$$Ax_o(a) \equiv Ax(a) \text{ v. } a = 40 \cdot 7^{3(a)_4} \cdot 11^{(a)_4} \text{ \&:} Tm[(a)_{44}]$$

$$\text{\& } Tm[(a)_{45}] \text{ \& } (a)_4 = 70 \cdot 11^{(a)_{44}} \cdot 11^{(a)_{45}}. \text{ v.}$$

$$(a)_4 = 70 \cdot \mathcal{P}_{\ln (a)_4}{}^{(a)_{\ln (a)_4}} \text{ \& } Tm[(a)_{\ln (a)_4}]$$

$$\text{\& } \ln[(a)_4] = 2^{(\ln (a)_4)_o} \cdot \mathcal{P}_{\ln[\ln (a)_4]} \cdot$$

(cf. defs. 21 and 22).

Def. 29. Prks(a, b) -- a is the number of a proof in S_o of the formula number b . We assume a predicate $<_o$ which will be a well-ordering of the natural numbers; in the text, different well-orderings are used.

$$Prks(a, b) \equiv :: Fl(b) \text{ \& } WF(b) \text{ \&:. } a = 2^b \text{ \&}$$

$$(Ew)[Gw(b, x) \text{ \& } Ax_o(x)].$$

$$\text{v: } a = 2^b \cdot 3^{(a)_1} \cdot 5^{(a)_2} \text{ \& } (a)_1 = (a)_{21} \text{ \& } Prks[(a)_2, (a)_{20}]$$

$$\text{\&. } Um[b, (a)_{20}] \text{ v } Ku[b, (a)_{20}]:$$

$$\text{v. } a = 2^b \cdot 3^{(a)_1} \cdot 5^{(a)_2} \cdot 7^{(a)_3} \text{ \& } (a)_{21} <_o (a)_1 \text{ \&}$$

$$(a)_{31} <_o (a)_1 \text{ \& } Prks[(a)_2, (a)_{20}] \text{ \& } Prks[(a)_3, (a)_{30}]$$

$$\text{\& } Cut[b, (a)_{20}, (a)_{30}].$$

$$\text{v: } a = 2^b \cdot 3^{(a)_1} \cdot 7^{(a)_3} \text{ \& } (a)_{31} <_o (a)_1 \text{ \& } Prk[(a)_3, (a)_{30}].$$

$$\text{\&. } Wk[b, (a)_{30}] \text{ v } \ldots \text{ v } Ge_2[b, (a)_{30}]: \quad \text{(cf. def. 21)}$$

$$\text{v. } a = 2^b \cdot 3^{(a)_1} \cdot 7^{(a)_3} \cdot 11^{(a)_4} \text{ \& } Cp[b, (a)_{30}, (a)_{40}]$$

$$\text{\& } Prks[(a)_3, (a)_{30}] \text{ \& } Prks[(a)_4, (a)_{40}] \text{ \& } (a)_{31} <_o (a)_1$$

$$\text{\& } (a)_{41} <_o (a)_1.$$

$$\text{v. } a = 2^b \cdot 3^{(a)_1} \cdot 11^{(a)_4} \cdot 19^{(a)_7} \text{ \& } (x)\, Prks[(a)_4(x),$$

$$\overline{st}\{\ln[(a)_7 + 1, \prod_{i \le \ln (a)_7} \mathcal{P}_i{}^{(x)_i}, (a)_7, b\} \text{ \&}$$

$((a)_4(x))_1 <_o (a)_1$ & $(y)[y \leq \ln((a)_7) \supset 2 < \{\ln (a)_7)_1]$

In the last clause, $\mathcal{P}_{((a)_7)_o} \ldots \mathcal{P}_{((a)_7)_{\ln (a)_7}}$ are the numbers of number variables such that for each x we suppose we have a proof, numbered $(a)_4(x) = U(\mu y T_1^{\bar{f}, \bar{a}}[(a)_4, x, y])$ of the result of simultaneous substitution of $0^{((x)_o)} \ldots 0^{((x)_{\ln (a)_7})}$ for these variables. Thus we suppose we have proofs of all the instances of substituting numerals for these variables.

By the same changes as in defs. 22 and 24, we can define the corresponding proof predicate Prsr(a, b) for $RA(S_o)$. As we have defined it, Prks(a, b) includes proofs with free class variables. This can be prevented by dropping the second alternand of the last alternand in the definition of Ax_o.

We note that in practice we shall always take the proof-generating functions $\{(a)_4\}$ from a recursively enumerable class of general recursive functions, so that the expression $(a)_4(x)$ could be replaced by $f[(a)_4, x]$ for some recursive f, in the number theoretic case, the function which enumerates all primitive recursive functions.

If arbitrary general recursive functions are admitted, then it appears that Prks is not arithmetical. Even with the restriction, it is not recursive or r. e. The predicate would be eliminated from our exposition, since we confine our interest to an r. e. subclass of the numbers a of "proofs". This subclass is the union of the ranges of our various transformations of proofs, starting with proofs in the proper formal systems Z_0 and $RA(Z_0)$.

Finally, we remark that although we have suppressed the function arguments, the proof predicate depends on $f_1 \ldots f_k, a_1 \ldots a_m$, both through the class of axioms, which depends on the valuation of def. 26, and through the fact that the proof-generating functions are defined relatively to $\bar{f}, \bar{a}$.

Def. 29. g(a) is to be a primitive recursive functionsuch that if a is the number of a formula A of ramified analysis, then g(a) is to be the number of a cut-free proof in Schütte's ramified second order calculus of - A v A . This function would be defined by arithmetizing the following argument:

1. A is a numerical prime formula of of the form $t \notin X \vee t \in X$. Then - A v A is an axiom.

2. If A is - B , by hypothesis of induction we have - B v B , hence B v - B , hence - - B v - B .

2. If A is B v C , then from - B v B we infer by weakening and interchanges, - B v (B v C) ; likewise we have - C v (B v C) , and - A v A by composition.

3. If - B(a) v B(a) has been proved, then by binding we obtain - (x)B(x) v B(a) , and by interchange and

generalization $-(x)B(x) \vee (x)B(x)$. Hence if A is $(x)B(x)$, things are all right. The situation is similar if A is $(Ex)B(x)$, $(X)B(X)$, or $(EX)B(X)$.

4. If A is $t \varepsilon xB(x)$ and we have $-B(t) \vee B(t)$, then we obtain $-A \vee A$ by abstractions and interchanges.

Considered as a proof in $RA(S_0)$, the order of this proof is $\leq$ twice the logical degree of A . Let $g'(a)$ be a primitive recursive function which gives the number of a proof of $-A \vee A$ in $RA(S_0)$.

If A is a formula of Z_0 , then $g(a)$ is the number of a first-order proof, and $g'(a)$ is the number of a proof in S_0 .

We now define a series of auxiliary functionals φ_i which are used in the elimination of cuts in S_0 and $RA(S_0)$. We shall suppress the arguments $f_1 \ldots f_k$, $a_1 \ldots a_m$ throughout. Since in the application we work with a fixed substitution for these, we can think of ourselves as defining functions relative to them.

First we define primitive recursive function $\psi_1(c, b, x)$ and a functional $\varphi_1(a, b, x)$ with the following properties: If c is the number of an alternation, then $\varphi_1(c, b, x)$ is the number of the formula which results from changing the $(i + 1)$st alternand from $- - B$ to B , if it happens that $(x)_i \neq 0$ and the $(i + 1)$st alternand of c is $- - B$, where B is the formula number b . Then if a is the number of a proof of c , $\varphi_1(a, b, x)$ is the number of a proof of $\psi_1(c, b, x)$. In particular, if a is the number of a proof of $- - B \vee N$, then $\varphi_1(a, b, 2)$ is the number of a proof of $B \vee N$.

If a has no infinite inductions, neither has $\varphi_1(a, b, x)$. If a has no bound class variables, neither has $\varphi_1(a, b, x)$. If the cuts of a are of no more than a certain level, binding degree, or degree, so are those of $\varphi_1(a, b, x)$. If a has infinite inductions and is of a certain order, then $\varphi_1(a, b, x)$ is of no larger order. If a transformation of proofs satisfies all these conditions, we shall say it is standardly simple. The functionals we define will operate on all the classes of proofs so far defined (with certain exceptions, in particular φ_3) except those with induction, and here some will.

Def. 30.
$$na(b) = 1 \quad \text{if} \quad b \neq 40 \cdot 7^{(b)_3} \cdot 11^{(b)_4}$$
$$= na[(b)_3] + na[(b)_4] \quad \text{otherwise.}$$
$$sq(c, x) = \prod_{1 < na[(c)_4]} p_1^{(x)_{na\,(c)_3 + 1}}$$
$$\psi_1(c, b, x) = b \quad \text{if} \quad c = 9b \text{ and } (x)_0 \neq 0$$
$$= 40 \cdot 7^{\psi_1[(c)_3, b, x]} \cdot 11^{\psi_1[(c)_4, b, sq(c,x)]} \quad \text{if} \quad c = 40 \cdot 7^{(c)_3} \cdot 11^{(c)_4}$$
$$= c \quad \text{otherwise.}$$

Clearly if c is an alternation, $na(c)$ is the number of its alternands. If $(x)_1 \neq 0$ and $na[(c)_3] \leq 1$, then

$(sq(c, x))_{i-na\ (c)_3} \neq 0$, so that if $- - B$ is the $(i+1)$st alternand of c in the second case, it is replaced if i functions as it should for $(c)_3$.

In order to define φ_1 recursively on the ways of constructing proofs in $RA(S_0)$, we need functions which pick out alternands in the premiss of an inference which are in the Formelbund of those in the conclusion for which $(x)_i \neq 0$ and $- - B$ is to be replaced. For example if the last inference of a proof is an interchange

$$\frac{\mathcal{M} \vee (\mathcal{B} \vee (\mathcal{A} \vee \mathcal{N}))}{\mathcal{M} \vee (\mathcal{A} \vee (\mathcal{B} \vee \mathcal{N}))}$$

then if $i \leq$ the number of alternands of $\mathcal{M}$ and $(x)_i \neq 0$, we want $(y)_i \neq 0$ for the number y which picks out the correspondent; if the i th alternand of the conclusion is an alternand of $\mathcal{A}$, then the $i + na(c)$ th alternand of the premiss is the correspondent, if c is the number of $\mathcal{B}$, etc. If we set

$$Cum_1(b, c, x) = \prod_{i<na(b)} p_i^{h(b,c,x,i)} \text{ , where}$$

$$\begin{aligned} h(b, c, x, i) &= (x)_i && \text{if } i < na[(b)_3] \\ &= (x)_{i+na\ (b)_{443}} && \text{if } na[(b)_3] \leq i < na[(b)_{43}] \\ &= (x)_{i-na\ (b)_{443}} && \\ & na[(b)_3] + na[(b)_{43}] \leq i < && na[(b)_3] + na[(b)_{43}] + na[(b)_{443}] \end{aligned}$$

$h(b, c, x, i) = (x)_i$ otherwise,

then it will pergoem this function if $Um_1(b, c)$ (def. 6, p. 265).

Similarly we can define Cum_i for $i = 2, 3, 4$ and

$$Cum(b, c, x) = Cum_i(b, c, x) \quad \text{if } Um_i(b, c)$$
$$i = 1 \ldots 4.$$

With each inference we can associate a function of this sort which can be easily defined; the case we have given is the most complex. We note that at a constructional inference the Formelbund containing the principal formula does not contimue.

Given the functions Cum , Cku, $Ccut_i$, etc. , we define functions $s_i(a, x)$, $i = 2 \ldots 6$, which pick out the appropriate function for the exponent of p_1 in the number of the proof number a .

For example (see defs. 21, 22, 29), if a is the number of a proof, then $(a)_2$ is either 0 or the number of a proof of a formula A_0 from which the last line of a is got by interchange, contraction, or cut with another premiss B_0 . Hence we dan set

$$\begin{aligned} s_2(a, x) &= Cum[(a)_0, (a)_{20}, x] \quad \text{if } Um[(a)_0, (a)_{20}]; \\ &= Cku[(a)_0, (a)_{20}, x] \quad \text{if } Ku[(a)_0, (a)_{20}] \\ &= Ccut_1[(a)_0, (a)_{20}, x] \quad \text{if } Cut[(a)_0, (a)_{20}, (a)_{30}] . \end{aligned}$$

(The two-premiss inferences require two Formelbund functions, one for each premiss. In s_4 , we neglect infinite induction.)

The other cases are similar. Now we set

$$\varphi_1(e, a, b, x) = a \quad \text{if} \quad a = 2^{(a)_0}$$

$$= \varphi_1[e, (a)_2, b, s_2(a, x)]$$

if $\ln(a) = 2$ & $\hat{\psi_1}[(a)_{20}, b, s_2(a, x)] = \hat{\psi_1}[(a)_0, b, x]$,

$$= 2^{\hat{\psi_1}[(a)_0, b, x]} \cdot 3^{(\varphi_1[e, (a)_2, b, s_2(a, x)])_1} \cdot 5^{\varphi_1[e, (a)_2, b, s_2(a, x)]}$$

if $\ln(a) = 2$ & $\hat{\psi_1}[(a)_{20}, b, s_2(a, x)] = \hat{\psi_1}[(a)_0, b, x]$,

$$= \varphi_1[e, (a)_3, s_3(a, x)]$$

if $\ln(a) = 3$ & $(a)_2 = 0$ & $\hat{\psi_1}[(a)_0, b, x] = \hat{\psi_1}[(a)_{30}, b, s_3(a, x)]$,

$$= 2^{\hat{\psi_1}[(a)_0, b, x]} \cdot 3^{(a)_1} \cdot \prod_{i \le 4} p_i^{\varphi_1[e, (a)_{i+2}, b, s_{i+2}(a, x)]}$$

otherwise, if $\ln(a) \le 6$

$$= 2^{\hat{\psi_1}[(a)_0, b, x]} \cdot 3^{(a)_1} \cdot 11^{F_1(e, a, b, x)} \cdot 19^{(a)_7}$$

if $\ln(a) = 7$, where $F_1(e, a, b, x)$ is a primitive recursive function which from e , a, b, x gives a Gödel number of the function(al)

$$\lambda n\, e\Big[(a)_5(n),\ \overline{st}\{\ln[(a)_7] + 1,\ \prod_{i \le \ln (a)_7} p_i^{2 \cdot 3^{(n)_i}},\ (a)_7,\ b\},\ x\Big].$$

$= a$ otherwise (in particular if $a = 0$).

By the recursion theorem, we can find a number e which is a Gödel number of $\lambda abx \varphi_1(e, a, b, x)$. Since $\lambda eabx \varphi_1(e, a, b, x)$ is primitive recursive, so is the fixed point. It follows that the functions which give the proofs of the premisses of infinite inductions in the transformed proofs are primitive recursive in the functions which do this in the original proofs. Therefore if $(a)_4$ is restricted to be the number of a primitive recursive function, the new proof obeys the restriction.

By induction on the proof predicates, we can easily see that the fixed point is defined for all numbers of proofs a , if b is the number of a formula, and that it yields a proof which has the properties claimed for it. Therefore if e is the mentioned number, we set:

$$\varphi_1(a, b, x) = \varphi_1(e, a, b, x) .$$

Def. 31. Similarly, we can define primitive recursive functions $\hat{\psi}_{21}(c, b_1, b_2, x)$, $\hat{\psi}_{22}(c, b_1, b_2, x)$, $\varphi_{21}(a, b_1, b_2, x)$, and $\varphi_{22}(a, b_1, b_2, x)$ with the following properties:

If b_i is the number of a formula B_i $(i = 1, 2)$, and c is the number of an alternation, then $\hat{\psi}_{21}(c, b_1, b_2, x)$ is the number of the alternation obtained from c by replacing $-(B_1 \vee B_2)$ by $-B_1$, if $-(B_1 \vee B_2)$ occurs as the $(j + 1)$st alternand and $(x)_j \neq 0$.

Then if a is the number of a proof of c , then $\varphi_{21}(a, b_1, b_2, x)$ is the number of a proof of $\hat{\psi}_{21}(c, b_1, b_2, x)$. The transformation is standardly simple.

Again, we note that if a is the number of a proof of $-(B_1 \vee B_2) \vee N$, then $\varphi_{21}(a, b_1, b_2, 2)$ is the number of a proof of $-B_1 \vee N$.

The fact that the functionals φ_1, φ_{21}, and φ_{22} are standardly simple transformations means that they are satisfactory for use in defining the ρ_1 of lemma 13.3. See pp. 142-5 and below, def. 42.

We now define a primitive recursive functional $\varphi_3(a, b, c, d, k)$ such that if b is the number of a formula A(x) , where the number of x is p_k , c and d are numbers of closed terms s and t respectively, and a is the number of a proof in $RA(S_o)$ of A(s) , then $\varphi_3(a, b, c, d, k)$ is the number of a proof in $RA(S_o)$ of A(t) .

<u>Def. 32</u>. First we define $\varphi_3(e, a, b, c, d, k)$.

$$\varphi_3(e, a, b, c, d, k) = 2^{su(d, 0, k, b)} \quad \text{if} \quad a = 2^{(a)_0} ;$$

(for by <u>def</u>. 29, if A(s) is an axiom, so is A(t) .)

$$= 2^{su(d,0,k,b)} \cdot 3^{(a)_1} \cdot \prod_{2 \leq i \leq 6} p_i^{\,e[e,(a)_i,m_i(a,b),c,d,k_i]}$$

if $1 < \ln(a) \leq 6$.

$m_i(a, b)$ is to be the function which describes a formula A'(x) such that in the given proof, A'(s) is (one of) the premiss(es) of the inference which yields A(s) . It is intended that in the new proof A'(t) will yield A(t) by the same inference.

This is done, as with the s_i , by the device of auxiliary functions Mum, Mku, etc., corresponding to each inference, and then observing that for $i = 2 \ldots 6$, $(a)_i$ must be the number of a proof of a premiss of one of a few inferences of which $A(s)$ is the conclusion.

For example

$$\mathrm{Mbi}_{11}(b_1, c_1, b) = 40 \cdot 7^{su[bi(b_1,c_1),0,ln((b)_3),(b)_3,ln(b)_3]} \cdot 11^{(b)_4} \quad \text{(cf. def. 11, p. 266)}$$

$$\mathrm{Mum}_1(b_1, c_1, b) = 40 \cdot 7^{(b)_3} \cdot 11 \exp$$
$$40 \cdot 7^{(b)_{443}} \cdot 11^{40 \cdot 7^{(b)_{43}} \cdot 11^{(b)_{444}}} .$$

$$M_3(a, b) = \mathrm{Mcut}_2[(a)_0, (a)_{30}, b] \text{ if } \mathrm{Cut}[(a)_0, (a)_{20}, (a)_{30}],$$
$$= \mathrm{Mcp}_1[(a)_0, (a)_{30}, b] \text{ if } \mathrm{Cp}[(a)_0, (a)_{30}, (a)_{40}],$$
etc. including
$$= \mathrm{Mbi}[(a)_0, (a)_{30}, b] \text{ if } \mathrm{Bi}_{1v2}[(a)_0, (a)_{30}]$$

We set $k_1 = (a)_{10} + 1$. This is to insure that we have a variable which does not occur in the premiss, so that the substitution for it will introduce only those occurrences of t which replace occurrences of s.

$$\varphi_3(a, b, c, d, k) = 2^{su(d,0,k,b)} \cdot 3^{(a)_1} \cdot 11^{F_3(e,a,b,c,d,k)} \cdot 19^{(a)_7}$$

if $ln(a) = 7$, where $F_3(e, a, b, c, d, k)$ is a primitive recursive function which gives a Gödel number of the function

$$\lambda n\, e\Big[(a)_4(n), \overline{st}\{ln[(a)_7] + 1, \prod_{i \le ln\,(a)_7} p_i^{2 \cdot 3^{(a)_i}}, (a)_7, b\}, c, d, k\Big] .$$

Again by the recursion theorem, we can find e_0 such that

e_0 is a Gödel number of $\lambda abcdk\,\varphi_3(e_0, a, b, c, d, k)$. For the same reason as in previous cases the proof-generating functions at infinite inductions are primitive recursive in those at infinite inductions in the old proof. By induction on the definition of proof, we see that the transformation is standardly simple.

To see that φ_3 gives a proof at all, note that nothing in the proof is affected by starting from the conclusion and removing some closed numerical terms in certain occurrences and replacing them by others, provided that this is carried through grosse Formelbünde, sothat inferences are transformed into new ones of the same kind. This is insured by our functions m_1 . Only axioms can be affected, and they are, in view of def. 29, replaced by new axioms if the new terms have the same numerical value as those they replace.

We now define a primitive recursive functional $\varphi_4(a, r, k, m)$ such that if a is the number of a proof of a formula $A(y)$, where $r = 0$ and k is odd and is the index of y , then if m is odd and is the index of z , $\varphi_4(a, r, k, m)$ is the number of a proof of $A(z)$. If $r \neq 0$, the same holds for class variables of level $r - 1$.

This transformation is also standardly simple. Moreover, we observe that since it follows from def. 29 that every line of a proof is strongly well-formed, no occurrence of z introduced by the transformation can be captured by a quantifier in the proof.

<u>Def. 33</u>. $\varphi_4(e, a, r, k, m) = 2^{su[2^{r}\cdot p_m, r, k, (a)_0]}$

if $a = 2^{(a)_0}$. Let su_0 abbreviate the above exponent.

$= 2^{su_0} \cdot 3^{(\varphi_4[e, (a)_2, r, k, m])_1} \cdot 5^{\varphi_4[e, (a)_2, r, k, m]}$

if $ln(a) = 2$ & $su_0 \neq su[2^{r}\cdot p_m, r, k, (a)_{20}]$,

$= \varphi_4[e, (a)_2, r, k, m]$

if $ln(a) = 2$ & $su_0 = su[2^{r}\cdot p_m, r, k, (a)_{20}]$,

$= 2^{su_0} \cdot 3^{(a)_1} \cdot \prod_{2 \leq i \leq 6} p_i^{\varphi_4[e, (a)_i, r, k, m]}$

if $2 < ln(a) \leq 6$ & $-[r = 0$ & $Ge_{1v2}((a)_0, (a)_{30})$ & $m = gev((a)_0, (a)_{30})$ .v. $r \neq 0$ & $Ge_{3v4}((a)_0, (a)_{50})$ & $m = gev((a)_0, (a)_{50})$ & $r = gev_0((a)_0, (a)_{50})]$,

$= 2^{su_0} \cdot 3^{(a)_1} \cdot 7 \exp \varphi_4\{e, \varphi_4[e, (a)_3, 0, m, (a)_{30} + 1], 0, k, m\}$

if $2 < ln(a) \leq 6$ & $r = 0$ & $Ge_{1v2}[(a)_0, (a)_{30}]$ & $m = gev[(a)_0, (a)_{30}]$ (note that since the number of a formula is always even, $(a)_{30} + 1$ is odd if a is the number of a proof),

$= 2^{su_0} \cdot 3^{(a)_1} \cdot 13 \exp \varphi_4\{e, \varphi_4[e, (a)_5, r, m, (a)_{50} + 1], r, k, m\}$

if $2 < ln(a) \leq 6$ & $Ge_{3v4}[(a)_0, (a)_{50}]$ & $m = gev[(a)_0, (a)_{50}]$ & $r = gev_0[(a)_0, (a)_{50}]$,

$= 2^{su_0} \cdot 3^{(a)_1} \cdot 11^{F_4(e, a, r, k, m)} \cdot 19^{g_4(a, r, k, m)}$

if $\ln(a) = 7$, where $F_4(e, a, r, k, m)$ and $g_4(a, r, k, m)$ are primitive recursive functions such that if $-\{r = 0$ & $(Ei)[i \leq \ln((a)_7)$ & $(a)_{7i} = k]\}$, $F_4(e, a, r, k, m)$ is a Gödel number of

$$\lambda n\ e[(a)_4(n), r, k, m]$$

and $g_4(a, r, k, m) = (a)_7$; if $r = 0$ & $(Ei)[i \leq \ln((a)_7)$ & $(a)_{7i} = k]$, then $F_4(e, a, r, k, m) = (a)_4$ and

$$g_4(a, r, k, m) = \prod_{i \leq \ln (a)_7} p_i^{j_4(a, r, k, m, i)} , \text{ where}$$

$$j_4(a, r, k, m, i) = (a)_{7i} \quad \text{if} \quad (a)_{7i} \neq k$$
$$= m \quad \text{if} \quad (a)_{7i} = k .$$

$\varphi_4(e, a, r, k, m) = a$ otherwise.

Again we choose an e_0 by the recursion theorem and let

$$\varphi_4(a, r, k, m) = \varphi_4(e_0, a, r, k, m) .$$

The reason for the complication in the infinite induction step is that the variable to be replaced may be one of the variables introduced by the infinite induction.

We now define a primitive recursive functional $\varphi_5(a, c, r, k)$ such that if a is the number of a proof of a formula $A(Y)$, where Y is the variable number $2^r \cdot p_k$, $r \neq 0$, and c is the number of a strongly well-formed class term T of level $\leq r - 1$, then $\varphi_5(a, c, r, k)$ is the number of a proof of $A(T)$. Moreover if $r = 0$, then if a

is the number of a proof of A(y) where y has number $\mathfrak{p}_k$, and c is the number of a term t , then $\varphi_5(a, c, r, k)$ is the number of a proof of A(t)

This transformation is also standardly simple except that if s is the number of a proof of finite order and $r \neq 0$, then the order might be increased by a finite amount.

Def. 34. Let su_1 abbreviate $su[c, r, k, (a)_{30}^{-}]$.

First we define functions $w_1(a, b)$, $w_2(a, b)$, $w_3(a, b)$, and $w_4(a, b)$ such that if a and b are number terms such that b is obtained from a by replacing occurrences of closed terms of equal value by others, then

$w_1(a, b)$ is the number of a term such that $a = \overline{st}\{ln[w_2(a, b)], w_3(a, b), w_2(a, b), w_1(a, b)\}$ and $b = \overline{st}\{ln[w_2(a, b)], w_4(a, b), w_2(a, b), w_1(a, b)\}$. I. e., $w_2(a, b)$ is the number of a string of variables, and $w_3(a, b)$ and $w_4(a, b)$ numbers of strings S_1 and S_2 of terms, such that a is obtained from $w_1(a, b)$ by substitution of S_1 for the variables $w_2(a, b)$, and b is obtained by substitution of S_2 .

If $Tm(a) \;\&\; Tm(b) \;\&\; (x)[2 < x \leq \max(a, b) \;\&.\; Of(0, x, a) \vee Of(0, x, b) :\supset . \mathfrak{p}_x = \bar{s}_1 \vee \ldots \vee \mathfrak{p}_x = s_m] \;\&\; val(a) = val(b)$, then

$$w_1(a, b) = \mathfrak{p}_{y_2(a,b)}$$

$$w_2(a, b) = 2^{w_1(a,b)}$$

$w_3(a, b) = 2^a \qquad w_4(a, b) = 2^b$

Otherwise, if $Pr(a)$ & $7 \leq a$ & $a = b$, then

$w_1(a, b) = a$

$w_i(a, b) = 1 \qquad i = 2, 3, 4.$

If 3 a and 3 b and $Gw(a/3, b/3)$, then

$w_1(a, b) = 3 \cdot w_1(a/3, b/3)$

$w_i(a, b) = w_i(a/3, b/3) \qquad i = 2, 3, 4.$

If $a = 5 \cdot \prod_{r_i \leq j < r_i + m_i} p_j^{(a)_j}$ & $b = 5 \cdot \prod_{r_i \leq j < r_i + m_i} p_j^{(b)_j}$

for some i , $1 \leq i \leq k$, and $(j)\{j < m_i \supset Gw[(a)_{r_i+j},$ $(b)_{r_i+j}]\}$, then we set

$$w_1^*(a, b) = \max_{j < m_i} w_1[(a)_{r_i+j}, (b)_{r_i+j}]$$

$$w_{1j}'(a, b) = st\{ln[w_2((a)_{r_i+j}, (b)_{r_i+j})], \prod_{p \leq ln\, w_2((a)_{r_i+j}, (b)_{r_i+j})} p_i^{(w_2(.))_p + w_1^*(a,b)}, w_2[(a)_{r_i+j}, (b)_{r_i+j}], w_1[(a)_{r_i+j}, (b)_{r_i+j}]\} \qquad (1)$$

for $j < m_i$. Then

$$w_1(a, b) = 5 \cdot \prod_{j < m_i} p_{r_i+j}^{w_{1j}'(a,b)}$$

$$w_2(a, b) = w_{21}'(a, b) * \ldots * w_{2m_i}'(a, b)$$

where $w_{2j}'(a, b)$ is the expression (1) (i. e. just that line), and if $a = \prod_{i \leq m} p_i^{(a)_i}$ & $b = \prod_{i \leq n} p_i^{(b)_i}$, $a * b = a \cdot \prod_{i \leq n} p_{m+i}^{(b)_i}$. [The purpose of raising the indices of the variables in $w_2(a, b)$ is to insure that we do not use

one which is already free in another arguments of the given term.] We note that from the first case it follows that if a variable is duplicated in the string $w_2(a, b)$, then by the properties of ν_2 the terms substituted for it are the same for its two occurrences in the string. By induction on the construction of equal-valued terms (def. 27), we see that the functions w_i accomplish what is claimed for them.

Now let

$$w(a, b, n) = \overline{st}\{ln[w_2(a, b)], \prod_{i<n} p_i^{(w_4(a,b))_i} \cdot p_n^{(w_2(a,b))_n} \prod_{n+1\leq i\leq ln\, w_2(a,b)} p_i^{(w_3(a,b))_i}, w_2(a, b), w_1(a, b)\}$$

$w(a, b, n)$ replaces variables before the $(n + 1)$st in the string w_2 by the terms for b, leaves the $(n + 1)$st alone, and replaces the later ones by the terms for a.

Now consider a formula $s \notin Y \vee s \in Y$, whose number is $40 \cdot 7^{3a} \cdot 11^{a}$, where $a = 70 \cdot p_p^{\,a}$, where $p = 2^r \cdot p_k$. Any formula equal-valued to this has number $40 \cdot 7^{3c_1} \cdot 11^{a}$, where $c_1 = 70 \cdot p_p^{\,b}$ and $Gw(a, b)$, if the term s is unchanged. Any axiom of the form $s' \in Y \vee s \in Y$ of $RA(S_o)$ can be obtained from $s \notin Y \vee s \in Y$ by this transformation.

Consider a formula $s' \notin T \vee s \in T$. By def. 29, if a is the number of T, $g'(70 \cdot p_c^{\,a})$ is the number

of a proof in $RA(S_0)$ of $s \not\varepsilon T \vee s \varepsilon T$. Then if
$w^1(a, b, n) = \underline{su}[(w_3(a, b))_n, 0, (w_2(a, b))_n, w(a, b, n)]$
and w^2 is the same with w_4 for w_3, then

$$\underline{\varphi_3}[g'(70 \cdot \mathfrak{p}_c{}^a), w(a, b, 0), w^1(a, b, 0), w^2(a, b, 0), (w_2(a, b))_0]$$

is the number of a proof of $s_0 \not\varepsilon T \vee s \varepsilon T$, where s_0 is the term number $w^2(a, b, 0)$.

Set $\psi_4(0, a, b, c) =$ the above φ_3-term.
If s_n is the term number $w^2(a, b, n)$, then if
$\psi_4(n, a, b, c)$ is the number of a proof of $s_n \not\varepsilon T \vee s \varepsilon T$,
then if

$$\psi_4(n + 1, a, b, c) = \underline{\varphi_3}[\psi_4(n, a, b, c), w(a, b, n + 1), w^1(a, b, n + 1), w^2(a, b, n + 1), (w_2(a, b))_{n+1}]$$

then $\psi_4(n + 1, a, b, c)$ is the number of a proof of
$s_{n+1} \not\varepsilon T \vee s \varepsilon T$.

Then by induction, if b is the number of s', then
$\psi_4[\underline{ln}[\underline{w_2}(a, b)], a, b, c)$ is the number of a proof in
$RA(S_0)$ of $s' \varepsilon T \vee s \varepsilon T$, whose order is $(g'(70 \cdot \mathfrak{p}_c{}^a))_1$.

We now define the functional $\varphi_5(e, a, c, r, k)$.
If $a = 2^{(a)_0}$ & $(a)_0 = 70 \cdot 7^{(a)_{03}} \cdot 11^{(a)_{04}}$ &
$(a)_{04} = 70 \cdot \mathfrak{p}_{2^r \cdot \mathfrak{p}_k}{}^{(a)_{04, 2^r \cdot \mathfrak{p}_k}}$ & $(a)_{03} = 3 \cdot 70 \cdot \mathfrak{p}_{2^r \cdot \mathfrak{p}_k}{}^{((a)_{03}/3)_{2^r \cdot \mathfrak{p}_k}}$, then $\underline{GW}[(a)_{04, 2^r \cdot \mathfrak{p}_k}, ((a)_{03}/3)_{2^r \cdot \mathfrak{p}_k}]$
must hold.

Then by the above, $\psi_4\{ln(w_2[(a)_{04, 2^r \cdot \mathfrak{p}_k}, ((a)_{03}/3)_{2^r \cdot \mathfrak{p}_k}]),$

$(a)_{04,2^{r}\cdot p_k}, ((a)_{03}/3)_{2^{r}\cdot p_k}$, c is the number of a proof in $RA(S_o)$ of $40 \cdot 7^{210\cdot p_c((a)_{03}/3)_{2^r p_k}} 11^{70\cdot p_c (a)_{04,2^r\cdot p_k}}$

Hence we can set in this case

$$\xi(a, c, r, k) = \varphi_4\{\ln(w_2[(a)_{04,2^r\cdot p_k}, ((a)_{03}/3)_{2^r\cdot p_k}]),$$
$$(a)_{04,2^r\cdot p_k}, ((a)_{03}/3)_{2^r\cdot p_k}, c\}$$

Let p_o abbreviate $(g'(70\cdot p_c{}^{(a)_{04,2^r\cdot p_k}}))_1$; let su_1 abbreviate $su[c, r, k, (a)_o]$.

$\varphi_5(e, a, c, r, k) = 2^{su_1}$ if $a = 2^{(a)_o}$ otherwise,

$= \varphi_5[e, (a)_2, c, r, k]$ if $\ln(a) = 2$ &

$su_1 = su[c, r, k, (a)_{30}]$

$= 2^{su_1} \cdot 3^{p_o +_o (a)_1} \cdot 5^{\varphi_5[e,(a)_2,c,r,k]}$

if $\ln(a) = 2$ otherwise,

(In the case $r = 0$, we set $p_o = 0$. We note that apart from this, the value of p_o depends only on c .

$= 2^{su_1} \cdot 3^{p_o +_o (a)_1} \cdot \prod_{2\le i\le 6} p_i{}^{5[e,(a)_i,c,r,k]}$

if $2 < \ln(a) \le 6$ & $-\{Ge_{1v2}[(a)_o, (a)_{30}]$ & Of 0, gev[$(a)_o$, $(a)_{30}$], c .v. $Ge_{3v4}[(a)_o, (a)_{50}]$ & Of $gev_o[(a)_o, (a)_{50}]$, $gev_1[(a)_o, (a)_{50}]$, c$\}$,

$= 2^{su_1} \cdot 3^{p_o +_o (a)_1} \cdot 7 \exp \varphi_5[e, \varphi_4\{(a)_3, 0, gev[(a)_o,$
$c + 1\}, c, r, k]$

if $\ln(a) = 3$ & $Ge_{1v2}[(a)_o, (a)_{30}]$ & Of$\{0, gev[(a)_o, (a)_{30}],$ c$\}$,

$$= 2^{su_1} \cdot 3^{p_0 +_0 (a)_1} \cdot 13 \exp \varphi_5 \Big[e, \varphi_4\{(a)_5, gev_0[(a)_0, (a)_{50}], gev[(a)_0, (a)_{50}], c + 1\}, c, r, k\Big],$$

$$= 2^{su_1} \cdot 3^{p_0 +_0 (a)_1} \cdot 11^{F_5(e,a,c,r,k)} \cdot 19^{g_5(a,c,r,k)}$$

if $\ln(a) = 7$, where F_5 and g_5 are primitive recursive functions such that

If $-(r = 0 \;\&\; (Ei)[i \leq \ln((a)_7) \;\&\; (a)_{7i} = k])$,

then $F_5(e, a, c, r, k)$ is a Gödel number of

$$\lambda n\, e\Big[(a)_4(n), \overline{st}\Big\{\ln((a)_7), \prod_{i \leq \ln (a)_7} p_i^{2 \cdot 3^{(n)_i}}, (a)_7, c\Big\}, r, k\Big],$$

and $g_5(a, c, r, k) = (a)_7$.

If $r = 0 \;\&\; (Ei)[i \leq \ln((a)_7) \;\&\; (a)_{7i} = k]$, then

$$g_5(a, c, r, k) = (a)_7 * \prod_{i < h_5'(a,c,r,k)} p_i^{h_5(a,c,r,k,i)}$$

where $h_5(a, c, r, k, 0) = \mu x \{x \leq c \;\&\; Of(0, x, c) \;\&\; (i)[i \leq \ln((a)_7) \supset (a)_{7i} \neq x]\}$,

$$h_5(a, c, r, k, n + 1) = \mu x\{h_5(a,c,r,k,n) < x \leq c \;\&\; Of(0, x, c) \;\&\; (i)[i \leq \ln((a)_7) \supset (a)_{7i} \neq x]\}$$

$$h_5'(a, c, r, k) = \mu x[x \leq c \;\&\; h_5(a, c, r, k, x) = 0].$$

In this case, $F_5(e, a, c, r, k)$ is a Gödel number of

$$n\, (a)_4\, (n) \prod_{i \leq \ln[g_5(a,c,r,k)]} p_i \exp k_1(a, c, k, n)$$

where $k_1(a, c, k) = (n)_i$ if $(a)_{7i} \neq k$

$$= val\Big[\overline{st}\Big\{\ln[g_5(a,c,k)] + 1, \prod_{i \leq \ln g_5(a,c,r,k)} p_i^{2 \cdot 3^{(n)_i}}, g_5(a, c, r, k), c\Big\}\Big] \quad \text{if } (a)_{7i} = k.$$

The expression $+_o$ refers to the function which expresses ordinal addition in the chosen well-ordering. Since in this use the first argument is a finite ordinal, there is no problem about the primitive recursiveness of this.

Thus $\varphi_5(e, a, c, r, k)$ is a primitive recursive functional. Choose e_o by the recursion theorem to be a Gödel number of $\lambda acrk\ _5(e, a, c, r, k)$, and set

$$\varphi_5(a, c, r, k) = \varphi_5(e_o, a, c, r, k) .$$

We note that in both cases of infinite induction, $F_5(e, a, c, r, k)$ is again the number of a functional primitive recursive in $(a)_4$ and e . Both this result and the primitive recursiveness of φ_5 are achieved at the price of possibly introducing into the proof of $A(t)$ or $A(T)$ vacuous infinite inductions, which spare φ_5 from involving the actual evaluation of functionals $(a)_4$.

For example, suppose a is the number of a proof of $A(y)$ and t is the numeral $0^{(n)}$. If the last step of the proof is an infinite induction whose premisses are proofs numbered $(a)_4(m)$ of the formulae $A(0^{(m)})$, then the last step of the new proof will be an infinite induction whose premisses are the results of substituting $0^{(m)}$ for y in $A(0^{(n)})$, i. e. $A(0^{(n)})$ itself. Then $(\varphi_5(a, c, r, k))_4$ is simply a function which for each m gives a proof of $A(0^{(n)})$, of lower order than the ones given by φ_5 . We shall have to evaluate the functions at such infinite inductions eventually (see lemma 13.6), but it is simpler to determine the complexity of our final functionals if this evaluation is put off as long as possible.

We now define a primitive recursive function $\psi_6(c, b, r, k, m, x)$ and a functional $\varphi_6(a, b, r, k, m, x)$ such that if c is the number of a formula not containing free occurrences of the variable y numbered p_k, and b is the number of the formula A(x), where x has number p_m, then $\psi_6(c, b, k, m, x)$ is the number of the formula obtained by replacing the i th alternand of c, wherever $(x)_i \neq 0$ and it is (x)A(x), by A(y). If a is the number of a proof of c, then $\varphi_6(a, b, r, k, m, x)$ is the number of a proof of $\psi_6(c, b, r, k, m, x)$.

All this holds if $r = 0$. If $r \neq 0$, then the corresponding holds for class variables of level $r - 1$.

The transformation φ_6 is standardly simple.

Def. 35. $\psi_6(c, b, r, k, m, x) = su(2^r \cdot p_k, r, m, b)$
if $c = 50 \cdot p_m{}^b \,\&\, r = 0$ .v. $c = 2^r \cdot 5^3 \cdot p_m{}^b \,\&\, r \neq 0 :\& \, (x)_0 \neq$

$= 40 \cdot 7^{\psi_6[(c)_3, b, r, k, m, x]} \cdot 11^{\psi_6[(c)_4, b, r, k, m, sq(c, x)]}$
if $c = 40 \cdot 7^{(c)_3} \cdot 11^{(c)_4}$

$= c$ otherwise.

$\varphi_6(e, a, b, r, k, m, x) = a$ if $a = 2^{(a)_0}$

$= \varphi_6[e, (a)_a, b, r, k, m, x]$
if $ln(a) = 2 \,\&\, \psi_6[(a)_{30}, b, r, k, m, s_2(a, x)] =$

$\psi_6[(a)_o,\ b,\ r,\ k,\ m,\ x]$,

$= 2^{\psi_6[(a)_o,b,r,k,m,x]} \cdot 3^{(\varphi_6[e,(a)_2,b,r,k,m,s_2(a,x)])_1}$

$\cdot\ 5^{\varphi_6[e,(a)_2,b,r,k,m,s_2(a,x)]}$

if $\ln(a) = 2$ otherwise ,

$= 2^{\psi_6[(a)_o,b,r,k,m,x]} \cdot 3^{(a)_1} \cdot$

$\prod_{2\leq i\leq 6} p_i^{\varphi_6[e,(a)_i,b,r,k,m,s_i(a,x)]}$

if $3 \leq \ln(a) \leq 6\ \&\ -\{r = 0\ \&\ Ge_{1v2}[(a)_o,\ (a)_{30}]\ \&{:}.(x)_o \neq 0$
$\&.\ (a)_o = 50 \cdot p_m{}^b\ v\ (a)_{03} = 50 \cdot p_m{}^b\ {:}v\ k = gev[(a)_o,\ (a)_{30}]{:}{:}$
$v{:}{:}r \neq 0\ \&\ Ge_{3v4}[(a)_o,\ (a)_{50}]\ \&{:}.(x)_o \neq 0\ \&.$
$(a)_o = 2^r5^3 \cdot p_m{}^b\ v\ (a)_{03} = 2^r5^3 \cdot p_m{}^b\ {:}v.k = gev[(a)_o,\ (a)_{50}]$
$\&\ r = gev_o[(a)_o,\ (a)_{50}]\}.$

$= \varphi_4\{\varphi_6[e,\ (a)_1,\ b,\ r,\ k,\ m,\ s_1(a,\ x)],\ r,$

$gev[(a)_o,\ (a)_{10}],\ k\}$

if $Ge_2[(a)_o,\ (a)_{30}]\ \&\ r = 0\ \&\ (x)_o \neq 0\ \&.(a)_o = 50 \cdot p_m{}^b$
$v\ (a)_{03} = 50 \cdot p_m{}^b{:}v{:}\ Ge_3[(a)_o,\ (a)_{50}]\ \&\ r \neq 0\ \&\ (x)_o \neq 0$
$\&\ (a)_o = 2^r5^3 \cdot p_m{}^b\ v\ (a)_{03} = 2^r5^3 \cdot p_m{}^b$
where $i = 3$ if $r = 0$, $i = 5$ if $r \neq 0$,

$= 2^{\psi_6[(a)_o,b,r,k,m,x]} \cdot 3^{(a)_1} \cdot 7\ \exp\ \varphi_6\{e,\ \varphi_4[(a)_3,$

$r,\ k,\ (a)_{30}+1],\ b,\ r,\ k,\ m,\ s_3(a,\ x)\}$

otherwise, if $Ge_{1v2}[(a)_o,\ (a)_{30}]\ \&\ r = 0\ \&\ k = gev[(a)_o,$
$(a)_{30}]$,

$= 2^{\psi_6[(a)_o,b,r,k,m,x]} \cdot 3^{(a)_1} \cdot 13\ \exp\ \varphi_6\{e,\ \varphi_4[(a)_5,$

$r,\ k,\ (a)_{50} + 1],\ b,\ r,\ k,\ m,\ s_5(a,\ x)\}$

otherwise, if $Ge_{3v4}[(a)_0, (a)_{50}]$ & $r = gev_0[(a)_0, (a)_{50}]$ & $k = gev[(a)_0, (a)_{50}]$

$$= 2^{\psi_6[(a)_0, b, r, k, m, x]} \cdot 3^{(a)_1} \cdot 11^{F_6(e, a, b, r, k, m, x)} \cdot 19^{(a)_7}$$

if $ln(a) = 7$, where $F_6(e, a, b, r, k, m, x)$ is a Gödel number of

$$\lambda n\, e\left\{(a)_4(n), \overline{st}[ln((a)_7) + 1, \prod_{i \leq ln\,(a)_7} p_i^{2 \cdot 3^{(n)_i}}, (a)_7, b], r, k, m, x\right\},$$

and F_6 is primitive recursive;

= a otherwise.

Again, we choose e_0 by the recursion theorem so that e_0 is a Gödel number of $\varphi_6(e_0, a, b, r, k, m, x)$ as a function of a, b, r, k, m, x, and set

$$\varphi_6(a, b, r, k, m, x) = \varphi_6(e_0, a, b, r, k, m, x)$$

Then φ_6 is primitive recursive and standardly simple. If $(a)_4$ is the number of a primitive recursive function then $F_6(e, a, b, r, k, m, x)$ is also.

Def. 36. Similarly, we can define primitive recursive functions $\psi_7(c, b, r, k, m, x)$ and a functional $\varphi_7(a, b, r, k, m, x)$ such that if c is the number of an alternation, and b is the number of a formula $A(x)$, where x is numbered p_m, and p_k is the number of a variable y, then $\psi_7(c, b, r, k, m, x)$ is the number of the formula obtained from c by, wherever the ith alternand is $-(Ex)A(x)$ and $(x)_i \neq 0$, replacing it by

$- A(y)$. If a is the number of a proof of c , then $\varphi_7(a, b, r, k, m, x)$ is the number of a proof of $\psi_7(a, b, r, k, m, x)$. If $r \neq 0$, the analogue for class variables holds.

The transformation is standardly simple, and the functionals at infinite inductions in the new proofs are primitive recursive in the ones they replace.

We now define the auxiliary functions used in case 4b-c of lemma 13.4 (pp. 147-9) and 4d and 4e of lemma 17.5 (pp. 215-6).

First we define a function $\varphi_{81}(a, c, r, k, b, p, q)$ such that if a is the number of a proof of a formula of the form $\mathcal{R}\ v\ (x)A(x)$ or $\mathcal{R}\ v\ (X)A(X)$, where the variable has number $2^r \cdot p_k$, and $2 < (q)_i$ for $i \leq \ln(q)$, and c is the number of a term t (class term T), then $\varphi_{81}(a, c, r, k, b, p, q)$ is the number of a proof of $\mathcal{R}^*\ v\ A^*(T)$, where $*$ indicates substitution of $0^{((p)_0)} \ldots 0^{((p)_{\ln q})}$ for the variables number $p_{(q)_0} \ldots p_{(q)_{\ln q}}$ respectively.

Def. 37. $\varphi_8^0(0, a, p, q) = \varphi_5[a, 2 \cdot 3^{(p)_0}, 0, (q)_0]$

$$\varphi_8^0(n + 1, a, p, q) = \varphi_5[\varphi_8^0(n, a, p, q), 2 \cdot 3^{(p)_{n+1}}, 0, (q)_{n+1}]$$

$$\varphi_8^1(a, p, q) = \varphi_8^0[\ln(q), a, p, q]$$

$$\varphi_{81}(a, c, r, k, b, p, q) = \varphi_5\{\varphi_6[\varphi_8^1(a, p, q), b, 0, k, k, na[(a)_0]], c, 0, k\} .$$

Similarly, we have a function $\varphi_{82}(a, c, r, k, b, p, q)$ which does the analogous with a proof of $-(Ex)A(x) \vee \mathcal{S}$, or $-(EX)A(X) \vee \mathcal{S}$, using φ_7 in place of φ_6 and $\mathcal{P}_0$ instead of $\mathcal{P}_{na[(a)_0]}$.

These transformations are standardly simple except that if $r \neq 0$ the order of a proof of finite order might be finitely increased (see def. 34).

Now we define a functional φ_9 which, from proofs of $\mathcal{R} \vee (x)A(x)$ and $-(x)A(x) \vee \mathcal{S}$, obtains a proof of $\mathcal{R} \vee \mathcal{S}$ without a cut on $(x)A(x)$.

$\psi_9(h, b, d, r, k, p, q, x)$ is to be such that if h is the number of an alternation, b the number of a formula $A(x)$ or $A(X)$ where the variable has number $2^r \cdot p_k$, $d = 0$ or d is the number of a formula R, $2 < (q)_1$ if $i \leq \ln(q)$, then if $(x)_i \neq 0$ and the $(i+1)$st alternand of h is obtained from $-(x)A(x)$ by substituting $0^{((p)_0)} \dots 0^{((p)_{\ln q})}$ for $\mathcal{P}_{(q)_0} \dots \mathcal{P}_{(q)_{\ln q}}$ respectively, then in $\psi_9(h \dots x)$ it is omitted if $d = 0$ and replaced by R otherwise.

If a is the number of a proof of h and c is the number of a proof of $(x)A(x)$ if $d = 0$, of $R \vee (x)A(x)$ otherwise, then $\varphi_9(a, c, b, d, r, k, p, q, x)$ is the number of a proof of $\psi_9(h \dots x)$ of order $\leq (c)_1 *_0 (a)_1$. The transformation has the other properties of a standardly simple one.

Def. 38. Let $s^*(u, p, q) = \overline{st}[\ln(q) + 1, \prod_{i \le \ln q} p_i^{2 \cdot 3^{(p)_i}}, q, u]$

$\psi_9(h, b, d, r, k, p, q, x) = d$ if $(x)_o \neq 0$ &: $h = s^*(150 \cdot p_k^{\,b}, p, q)$ & $r = 0$ .v. $h = s^*(2^r 3 \cdot 5^{3 \cdot} p_k^{\,b}, p, q)$ & $r \neq 0$

$= \hat{\psi}_9[(h)_3, b, d, r, k, p, q, x]$

if $h = 40 \cdot 7^{(h)_3} \cdot 11^{(h)_4}$ & $\hat{\psi}_9[(h)_4, b, d, r, k, p, q, sq(h, x)] = 0$,

$= \hat{\psi}_9[(h)_4, b, d, r, k, p, q, sq(h, x)]$

if $h = 40 \cdot 7^{(h)_3} \cdot 11^{(h)_4}$ & $\hat{\psi}_9[(h)_3, b, d, r, k, p, q, x] = 0$,

$= 40 \cdot 7 \exp \hat{\psi}_9[(h)_3, b, d, r, k, p, q, x] \cdot 11 \exp \hat{\psi}_9[(h)_4, b, d, r, k, p, q, sq(h, x)]$

if $h = 40 \cdot 7^{(h)_3} \cdot 11^{(h)_4}$ otherwise ,

$= h$ otherwise.

$\varphi_9(e, a, c, b, r, k, p, q, x) = a$ if $a = 2^{(a)_o}$

$= 2^{ps_9} \cdot 3^{(\varphi_9[e,(a)_2,c,b,r,k,p,q,s_2(a,x)])_1} \cdot 5 \exp \varphi_9[e,(a)_2,c,b,r,k,p,q,s_2(a,x)]$

if $\ln(a) = 2$ & $ps_9 \neq \varphi_9[(a)_{20}, b, s(c), r, k, p, q, s_2(a, x)]$,

where ps_9 abbreviates $\varphi_9[(a)_o, b, s(c), r, k, p, q, x]$

and $s(c) = (c)_{03}$ if $(c)_o = 40 \cdot 7^{(c)_{03}} \cdot 11^{(c)_{04}}$

$= 0$ otherwise.

$= \varphi_9[e, (a)_2, c, b, r, k, p, q, s_2(a, x)]$

if $\ln(a) = 2$ otherwise,

$$= 2^{ps_9} \cdot 3^{(c)_1 +_o (a)_1} \cdot \prod_{2 \le i \le 6} p_i^{\varphi_9[e,(a)_i,c,b,r,k,p,q,s_i(a,x)]}$$

if $2 < \ln(a) \le 6$ & $-\{r = 0$ & $(x)_o \ne 0$ & $Bi_2[(a)_o, (a)_{30}]$ &. $(a)_o = s^*(150 \cdot p_k^{\ b}, p, q)$ v $(a)_{03} = s^*(\ \ )$:v: $r \ne 0$ & $(x)_o \ne 0$ & $Bi_4[(a)_o, (a)_{50}]$ &. $(a)_o = s^*(2^r \cdot 3^{\tilde{r}} 5^3 \cdot p_k^{\ b}, p, q)$ v $(a)_{03} = s^*(\ \ )\}$,

$$= 2^{ps_9} \cdot 3^{(c)_1 +_o (a)_1} \cdot 5^{\varphi_{81}[c,bi((a)_o,(a)_{10}),r,k,b,p,q]} \cdot 7^{\varphi_9[e,(a)_i,c,b,r,k,p,q,s_i(a,x)]}$$

if $2 < \ln(a) \le 6$ otherwise, where $i = 3$ if $r = 0$, $= 5$ if $r \ne 0$

$$= 2^{ps_9} \cdot 3^{(c)_1 +_o (a)_1} \cdot 11^{F_9(e,a,c,b,r,k,p,q,x)} \cdot 19^{(a)_7}$$

where F_9 is a primitive recursive function which gives a Gödel number of

$$\lambda n\, e[(a)_4(n),\ c,\ b,\ r,\ k,[\textstyle\prod_{i \le \ln q} p_i^{(p)_i}] * n,\ q^*(a)_7,\ x] .$$

Then we again define φ_9 by choosing an e_o by the recursion theorem so that e_o is a Gödel number of $\lambda acbrkpqx\ \varphi_9(e_o, a, c, b, r, k, p, q, x)$, and setting $\varphi_9(a, c, b, r, k, p, q, x) = \varphi_9(e_o, a, c, b, r, k, p, q, x)$.

In the proofs of lemmas 13.4 and 17.5, if a is the number of the reduced proof of $-(x)\mathcal{B}(x)$ v $\mathcal{S}$, and c is the number of the reduced proof of $\mathcal{R}$ v $(x)\mathcal{B}(x)$, then the number of the reduced proof of $\mathcal{R}$ v $\mathcal{S}$ is $\varphi_9(a, c, b, r, k, 1, 1, 2) = \varphi_9^o(a, c, b, r, k)$.

Def. 39. Similarly, we can define a function ψ_{10} and a functional φ_{10} such that if h is the number of an alternation, b, r, k, p, q as before, d = 0 or the number of a formula S, then if $(x)_i \neq 0$ and the (i + 1)st alternand of h is obtained from (Ex)A(x) by substituting $0^{((p)_0)} \dots 0^{((p)_{\ln q})}$ for $\mathcal{P}_{(q)_0} \dots \mathcal{P}_{(q)_{\ln q}}$ respectively, then in $\psi_{10}(h \dots x)$ it is omitted if d = 0 and replaced by S otherwise.

If a is the number of a proof of h and c is the number of a proof of $-$ (Ex)A(x) v S, then $\varphi_{10}(a, c, b, r, k, p, q, x)$ is the number of a proof of $\psi_{10}(h \dots x)$ of order $\leq (c)_1 +_o (a)_1$. The transformation has the other properties of a standardly simple one.

Both φ_9 and φ_{10} are primitive recursive in the function $+_o$ which represents ordinal addition, and the functionals at infinite inductions in the new proofs are primitive recursive in those of the old proofs and $+_o$.

We now define functions ψ_{11} and ψ_{12} and functionals φ_{11} and φ_{12} such that if c is the number of an alternation, m the number of a term, b of a formula A(x) where x has number $\mathcal{P}_k$, then if $(x)_i \neq 0$ and the (i + 1)st alternand of c is $t \varepsilon \hat{x}A(x)$, then in $\psi_{11}(c, b, m, k, x)$ it is replaced by A(t). If it is $t \not\varepsilon \hat{x}A(x)$, then in $\psi_{12}(c, b, m, k, x)$ it is replaced by $-$ A(t). If a is the number of a proof of c, then

$\varphi_{11}(a, b, m, k, x)$ is the number of a proof of $\psi_{11}(a, b, m, k, x)$ and $\varphi_{12}(a, b, m, k, x)$ is the number of a proof of $\psi_{12}(c, b, m, k, x)$. The transformation is standardly simple. We give the definitions only of ψ_{11} and φ_{11}; the others are similar.

Def. 40. $\psi_{11}(c, b, m, k, x) = su(m, 0, k, b)$ if $c = 70 \cdot p_b^{\,m}$ and $(x)_0 \neq 0$

$= 40 \cdot 7^{\psi_{11}[(c)_3, b, m, k, x]} \cdot 11^{\psi_{11}[(c)_4, b, m, k, sq(c, x)]}$

if $c = 40 \cdot 7^{(c)_3} \cdot 11^{(c)_4}$

$= c$ otherwise.

$\varphi_{11}(\phi_1(a, b, m, k, x) = a$ if $a = 2^{(a)_0}$

$= \; = 2^{\psi_{11}[(a)_0, b, m, k, x]} \cdot 3^{(\varphi_{11}[e, (a)_2, b, m, k, s_2(a, x)])_1} \cdot$

$\cdot \; 5^{\varphi_{11}[e, (a)_2, b, m, k, s_2(a, x)]}$

if $\ln(a) = 2$ & $\psi_{11}[(a)_0, b, m, k, x] = \psi_{11}[(a)_{20}, b, m, k, s_2(a, x)]$

$= \varphi_{11}[e, (a)_2, b, m, k, s_2(a, x)]$

if $\ln(a) = 2$ otherwise,

$= 2^{\psi_{11}[(a)_0, b, m, k, x]} \cdot 3^{(a)_1} \cdot \prod_{2 \leq i \leq 6} p_i^{\varphi_{11}[e, (a)_i, b, m, k, s_i(a, x)]}$

if $2 < \ln(a) \leq 6$ & $-\{Abs[(a)_0, (a)_{60}]$ & $(x)_0 \neq 0$ & $(a)_0 = 70 \cdot p_b^{\,m} \vee (a)_{03} = 70 \cdot p_b^{\,m}\}$,

$= \varphi_{11}[e, (a)_6, b, m, k, s_6(a, x)]$

if $2 < \ln(a) \leq 6$ otherwise,

$= 2^{\psi_{11}[(a)_0, b, m, k, x]} \cdot 3^{(a)_1} \cdot 11^{F_{11}(e, a, b, m, k, x)} \cdot 19^{(a)_7}$

if $\ln(a) = 7$, where F_{11} is a primitive recursive function such that $F_{11}(e, a, b, m, k, x)$ is a Gödel number of

$\lambda n\ e[(a)_4(n), s^*(n, (a)_7, b), s^*(n, (a)_7, m), k, x]$,

$= a$ otherwise.

Then $\varphi_{11}(a \dots x)$ is defined by the recursion theorem as before.

Before we go on to define the functionals ρ_1, ρ_2 of the text, we define one more auxiliary functional, namely the functional $Sp(\bar{f}, \bar{a}, b)$ of lemma 13.2 and 17.3, which gives for each proof in $RA(Z_0)$ with no function symbols not among $f_1 \dots f_k$, of a formula with no free number variables not among $f_1 \dots f_k$, a proof in $RA(S_0)$ of order $< \omega\cdot(q + 1)$, where q is the maximum number of inductions in any branch, level $\leq n$, where n is the maximum level of inductions and cuts, and binding degree $\leq p$, where p is the maximum binding degree of inductions and cuts of level n in the given proof. The proof in S_0 or $RA(S_0)$ also has a top degree no greater than the maximum top degree of the inductions and cuts in the given proof.

The definition is by a recursion parallel to def. 24 (cf. defs. 21, 22, 23).

<u>Def. 41</u>. Let $in(a) = 0$ if $a = 2^{(a)_0}$

$$= \max_{2 \leq i \leq 6} \{in[(a)_i]\}$$

if $2 \leq ln(a) \leq 6 \ \& \ a \neq 2^{(a)_0} \cdot 5^{(a)_2} \cdot 11^{(a)_4}$,

$$in(a) = max[in((a)_2),\ in((a)_4)] + 1$$

if $a = 2^{(a)_0} \cdot 5^{(a)_2} \cdot 11^{(a)_4}$

$= 0$ otherwise.

Then if $Prir[a,\ (a)_0]$ (and a fortiori if $Prki[a,\ (a)_0]$), $in(a)$ is the maximum number of inductions in any branch of the proof number a. Then

$$Sp(e,\ \bar{f},\ \bar{a},\ a) = a \quad \text{if} \quad a = 2^{(a)_0}$$

$$= 2^{(a)_0} \cdot 3^{(Sp[e,\bar{f},\bar{a},(a)_2])_1} \cdot 5^{Sp[e,\bar{f},\bar{a},(a)_2]}$$

if $in(a) = 2$,

$$= 2^{(a)_0} \cdot 3 \exp \max_{\substack{0 \\ 2\le i\le 6}}[(Sp[e,\ \bar{f},\ \bar{a},\ (a)_i])_0 +_0 1_0] \cdot$$

$$\cdot \prod_{2\le i\le 6} p_i^{Sp[e,\bar{f},\bar{a},(a)_i]}$$

if $2 \le in(a) \le 6$, unless $a = 2^{(a)_0} \cdot 5^{(a)_2} \cdot 11^{(a)_4}$.

$$= 2^{(a)_0} \cdot 3^{wn[in(a)]} \cdot 11^{F_0(e,a)} \cdot 19^{g_0(a)}$$

if $a = 2^{(a)_0} \cdot 5^{(a)_2} \cdot 11^{(a)_4}$, where $wn(m)$ is the notation in the chosen well-ordering for $\omega \cdot m$ ($wn(m) = 2^m - 1$ in $\underset{1}{<}$, $= 5^m$ in $\underset{2}{<}$, $= 3^m$ in $\underset{p+3}{<}$ and $L(n,\ a,\ b,\ 0)$, $= \nu_2(0,\ 3^m)$ in $<_n$ if $n \ne 0$).

To define F_0 and g_0 , we first define a function

$$Fv(b,\ 0) = 2^3 \quad \text{if} \quad Of(0,\ 3,\ b)\ \&\ s_1 \ne p_3\ \&\ \dots\ \&\ s_m \ne p_3 ,$$

$= 1$ otherwise .

$$Fv(b,\ n + 1) = Fv(b,\ n) \quad \text{if} \quad -\ Of(Op\ n + 4,\ b)\ v$$

$$s_1 = p_{n+4}\ v\ \dots\ v\ s_m = p_{n+4} ,$$

(cf. def. 26 for the s_i)

$Fv(b, n + 1) = Fv(b, n) \cdot p_{lh\, Fv(b,n)}{}^{p_{n+4}}$ otherwise.

(For lh see IM p. 230.)

Then $Fv(b, n)$ is a number which encodes the numbers of the free variables of the expression number b, other than the selected variables $a_1 \ldots a_m$.

$$\begin{aligned} int(a, b, c) = (\mu y\{y < 2^{a}3^{b} \ \&\ b = su[2, 0, (y)_0, (c)_3/3] \\ \&\ (c)_4 = su[3(y)_0, 0, (y)_0, (c)_3/3] \ \& \\ a = su[(y)_1, 0, (y)_0, (c)_3/3]\})_1 . \end{aligned} \qquad (2)$$

Then if a is inferred from b and c by induction, $int(a, b, c)$ is the number of the term substituted for the induction variable in the conclusion (cf. def. 23).

Let $int^*(a) = int[(a)_0, (a)_{20}, (a)_{40}]$.

Then $g_0(a) = Fv[int^*(a), (a)_0]$.

Let $F^*(e, a)$ be a primitive recursive function which gives a Gödel number of a function H (recursive in $\bar{f}, \bar{a}$) such that

$$H(0) = e[(a)_2]$$

$$H(n + 1) = 2^{su[2\cdot 3^{n+1}, [illegible] 0,\ inv^*(a),\ (a)_{40}/3]} \cdot 3^{(H(n))_1 +_0 1} \cdot 5^{H(n)} \cdot 7^{e\, G[(a)_4,\, inv^*(a),\, n]_1}$$

where $inv(a, b, c)$ is (2) with the subscript 0 instead of 1, $inv^*(a)$ is defined as $int^*(a)$, and G is a function which substitutes the numeral $0^{(n+1)}$ for the variable $inv^*(a)$ in the proof $(a)_4$ in $RA(Z_0)$ [i. e. it yields the proof of $- A(0^{(n)}) \vee A(0^{(n+1)})$; it is defined like φ_5 above, only simpler].

Then $F_o(e, a)$ is a primitive recursive function which gives a Gödel number of

$$\lambda n\, \varphi_3\Big(\{F^*(e, a)\}[\text{val } s^*(\text{int}^*(a), n, g_o(a))], (a)_{4 \cdot 3}/3$$
$$2 \cdot 3 \exp[\text{val } s^*(\text{int}^*(a), n, g_o(a))],$$
$$s^*[\text{int}^*(a), n, g_o(a)], \text{inv}^*(a)\Big) .$$

Then we choose e_o by the recursion theorem so e_o is a Gödel number from $\bar{f}$, $\bar{a}$ of $\lambda a Sp(e_o, \bar{f}, \bar{a}, a)$. Then we set $Sp(\bar{f}, \bar{a}, a) = Sp(e_o, \bar{f}, \bar{a}, a)$. Then Sp is primitive recursive.

Now we define the function ρ_1 used in the proofs of lemma 13.3 and 17.4. We define a function ρ_1 which removes the truth-functional structure from <u>all</u> cuts in proofs in $RA(S_o)$, although if the top degree is bounded it is only of the cuts of level n that we know that iteration of this function as many times as the top degree will produce a proof in which they are truth-functionally simple. Note that abstraction is handled with truth-functional structure. This function is adequate for the purposes of both lemma 13.3 and 17.4. It is primitive recursive in the representation of ordinal addition.

<u>Def. 42</u>. $\rho_1(a) = a \quad \text{if} \quad a = 2^{(a)_o}$

$$= 2^{(a)_o} \cdot 3^{(a)_2 + 8(a)_1 \cdot]} \prod_{2 \le i \le 6} p_i^{\rho_1[(a)_i]}$$

if $\ln(a) > 2$ and $\ln(a) \le 6$, unless $a = 2^{(a)_o} \cdot 3^{(a)_1} \cdot 5^{(a)_2} \cdot 7^{(a)_3}$ $\&. 3 | cf[(a)_o, (a)_{20}, (a)_{30}] \vee cf^*(a) = 40 \cdot 7^{(cf^*(a))_3}$.

$\cdot\ 11^{(cf^*(a))_4}$ v. $cf^*(a) = 70 \cdot \mathcal{P}_{\ln cf^*(a)}{}^{(a)_{\ln cf^*(a)}}$ &

$\ln cf^*(a) = 5^{(\ln cf^*(a))_2} \cdot \mathcal{P}_{\ln[\ln cf^*(a)]}{}^{(\ln cf^*(a))_{\ln[\ln\ ]}}$.

Let $R_1(a, b, c)$ be a primitive recursive function such that if a is the number of a proof of $\mathcal{B} \vee \mathcal{S}$, b the number of a proof of $\mathcal{R} \vee -\mathcal{B}$, $(a)_1 <_0 c$, $(b)_1 <_0 c$, $R_1(a, b, c)$ is the number of the proof of $\mathcal{R} \vee \mathcal{S}$ constructed by the figure on page 144, of order c

Let $R_2(a, b, c, d)$ be a primitive recursive function such that if a is the number of a proof of $\mathcal{R} \vee (\mathcal{B} \vee \mathcal{B}')$, b the number of a proof of $-\mathcal{B} \vee \mathcal{S}$, c is the number of a proof of $-\mathcal{B}' \vee \mathcal{S}$, $(a)_1 +_0 1_0, (b)_1 +_0 1_0, (c)_1 +_0 1_0 <_0 c$, then $R_2(a, b, c, d)$ is the number of a proof of order c constructed by the figure on page 145.

Then if $a = 2^{(a)_0} \cdot 3^{(a)_1} \cdot 5^{(a)_2} \cdot 7^{(a)_3}$ and one of the above cases obtains,

$$\rho_1(e, a) = R_1\{\varphi_1[\rho_1(e, (a)_3), cf^*(a)/3, 2], \rho_1[e, (a)_2], (a)_1 +_0 (a)_1\}$$

if $3\ cf^*(a)$

$$= R_2\{\rho_1[e, (a)_2], \varphi_{21}[\rho_1(e, (a)_3), (cf^*(a))_3, (cf^*(a))_4, 2], \varphi_{22}[\rho_1(e, (a)_3), (cf^*(a))_3, (cf^*(a))_4, 2], (a)_1 +_0 (a)_1\}$$

if $cf^*(a) = 40 \cdot 7^{(cf^*(a))_3} \cdot 11^{(cf^*(a))_4}$,

$$= 2^{(a)_0} \cdot 3^{(a)_1 +_0 (a)_1} \cdot 5 \exp \varphi_{11}\{\rho_1(e, (a)_2),$$

$(\ln cf^*(a))_{\ln[\ln cf^*(a)]}$, $(cf^*(a))_{\ln cf^*(a)}$, $\ln[\ln cf^*(a)]$, $\varphi_{na[(a)_2]}\} \cdot 7 \exp \varphi_{12}\{\rho_1[e, (a)_3], (\ln cf^*(a))_{\ln[\ln cf^*(a)]}, (cf^*(a))_{\ln cf^*(a)}, \ln[\ln cf^*(a)], 2\}$

if $cf^*(a) = 70 \cdot \varphi_{\ln cf^*(a)}{}^{(cf^*(a))_{\ln cf^*(a)}}$ &

$\ln cf^*(a) = 5^{(\ln cf^*(a))_2} \cdot \varphi_{\ln[\ln cf^*(a)]}{}^{(\ln cf^*(a))_{\ln[\ln\ ]}}$.

It is a mechanical task to write down the definitions of R_1 and R_2 .

If $\ln(a) = 7$, then

$\rho_1(e, a) = 2^{(a)_0} \cdot 3^{(a)_1 +_0 (a)_1} \cdot 11^{K_1(e,a)} \cdot 19^{(a)_7}$,

where $K_1(e, a)$ is a Gödel number of $\lambda n\ e\ ,[(a)_4(n)]$.

$\rho_1(e, a) = a$ otherwise.

Then $\rho_1(a)$ is defined in the usual way by the recursion theorem. Since our auxiliary functionals are all primitive recursive, ρ_1 is primitive recursive in the function $\lambda x(x +_0 x)$, for our chosen well-ordering.

We now define the functional ρ_2 of lemmas 13.4 and 17.5, similarly ignoring the level of the cut terms, so that we deviate from the text (pp. 214-218). We pare off all outermost quantifiers of cuts on quantifications, and eliminate all cuts on prime formulae $t \varepsilon Y$, although in the application with argument $\sigma_1(a, b)$, it is only of those of level n that we know that they are all the cuts of that level in the proof.

Def. 43. $\rho_2(e, a) = a$ if $a = 2^{(a)_0}$

$$\rho_2(e, a) = 2^{(a)_0} \cdot 3^{(\rho_2[e,(a)_2])_1} \cdot 5^{\rho_2[e,(a)_2]}$$

$$\text{if } \ ln(a) = 2$$

$$= 2^{(a)_0} \cdot 3^{W[(a)_1]} \cdot \prod_{2 \le i \le 6} p_i^{\rho_2[e,(a)_i]}$$

if $2 < i \leq 6$, where $W(c)$ is the arithmetical representation in terms of our chosen ordering of $\lambda a\,\omega^a$, unless $a = 2^{(a)_0} \cdot 3^{(a)_1} \cdot 5^{(a)_2} \cdot 7^{(a)_3}$ &:cf*(a) = 50 $\cdot p_{ln\ cf*(a)}$ exp $(af*(a))_{ln\ cf*(a)}$ v cf*(a) = 100 $\cdot p_{ln\ cf*(a)}$ exp $(cf*(a))_{ln\ cf*(a)}$ v. cf*(a) = $2^{(cf*())_0} \cdot 5^{(cf*())_2} \cdot p_{ln\ cf*(a)}$ exp $(cf*(a))_{ln\ cf*()}$ &. $(cf*(a))_2 = 3$ or 4 : v cf*(a) = 70 $\cdot p_{ln\ cf*(a)}$ exp $(cf*(a))_{ln\ cf*(a)}$ & $ln[cf*(a)] = 2^{(ln\ cf*(a))_0} \cdot p_{ln[ln\ cf*(a)]}$.

In this case, if cf*(a) = 50 $\cdot p_{ln\ cf*(a)}{}^{(cf*(a))_{ln\ cf*()}}$ v cf*(a) = $2^{(cf*(a))_0} \cdot 5^3 \cdot p_{ln\ cf*(a)}{}^{(cf*(a))_{ln\ cf*(a)}}$,

$$\rho_2(e, a) = \varphi_9^0\{\rho_2[e, (a)_3], \rho_2[e, (a)_2], (cf*(a))_{ln\ cf*(a)}, p_1(a), ln[cf*(a)]\}$$

where $p_1(a) = (cf*(a))_0$ if $(cf*(a))_2 = 3$ v $(cf*(a))_2 = 4$

$= 0$ if $(cf*(a))_2 = 2$.

If (cf*(a)) = 100 $\cdot p_{ln\ cf*(a)}{}^{(cf*(a))_{ln\ cf*(a)}}$ v cf*(a) = $2^{(cf*(a))_0} \cdot 5^4 \cdot p_{ln\ cf*(a)}{}^{(cf*(a))_{ln\ cf*(a)}}$,

$$\rho_2(e, a) = \varphi_{10}\{\rho_2[e, (a)_2], \rho_2[e, (a)_3], (cf*(a))_{ln\ cf*(a)}, p_1(a), ln[cf*(a)], 1, 1, p_{na[(a)_2]}\} .$$

If cf*(a) = 70 $\cdot p_{ln\ cf*(a)}{}^{(cf*(a))_{ln\ cf*(a)}}$ & $ln[cf*(a)] = 2^{(ln\ cf*(a))_0} \cdot p_{ln[ln\ cf*(a)]}$, then

$\rho_2(e, a) = \varphi_{13}\{\rho_2[e, (a)_3], \rho_2[e, (a)_2], (cf*(a))_{ln\ cf*()},$

$(ln\ cf*(a))_o, ln[ln\ cf*(a)], 1, 1, 2\},$

where $\varphi_{13}(a, c, m, r, k, p, q, x)$ is a function defined similarly to φ_9 ; instances of R are introduced in place of formulae t $\not\in$ Y ; see page 218.

$\rho_2(e, a) = 2^{(a)_o} \cdot 3^{W[(a)_1]} \cdot 31^{K_1(e, a)} \cdot 19^{(a)_7}$

if $ln(a) = 7$

= a otherwise.

Since the auxiliary functionals are primitive recursive in $x\lambda xy(x +_o y)$, and $\rho_2(e, a)$ is defined primitive recursively in them and W , $\rho_2(e, a)$ is primitive recursive in $+_o$ and W , as claimed in lemma 17.5. Then $\rho_1(a)$ is defined in the usual way by the recursion theorem, and is also primitive recursive in $+_o$ and W .

We now define the function σ_4 of lemma 17.7.

<u>Def. 44</u>. $\sigma_4(e, a, n) = a$ if $a = 2^{(a)_o}$

$= 2^{(a)_o} \cdot 3^{(\sigma_4[e,(a)_2,n])_1} \cdot 5^{\sigma_4[e,(a)_2,n]}$

if $ln(a) = 2$,

$= 2^{(a)_o} \cdot 3^{E[(a)_1]} \cdot \prod_{2 \le i \le 6} p_i^{\sigma_4[e,(a)_i,n]}$ if $2 < ln(a) \le 6$

unless $a = 2^{(a)_o} \cdot 3^{(a)_1} \cdot 5^{(a)_2} \cdot 7^{(a)_3}$ & $Lv[cf*(a)] = n$,

where E is the arithmetical representation of $\lambda\alpha\ \varepsilon_\alpha$,

and $Lv(b) = \mu y[y \le b\ \&.Fla(y, b) v\ CT(y, b)]$, i. e. the level of b .

Let d*(b) be the binding degree of the formula number

b ; let $t^*(b)$ be the top degree of the formula number b .

If $a = 2^{(a)_0} \cdot 3^{(a)_1} \cdot 5^{(a)_2} \cdot 7^{(a)_3}$ & $(a)_2 \neq 0$ & $Lv[cf^*(a)] = n$, then

$$\sigma_4(e, a, n) = \sigma_3(a_1, t^*[cf^*(a)], n, d^*[cf^*(a)]) ,$$

where $a_1 = 2^{(a)_0} \cdot 3^{E(\max_0[(a)_{21}, (a)_{31}]) +_0 1_0} \cdot$

$$\cdot\ 5^{\sigma_4[e,(a)_2,n]} \cdot 7^{\sigma_4[e,(a)_3,n]}$$

$$\sigma_4(e, a, n) = 2^{(a)_0} \cdot 3^{E[(a)_1]} \cdot 11^{K_1(e, a)} \cdot 19^{(a)_7}$$

if $\ln(a) = 7$,

$= a$ otherwise.

Then $\sigma_4(a, n)$ is defined in the usual way by the recursion theorem.

Since σ_3 (defined in the text, p. 220) is primitive recursive in $+_0$ and W , and σ_4 has been defined primitive recursively in E and σ_3 , it is primitive recursive in $+_0$, W, and E, as claimed in lemma 17.7.

Finally, we shall define the functional Γ of lemmas 13.6 and 17.9. In order to arrive at this, we need one more auxiliary functional; a functional φ_{14} such that if a is the number of a proof of an alternation C , and b is the number of a prime numerical formula, then $\varphi_{14}(a, b, x)$ is the number of a proof of the formula resulting from C by, if b is true, deleting its negation if it is the (1 + 1)st alternand, and if b is false, deleting b itself under these conditions. We first define a function φ_{14}.

Def. 44. Let Pf(b) hold if and only if b is the number of a prime formula of Z_0 with no function symbols other than $f_1 \ldots f_k$, and no variables other than $a_1 \ldots a_m$.

$$\psi_{14}(c, b, x) = 0 \text{ if } (x)_0 \neq 0 \;\&\!: b = c \;\&\; \mathrm{Val}(b) = 1.$$

$$\mathrm{v.}\; c = 3b \;\&\; \mathrm{Val}(b) = 0\!: \;\&\; \mathrm{Pf}(b)$$

If $c = 40 \cdot 7^{(c)_3} \cdot 11^{(c)_4}$, then

$$\psi_{14}(c, b, x) = \psi_{14}[(c)_3, b, x] \text{ if } \psi_{14}[(c)_4, b, sq(c, x)] = 0$$

$$= \psi_{14}[(c)_4, b, sq(c, x)] \text{ if } \psi_{14}[(c)_3, b, x] = 0$$

$$= 40 \cdot 7 \exp \psi_{14}[(c)_3, b, x] \cdot 11 \exp \psi_{14}[(c)_4, b, sq(c, x)] \text{ otherwise.}$$

In all other cases, $\psi_{14}(c, b, x) = c$.

$$\varphi_{14}(a, b, x) = 2^{\psi_{14}[(a)_0, b, x]} \text{ if } a = 2^{(a)_0}$$

$$= 2^{(a)_0} \cdot 3^{(a)_1} \prod_{2 \leq i \leq 6} p_i^{\psi_{14}[e, (a)_i, b, s_i(a, x)]}$$

if $2 \leq \ln(a) \leq 6 \;\&\; \psi_{14}[(a)_0, b, x] \neq \psi_{14}[(a)_{20}, b, s_2(a, x)] \;\&\; \psi_{14}[(a)_0, b, x] \neq \psi_{14}[(a)_{30}, b, s_3(a, x)]$

$$= \varphi_{14}[e, (a)_i, b, s_i(a, x)]$$

if $2 \leq \ln(a) \leq 6 \;\&\; \psi_{14}[(a)_0, b, x] = \psi_{14}[(a)_{i0}, b, s_i(a, x)]$ $(i = 2, 3)$

$$= 2^{\psi_{14}[(a)_0, b, x]} \cdot 3^{(a)_1} \cdot 11^{F_{14}(e, a, b, x)} \cdot 19^{(a)_7}$$

if $\ln(a) = 7$, where $F_{14}(e, a, b, x)$ gives a Gödel

number of $\lambda n\, e[(a)_4(n), b, x]$,

= a otherwise.

Then $\varphi_{14}(a, b, x)$ is defined in the usual way by the recursion theorem. The transformation is standardly simple, but does introduce initial formulae which, although they are verifiable, are not axioms of $RA(S_o)$.

Def. 45. Let $st^*(b) = s^*[b, 1, Fv(b, b)]$. $st^*(b)$ is the number of the result of substituting 0 for each free variable (except the a_1) of b .

$$Q(a) = 2^{st^*[(a)_o]} \quad \text{if} \quad a = 2^{(a)_o}$$

$$= 2^{st^*[(a)_o]} \cdot \prod_{2 \le i \le 6} p_i^{Q[(a)_i]}$$

unless $a = 2^{(a)_o} \cdot 3^{(a)_1} \cdot 5^{(a)_2} \cdot 7^{(a)_3} \,\&\, (a)_2 \neq 0$ $\&\, Pf(st^*[cf^*(a)])$.

In this case, if $Val(st^*[cf^*(a)]) = 1$, then

$$Q(a) = 2^{st^*[(a)_o]} \cdot 7^{\varphi_{14}[Q((a)_2), st^*(cf^*(a)), p_{na[(a)_2]}]}$$

If $Val(st^*[cf^*(a)]) = 0$, , then

$$Q(a) = 2^{st^*[(a)_o]} \cdot 7^{\varphi_{14}(Q[(a)_3], st^*[cf^*(a)], 2)}$$

If $ln(a) = 7$, then

$$Q(a) = Q[(a)_4(1)] \text{ ; i. e.}$$

$$= Q(f[(a)_4, 1]) ,$$

where f is an enumerating function for the class of functions (recursive in $\bar{f}, \bar{a}$) whose Gödel numbers are admitted as $(a)_4$ (cf. p. 275 above).

Then in the case of lemma 13.6,

$\Gamma_p(a, b, r) = Q[\sigma'_p(a, b), wor(p, b, r)]$.

I have given the order as a second argument for Q because the recursion is properly on this. σ is the functional of lemma 13.5; p is given as a subscript because if the ordering chosen is $<_{q+1}$, then $\sigma_p(a, b)$ is defined only if $p \leq q$.

In the case of lemma 17.9

$\Gamma_{pq}(a, b, r) = Q[\sigma_{5nq}(a, b), Er(n, q, b, r)]$,

where the same comments apply. Er is a function which gives a notation for $\varepsilon^n[\omega_q(\omega \cdot 2^{b+1}r)]$. Here we suppose the ordering is $<_{p+1}n$ for some $p \geq q$; if $<_n$ with the ordering D(n, a, b, 0) as $<_o$ were chosen, then $\sigma_5(a, b, n, q)$ would be defined for all q , and therefore it could be an argument instead of a subscript. To make n an argument, it is necessary to use $<_\omega$.

APPENDIX II

Ordinal Functions

In this appendix, we shall give recursive definitions of the representations in terms of our well-orderings of the ordinal operations used in the proofs of theorems 13 and 17.

Def. 1. $sc(a, 0) = \nu_2[\nu_2^1(a), \nu_2^2(a) + 1]$

$sc(a, p + 1) = 2a$ if $a \neq 0$

$= 1$ if $a = 0$.

$sc(a, p)$ is the successor of a in the ordering $\underset{p+1}{<}$ (with the standard $\underset{1}{<}$; we shall assume this throughout).

Def. 2. $ad(a, b, 0) = \nu_2[\nu_2^1(a) + \nu_2^1(b), \nu_2^2(b)]$

$ad(a, b, p + 1) = \prod_i \mathcal{P}_i^{h(a,b,p,i)}$ if $b \neq 1$, where

$h(a, b, p, i) = (b)_i$ if $(Ex)[x \leq \ln(b) \;\&\; (b)_x \neq 0 \;\&\; i \underset{p+1}{<} x]$

$= (a)_i$ if $(x)[x \leq \ln(b) \;\&\; (b)_x \neq 0. \supset x \underset{p+1}{<} i]$

$= (a)_i + (b)_i$ otherwise.

$ad(a, b, p + 1) = sc(a, p + 1)$ if $b = 1$.

Then $ad(a, b, p)$ is the ordinal sum of a and b in $\underset{p+1}{<}$.

Def. 3. $w(0) = 11$

$w(p + 1) = \mathcal{P}_{w(p)}$.

Then $w(p)$ is a notation for $\omega_p(\omega^2)$ in $\underset{p+2}{<}$.

For since 4 is a notation for 2 in $\underset{1}{<}$ $[4 = \nu_2(0,2)]$, $\mathcal{P}_4 = 11$ is the notation for ω^2 in $\underset{2}{<}$, and if k is the notation for $\omega_p(\omega^2)$ in $\underset{p+2}{<}$, then $\mathcal{P}_k$ is the notation for $\omega^{\omega_p(\omega^2)} = \omega_{p+1}(\omega^2)$ in $\underset{p+3}{<}$.

Def. 4. $C^+(a, 0) = 0$ if $a = 0$.

$= 2^{\nu_2^2(a)-1}$ if $\nu_2^1(a) = 0$

$= 2^{\nu_2^2(a)} \cdot 5^{\nu_2^1(a)}$ otherwise.

$$C^+(a, p+1) = \prod_{i \leq ln(a)} \mathcal{P}_{C^+(i,p)}{}^{(a)_i} \quad \text{if } a \neq 0, 1$$

$= a$ otherwise.

Then if a represents α in $\underset{p+1}{<}$, then $C^+(a, p)$ represents α in $\underset{p+2}{<}$.

Def. 5. $wi(p, 0) = w(p)$

$wi(p, q+1) = C^+[wi(p \dot{-} 1, q), p]$ if $q < p$

$= 0$ otherwise .

Then if $q \leq p$, $wi(p, q)$ represents in $\underset{p+2}{<}$ the ordinal $\omega_{p-q}(\omega^2)$. This is evident if $q = 0$, and follows from the corresponding for $p - 1$ otherwise.

Def. 6. $C^-(a, 0) = \nu_2[(a)_2, (a)_o \dot{-}]$ if $(a)_2 \neq 0$

$= 2((a)_o + 1)$ if $a = 2^{(a)_o}$

$= 0$ otherwise.

$$C^-(a, p+1) = \prod_{i \leq ln(a)} \mathcal{P}_{C^-(i,p)}{}^{(a)_i} \quad \text{if } a \neq 0, 1$$

$= a$ otherwise.

Then if $a \underset{p+2}{<} w(p)$, $C^+[C^-(a, p), p] = a$; i. e. $C^-(a, p)$ is a notation in $\underset{p+1}{<}$ for the ordinal which a represents in $\underset{p+2}{<}$.

This is proved by induction on p. For $a \underset{2}{<} \mathcal{P}_4$ if and only if for any i for which $(a)_i \neq 0$, $i \underset{1}{<} 4$, i. e., $a = 2^{(a)_0} \cdot 5^{(a)_2}$, in which case if $(a)_2 \neq 0$

$$C^+[\underset{-}{C}^-(a, 0), 0] = 2^{\nu_2^2(\nu_2[(a)_2,(a)_0])} \cdot 5^{\nu_2^1(\nu_2[(a)_2,(a)_0])}$$
$$= 2^{(a)_0} \cdot 5^{(a)_2} = a .$$

If $(a)_2 = 0$, $C^-(a, 0) = 2((a)_0 + 1)$

$$= [2((a)_0 + 1) + 1] - 1$$
$$= \bar{\nu}_2[0, (a)_0 + 1] .$$

Hence $C^+[\underset{-}{C}^-(a, 0), 0] = 2^{(a)_0} = a$.

Suppose our claim holds for p. If $a \leq 1$ it obviously holds for $p + 1$. Otherwise

$$C^+[\underset{-}{C}^-(a, p + 1), p + 1] = C^+[\prod_{-i \leq \ln(a)} \mathcal{P}_{C^-(i,p)}{}^{(a)_i}, p + 1].$$

Now since $a \underset{p+3}{<} w(p + 1)$, if $(a)_i \neq 0$, $i \underset{p+2}{<} w(p)$.

Therefore by the hypothesis of induction

$$C^+[\underset{-}{C}^-(i, p), p] = i \quad \text{for such } i .$$

$$C^+[\underset{-}{C}^-(a, p + 1), p + 1] = \prod_{\substack{i \leq \ln a \\ (a)_i \neq 0}} \mathcal{P}_{C^+[C^-(i,p),p]}{}^{(a)_i}$$
$$= \prod_{\substack{i \leq \ln a \\ (a)_i \neq 0}} \mathcal{P}_i{}^{(a)_i} = a, \text{ q. e. d.}$$

<u>Def. 5.</u> $wp(a, p, 0) = a$

$$wp(a, p, q + 1) = \mathcal{P}_{\underset{-}{C}^-[wp(a, p, q), p]},$$
$$\text{if } q \leq p \ \& \ a \underset{p+2}{<} wi(p, q) .$$

Then clearly if $0 < q \leq p$, $a \underset{p+2}{<} wi(p, q - 1)$ and a represents α [which must be $< \omega_{p-q}(\omega^2)$], then wp(a, p, q) represents $\omega_q(a)$. If q = 0 , this holds without the hypotheses; if it holds for q and $a <_{p+2} wi(p, q)$, then $\omega_q(a) < \omega_p(\omega^2)$, i. e. $wp(a, p, q) <_{p+2} w(p)$. Then by the above, $C^-[wp(a,p,q), p]$ repşesents $\omega_q(a)$ in $<_{p+1}$. Therefore wp(a, p, q + 1) represents $\omega_{q+1}(a)$ in $<_{p+2}$.

We note that $\nu_2(r, 0)$ represents $\omega \cdot r$ in $<_1$. If we set $C(0, a) = a$; $C(n + 1, a) = C^+[C(n, a), n + 1]$, then $C[p, \nu_2(r, 0)]$ represents $\omega \cdot r$ in $<_{p+1}$.

<u>Def. 8</u>. $wor_p(q, b, r) = wp\, C[p, \nu_2(2^{b+1}r, 0)], p - 1, q$ is by the above a notation for $\omega_q(\omega \cdot 2^{b+1}r)$ in $<_{p+1}$, if $q \leq p$, and therefore fulfills the functions required of wor in lemma 13.6. It is primitive recursive.

The function $+_o$ assumed in appendix I is, if $<_{p+1}$ is the chosen ordering, $\lambda xyad(x, y, p)$. The function W is $\lambda x\, wa(x, p - 1, 1)$. These are primitive rècursive. This completes the proof that the functionals of lemmas 13.3-5 are primitive recursive if the orderings $<_{p+1}$ are used.

We now proceed to define the functions corresponding to ordinal addition, exponentiation by ω, and the function $\lambda a\, \varepsilon_a$ in the orderings $<_n$. In the first two cases we shall use the procedure of ch. V. §2 where the orderings themselves are defined: namely we shall define the functions for $<_n$ and then for the intermediary orderings $L(n, a, b, i)$, and then for $<_{n+1}$. The situation is complex, and the most we can give is an involved simultaneous recursion, which shows that additon and exponentiation by ω are primitive recursive if $n = 0$ and ordinal recursive on $<_{n-1}$ if $n \neq 0$. $\lambda a\ \varepsilon_a$ proves to be primitive recursive.

Def. The definitions of ch. V §2 were incomplete in that we did not define Suc_o, $pred_o$, etc. for the case where the ordering $<_o$ was among $<_q$. We now define the predicates and functions which fill this gap. The definitions are self-explanatory.

Def. 9. $Suc_o(a, 0) \equiv \nu_2^2(a) \neq 0$

$Suc_o(a, p + 1) \equiv . a = 1 \lor 2 | a$

($Suc_o(a, p)$ holds if a isa successor element in $<_{p+1}$.)

Def. 10. $Lim_o(a, p) \equiv . a \neq 0\ \&\ - Suc_o(a, p)$

Def. 11. $pred_o(a, 0) = \nu_2[\nu_2^1(a), \nu_2^2(a) \dot{-} 1]$

$pred_o(a, p + 1) = 0$ if $a = 1$

$= a/2$ otherwise

Def. 12. $lim_o(r, m, a, 0) = \nu_2[\nu_2^1(a) \dot{-} 1, m]$

$lim_o(m, a, p + 1) = \prod p_i^{h(m,a,p,i)}$

where $h(m, a, p, i) = (a)_i$ if $r <_p i$

$= (a)_i - 1$ if $r = i$

$= m$ if $Suc_o(r, p)\ \&\ i = pred_o(r, p)$

$h(m, a, p, i) = 1$ if $\mathrm{Lim}_o(r, p)$ & $i = \mathrm{lim}_o(m, r, p)$,

and $r = \mu x\{x \leq \mathrm{ln}(a)$ & $(a)_x \neq 0$ & $(y)[y \leq \mathrm{ln}(a)$ & $(a)_y \neq 0.$

$\supset x \underset{p}{\leq} y]\}$.

<u>Def. 13</u>. $\mathrm{ub}_o(m, p) = \nu_2(m, 0)$ if $p = 0$

$= \varphi_{\mathrm{ub}_o(m,p-1)}$ if $p \neq 0$.

We now seek to define the function $G(n, j, i)$, whose existence was implicitly claimed on page 208, such that if $j <_n i$ & $\mathrm{Lim}_n(i)$, then $G(n, j, i)$ is the least m such that $j <_n \mathrm{lim}_n(m, i)$. We define two auxiliary functions.

<u>Def. 14</u>. $F'(n, a, i) = \mathrm{dp}(a)$ if $i = 0 \vee \mathrm{Suc}_n(i)$

$= \nu_2^1(a) + 1$ if $\mathrm{Lim}_n(i)$.

Then $F'(n, a, i)$ is the least m such that

$L[n, a, \mathrm{ub}(n, m, i), i)]$.

<u>Def. 15</u>. If $i = 0$,

$F(n, a, b, i) = 0$ if $a = 0$.

Let $r_{n1}(a, b) = \mu x\{x < \max(a, b)$ & $(a)_x \neq (b)_x$ & $(y)[y < \max(a, b)$ & $L(n, x, y, i). \supset (a)_y = (b)_y]\}$. Suppose henceforhh $a, b, \neq 0$. [For $r_{n1}(a)$ see page 206.]

$F(n, a, b, i) = 0$ if $\mathrm{L}[n, r_{no}(b), r_{no}(a, b), 0]$

$\vee\ (a)_{r_{no}(b)} + 1 < (b)_{r_{no}(b)}$,

$= (a)_{\mathrm{pred}[n, r_{no}(b), 0]} + 1$ if $\mathrm{Suc}[n, r_{no}(b), 0]$

$= \mu x\{x \leq \mathrm{ln}(a)+1$ & $(y)[x \leq y \leq \mathrm{ln}(a)+1.$

$\supset (a)_{\mathrm{lim}[n, y, r_{no}(b), i]} = 0]\}$

if $\mathrm{Lim}[n, r_{no}(b), 0]$

If $Suc_n(i)$,

$$F(n, a, b, i) = 0 \text{ if } a = 0 \vee L[n, r_{ni}(b), r_{ni}(a, b), i] .$$

$$= F'[n, (a)_o, pred_n(i)]$$

if $Suc_n[n, r_{ni}(b), i] \& Suc_n[n, (b)_{r_{ni}(b)}, pred_n(i)]$,

$$= F[n, (a)_{r_{ni}(b)}, (b)_{r_{ni}(b)}, pred_n(i)]$$

if $Suc[n, r_{ni}(b), i] \& Lim[n, (b)_{r_{ni}(b)}, pred_n(i)]$,

$$= \mu x\{x \leq ln(a)+1 \ \& \ (y)[y \leq ln(a)+1 \ \&. \ x = y \vee L(n, x, y, i) : \supset (a)_{lim[n,m,r_{ni}(a),i]} = 0\}$$

if $Lim[n, r_{ni}(b), i] \& Suc[n, (b)_{r_{ni}(b)}, pred_n(i)]$.

If $Lim_n(i)$,

$$F(n, a, b, i) = 0 \text{ if } \nu_2^1(a) + 1 < \nu_2^1(b) \text{ v. } \nu_2^1(a) + 1 = \nu_2^1(b) \ \& \ \nu_2^2(b) \neq 0$$

$$= F'[n, \nu_2^2(a), \nu_2^1(a)]$$

$$\text{if } \nu_2^1(a) + 1 = \nu_2^1(b) \ \& \ \nu_2^2(b) = 0 ,$$

$$= F[n, \nu_2^2(a), \nu_2^2(b), lim_n(\nu_2^1(a), i)]$$

otherwise.

Then if $Lim(n, b, i)$ and $L(n, a, b, i)$, then $F(n, a, b, i)$ is the least m such that $L[n, a, lim(n, m, b, i), i]$.

Def. 16. $G_o(a, b, p) = 0$ if $\nu_2^1(a) + 1 < \nu_2^1(b)$

$$= \nu_2^2(a) + 1 \quad \text{otherwise.}$$

$$G_o(a, b, p + 1) = 0 \text{ if } r^p(b) \underset{p}{<} r^p(a, b)$$

where $r^p(b) = \mu x\{x \leq ln(b) \ \& \ (b)_x \neq 0 \ \& \ (y)[y \leq ln(b) \ \&$

$(b)_y \neq 0 . \supset x \underset{p+1}{<} y]\}$, and $r^p(a, b) = \mu x\{x < \max(a, b)$ $\& (a)_x \neq (b)_x \& (y)[y < \max(a, b) \& x \underset{p+1}{<} y . \supset (a)_y = (b)_y]\}$.

$$G_o(a, b, p + 1) = (a)_{\mathrm{pred}_o[r^p(b), p]} + 1 \text{ if } \mathrm{Suc}_o[r^p(b), p] ,$$

$$= \mu x\{x \leq \ln(a) + 1 \& (y)[x \leq y \leq \ln(a) + 1 \supset (a)_{\lim_o[m, r^p(b), p]} = 0]\}$$

if $\mathrm{Lim}_o[r^p(b), p]$.

Then $G_o(a, b, p)$ is such that if $j \underset{p+1}{<} i$ and $\mathrm{Lim}_o(i, p)$, then $G_o(j, b, p)$ is the least m such that $j \underset{p+1}{<} \lim_o(m, i, p)$.

Def. 17. $G(0, a, b) = F(0, a, b, 0)$ if $<_o$ is $L(n, a, b, 0)$

$$= G_o(a, b, p) \text{ if } <_o \text{ is } \underset{p+1}{<} .$$

$$G(n + 1, a, b) = 0 \text{ if } \nu_2^1(a) <_n \nu_2^1(b) \& . \nu_2^2(b) \neq 0$$

$$\vee \nu_2^1(b) \neq \mathrm{sc}_n[\nu_2^1(a)] ,$$

$$= F'[n, \nu_2^2(a), \nu_2^1(b)]$$

if $\nu_2^1(b) = \mathrm{sc}_n[\nu_2^1(a)] \& \nu_2^2(b) = 0$

$$= F[n, \nu_2^2(a), \nu_2^2(b), \mathrm{sc}_n(\nu_2^1(a))]$$

if $\nu_2^1(a) = \nu_2^1(b)$.

Def. 18. $E(n, j, i) = \underline{E}[n, j, \mathrm{pred}_n(i)]$

if $\mathrm{Suc}_n(i) \& j <_n \mathrm{pred}_n(i)$,

$$= \varphi_{\mathrm{sc}[n,0,i]}^{\mathrm{sc}[n,0,\mathrm{pred}_n(i)]}$$

if $i = \mathrm{sc}_n(j)$,

$$= \nu_2\{0, E[n, j, \lim_n(0, i)]\}$$

if $j <_n \lim_n(0, i) \& \mathrm{Lim}_n(i)$

$$= \nu_2[G(n, j, i), 0]$$

if $\text{Lim}_n(i)$ & $j = \text{lim}_n[G(n, j, i) - 1, i]$ [clearly if $j = \text{lim}_n(m, i)$, then $G(n, j, i) = m + 1$],

$E(n, j, i) = \nu_2\big(G(n, j, i), E\{n, j, \text{lim}_n[G(n, j, i), i]\}\big)$,

if $\text{Lim}_n(i)$ & $\text{lim}_n[G(n, j, i) - 1, i] <_n j$.

Then if $j <_n i$, $E(n, j, i)$ is a notation for $\varepsilon_{/j/}$ in $L(n, a, b, i)$. We note that the definition involves ordinal recursion on $<_n$.

Def. 19. $\text{Fin}(n, a, i) \equiv. a = 0 \vee a = 2^{(a)_0}$ if $i = 0$,

$\equiv. a = 0 \vee a = 2^{(a)_0}$ & $\text{Fin}[n, (a)_0, \text{pred}_n(i)]$ if $\text{Suc}_n(i)$,

$\equiv. \nu_2^1(a) = 0$ & $\text{Fin}[n, \nu_2^2(a), \text{lim}_n(0, i)]$ if $\text{Lim}_n(i)$

$\text{Fin}(n, a, i)$ holds if a represents a finite ordinal in $L(n, a, b, i)$.

We now define by simultaneous ordinal recursion four functions:

$\text{Ad}(n, a, b, i)$ If $/a/_{ni}$ is the ordinal represented by a in $L(n, a, b, i)$, then $\text{Ad}(n, a, b, i)$ represents $/a/_{ni} + /b/_{ni}$.

$cv^+(n, a, j, i)$ If $j \leq_n i$, then $/a/_{nj} = /cv^+(n, a, j, i)/_{ni}$.

$cv^-(n, a, j, i)$ If $j <_n i$ & $L[n, a, E(n, j, i), i]$ or $j = i$, then $/a/_{ni} = /cv^-(n, a, j, i)/_{nj}$.

Sbe(n, a, j, i) If $j <_n i$ and $L[n, E(n, j, i), a, i] \vee E(n, j, i) = a$, then $Ad[n, E(n, j, i), Sbe(n, a, j, i), i] = a$.

The definitions are so constructed that for a given i, Ad, cv^+, cv^- are defined in terms of Ad, cv^+, cv^-, Sbe for certain $h <_n i$, while Sbe in addition involves cv^+ for i.

Def. 20a. $Ad(n, a, b, i) = a$ if $b = 0$,

$= b$ if $a = 0$.

Otherwise if $i = 0$,

$Ad(n, a, b, i) = a \cdot 2^{(b)_0+1}$ if $b = 2^{(b)_0}$,

$= \prod p_j^{h_1(a,b,j)}$ otherwise, where if

$s_{ni}(b) = \mu x\{x \leq ln(b) \;\&\; (b)_x \neq 0 \;\&\; (y)[y \leq ln(b) \;\&\; (b)_y \neq 0. \supset L(n, y, x, i) \vee y = x]\}$ (cf. r_{ni}, p. 206),

$h_1(a, b, j) = (a)_j$ if $L[n, s_{no}(b), j, 0]$,

$= (a)_j + (b)_j$ if $s_{no}(b) = j$,

$= (b)_j$ otherwise.

If $Suc_n(i)$,

$Ad(n, a, b, i) = \prod_{i \neq 0} p_i^{(a)_i} \cdot 2 \exp' Ad\{n, (a)_0, sc[n, (b)_0, pred_n(i)], pred_n(i)\}$

if $b = 2^{(b)_0} \;\&\; Fin[n, (b)_0, pred_n(i)]$,

$= \prod p_j^{h_2(n,a,b,i,j)}$ otherwise, where

$h_2(n, a, b, i, j) = (a)_j$ if $L[n, s_{ni}(b), j, i]$,

$= Ad[n, (a)_j, (b)_j, pred_n(i)]$ if $j = s_{ni}(b)$,

$= (b)_j$ otherwise.

If $\mathrm{Lim}_n(i)$,

$$\begin{aligned}
\mathrm{Ad}(n, a, b, i) &= b \quad \text{if } \nu_2^1(a) < \nu_2^1(b) , \\
&= \nu_2\Big(\nu_2^1(a), \mathrm{Ad}\big[n, \nu_2^2(a), cv^+\{n, \nu_2^2(b), \mathrm{lim}_n(0, i), \mathrm{lim}_n[\nu_2^1(a), i]\}, \mathrm{lim}_n(\nu_2^1(a), i)\big]\Big)
\end{aligned}$$

if $\nu_2^1(b) = 0$,

$$\begin{aligned}
&= \nu_2\Big[\nu_2^1(a), \mathrm{Ad}\Big(n, \nu_2^2(a), \mathrm{Ad}\Big\{n, E[n, \mathrm{lim}_n(\nu_2^1(b) - 1, i), \mathrm{lim}_n(\nu_2^1(a), i)], \\
&\quad cv^+[n, \nu_2^2(b), \mathrm{lim}_n(\nu_2^1(b), i), \mathrm{lim}_n(\nu_2^1(a), i)], \\
&\quad \mathrm{lim}_n[\nu_2^1(a), i]\Big\}, \mathrm{lim}_n[\nu_2^1(a), i]\Big)\Big]
\end{aligned}$$

if $\nu_2^1(b) \neq 0$ & $\nu_2^1(b) \leq \nu_2^1(a)$.

The complication of this definition arises from the fact that if $m \neq 0$, then $/\nu_2(m, a)/_{ni} = /\mathrm{lim}_n(m-1,i)/ + /a/_{n,\mathrm{lim}_n(m,i)}$. Therefore in order to compute $\mathrm{Ad}[n, c, \nu_2(m, a), i]$ for a given c with $m \leq \nu_2^1(c)$, it is necessary to add to $\nu_2^2(c)$ a replica not of a but of $\mathrm{Ad}\{n, E[n, \mathrm{lim}_n(m - 1, i), \mathrm{lim}_n(m, i)], a, \mathrm{lim}_n(m, i)\}$

<u>Def. 20b</u>. $cv^+(n, a, j, i) = a$ if $j = i$ or $a = 0$.

Otherwise if $\mathrm{Suc}_n(i)$,

$$\begin{aligned}
cv^+(n, a, j, i) &= 2 \exp \mathrm{pred}\{n, cv^+[n, a, j, \mathrm{pred}_n(i)], \mathrm{pred}_n(i)\} \quad \text{if } \mathrm{Fin}(n, a, j) , \\
&= 2 \exp cv^+[n, a, j, \mathrm{pred}_n(i)] \quad \text{otherwise.}
\end{aligned}$$

If $\mathrm{Lim}_n(i)$,

$$cv^+(n, a, j, i) = \nu_2\{0, cv^+[n, a, j, \mathrm{lim}_n(0, i)]\}$$

if $j \leq_n \mathrm{lim}_n(0, i)$,

$$= \nu_2\Big[k_o, cv^-\Big\{n, \mathrm{Sbe}\Big(n, cv^+[n, a, j,$$

$$\lim_n(m + 1,\ i)],\ \lim_n(k_o,\ i),\ \lim_n(m + 1,\ i)\Big),$$
$$\lim_n(k_o,\ i),\ \lim_n(m + 1,\ i)\}\Big]$$

if $\lim_n(m,\ i) <_n j \leq_n \lim_n(m + 1,\ i)$ & $L\{n,\ a,\ E[n,\ \lim_n(m,\ i),\ j],\ j\}$, where $m = G(n,\ j,\ i) - 1$ unless $j = \lim_n[G(n,\ j,\ i) - 1,\ i]$, in which case $m = G(n,\ j,\ i) - 2$; k_o is the greatest $k \leq m$ such that $L\{n,\ a,\ E[n,\ \lim_n(k,\ i),\ j],\ j\}$.

$$cv^{+}(n,\ a,\ j,\ i) = \nu_2\{m + 1,\ Sbe[n,\ a,\ \lim_n(m,\ i),\ \lim_n(m + 1,\ i)]\}$$

if m is as in the last case, and $-\ L[n,\ a,\ E(n,\ \lim_n(m,\ i),\ j),\ j]$.

Def. 20c. $cv^{-}(n,\ a,\ j,\ i) = a$ if $j = i$ or $a = 0$.

Otherwise if $Suc_n(i)$,

$$cv^{-}(n,\ a,\ j,\ i) = cv^{-}[n,\ (a)_o,\ j,\ pred_n(i)]$$

if $-\ Fin[n,\ (a)_o,\ pred_n(i)]$,

$$= cv^{-}\{n,\ sc[n,\ (a)_o,\ pred_n(i)],\ j,\ pred_n(i)\}$$ if $Fin[n,\ (a)_o,\ pred_n(i)]$.

If $Lim_n(i)$,

$$cv^{-}(n,\ a,\ j,\ i) = cv^{-}[n,\ \nu_2^2(a),\ j,\ \lim_n(0,\ i)]$$

if $j <_n \lim_n(0,\ i)$,

$$= cv^{-}\Big(n,\ Ad\{n,\ E[n,\ \lim_n(\nu_2^1(a) - 1,\ i),\ \lim_n(\nu_2^1(a),\ i)],\ \nu_2^2(a),\ \lim_n[\nu_2^1(a),\ i]\},\ j,\ \lim_n[\nu_2^1(a),\ i]\Big)$$

if $j <_n \lim_n[\nu_2^1(a),\ i]$ & $\nu_2^1(a) \neq 0$.

$$= cv^{+}\Big(n,\ Ad\{n,\ E[n,\ \lim_n(\nu_2^1(a) - 1,\ i),\ \lim_n(\nu_2^1(a),\ i)],\ \nu_2^2(a),\ \lim_n[\nu_2^1(a),\ i]\},\ j,\ \lim_n[\nu_2^1(a),\ i]\Big)$$

if $\lim_n[\nu_2^1(a), i] \leq_n j \ \& \ \nu_2^1(a) \neq 0$,

$= cv^+[n, \nu_2^2(a), \lim_n(0, i), j]$

if $\lim_n(0, i) \leq_n j \ \& \ \nu_2^1(a) = 0$.

Def. 20d. If $Suc_n(i)$,

$Sbe(n, a, j, i) = a$ unless $a = 2^{(a)_0} \cdot 3^{(a)_1}$ [note that if $Suc_n(i)$, $sc(n, 0, i) = 1$] &: $Fin[n, (a)_1, pred_n(i)]$ & $(a)_1 \neq 0$ & $j = pred_n(i)$ .v. $(a)_1 = 0$ & $j <_n pred_n(i)$.

$Sbe(n, a, j, i) = 2^{(a)_0} \cdot 3^{pred[n,(a)_1,pred_n(i)]}$

if $j = pred_n(i)$,

$= 2^{Sbe[n,(a)_0,j,pred_n(i)]}$

if $j <_n pred_n(i)$.

If $Lim_n(i)$,

$Sbe(n, a, j, i) = \nu_2\{0, Sbe[n, \nu_2^2(a), j, \lim_n(0, i)]\}$

if $\nu_2^1(a) = 0$ [we must have $j <_n \lim_n(0, i)$],

$= a$

if $\nu_2^1(a) \neq 0$ & $j <_n \lim_n[\nu_2^1(a) - 1, i]$,

$= cv^+[n, \nu_2^2(a), j, i]$

if $\nu_2^1(a) \neq 0$ & $j = \lim_n[\nu_2^1(a) - 1, i]$,

$= cv^+\{n, Sbe[n, \nu_2^2(a), j, \lim_n(\nu_2^1(a), i)], \lim_n[\nu_2^1(a), -1], i\}$

if $\nu_2^1(a) \neq 0$ & $\lim_n[\nu_2^1(a) - 1, i] <_n j <_n \lim_n[\nu_2^1(a), i]$.

Def. 21. $a +_0 b = ad(a, b, p)$ if $<_0$ is $\underset{p+1}{<}$.

$= Ad(0, a, b, 0)$ if $<_0$ is $L(n, a, b, 0)$

$a +_{n+1} b = b$ if $\nu_2^1(a) <_n \nu_2^1(b)$.

$a +_{n+1} b = \nu_2\{0, Ad[n, \nu_2^2(a), \nu_2^2(b), sc_n(0)]\}$
if $\nu_2^1(a) = \nu_2^1(b) = 0$,

$$= \nu_2\left[\nu_2^1(a), Ad\left(n, \nu_2^2(a), Ad\{n, E[n, \nu_2^1(b), sc_n(\nu_2^1(a))], \nu_2^2(b), sc_{\underline{n}}[\nu_2^1(a)]\}, sc_{\underline{n}}[\nu_2^1(a)]\right)\right]$$

otherwise.

Then $+_n$ represents addition on $<_n$. If $n = 0$, it is primitive resursive; for fixed n , $+_{n+1}$ is ordinal recursive on $<_n$. As a function of n , $+_n$ could in all probability be shown to be ordinal recursive on the ordering $<_\omega$ of page 227.

We next seek to define a function w_n which will represent exponentiation by ω. The first auxiliary function, $LM(n, a, j, i)$, gives for $j <_n i$ a notation in $L(n, a, b, i)$ for $\varepsilon_{/j/} \cdot /a/_{ni}$. The second function $W(n, a, i)$ represents exponentiation by ω in $L(n, a, b, i)$.

<u>Def. 22</u>. If $Suc_n(i)$ & $j = pred_n(i)$,

$LM(n, a, j, i) = 0$ if $a = 0$,

$$= \prod p_{h_3(n,a,j,i,s)}^{h_4(a,s)} \text{ otherwise, where}$$

$h_3(n, a, j, i, s) = sc(n, s, i)$ if $Fin(n, s, i)$,

$= 0$ otherwise;

$h_4(a, s) = sc[n, (a)_s, pred_n(i)]$ if $s = 0$ & $a = 2^{(a)_0}$

$= (a)_s$ otherwise.

If $Suc_n(i)$ & $j <_n pred_n(i)$,

$LM(n, a, j, i) = 0$ if $a = 0$,

$$LM(n, a, j, i) = E(n, j, i) \text{ if } a = 1$$
$$= \prod \rho_s^{h_5(n,a,j,i,s)} \text{ otherwise, where}$$
$$h_5(n, a, j, i, s) = (a)_s \text{ if } s \neq 0,$$
$$= LM\{n, sc[n, (a)_o, pred_n(i)], j, pred_n(i)\}$$
if $s = 0 \ \& \ a = 2^{(a)_o} \ \& \ Fin[n, (a)_o, pred_n(i)]$,
$$= LM[n, (a)_o, j, pred_n(i)]$$
otherwise.

If $Lim_n(i)$,

$$LM(n, a, j, i) = \nu_2\{0, LM[n, \nu_2^2(a), j, lim_n(0, i)]\}$$
if $\nu_2^1(a) = 0 \ \& \ j <_n lim_n(0, i)$,
$$= cv^+\{n, 3 \exp cv^+[n, \nu_2^2(a), lim_n(0, i), j], sc_n(j), i\}$$
if $\nu_2^1(a) = 0 \ \& \ lim_n(0, i) \leq_n j$,
$$= cv^+\Big[n, Ad\Big(n, LM\{n, E[n, lim_n(\nu_2^1(a) - 1, i), lim_n(\nu_2^1(a), i)], j, lim_n[\nu_2^1(a), i]\}, LM\{n, \nu_2^2(a), j, lim_n[\nu_2^1(a), i]\}, lim_n[\nu_2^1(a), i]\Big), Lim_n[\nu_2^1(a), i], i\Big]$$
if $\nu_2^1(a) \neq 0 \ \& \ j <_n lim_n[\nu_2^1(a), i]$,
$$= cv^+\Big(n, 3 \exp Ad\{n, E[n, lim_n(\nu_2^1(a) - 1, i), j], cv^+[n, \nu_2^2(a), lim_n(\nu_2^1(a), i), j], j\}, sc_n(j), i\Big)$$
if $\nu_2^1(a) \neq 0 \ \& \ lim_n[\nu_2^1(a), i] \leq_n j$.

Def. 23. $W(n, a, i) = 1$ if $i = 0 \ \& \ a = 0$,
$$= \rho_a \text{ if } i = 0 \ \& \ a \neq 0 .$$

If $a \neq 0, 2^{(a)_o} \ \& \ Suc_n(i)$, let

$$s_1(n, a, i) = \prod_{j \neq 0} \rho_{h_6(n,i,j)}^{(a)_j} \text{, where}$$

$h_6(n, i, j) = pred(n, j, i)$ if $Fin(n, j, i)$,

$= j$ otherwise.

Then if $Suc_n(i)$,

$W(n, a, i) = 1$ if $a = 0$,

$= 2 \exp W\{n, sc[n, (a)_o, pred_n(i)], pred_n(i)\}$

if $a = 2^{(a)_o}$ & $Fin[n, (a)_o, pred_n(i)]$,

$= 2 \exp W[n, (a)_o, pred_n(i)]$

if $a = 2^{(a)_o}$ & $- Fin[n, (a)_o, pred_n(i)]$,

$= \mathcal{P}_{s_1(n,a,i)} \exp W[n, (a)_o, pred_n(i)]$

otherwise.

If $Lim_n(i)$,

$W(n, a, i) = \nu_2\{0, W[n, \nu_2^2(a), lim_n(0, i)]\}$ if $\nu_2^1(a) = 0$,

$= cv^+\big(n, LM\{n, W[n, \nu_2^2(a), lim_n(\nu_2^1(a), i)],$

$lim_n[\nu_2^1(a) - 1, i], lim_n[\nu_2^1(a), i]\}, lim_n[\nu_2^1(a) - 1, i],$

$lim_n[\nu_2^1(a), i]\big)$ if $\nu_2^1(a) \neq 0$.

Def. 24. $w_o(a) = wp(a, p - 1, 1)$ if $<_o$ is $\underset{p+1}{<}$ (defined only if $p \neq 0$ & $a \underset{p+1}{<} w(p - 1)$),

$= W(0, a, 0)$ if $<_o$ is $L(n, a, b, 0)$.

$w_{n+1}(a) = \nu_2\{0, W[n, \nu_2^2(a), sc_n(0)]\}$ if $\nu_2^1(a) = 0$,

$= \nu_2\big(\nu_2^1(a), LM\{n, W[n, \nu_2^2(a), sc_n(\nu_2^1(a))], \nu_2^1(a),$

$sc_n[\nu_2^1(a)]\}\big)$ if $\nu_2^1(a) \neq 0$.

Then w_o is primitive recursive, and w_{n+1} is ordinal recursive on $<_n$

Finally we define a function $E_n(a)$ such that if a

is a notation in $<_n$ for the ordinal α and $n \neq 0$, then $E_n(a)$ is a notation for ε_α. This will be defined only if $\alpha < \varepsilon^{n-1}(\alpha_0)$, where α_0 is the type of $<_0$.

Def. 25. $e(n, 0) = 6$; $e(n, a + 1) = \nu_2(a + 1, 0)$.

If a represents α in $<_n$, then $e(n, a)$ represents ε_α in $<_{n+1}$.

Def. 26. $H(0, 0) = \mathcal{P}_2 = 5$; $H(0, p + 1) = \mathcal{P}_{H(0,p)}$.

$H(0) = \nu_2(1, 0)$ if $<_0$ is $L(n, a, b, 0)$.

$= H(0, p)$ if $<_0$ is $\underset{p+1}{<}$,

$H(n + 1) = \nu_2[H(n), 0]$.

$H(n)$ represents $\bar{\varepsilon}^n(\alpha_0)$ in $<_{n+1}$.

Def. 27. $c_0(0, a) = \nu_2[(a)_1, (a)_0]$ if $a = 0 \vee (a)_1 \neq 0$

$= 2[(a)_0 + 1]$ if $a = 2^{(a)_0}$.

$c_0(p + 1, a) = \prod \mathcal{P}_{c_0(p,1)}^{(a)_1}$

$c^-(0, a) = \nu_2^2(a)$ if $<_0$ is $L(n, a, b, 0)$,

$= c_0[p, \nu_2^2(a)]$ if $<_0$ is $\underset{p+1}{<}$.

$c^-(n + 1, a) = \nu_2\{c^-[n, \nu_2^1(a)], \nu_2^2(a)\}$

If $i <_{n+1} H(n)$, then $c^-(n, i)$ represents in $<_n$ the ordinal which i represents in $<_{n+1}$.

Def. 28. $E_{n+1}(a) = e[n, c^-(n, a)]$

This completes the proof that the functionals Γ_{nq} of pp. 224-6 are ordinal recursive on $<_n$ with $\underset{q+1}{<}$ as $<_0$, and that the functionals Γ_n are ordinal recursive on $<_n$ with $L(0, a, b, 0)$ as $<_0$. It could also be shown that the functional Γ of page 227 is ordinalrrecursive on $<_\omega$.

BIBLIOGRAPHY

Ackermann, W. [1] Begründung des tertium non datur mittels der Hilbertschen Theorie der Widerspruchsfreiheit, Mathematische Annalen, vol. 93 (1924/5), pp. 1-36.

[2] Zur Widerspruchsfreiheit der Zahlentheorie, Ibid., vol. 117 (1940), pp. 162-194.

Axt, Paul, On a subrecursive hierarchy and primitive recursive degrees, Transactions of the American Mathematical Society, vol. 92 (1959), pp. 85-117.

Brouwer, L. E. J. [1] Ueber die Bedeutung des Satzes vom ausgeschlössenen Dritten in der Mathematik, insbesonder in der Funktionentheorie, Journal für die reine und angewandte Mathematik, vol. 154 (1925), pp. 1-7.

[2] Mathematik, Wissenschaft, und Sprache, Monatshefte für Mathematik und Physik, vol. 36 (1929), pp. 153-64.

[3] Beweis, dass der Begriff der Menge höherer Ordnung nicht als Grundbegriff der intuitionistischen Mathematik in Betracht kommt, Proceedings of the Dutch Academy of Sciences, section A., vol. 45 (1942), pp. 791-5.

[4] Points and Spaces, Canadian Journal of Mathematics, vol. 6 (1954), pp. 1-17.

Dreben, Burton, On the completeness of quantification theory, Proceedings of the National Academy of Sciences, vol. 38 (1952), pp. 1047-52.

Gentzen, Gerhard [1] Untersuchungen über das logische Schliessen, Mathematische Zeitschrift, vol. 39 (1934), pp. 176-210, 405-431.

[2] Die Widerspruchsfreiheit der reinen Zahlentheorie, Mathematische Annalen, vol. 112 (1936), pp. 493-565.

[3] Neue Fassung des Widerspruchsfreiheitsbeweises für die reine Zahlentheorie, Forschungen zur Logik und zur Grundlegung der exakten Wissenschaften, Neue Folge, vol. 4 (1938), pp. 19-44.

[4] Beweisbarkeit und Unbeweisbarkeit von Anfangsfällen der transfiniten Induktion in der reinen Zahlentheorie, Mathematische Annalen, vol. 119 (1943), pp. 140-161.

Gödel, Kurt, [1] Zur intuitionistischen Arithmetik und

Zahlentheorie, Ergebnisse eines mathematischen Kolloquiums, Heft 4 (1933), pp. 34-38.

[2] Ueber eine bisher noch nicht benützte Erweiterung des finiten Standpunktes, Logica: Studia Paul Bernays dedicata (Neuchâtel, Éditions du Griffon, 1959), pp. 76-84.

Heyting, A. [1] Intuitionism: An Introduction. Amsterdam, North Hölland Publishing Company, 1956.

[2] Blick von der intuitionistischen Warte, Logica, pp. 128-41.

Hilbert, David [1] Ueber das Unendliche, Mathematische Annalen, vol. 95 (1926), pp. 161-90.

[2] Grundlagen der Geometrie, 7th edition. Leipzig and Berlin, B. G. Teubner, 1930. Appendices VI-X, which are abridged reprints of articles on foundations, are omitted from the 8th edition (Stuttgart, 1956).

Hilbert, David, and Paul Bernays, Grundlagen der Mathematik. Berlin, Verlag von Julius Springer. Vol. I, 1934; Vol. II, 1939.

Kleene, S. C. [1] On notation for ordinal numbers, Journal of Symbolic Logic, vol. 3 (1938), pp. 150-5.

[2] On the forms of the predicates in the theory of constructive ordinals, American Journal of Mathematics, vol. 66 (1944), pp. 41-58; vol. 77 (1955), pp. 405-28.

[3] Introduction to Metamathematics. New York, D. Van Nostrand Co., 1952

[4] Arithmetical predicates and function quantifiers, Transactions of the American Mathematical Society, vol. 79 (1955), pp. 312-40.

[5] Hierarchies of number-theoretic predicates, Bulletin of the American Mathematical Society, vol. 61 (1955), pp. 193-213.

[6] Extension of an Effectively Generated Class of Functions by Enumeration, Colloquium Mathematicum, vol. 6 (1958), pp. 67-77.

[7] Quantification of number-theoretic functions, Compositio Mathematica, vol. 14 (1959), pp. 23-40.

[8] Countable functionals, Constructivity in Mathematics, ed. A. Heyting (Amsterdam, North Holland Publishing Company, 1959), pp. 81-100.

[9] Realizability, Ibid. pp. 285-9.

[10] Recursive functionals and quantifiers of finite types I, Transactions of the American Mathematical Society, vol. 91 (1959), pp. 1-52.

Kreisel, G. [1] On the interpretation of non-finitist proofs, Journal of Symbolic Logic, vol. 16 (1951), pp. 241-67; vol. 17 (1952), pp. 43-58.

[2] On the concepts of completeness and interpretation of formal systems, Fundamenta Mathematicae, vol. 39 (1952), pp. 103-27.

[3] Some concepts concerning formal systems of number theory, Mathematische Zeitschrift, vol. 57 (1952), pp. 1-12.

[4] A Variant to Hilbert's theory of the foundations of arithmetic, British Journal for the

Philosophy of Science, vol. 4 (1953), pp. 107-29.

[5] Models, translations, and interpretations, Mathematical Interpretation of Formal Systems (Amsterdam, North Holland Publishing Company, 1955), pp. 26-50.

[6] The mathematical significance of consistency proofs, Journal of Symbolic Logic, vol. 23 (1958), pp. 155-82.

[7] Interpretation of Analysis by means of constructive functionals of finite types, Constructivity in mathematics, pp. 101-28.

[8] Hilbert's programme, Logica, pp. 142-68.

Kreisel, G., and H. Wang, Some applications of formalized consistency proofs, Fundamenta Mathematicae, vol. 42 (1955), pp. 101-110.

Kreisel, G., J. Shoenfield, and H. Wang, Number-theoretic concepts and recursive well-orderings, Archiv für mathematische Logik und Grundlagenforschung, vol. 5 (1960), pp. 42-64.

Parsons, Charles [1] Elimination of a restricted infinite induction (abstract), Journal of Symbolic Logic, vol. 23 (1958), p. 106

[2] The ω-consistency of ramified analysis, Archiv fur math. Logik und Grundlagenforschung, to appear.

Péter, Rosza, Rekursive Funktionen, 2d edition. Budapest, Verlag der ungarischen Akademie der Wissenschaften, 1957.

Quine, W. V. [1] Mathematical Logic, revised edition. Cambridge, Mass., Harvard University Press, 1951.

[2] A proof procedure for quantification theory, Journal of Symbolic Logic, vol. 20 (1955).

Schütte, Kurt [1] Schlussweisen-Kalküle der Prädikatenlogik, Mathematische Annalen, vol. 122 (1950/1), pp. 47-65.

[2] Beweistheoretische Erfassung der unendlichen Induktion in der reinen Zahlentheorie, Ibid. vol. 122, pp. 369-89.

[3] Beweistheoretische Untersuchung der verzweigten Analysis, Ibid. vol. 123 (1952), pp. 123-47.

[4] Beweistheorie. Berlin-Göttingen-Heidelberg, Springer-Verlag, 1960.

Shoenfield, J. [1] On an effective ω-rule, Bulletin de l'Academie polonaise des sciences, vol. 7 (1959), pp. 405-7.

[2] New proofs of theorems of Kreisel, Notices of the American Mathematical Society, vol. 6(1959), p. 906. (Abstract.)

Spector, Clifford, "Recursive well-orderings, Journal of Symbolic Logic, vol. 20 (1955), pp. 143-63.

Tarski, Alfred, Andrzej Mostowski, and R. M. Robinson, Undecidable Theories. Amsterdam, North Holland Publishing Company, 1953.

INDEX OF DEFINITIONS

Definition Number	Concept	Page	References
1	finitary interpretation	7	Kreisel [1], [2] ("interpretation"-simply), [3], [4], [5].
2	strong interpretation	9	Kreisel [1]
3	numerical scheme	10	Kreisel [1] ("systematically-decidable finite scheme")
4	does not occur		
5	numerical system	12	
6	verifiable	13	HB *passim*, esp. I, §2.
7	substitution (for free function variables)	13	cf. IM pp. 275-6, 290 ff.
8	verifiable (with free function variables)	14	Kreisel [1]
9	ν_2, ν_2^1, ν_2^2 (pairing functions)	14	Ackermann [2]
10	ν_{n+3}, ν_{n+3}^1	15	
11	formula of recursive number theory	18	
12	full finitary formula	18	
13	formula of elementary number theory	19	
14	system of elementary number theory	19	
15	system of elementary number theory without induction, with induction	19	
16	recursive satisfaction	27	Kreisel [1] ("comput-

			able satisfaction") IM p. 465 ("effectively", "general recursively true" for satisfiable)
17	1-consistent	32	
18	1*-consistent	33	
19	Herbrand alternation	41	Dreben, cf. HB II 151 ff.
20	Herbrand interpretation	43	Kreisel [1]
21	uniformly 1*-consistent	54	
22	logical degree	67	Schütte [1], [2], [4] p. 77
23	no-counter-example interpretation	79	Kreisel [1], [3], [4], [5].
24	externally consistent	95	HB II, 282-3; Kreisel [3]
25	simply representable functional	98	cf. Kreisel [3] "functional of $Z_{\bar{\mu}}$"
26	primitive recursive functional	119	Kleene [10], IM p. 234; <u>not</u> Gödel [2]
27	numeralwise expresses	120	IM p. 195 (for number arguments)
28	numeralwise represents	120	IM p. 200 (for number arguments)
29	strongly represent	120	cf. IM pp. 244-5.
30	probably recursive	121	cf. HB I 401 ff., Kreisel [1]
31	well-orderings $<_p$ of type $\omega_{p-1}(\omega^2)$.	122	Ackermann [2], Kreisel [1], HB II 361
32	ordinal recursive functionals of degree p	123	Kreisel [1] (order p)
33	binding degree of a first-order formula	125	
34	principal, side, second-	130	IM p. 443, Schütte [1],

	ary formulae or inference; principal term, principal variable, cut formula		[2], [3], [4] §§18-19
35	<u>kleiner Formelbund</u>	132	Schütte [1]-[3] (<u>Formelbund</u> simply), [4] pp. 83-6
36	<u>grosser Formelbund</u>	133	Schütte [4] pp. 83-6
37	truth-functional (tf-) degree	142	
38	formal transfinite induction with respect to $<^*$	163	HB II 361
39	ramified analysis on $\mathfrak{F}$	187	Schütte [3]
40	top degree	191	Schütte [4] p. 249 (<u>Beizahl</u>)
41	binding degree of formula of ramified analysis	192	Schütte [3]
42	immediate subformula	192	cf. IM p. 449
43	proper subformula	194	
44	well-orderings $<_n$ of type $\varepsilon^n(\alpha)$	199-208	
45	ordinal recursive functionals of level n	209	
46	ordinal recursive functionals of level n and degree p, ordinal recursive functionals of level n and degree ω	209	
47	ω-consistent	245	Kreisel [1], [3], [5]